高等院校英语语言文学专业研究生系列教材(修订版)

总主编 戴炜栋

中西文化比较教程

Chinese and Western Cultures: A Course of Comparative Study

叶胜年 著

上海外语教育出版社
SHANGHAI FOREIGN LANGUAGE EDUCATION PRESS

图书在版编目（CIP）数据

中西文化比较教程 / 叶胜年著.
—上海：上海外语教育出版社，2010（2021重印）
（高等院校英语语言文学专业研究生系列教材（修订版））
ISBN 978-7-5446-1797-0

Ⅰ.①中… Ⅱ.①叶… Ⅲ.①比较文化－中国、西方国家－研究生－教材
Ⅳ.①G04

中国版本图书馆CIP数据核字（2010）第118723号

出版发行：**上海外语教育出版社**
（上海外国语大学内）　邮编：200083
电　　话：021-65425300（总机）
电子邮箱：bookinfo@sflep.com.cn
网　　址：http://www.sflep.com
责任编辑：包　洁

印　　刷：江苏凤凰数码印务有限公司

开　　本：700×1000　1/16　印张19.5　字数464千字
版　　次：2010年12月第1版　2021年8月第7次印刷

书　　号：ISBN 978-7-5446-1797-0 / G・0648
定　　价：33.00 元

本版图书如有印装质量问题，可向本社调换
质量服务热线：4008-213-263　电子邮箱：editorial@sflep.com

编委会

主 任：戴炜栋

委 员：（以姓氏笔画为序）

文秋芳	北京外国语大学	邹 申	上海外国语大学
王守仁	南京大学	陈建平	广东外语外贸大学
冯庆华	上海外国语大学	陈法春	天津外国语学院
申 丹	北京大学	罗选民	清华大学
石 坚	四川大学	胡文仲	北京外国语大学
刘世生	清华大学	赵忠德	大连外国语学院
刘海平	南京大学	殷企平	杭州师范大学
庄智象	上海外国语大学	秦秀白	华南理工大学
朱永生	复旦大学	梅德明	上海外国语大学
何兆熊	上海外国语大学	黄国文	中山大学
张绍杰	东北师范大学	黄源深	上海对外贸易学院
李建平	四川外国语学院	程晓堂	北京师范大学
李绍山	解放军外国语学院	程爱民	南京大学
杨信彰	厦门大学	蒋洪新	湖南师范大学

总序

随着我国经济的飞速发展，社会对以研究生为主体的高层次人才的需求日益增长，我国英语语言文学专业的研究生教育规模也在不断扩大。要使研究生教育持续健康地发展，培养学生创新思维能力和独立研究与应用能力，必须全面系统地加强基础理论与基本方法的训练。而要实现这一目标，就必须有一套符合我国国情的、系统正规的英语语言文学专业研究生主干教材。

基于这一认识，上海外语教育出版社于21世纪之初邀请全国英语语言文学专业各研究领域中的知名专家学者，编写了"高等院校英语语言文学专业研究生系列教材"，迄今已陆续出版了二十余种。这套系列教材集各高校之所长，优势互补，形成合力，在教材建设方面，把我国英语语言文学专业的研究生培养工作推上了一个新的台阶，规范了我国英语语言文学专业的研究生课程，为高校培养基础扎实、知识面广、富有开拓精神、符合社会需要的高质量研究生提供了条件。

该系列教材的编写结合了我国英语语言文学专业研究生教学的实际情况与需要，强调科学性、系统性、先进性和实用性，力求体现理论与应用相结合，介绍与研究相结合，史与论相结合，原创与引进相结合，全面融会贯通。每一种教材都能够反映出该研究领域的新理论、新方法和新成果。系列教材推出后不仅被作为我国英语语言文学专业研究生的主干教材，也被作为中国语言文学专业的教师与学生的参考用书。

在多年的使用过程中，全国各高校的英语语言文学专业的专家学者和教师对该系列教材提出了许多建设性的建议。近几年，英语语言文学研究也有了新的发展。为了吸纳这些建设性建议及最新的学科研究成果，进一步完善教材，我们对该系列教材进行了修订。此次修订的主要方面有：内容上查漏补缺，进一步提升教材质量；理论上与时俱进，反映最新的学科研究成果；体例上规范统一，提高学术的严谨性；资料上充实丰富，增加教学资源；版式上全新设计，增强教材的易教性。此外，我们还对该系列教材的选题进行了拓展和延伸，在邀请国内专家学者编写原创教材的同时，精选国外原版教材引进出版。修订后的"高等院校英语语言文学专业研究生系列教材"在选题上中西合璧，覆盖了英语语言文学专业各学科的主要课程，学科方向将更齐全，更能满足我国英语语言文学专业研究生教育在学科建设方面的需求。

教材建设是学科建设的一项重要基本建设，对学科发展有着深远的影响。我们相信，在新世纪推出的这套系列教材，必将大大推动我国英语语言文学专业研究生教育事业的发展，促进我国英语语言文学研究水平的提高。

戴炜栋

2009 年 5 月

PREFACE

Here is a textbook designed for the need of acquiring by comparison a more comprehensive and further understanding of cultural essentials of both China and the West based on a preliminary introduction first made to a group of graduate students about eight years ago. The book falls into nine chapters handling respectively different areas of culture which, I assume, have contributed a great deal to the development of human civilization as a whole no matter how they vary in form, content, performance and popularity.

The nine chapters are largely pertinent to four areas, namely ideology, literature and art, language and science. Among these four respects, the ideological field is of primary importance for it always, in whichever stage of human development, determines the direction, speed and scope of the other fields, such as art, literature, language and science. One could locate different traces of evolvement in these traditional forms of the humanities by focusing on function as well as the general temperament or established features of each category. A comparative study might help expose and identify the advantage and disadvantage of the form concerned on each side in terms of historical retrospect, effect-focused investigation, constitutional calculation, moral judgment and aesthetic estimation without caring much for racial and ethnical distinction which once cast shadows over our points of view. The reader certainly does not have to be limited by the author's perspective though the comparative comments could work as a kind of guidance in reading through the book and following the right way of reading and identification.

With more contact with foreign, especially Western culture in the last three decades, most of the Chinese, either the academic or the non-academic, have regarded it necessary to know about what has happened outside China and fill up a vacancy or gap left by some historical or political events with an amount of information collected from Western culture to deal with academic need as a necessary inspiration to expanding one's perspective or useful reference to seeking background information, or even to deal with daily need in relation to the West. More often than not they have encountered more and more occasions on which they have to think or make use of Western culture as a necessary addition to their own national culture. In a way one can say a connection and even a mixture of Chinese and Western cultures is a frequent occurrence or an inevitable trend. We have to prepare ourselves for the consequence of such a trend, which should serve as an important purpose of this book, such as the interaction of the two cultures and mutual influence upon each other, including the existent and potential contributions of Western culture to our national culture, which has provided the basis as well as the motivation for picking up as a serious subject comparative studies of Chinese and Western cultures.

As to the dynamics of comparative studies, I would particularly refer to the essence of comparison used both as a purpose and as a method. We do not intend to offer everything concerning comparative studies between Chinese and Western cultures, but rather attempt to build up a basic framework or platform on which we could start to work alongside some fundamental principles and precepts, such as parallelism, mutual reference, generalization, deduction, inference, contrasts or emulation, all of which would go into and interact with our deepening understanding of the cultural similarities and dissimilarities of the two sides. These specific methods or techniques would usually bring into play their potential and sharpen the wits of learners by means of group discussions or individual meditations, both of which I would be pleased to recommend as basic form of learning either in or out of class. It is the reason why some questions and lists of further reading are attached to each chapter. Hopefully they could help heighten the efficiency of learning.

I would hesitate to offer any specific advice to the details of teaching or learning, but would happily help define a general syllabus by which one could find some reference to his or her work on the course. Usually forty teaching periods or so are needed for the teaching of the whole book. Maybe a distribution of four to five periods per chapter is reasonable apart from an additional amount for the introduction and conclusion. I would propose a normal procedure of teaching to be composed of three steps: lecturing, discussion and conclusion. Lecturing as the leading part of the whole processs would regularly take two periods by focusing on the basic elements of the chapter concerned, embodying a collection of necessary information, the identification of the perimeter of the subject and preparation for later discussion. The second step is principally used to further the student's understanding of the essential points of the lecture and train his or her ability to research into relevant areas based on the questions and reading lists attached to each chapter. The last step is a necessary summary of the discussion as well as a brief account of the central ideas of the chapter. The reading list might work to extend students' desire to more details of some aspect of knowledge concerned, which points to a direction for those who want to further their studies.

CONTENTS

CHAPTER 1 Introduction 1

    Motivations and grounds for making comparative studies 1
    The essentials of comparative culture in the present book 2
    1.2.1   The leading role of ideology 2
    1.2.2   Literature and art as part of cultural tradition 7
    1.2.3   A variety of cultural subjects 12
    Gap yet to be bridged 14

CHAPTER 2 A Comparison of Ancient Chinese and Western Philosophies 16

    A survey of ancient Chinese philosophy 16
    2.1.1   Confucianism 17
    2.1.2   Taoism 22
    2.1.3   Legalism 25
    2.1.4   Mohism 27
    A survey of ancient Western philosophy 28
    2.2.1   The inception of Western philosophy 28
    2.2.2   The representative figures or schools 29
    Comparative comments 36
    2.3.1   Economic, political and intellectual circumstances 37
    2.3.2   Philosophical and academic ideas 40
    A case study 45
    2.4.1   Setting for the birth of Confucius and Socrates' ideologies ... 45
    2.4.2   Personal and academic experiences 46
    2.4.3   Religious faith 46
    2.4.4   Political views 47
    2.4.5   Philosophical and cognitive issues 48
    2.4.6   Ethical ideas 48

CHAPTER 3　A Comparison of Middle-Age Chinese and Western Philosophies 51

　　Social and intellectual background 51
　　Chinese representative philosophies 53
　3.2.1　Fan Zhen 53
　3.2.2　Zhu Xi 55
　3.2.3　Wang Shouren 57
　　Western representative philosophies 58
　3.3.1　Neoplatonism 58
　3.3.2　Scholasticism 59
　3.3.3　The Christian Reformation and Martin Luther 62
　　Comparative comments 64
　3.4.1　The establishment and defence of the orthodox ideology 65
　3.4.2　Historical reasons behind the faiths 66
　3.4.3　The view of Confucianism and Christianity 67
　3.4.4　Influence on the attitude towards nature and learning 68
　3.4.5　Mysterious and religious factors within the ideological tendency 69
　　A case study 70
　3.5.1　Motivation for scholarly modifications 71
　3.5.2　Epistemology and metaphysics 73
　3.5.3　Ethical principles 76
　3.5.4　Political, social and intellectual concerns 79

CHAPTER 4　A Comparison of Modern Chinese and Western Philosophies 83

　　Social and intellectual scene for modern philosophy 84
　　The Chinese representative thinkers 85
　4.2.1　Wang Fuzhi 85
　4.2.2　Gong Zizhen 87
　4.2.3　Kang Youwei 88
　4.2.4　Sun Yatsen 91
　　The development of modern Western philosophy and its representative figures
　　.. 93
　4.3.1　The Renaissance: F. Bacon and T. Hobbes 93
　4.3.2　Empiricism and J. Locke 95
　4.3.3　J. Rousseau and the French Revolution 97
　4.3.4　J. Mill, F. Nietzsche and the dawn of the new era 98
　　Comparative comments 101
　4.4.1　Social and intellectual conditions 101

4.4.2	Contribution to social progress	103
4.4.3	Philosophical and social significances in theoretical exploration	104
4.4.4	Critical spirit	105
4.4.5	The range and depth of intellectual influence	106
	A case study	107
4.5.1	A reflection on social change	107
4.5.2	Strong sense of critical spirit	108
4.5.3	Social and intellectual analyses	109
4.5.4	Political significance in academic study	110

CHAPTER 5 A Comparison of the Chinese and English Languages 113

	The origin and development of the Chinese and English languages	113
5.1.1	The development of the Chinese language	113
5.1.2	The development of the English language	114
	The main features of the Chinese language	116
5.2.1	The ideographic language in general	116
5.2.2	Flexibility in sentence structure	117
5.2.3	Sense of tense and inflection	117
5.2.4	Elliptical elements	118
5.2.5	Chinese as a tonal language	118
5.2.6	Chinese pronunciation	119
5.2.7	Chinese vocabulary	119
5.2.8	Chinese grammar	120
	The main features of the English language	121
5.3.1	Shape-and-inflection structure	121
5.3.2	Sound-identified language	122
5.3.3	Accent as the sign for differentiation in meaning or part of speech	123
5.3.4	The constitution of a variety of rhyme and rhythm	123
5.3.5	The expansion of vocabulary by borrowing from other languages	124
5.3.6	Varieties of English established in the modern age	125
	Comparative comments	126
5.4.1	The origin of the two languages	126
5.4.2	Diverse linguistic applications and features	128
5.4.3	Historical changes in language form	130
5.4.4	Psychological and aesthetic effects of the two languages	132
5.4.5	External influences	134
5.4.6	Academic study	136

CHAPTER 6 A Comparison of Chinese and Western Poetry 140

    An account of the development of Chinese and Western poetry 140
- 6.1.1 The story of Chinese poetry 140
- 6.1.2 The story of Western poetry 143

    Central concerns in Chinese and Western poetry 144
- 6.2.1 Political issues 145
- 6.2.2 Social concerns 146
- 6.2.3 Personal concerns 147

    Aesthetic sense in poetic production 150
- 6.3.1 Emotional touches on various occasions 150
- 6.3.2 Awareness of natural charm 151
- 6.3.3 Philosophical meditations 153
- 6.3.4 Imagination 155
- 6.3.5 Cultural taste 157
- 6.3.6 Social satire 160

    Poetic form 162
- 6.4.1 Sound pattern 163
- 6.4.2 Imagery 165

    A case study 167

CHAPTER 7 A Comparison of Chinese and Western Fictions 173

    Historical development of Chinese and Western fictions 173
- 7.1.1 An account of fiction development in China 173
- 7.1.2 An account of Western fiction development 176

    General sense of fiction as a literary genre 178
- 7.2.1 Story development in early fiction 179
- 7.2.2 Historical aspect of fiction 180
- 7.2.3 Moral value of fiction 181
- 7.2.4 Social significance of fiction 182
- 7.2.5 Preparation for modern fiction 183

    Central concern and subject matter 184
- 7.3.1 Historical and political concerns 185
- 7.3.2 Social convention 187
- 7.3.3 Love romance 188
- 7.3.4 Myth and supernatural tales 190

    Writing methods 191
- 7.4.1 Language features 191
- 7.4.2 Narrative structure and perspective 193
- 7.4.3 Characterization and psychological writing 194

7.4.4	The use of imagery and other rhetorical devices	196
7.4.5	Satirical and critical tone	198
	Case studies	200
7.5.1	A comparative study of *san-guo-yan-yi* and *War and Peace*	200
7.5.2	A comparative study of *hong-lou-meng* and *The Sound and the Fury*	203

CHAPTER 8 A Comparison of Chinese and Western Paintings ... 207

	The development and main features of Chinese painting	207
8.1.1	Beginning of Chinese painting and its early development	207
8.1.2	Vigour and variety of Chinese painting in the middle period	209
8.1.3	The signs of change in the modern Chinese painting	213
	The origin and development of Western painting	216
8.2.1	The initial stage of Western painting	216
8.2.2	Vigorous growth in Western painting since the Renaissance	217
8.2.3	The dawn of the modern painting and modernist achievement	219
	Comparative comments	223
8.3.1	The origin and development of paintings	223
8.3.2	Form and style of paintings	225
8.3.3	Subject and object	228
8.3.4	Practice and theory	229
8.3.5	Tradition and experiment	232

CHAPTER 9 A Comparison of Science between China and the West ... 235

	A survey of Chinese scientific development	236
9.1.1	The early achievement in Chinese maths and astronomy	236
9.1.2	Contributions of Chinese earth science and medicine	237
9.1.3	Scientific records in Chinese agriculture	238
9.1.4	Chinese early inventions in comparison with those of the West	239
	A survey of Western scientific development	241
9.2.1	The birth of Western science and its early development	241
9.2.2	Western scientific development in the Middle Ages	242
9.2.3	The awakening of the Western sense of science on the threshold of the modern age	244
9.2.4	Western science in the modern age	247
	Comparative comments	250
9.3.1	Initiation of science from mathematics	251

	9.3.2	Part-time engagement with scientific research	251
	9.3.3	Close relation between science and practice	252
	9.3.4	Dependence of science on economy and other developments	253
	9.3.5	Intellectual and rational influences	253
	9.3.6	Practical effects and social status	254

Epilogue ... 263

Chronological Table of Major Chinese and Western Cultural Events / Figures ... 266

Bibliography ... 295

Chapter 1

Introduction

Globalization, as a current phenomenon, requires further understanding on the part of the average Chinese, of foreign, especially Western culture, or Western ways of living and thinking. Such a need for comprehension comes from frequent use of Western ideas and technology in their daily life and work in almost every aspect of social and economic and cultural developments. Many people have greatly benefited from acquiring such knowledge and understanding, which has subsequently accelerated the process of economic and cultural globalization. Nonetheless, cultural acquisition and understanding is never unilateral but always bilateral. Consequently, there arises an issue of how to handle the relationship between native culture and external culture. Generally no nation would expect to easily give up its own national and cultural identity though national differences could be narrowed and bridged in the process of globalization. People would often, consciously or unconsciously, first take up and then compare what they have acquired to see if they have actually added something to their established way of thinking and behaving. In doing so, they have started to build up a new culture. It is also the case with the development of national identity. This may be the original motivation for making comparisons at the beginning of a course of cultural studies.

1.1 Motivations and grounds for making comparative studies

The necessity for preserving and improving national culture is today acknowledged universally since it has much to do with social and intellectual developments as well as the establishment of the national identity of a country. Traditional culture is certainly one of the most charming elements of national identity. But doubtless, the inadequacies in any tradition have, in a way, retarded social and intellectual developments. When one feels proud of the long history of one's country and its glorious cultural accomplishment, one has a sense of pity if it has suffered from backwardness and weakness.

This is especially true in modern times when countries with a long history, like China, Egypt, India or even Iraq, declined while the West arose. Comparative study of cultures, from the scholar's perspective, partially helps to sum up the historical lessons of backwardness and inadequacies in addition to the advanced experience and brilliant achievement. It also helps to heighten one's consciousness of the social, cultural and intellectual conditions that give rise to any example of downgrading inclination at a particular stage of modern history.

One of the attractions of comparative studies is the academic freedom and advantages one can enjoy in doing research. Comparative study enables us to explore more easily and to discern more clearly, a more precisely identified range of strengths and weakness on both sides. One can try to put aside all the unnecessary prejudices, political, racial or social, and only focus on one's academic concerns. I trust that comparative study, as an independent discipline as well as a useful method, can aim to develop and establish one's view of certain subjects more consciously, more sharply and more effectively. It can be dangerous to pursue development without understanding one's own culture and the culture of other nations. It is a lesson we should learn from our history and it can benefit our current ways of handling increasingly complicated world affairs.

The essentials of comparative culture in the present book

As mentioned above, herein lie three aspects of cultural affairs for our current comparative study, namely the ideological, the literary and artistic, and the other areas of the humanities. Among these three aspects, the ideological field is of primary importance for it always, in whichever period of human civilization, contributes to the direction, speed and scope of the other developments.

1.2.1 The leading role of ideology

In a way, ideology is a decisive factor in human civilization and social development. It has been discussed by quite a number of distinguished thinkers in both China and the West. Among them is perhaps Jean-Jacques Rousseau who, as one of the most eloquent speakers for Western culture, argues in his famous *Discourse on the Origin and Foundation of Inequality among Mankind* that human beings were initially little more than animals except for their special sympathy for their own species. Only through the development of reason and language, he asserts, were humans, while retaining this sympathy, able to understand their individual selves. This leads to a natural community and the closest thing to what he considers humanity's perfect moment. He also suggests, in *The Social Contract or Principles of Political Right*, the practical role of the legislator, and introduces the concept of the general will, as well as the solution to the conflicts between the particular and the universal, the individual and the citizen, and the actual and the moral. All these ideas initiated by Rousseau have provided a theoretical foundation for the later development of a new society established by the bourgeoisie. ① It is impossible to conceive of the bourgeois revolution or capitalist social development without Rousseau's thinking.

Ideology is also central to the development of Chinese civilization. Whether we like or dislike Confucianism, we have to admit that it dominated Chinese social and intellectual developments for about two thousand years. In spite of the ups and downs in the social and intellectual conditions in the long history of Chinese civilization, Confucianism helped maintain a fairly stable though sometimes turbulent or even critical and risky situation. No matter whether such a trend was good or bad for the ordinary Chinese, no one could deny that it was Confucianism that preceded and decided the spirit and nature of Chinese civilization with its social, economic and cultural accomplishments.

Apart from the important role played by ideology, especially by ruling ideology, we also take interest in how these ideas work under different conditions and contribute to social and intellectual developments. Ideology received due attention from society in the early days of both civilizations. It was used as part of the ruling strategies in respective competitive struggles between ideas during the Spring-Autumn and Warring States Periods in China and the Plato-Aristotle period of Greek civilization. Ideology established itself at the time as an independent factor, automatically working for the formation of certain generally accepted moral, ethical, academic, social and intellectual principles. These principles, even if they were rough and incomplete, started to apply to human behaviours as a guiding rule and thus became a kind of necessity in social and intellectual developments. Some of these principles were accepted and put into the building of certain legal system either in China or in the West. For instance, the ritual principles of the Zhou Dynasty or some of the pre-Socrates laws in a number of Greek city states, could be regarded as such demonstrations. During the early days of human civilizations, ideology seemed to take its own course and worked separately, principally as an unofficial force, with little interference from the government. Its position was humble yet independent, and crucial in terms of cultural and intellectual influence without any privilege. However, with the passage of time, such intellectual conditions were changed due to the increasing

---

① See *The Cambridge Dictionary of Philosophy*, p. 800, Robert Audi (ed.), Cambridge University Press, 1999.

concern for and practicable contribution of ideology.

The ruling class, no matter what its origin, was generally well educated and became aware of the significance of intellectual factors in the execution of its reign and policies. Perhaps it was rare that intellectual power would run at liberty into uncontrolled operation of society, which largely depended on the wisdom of certain politicians. But once such a practice was under way, its effectiveness and efficiency were witnessed as what happened during the Spring-Autumn Period in China and Pericle's time in Greece. Nonetheless, excessive care for ideology soon became a fashion in certain stages of human civilizations. In China it was initiated in the Western Han Dynasty when Dong Zhongshu, an official at the time, proposed to establish Confucianism as the only officially recognized ideology. Three or four centuries later, a similar event occurred in the Roman Empire when Constantine the Great made Christian worship lawful and his successor declared Christianity to be the only state religion and authoritative ideology. As a result of these two events, there came an epoch-making period when one particular ideology worked as an official instrument and prevailed over other kinds of ideology. Thus ideology lost its previous independence and freedom to perform its intellectual duty.

Meanwhile other schools of ideology were either held in disfavour or ignored and dwindled or even closed down in the face of the privileged position granted to the officially recognized ideology, such as Confucianism and Christianity. It was almost the same gloomy situation in both cases that prevailed over the long period between the ancient time and the modern age after the raising of the two ideologies to official status. Politically autocratic, intellectually depressed in the middle period on both sides, tens upon hundreds of years passed, with little achievements and much spiritual suffering to the ordinary people. No matter how many dynasties were removed or replaced on either side, the dominant position and the intellectual leadership of Confucianism and Christianity remained unchanged until the end of this period. Misuse of power by either the ruling ideological group or the ruling class dominated by the ruling ideology led to corruption, disintegration, civil war and misconduct or other evils, marking the darkest period within human history. Obviously social, economic and cultural developments were greatly retarded too during the period.

Perhaps, owing to the suffocating circumstances imposed on their life and work, writers and artists in the West during the Renaissance started to take a way different from Christian tradition and tried to evoke classical ideology as a new spiritual guideline for their creative work. If the artistic and literary achievements could confirm the justification and necessity of the Renaissance, the strength of ideology continued in political and other fields through its growing influence to be expanded against the bondage of Christianity and feudalism.

The rise of the Enlightenment was no accident, given that more and more people were conscious of the significance of intellectual issues. Social conditions and heightened consciousness allowed the ideas of Voltaire, Montesquieu and Rousseau to work beyond the intellectual level of general public. Eventually they aroused the conscience and awareness of the majority of the French when the bourgeois revolution overthrew the feudal and autocratic dynasties. Two decisive factors contributed to the eventual victory of the bourgeois revolution. One was certainly the foresight and wisdom of a few bourgeois revolutionary thinkers such as Rousseau, Voltaire and Montesquieu. The other, which was perhaps even more crucial and contributive, was that the capitalist mode of production had prepared the necessary social and economic conditions as a result of which the ordinary people shifted from a feudalistic to a capitalist way of living. Because of that change, people had the desire to seek freedom and resist autocracy and willingly accepted political changes arising from the bourgeois revolution. In that sense, ideology was to suit the social demands and general circumstances of the majority. No matter what kind of ideology came into fashion in the West in the last few centuries, the ruling class or the bourgeoisie always kept its sway by allowing intellectual freedom as a mediator among diverse views and ideas. Tolerance and a critical spirit worked as the two most important factors from then on, allowing for competition among ideological schools that flourished numerously and promoted social development as a result of intellectual emancipation.

China by comparison seemed a bit late in changing from autocracy to democracy. Not until the beginning of the 20th century did China finally give up its autocratic dynasty, about two centuries later than the West. Among various reasons accounting for the phenomenon, one could refer to tradition, both political and cultural. Politically, China used to emphasize centralization and unification. No matter in which period of history, eventual success or victory of a noble ideal was always marked by national unification or centralized rule though the country did experience a number of periods of disintegration. In the West, national unification and centralization of power was only an occasional experience. Beginning in ancient Greece, for most of the time the West was marked by separation or division, though it also went through transient periods of unification and peace, such as the period of the Roman Empire or Charlemagne's Holy Roman Empire. The long period of split offered the possibility of the existence of diverse political entities and the development of distinctive national cultures. Culturally and intellectually, for most of its long history, China seldom, if ever, cared for democracy as the basis for making a decision either within a family or within a government. Human relations were mostly established on the basis of hierarchy denoting superiority and inferiority determined by age, sex, rank, expertise and blood relationships. This was certainly quite different from if not exactly the opposite (in principle anyway) to the Western way of handling matters. Beginning from the period of the Greek city states, Western democracy has tended to work as the basis for making decisions and thus affected ways of thinking and ways of dealing with daily affairs, both at a personal level and at a business or administrative level, even though the execution of such a principle was disturbed periodically or even constantly in Western historical development, especially during the Middle Ages.

Another reason for the distinction between Chinese and Western ideologies resides in the attitudes to different or contrary opinions. Generally, many autocratic rulers on both sides took hostile and forceful measures to impose their ideas, seldom accepting if not totally refusing the opinions not in their favour. This gave rise to countless wars, killings, persecutions and suppressions for the sake of establishing or maintaining the so-called status or prestige of the rulers concerned. But this tendency was tremendously reduced in the West after the Renaissance, as was exemplified in Britain's Glorious Revolution in 1688 which greatly reduced the monarch's power to that of ceremonial significance. A non-bloody shift of power in Britain proved the possibility that one could use non-violence to achieve political ends or to reduce or remove political differences. The sense of compromise and reconciliation afterwards spread widely among Western countries as a principle to solve controversial problems and as a choice to avoid violence, as demonstrated in Denmark, Sweden, Luxembourg and Belgium where constitutional monarchy was established through a compromise between the monarch and the bourgeoisie.

Comparatively, Chinese ruling ideology seemed more unrelenting and lacked tolerance in its way of handling political differences. Just think of the countless civil wars throughout Chinese history. Those wars all went in parallel with similar events in Western history, which indicated that violence was inevitable during times of transition or instability. The point is that China showed little desire to change from using violence as a major way of coping with diversities in conflicts of politics or ideological points of view, even at the time when the West turned to non-violence. Furthermore, the Chinese use of violence was not confined to the political arena. One example is that the efforts to consolidate the political power developed into the need to suppress intellectual divergences, such as the mass persecution and execution of scholars for the so-called literal imprisonment during the Kangxi-Qianlong reign of the Qing Dynasty. It would have been a period in Chinese history very close to becoming like the Enlightenment in the West but for the violent suppression by the ruling class. The violent way to handle intellectual issues also occurred in the West, such as the brutal persecution by Inquisition of the scientists and other innocent people who were brought on trial or put on fire for execution on charge of infidelity because of their belief in science or the ideas other than Christianity. But the Western intellectual tradition, on the whole, was comparatively not as harsh as that in China.

The third reason might relate to the tradition of rational thinking, which once made up the core of Western classicism and contributed to the motivation of later intellectual development. For instance, the Renaissance and the Enlightenment were both influenced by rationalism, which served as a guiding rule to repudiate Christian mysticism and to uphold humanism and scientific knowledge. In comparison, Chinese ideology appeared inadequate in scientific and rational tradition though a school of Confucianism relevant to rational idea came onto the scene of the ruling ideology during the Song and the Ming Dynasties.[①] But generally Chinese ideology seemed more obsessed by autocracy, blind faith and superstition, which sometimes appeared negative and even stubbornly harmful in the long run of Chinese history and hindered further development of this country.

Lack of critical spirit and overemphasis on intellectual and ideological unification were peculiar to traditional Chinese ideology and greatly reduced its ability to tolerate different ideas or moderate the overuse of political power which led to corruption. This manifest tendency affected nearly every aspect of social and individual life in China.

1.2.2 Literature and art as part of cultural tradition

Literature is a traditional area of cultural activity for both sides. One could find both similarities and dissimilarities in literary origins, function, theme, subject matter, style and technique between China and the West. These can be demonstrated, for example, in poetry and fiction. A number of points are worthy of notice.

Together with art, literature is generally regarded as a product of social development at a certain stage to meet the spiritual needs of human beings. It is characterized by both amusement and didacticism in the sense that literature and art are created to make people happy and relaxed in spirit while improving them morally. The dual purpose has worked almost from the beginning and has applied unchallengedly to every aspect of literature and art till the arrival of modernism. Some radical schools of modernism, like Dadaism and futurism, attempt to deny all traditional forms and ideas and thus are trapped into a dead end. Therefore, though the focus of the dual motivation could vary with each side and even each individual work, the range of variety and diversity in art and literature should be confined to the dual purpose to evade polarity arising out of social and cultural divergence between China and the West.

The origin of literature and art has something to do with the need to record and convey human feelings, as is confirmed by the Chinese expression "poetry

---

① The representative figure of this school is Zhu Xi, who claims the whole universe is based on *li* (reason) and *qi* (gas) which are used to lay down a theoretical foundation to interpret and benefit the feudal reign of autocracy and impose the dominance of feudal ethics so that concentrated centralism could be consolidated and eternalized as a unified nation.

serves to express aspiration". Whether or not one could freely manifest one's feelings and by what standard one's feelings could be judged then become central to the quality of a literary work. This in turn leads to the moral values one should accept in reading poems and stories and gives different sets of moral codes which would vary according to time and space in close relation to certain social and intellectual developments. Apart from that difference, however, people are bound by some general tenets or human values, such as love and hatred, evil and good, poor and rich, beautiful and ugly. It is these general principles that people, in both China and the West, could share in understanding and making judgments about the best literary writings. This can be verified and amplified by an exchange of ideas in cultural and literary communications as part of the globalizing process, which again highlights the need to reduce, if not remove, various barriers between different cultures, like those between China and the West. Then what constitutes the chief cultural differences in such literary genres as poetry and fiction should attract considerable attention here since they concern the means to bridge the cultural gap and eventually to achieve a coming together.

By comparison with fiction and other literary genres, poetry cares more for its form and emotional expressions, in terms of its rhythm and rhyming patterns, figurative language, structures and choice of ideas. Rhyming devices once played a crucial role in Chinese *shi* and *ci* poetry, which were in fashion for a pretty long period of time. The difficulties in poetic composition limited the number of poets and poetry as a genre had to take its solitary course without the involvement of the ordinary people. Though Western poetry was less complicated than its Chinese counterpart in rhyming device, its composition also had to rely on the educated, such as aristocrats and scholars who conveyed their feelings through verse without considering the use of prose form until long after the Renaissance.

Working with the different tones of a limited number of characters, Chinese poets had to be very patient, deliberate and talented in choosing the right character to match their ideas. Complexities of poetic techniques and designs might work in composing short lyrical poems, but would appear difficult in making long narrative verse. This might explain why Chinese classical poetry lacked long narrative epics in its extended poetic tradition. In comparison, Western classical poetry was more flexible in using rhymes without caring too much about perfect accuracies and word-for-word or even syllable-for-syllable connection in compositions, as was the case with its Chinese counterpart. Hence it was no accident that the epic, as a form of poetry, gained popularity and stature in Western poetic composition from Homer on.

The relationship between literature and politics is another important aspect when considering the difference between China and the West. On the one hand, poets and writers are consciously or unconsciously motivated by their political inclinations in their writings. They have expressed their approval or disapproval, likes or dislikes of certain social circumstances in relation to their characters or the themes they drew on. On the other hand, literary or artistic works have to be influenced by the political situation or social trends when they are conceived. In a word, no one can really get rid of political influences since they exist in a certain dimension of society. Such manifestations are more evident in Chinese literature, since Chinese culture has a strong tradition that literary compositions should serve the society of their time, as was first proposed by Bai Juyi, a famous poet and critic in the Tang Dynasty. Bai once said: "Poetry should work to provide additional observation of current affairs and help to convey human feelings."[1] In ancient China the number of poets or artists was very much limited. They were either officials or scholars, unworried about their daily necessities. It was a common view that a good scholar should have an official expectation of sustenance and support as part of Confucianist intellectual inheritance. Such a tradition perhaps determined the tendency for many men of letters to have political ambitions throughout the long period of Chinese feudal society. Therefore, political concerns or aspirations were constant subjects in their poems or essays or artistic works. This probably gave rise to a typical inadequacy among many Chinese intellectuals who lost their precious status of intellectual independence by depending heavily on political expectations. It is also one of the major reasons why China could scarcely foster and cherish a robust and tolerably independent intellectual climate.

Comparatively speaking, Western writers were less concerned with this aspect for they were usually faced with more choices. An official career, compared with those in such areas as clergy or business, was not necessarily the best choice. Contrary to the ancient Chinese poets and artists, many Western writers were actually from the priesthood or aristocracy, an origin which seemed at the time to be less socially and politically demanding and have less expectation, thus providing more freedom for what they chose to write about.

Censorship is another area for cultural comparisons. Theoretically speaking, Chinese creative work did not have any censorship to follow except for spiritual bondage through Confucianism. Yet in practice no literary or artistic work dared to offend the emperor or the officials of the time and this bound people to allegiance like an invisible net. However, there were always some daring writers or artists who ignored and broke through conventional ideas to indicate their discontent with, or even resistance to, the ruler of the day. This was the case with a number of distinguished poets like Qu Yuan, Du Fu, Li Bai, Bai Juyi, artists like Ba Da Shan Ren and the Eight Eccentrics of Yangzhou. A lot of books were put on the censorship list once they were deemed to contain anything offensive. Almost every dynasty in Chinese history had a rule, forbidding all

---

[1] See *Chinese Literary History* (II), p. 449, Institute of Literary Research of Chinese Academy of Science, People's Literature Press, 1962.

books to mention anything positive about the previous dynasty or government.

The Western cultural tradition emphasized the restrictive role of the moral code though it was seemingly more tolerant of political offences. Yet dissidents also suffered similar persecution during the Middle Ages, such as what occurred to Dante with his *The Divine Comedy*. In spite of this, one could find a number of poems or novels or art works, which were characterized by political dissidence but received little or no censorship (although they might be ostracized) after the bourgeoisie took over power. English romantics like Byron and Shelley, for instance, time and again expressed their strong desire to stage a revolution against the ruling class in their romantic and sometimes overemotional poems. Novels by Charles Dickens, William Thackeray, Stendhal and Victor Hugo also showed strong sympathies for the poor and expressed the wish that the capitalist exploiting system would decline. But their works seemed to meet with surprisingly little censorship or banning in their circulation. Of course, undeniably the Roman Catholic church with its infamous list of prohibited books, issued by its department of Propaganda, did exert significant influence on some parts of the Western world.

In addition to these political concerns in subject matter, literature and art have demonstrated a great variety in terms of what to write about or what to represent in individual works. Overall, four groups of subject matter seem most popular. The first group is certainly of love, marriage and associated social conventions. The second group is about social satire targeting mainly the rich, the ruling classes, clerics, scholars and other privileged people. The third group is of military affairs based on some famous historical victories, defeats or simply local wars. The fourth group is concerned with adventures or myths with a focus on wild imagination or fantasies. These four categories probably constitute the majority of literary works, both narrative poetry and prose, in China and the West. Since poetry is usually for spontaneous or occasional emotions, especially on the Chinese side, prose is more appropriate for longer narration, though there are a number of epics in the Western poetic tradition. In modern times, poetry certainly contributes more to lyrical purpose and assumes shorter and more visible form in comparison with fiction. This of course has not contained drama, opera or the ballet which are not the targets of our discussion on account of the limited space of the book.

Though these four areas apply constantly to the subject matter of literature in both China and the West, the priority is different in the respective works of literature and art. Social satire and adventure / fantasy are more commonly than not seen in Western works while scholar-beauty love affairs or official-career experiences occupy an important position on the Chinese side. However, these diversities in subject matter have greatly narrowed in the modern age when Chinese literature and art have gradually merged into the world fashions represented by Western preferences. For instance, social satire seemed to become a favourite category for Chinese writers at the turn of the 20th century when quite a number of novels appeared to aim at exposing social darkness and negative figures by ironic descriptions and commentaries.

Another important feature of literature and art relates to general modes of development and techniques, which shows more and more connections between the two cultures, such as classicism, realism, romanticism and modernism. Both sides were attracted by realism though the term was not coined in the early stage. Representation of social life has been found in the remnants of works and artifacts from ancient times. If the realist mode leads to almost no differences between the two sides, romanticism certainly means something different in China as opposed to the West. Chinese art and literature have never had any theory or movement equivalent to those in the West, yet China's early poets, like Qu Yuan and Li Po, appeared to express their romantic ideas through their wild imaginations or strong attraction to nature and the expression of powerful emotion. Western Romantics, however, appeared more influential as a group. The Romantic Movement launched in the 19th century was much later than the appearance of individual romantics in China. The romantic ideas of the Western writers were not only represented in their poems, music, paintings or novels but were transformed into some theoretical principles which promoted later the development of art and literature, by supplying as useful fodder for the formation of other cultural movements like modernism.

Modernism, in a way, is a continuation of romanticism. The turn to inward representation actually started with the Romantics as was confirmed by their emotional exclamation of excitement over nature. A focus on psychological representation is a natural result of intensive emotional expression. As mentioned above, a rebellious resistance to tradition can be seen in the writings of Romantics like Byron and Shelley who show their courage and determination to break free from the old ideas and social order. Their contemporaries Wordsworth, Coleridge and Keats are comparatively mild in temperament and manifest a stronger sense of aesthetics in their poetic works. A pursuit of new artistic forms is also characteristic of the Romantics, many of whom went abroad and took an interest in alien and fantastic culture after joining in the fashion of collecting folk songs or old tales. Of course, romanticism is not equal to modernism, which went even further to extremes. It attempted to deny all the traditional forms by delving into states of depression, alienation, displacement and absurdity in the human psyche. Beginning with French Symbolism, many schools of modernism embarked on routes of experimentation, greatly changing conventional ideas and forms to suit their subjective inward needs. Consequently, modernism has produced a large number of experimental works totally different in form from their predecessors and rebellious in content and spirit against the status quo and tradition of the time. Though modernism in its extreme forms (imagism, futurism, cubism, etc.) did not last long, its critical spirit and ways of exploring new techniques or new modes of writing, such as care for inward description, would certainly be passed onto later generations (e.g. surrealism, pop art and even postmodernism) as a heritage for the whole human race.

In many ways, art has shared with literature many features like the desire to create, originality and imagination, even though it is quite different in forms and methods of production. Both Chinese art and literature have been influenced by their Western counterparts, which initiated totally new ideas and forms. Chinese modernism thus gained headway in the first half of the 20th century and came into a new stage of development after the 1980s. It is noteworthy that modernism has merged into the mainstream of art and literature by making itself part of the accepted techniques of creation. In that sense, modernism is not extinct but has adapted to creative needs and new developments of art and literature. The best example is perhaps the popularity of the psychological approach and the use of symbolism. As a reaction against modernism, postmodernism owes a great deal to its predecessor.

1.2.3 A variety of cultural subjects

Language is the basis for all communications in ideology, culture, literature and art, though it has its own laws of operation. As a matter of fact, language contributes to almost every aspect of human life and hence works as the most fundamental and essential instrument at our human's disposition. But such a contribution is often ignored as it is often taken for granted that language practice is a natural endowment granted to human beings by God without any hindrance. Perhaps it is for this reason that linguistic study did not receive the public acknowledgement it deserved for its value to humanity. It could also explain the reason why nowadays more and more attention has been drawn to the subject since it has been proven to be closely related to the science of information and other advanced technologies.

In spite of the huge distinction between the Chinese and English languages, as manifested in orthography, pronunciation, vocabulary and grammar, the two languages have much in common. For example, they both never evade their responsibilities to work for their respective cultures as instruments of communication. Though Chinese is used by the largest number of people in the world, its popularity is still second to English, in that the use of Chinese is still limited by the extent of its social and economic development, especially in terms of the need for scientific and technological information conveyed by a certain language. Therefore a language is actually a symbol of a certain level of development in civilization and a measure of the culture's social, economic and intellectual status in the world. No wonder China has to borrow a great deal from the West in both technology and language. One example is the adoption of Roman letters as phonetic symbols for Chinese pronunciation at the turn of the

19th century. Another is the common use of Arabic numbers. Though Chinese has benefited from English and other foreign languages, it appears that Chinese maintains its own system as an ideographic language and has opened a new and prospective road for human civilization.

With the progress of modern science and technology, linguistic study has reached a new phase by introducing ideas that are more scientific and methods, including computerizing samples and calculation and sociological, psychological and even neurological approaches. These provide new means of exploring the depths of human language and establish interdisciplinary subjects in research. Chinese and English, since they are based on separate image- or sound-oriented systems, seem to work in opposite directions, yet have achieved balanced results in terms of speed and efficiency. Probably neither could really afford to reject the other unless some absolutely definite requirement comes out of world manufacturing and business as a whole. This is almost impossible to imagine within a century or two and is therefore beyond our expectation. However, one thing is certain that more and more contact with and influence upon each other is an inevitable part of the process of globalization. In a sense this is what has occurred in the fields of ideology, art and literature.

Language is a science in some ways, for it is intended to be a more objective and operational instrument for human beings. Yet generally language is not included in the conceptual areas of science and technology. It is regarded as a subject more related to humanity itself rather than existing outside the humanities. Yet it is different from the other subjects of the humanities, such as art and literature, which are more subjective. The objective of science usually refers to the understanding of nature, an area considered exterior to human society though in its initial sense the word was just confined to knowledge.

The word "science" is taken from the West through Japan, meaning knowledge. It is doubtless one of the most substantial as well as most fashionable terms in the world today. It is not just because of its practical significance through its ability to create huge wealth, but because of its increasingly widening popularity in a cultural sense, applying to our daily life. Scientific development is the key issue facing humanity, because it will determine the future of the human society. Consequently, the study of science is concerned not only with the material progress of mankind, but with the spiritual acquisitions of the current age.

In this sense, the term "science" is a yardstick to measure the degree and level of human civilization. One of the basic disparities between China and the West lies in the awareness of the meaning of science. An aspect of Chinese intellectual insufficiency is its lack of concern for science, which originated from ancient times when scientific research was not given its rightful status alongside other subjects in the curriculum of the major philosophers. Though some of the great scholars like Lao Zi and Mo Zi produced some good points about science, their ideas were either neglected or they themselves could not go on with their specific scientific investigation or care. Thus their assertions could not take shape as a comparatively complete set of independent ideas without further inquiry into nature based on science. One could give a number of reasons why Chinese civilization fell behind in later social, economic and intellectual developments in comparison with Western civilization, even though early Chinese civilization achieved a fairly good headway in this respect. Among them is the ignorance of science which served probably as one of the major factors leading to unsound ways of thinking, ill management of the country during the long period of autocratic reign and intolerance of different or progressive ideas.

Comparatively, the rapid growth of social development and productive forces initiated by the bourgeois revolution and Industrial Revolution in the modern West, is also partly due to the care for a scientific way of thinking established during the Renaissance and the Enlightenment, which encouraged scientific inquiries as part of the heritage of the Western cultural tradition. By contrast, the shortage of scientific development in China is ascribed to the slow development of Chinese society, economy and culture as a result of narrow and limited outlook originating from autocracy and long-term tradition of ignoring science and practical knowledge.

The function of science is of course not just confined to social and economic developments, but extends to intellectual development. The popularity of science in the West has greatly accelerated social and intellectual progress, which was confirmed by the Encyclopaedia Movement in France in the 18th century. The gap between China and the West was further expanded if one takes into account the role of science in modern intellectual development. The prolonging of the autocratic systems due to the sluggish advance in social, economic and scientific developments in old China, goes some way to explain the necessity of the Chinese revolution which has eventually brought about the Chinese modernization with a focus on the development of science.

1.3 Gap yet to be bridged

In the sense of scientific contribution, one should consider how China has benefited from the introduction of Western science since the early 20th century. The gap of course could not be easily bridged or removed, yet it has been narrowed in the past century. We can be confident that some day China will catch up and even go ahead because science is fair and freely available to every culture. It is not just up to the upgrading of sophisticated technology for the sake of improving material convenience or comfort, but depends on the popularity of science when everybody adopts it as a way of thinking and living. This must take a much longer period to come into effect because China itself is immense and education is more than just a luxury for such a large population. By the time the majority of average Chinese are able to enjoy a scientific outlook towards the world, with regard to both nature and human society, the Chinese people will find themselves not only at a high level of material comfort, but at a high level of spiritual comfort.

Questions for discussion and comprehension

1. What is the meaning for picking up cultural comparison as a subject to deal with Chinese and Western cultures?
2. Why do we have to place philosophy and ideology in a position of priority in terms of cultural studies?
3. What do you think of the relations of some general concerns and some specific areas within cultural comparison? Give one or two examples.

List of proposed books for further reading

1. 季羡林、张光(王磷)编选,1997,《东西文化议论集》,北京:经济日报出版社。
2. 韦政通,1988,《中国的智慧》,北京:中国和平出版社。
3. 郁龙余(编),1989,《中西文化异同论》,北京:生活·读书·新知三联书店。
4. 周一良(主编),1987,《中外文化交流史》,郑州:河南人民出版社。
5. 许苏民,1992,《比较文化研究史》,昆明:云南人民出版社。
6. 张隆溪(编),1982,《比较文学译文集》,北京:北京大学出版社。
7. Bode, Derk, *Chinese Ideas in the West*, Washington: American Council on Education, 1980.
8. Fernandez-Armesto, Felipe, *Millennium: A History of the Last Thousand Years*, Riverside, NJ: Simon and Schuster Inc., 1995.

Chapter 2

A Comparison of Ancient Chinese and Western Philosophies

As perhaps the most crucial factors in the intellectual development of the human race, philosophy and ideology are usually regarded as a product of human spirit and always serve as guiding principles for theoretical exploration and the enduring progress of human civilization. The advance and maturity of human civilization is closely related to and even decided by the operation of its ideology. The historical experiences of both China and the West have witnessed such a tendency which pervaded the long periods of intellectual and ideological formation, development and exploration before the current age of established ideology.

In spite of the general trend of ideological development common to both sides, cultural gap and social diversities contributed to the emergence of huge differences in the national identities as were manifest in ideologies and philosophies peculiar to China and the West. It is interesting to note the ideological similarities and dissimilarities between China and the West, which have shaped the intellectual conditions of these cultures and produced vast differences between the two great civilizations. This chapter will focus on the ancient period for a comparative study of the two cultures.

2.1 A survey of ancient Chinese philosophy

Chinese philosophy started to become apparent in the 6th century BC and reached its climax in the Spring-Autumn Period when Confucianism and other ideological schools were born and contested with each other to establish their different viewpoints on both the social and natural worlds. Many philosophers appeared with their marvellous opinions on some fundamental issues of the world they lived in, such as heaven, earth, natural phenomena and human society. Among them are Lao Zi, Confucius, Mo Zi, Mencius, Zhuang Zi, Xun Zi and Han Fei.

Chinese philosophy as represented by Confucianism, takes up a crucial position in the historical development of Chinese civilization where it has worked as the only caretaker of ideology not long after its birth. Its intellectual permeation and infiltration into wide-covering areas shows its powerful influence and tremendous contribution in terms of looking after the world outlook of the ordinary people and national superstructural dimensions, which are usually supervised in the West by both philosophy and religion. The latter seemed weak in China and was in a way replaced by philosophy which was dominant not only in academic studies and daily life for the ordinary people but also in politics. The best example is Confucianism which as the major philosophical school in China ruled over Chinese political and intellectual fields for over two thousand years. According to Professor Feng Yulan, "Regardless of the differences between the schools of Chinese philosophy, the philosophy of every school represents, at the same time, its political thought. This does not mean that in the various schools of philosophy there are no metaphysics, no ethics, no logic. It means only that all these factors are connected with political thought in one way or another, just as Plato's Republic represents his whole philosophy and at the same time is his political thought."[1]

The following is a brief account of their basic conditions and major views of the principal schools of ancient Chinese philosophy.

2.1.1 Confucianism

1 A brief account

The Ru School existed before the time of Confucius and its members were principally ritualists or teachers. Confucius, as one of the group, must have been influenced by its major concerns but seemed more concerned with the then chaotic situation of society. He tried to find remedies by restoring and manipulating some traditional values and norms. Since he was an eloquent teacher and propagandist, he soon gathered a large group of students and followers who shared his concerns and beliefs and then developed into a Confucianist school.

Confucianism is characterized by a common ethical ideal, which contains an affective concern for all living beings, varying in origin and nature, depending on how such things relate to them. It has a reverential attitude towards others which is manifested in the observance of formal rules of conduct, such as the way to receive guests. Confucius' followers also advocate a firm commitment to proper conduct so that one is not upset or disabled by adverse circumstances, such as poverty or death.

---

[1] See *A Short History of Chinese Philosophy*, p. 26, Feng Yulan, Press of Tianjin Social Science Academy, 2007.

According to Confucius, everyone in the political realm is supposed to have the ability to attain these ideals. A ruler who embodies the ideals would care about and provide for the people, who would be in turn attracted to and respectful of him. It was 400 years or so after Confucius' death that Confucianism was established as the dominant national ideology for both the government and people to follow. From then on, Confucianism remained dominant in Chinese social and intellectual life throughout the approximately two thousand years of feudalism despite changes of dynasties and political turmoils and social upheavals.

2 **Confucius** (about 551−479 BC)

Born into a bankrupt aristocratic family in Lu①, Confucius once served a short while (3 months) as a petty official in the kingdom. After living a life of poverty together with his widowed mother due to the early death of his father who was also a petty official in Lu, he subsequently devoted the rest of his life to his academic career. As a thinker, historian and teacher, Confucius contributed tremendously to the establishment of Confucianism, the ideological and philosophical school named after him, which dominated Chinese ideology and society for more than 2,000 years.

Confucius' major ideas could be summarized into the following points.

- *li* (rites for conducts)

Here *li* refers to the set of rites or rules established by the Zhou Dynasty, which normalized the proper behaviours of a variety of classes and grades in society. Since Confucius lived in a time when many of the local aristocrats and lords held most of the political power and ignored the ordinances of the central government of the Zhou Dynasty, he advocated strongly the necessity of recovering *li* and reestablishing the original rites. He opposed the violation of any *li*. This is illustrated in Confucius' critical remarks at Jishi for Jishi's use of a dancing rite normally organized for the emperor, which he called overstepping authority.

- *jen* (humanity or goodness or benevolence)

Jen refers to an all-encompassing ethical ideal for all human beings and specifically to the desirable attribute of having an emotional concern for all living things. It could serve as a principle to guide ordinary human relationships, viz. being kind to others on the one hand, and to show the ruler ways of reigning by being tolerant of the insufficiencies or wrongdoings of his subjects on the other. It could also be explained as being strict with one's behaviour in conforming to the rites.

Jen aims to achieve harmony which is regarded as a standard to judge or

---

① Lu was an ancient kingdom during the Spring-Autumn Period, currently Shandong Province.

handle the relationship either between man and nature or between man and man. Also harmony is expected to be obtained by the happy mean①(中庸之道).

Heaven is characteristic of human nature and has will-power as the supreme lord of nature and society. It is opposite to Lao Zi's concept of heaven which is personified as a man.

Heaven is irresistible and with absolute authority demonstrated by stressing the so-called Heavenly Fate. Confucius is uncertain of ghosts or spirits which makes him suspect their existence and the spiritual nature of life and death.

Confucius believes that no difference or discrimination in education should be allowed and therefore all people, whatever their origin, are entitled to receive education. The content of education should be of four kinds, i. e. literacy (culture and knowledge), behaviour, loyalty and credibility. Among the four components, Confucius values most highly the ethical education in relation to ethical or moral behaviours.

Confucius argues that people should care more for book knowledge than for physical labour and knowledge of production. They should care more for indirect and perceptible experiences than for direct experiences.

Confucius advocates a practical attitude towards knowledge and takes an earnest view of it, i. e. knowledge should be based on authenticity. He also claims that reviewing old knowledge produces new knowledge.

3 Mencius (about 372–289 BC)

Mencius was born into a poor family and brought up by his widowed mother who had overcome many difficulties and offered him his initial education. Mencius later studied under one of the followers of Confucius, called Zi-si who had once learned from Tzeng-zi, a student of Confucius. Basically Mencius is regarded as belonging to the Confucian school. Throughout his life, Mencius tried to develop Confucius' ideas about *jen* (humanity) and travelled round a number of kingdoms in China to convince the lords and aristocrats of the advantages of his theory about *jen*. Unfortunately his efforts at persuasion did not seem to succeed and he had to spend most of his life making further researches and disseminating Confucius' theory by teaching.

Mencius' main ideas go into the following divisions.

Mencius' politics is of benevolent origin. He advocates a benevolent reign by

---

① The happy mean is an ethical concept drawn from Confucianism, suggesting that one should choose to be neutral and take no prejudice in handling worldly affairs.

the ruler over his subjects, but maintains that kindness in rulers could not only increase agricultural, forestry and fishing production, but would induce more people to come willingly to add to the prosperity of the kingdom. Merciful ruling would win and tyranny would fail according to Mencius.

Mencius proposes an extraordinary relationship among the ordinary people, the state and the ruler. He holds that the ordinary people deserve the first priority, next to them is the state while the ruler is the last in terms of the difficulties arising from handling them.

Mencius values the treatment of different trades of people. He says that intellectuals should be treated respectfully in order to bring their talent into full play. He says that traders should be relieved of their overheavy taxation in trading and farmers of extra tax on their farmland by recovering their assigned land and the city-dweller should be exempted from tax on their houses.

Mencius is firmly opposed to war. He argues that war brings disasters and killing and a political victory does not depend on wars but on the people's support.

Mencius later divides the whole population into the ruler and the ruled. He claims that the people who perform mental work ought to be the ruling class while the physical workers should be the ruled.

Mencius maintains that human nature is good and that everyone has a sense of compassion, hatred for evil, modest decline[①] and an ability to tell right from wrong, these being sprouts respectively of *jen* (humanity), *yi* (righteousness), *li* (rite) and *zhi* (wisdom).

Mencius' self-cultivation is of particular contribution to the construction of later Chinese ethical development. He asserts that one should not be corrupted by wealth, or shaken by poverty, or bent by violence, if one is to be entitled to the name of a hero.

According to Mencius, one should value moral principles in one's communication with friends and should not try to take advantage of one's age or wealth to build up one's superiority over others.

Mencius says that one should stick to the principles of *jen* and *yi* as a life pursuit without shrinking from them and should be prepared to lose one's life for the sake of being humane and righteous.

Mencius argues that one should prepare oneself to go through all kinds of hardships, to be tortured mentally, to labour and be hungry, to be exhausted and disturbed before one is entrusted with great responsibilities. As well one should be able to adhere to one's own principles and look after oneself when circumstances

---

① Modest decline is one of the Chinese traditional etiquettes, as shown in not accepting the first offer by a host to indicate a modest or humble manner.

are difficult. One should be able to provide assistance to the rest of the world when circumstances are favourable. Finally one must control one's desire for material possessions and benefits so that one can preserve, totally or partly, one's virtue of being good.

4 Xun Zi (about 313 – 238 BC)

Xun Zi was from the Zhao Kingdom at the end of the Warring States Period. He was known as a Confucian philosopher for his opposition to Mencius' conception of the inherent goodness of human nature. He once served as a county magistrate at Lanling, the Chu Kingdom and then settled there for the rest of his life. He was famous for his learning and talent in reasoning, which was indicated in his lectures at Jixia, the capital of the Qi Kingdom and by his visit to the Qin Kingdom where he tried to persuade the king to accept his political advice. Most of his ideas were recorded in *Xun Zi*, a collection of 32 pieces.

Xun Zi's main ideas are presented as the following.

Xun Zi claims that nature has its own laws of change and movement, independent of man's existence, unaffected by good men like Yao or bad men like Jie. Fortune occurs when you handle it in the right way. One should not make complaints against heaven about disasters, which come about by natural laws. The best thing man could do is not to sing in praise of or admire heaven, but to control and make use of it. Generally Xun Zi is a materialist.

(ritual propriety)

The reason for the formation of ritual propriety lies in man's desire which leads to conflicts and chaos when unsatisfied. Therefore, ritual propriety was established as a criterion to reconcile clashes, to divide classes, to readjust man's desires and to satisfy man's requests.

Li has three basic functions: delimiting, which draws the boundaries of proper conduct; supportive, which provides channels for satisfaction; dignifying, which provides sources for ennobling personal character in accordance with *jen* (humanity) and *yi* (righteousness).

For Xun Zi, the essential part of human nature is bad, in the sense of possessing a motivational problem in seeking to satisfy his/her desire. This tendency could only be checked and guided by *li* (propriety) and *yi* (righteousness) which point to a proper direction towards which all human beings could strive.

Opposed to both empiricism and rationalism, Xun Zi argues that perceptual knowledge could serve as the starting point for the acquisition of knowledge, but perceptual knowledge could mislead and cause errors if one takes it as the only means of acquiring knowledge.

Xun Zi argues that knowledge comes from continuous learning which enables one to acquire new knowledge and to make progress. He assumes that knowledge shows its function by practice. He presents the process of how knowledge acquisition starts and then accumulates by steps and sections in his *quan-xue-pian* (《劝学篇》, Advice for Learning).

Critical of the views of ghosts and gods, Xun Zi asserts that the idea about ghosts and gods is a result of misconception or illusion which gives rise to false appearances. Hence one should not offer any judgment when one is confused.

Xun Zi puts forward some logical concepts like conception, judgment and inference, explaining that conception is used to elucidate substantial matter, that judgment works together with conception to express the same idea, that inference is based on judgment and conception for the development of an argument. He cares for the functions of both inductive reasoning and deductive reasoning though the latter seems weakened in his system of logical reasoning.

2.1.2 Taoism

1 A brief account

Taoism is a Chinese philosophy identified basically with the *Tao-qiao* (school of "the way"), represented by Lao Zi and Zhuang Zi. Taoists are the first to use *Tao* (way) to describe the comprehensive structure and dynamics of the cosmos, believing that there is a way the world should be, and a way that it is; human beings can understand this and need to have and follow such knowledge if they and the world are to exist in harmony; the world was once in such a state of harmony.

Taoists are metaphysical and ethical realists, but epistemological skeptics as language skeptics. They further deny that one can strive successively to attain the way. Taoist self-cultivation is a process not of accumulation but of paring away. One must remove the social fabric, forsake one's cultural conditioning and abandon rational thought, to be led instead by one's spontaneous inclinations. With a *hsu* (tenuous, empty) mind, one could perceive the *li* (reason) of the cosmos and live by *wu-wei* (non-action).

Taoist ideas are represented respectively by Lao Zi and Zhuang Zi.

2 Lao Zi (about 580−500 BC)

Lao Zi is the founder of Taoism and is also known as Lao Dan, or Li Er. He came from Ku County (Luyi of Henan Province at present) and once served as an official in charge of history during the Zhou Dynasty before he retired into seclusion at the sight of the decline of the royal family of the Zhou. He wrote and left to posterity the famous *tao-te-ching* (《道德经》, Classic of Tao and Te). There is another view that he is just a legendary figure.

Here are the major ideas of Taoism.

Lao Zi believes that heaven is composed of material, like the earth which is opposed to it. He does not deny there is such a thing as the existence of God in the world. He insists that the world should be determined by *Tao* which is above God. According to him, *Tao* provides a foundation for everything in the world, which suggests that *Tao* takes actions. However, it does so not through will, or on purpose. Therefore it also means it is *wu-wei* or takes no action. Thus Lao Zi established an atheist and materialist doctrine.

According to Lao Zi, *Tao* consists of five features. First, *Tao* is a kind of mixture of primitive matter which produces everything in the world. Second, *Tao* is substantial matter which is both primitive and moving eternally, born before the heaven and the earth. Third, *Tao* is different from everything specific by nature. *Tao* is the general source of everything in the universe, a lightless and shapeless image. Fourth, *Tao* could not be perceived by human senses and is unable to be seen or heard or touched. Fifth, *Tao* is a law of nature operating between opposites.

Simple dialectics make the earliest appearance in Lao Zi's doctrine. For example, the present relationships between man and nature or between opposites of objects are characteristic by some simple dialectical ideas.

The opposition of things is proposed in Lao Zi's work as one of the remarkable statements characteristic of the ancient Chinese philosophy. Everything develops in the direction of its opposite; so-called misfortune depends on fortune while fortune is related to misfortune. More examples show such a tendency, like the weak and the strong, life and death, less and more, bent and straight, honour and humiliation.

Quantity and quality are another crucial concepts created by the Chinese philosophy. Lao Zi advocates that the thick wood comes from a fine grain while the nine-floored tower starts from a pile of earth.

The characteristic of natural laws is frequently mentioned in Taoism. *Tao* is fair to everyone without any bias or favours and always helps those who follow and adapt themselves to the circumstances of nature, just as the people who pull the bow to shoot arrows by adjustment of the bow.

- Critical attitude

Lao Zi is critical of the ruling class for its luxurious way of living and ignorance of the actual living conditions of the average people. His opposition to wars is clearly presented; the war is regarded as something unlucky in bringing about famine and disasters.

· Opposition to commercial economy and exploitation

Lao Zi advocates egalitarianism because the heavenly *Tao* is to reduce the surplus to add to the insufficient whereas man's *Tao* is the reverse.

· The concept of *wu-wei* (non-action)

Lao Zi argues that the ruler should reign by *wu-wei*, avoiding interference with the ruled, which is like the relationship between the heavenly *Tao* and everything in the world. Such a ruler would have the support and obedience of his subjects.

· Social retreat

Lao Zi claims that society should return to the primitive form of society where there were no classes and clashes or oppression and exploitation.

3 Zhuang Zi (about 369 – 286 BC)

Zhuang Zi is another important figure of Taoism. He has contributed to Taoism by offering a number of new interpretations of its spiritual and epistemological aspects. Zhuang Zi came from an impoverished aristocratic family and lived a poor life. He once worked as a janitor of a painting-yard before he retired into complete seclusion. He was said to be so poor that he had to borrow rice for food and had to wear patched clothes in meeting the king of Wei. He had a limited number of academic visitors, friends and students during his lifetime. He refused to accept the invitations to take up the official post of prime minister. As he said to the envoy from the Chu Kingdom, he preferred to be unofficial in order to have spiritual pleasure.

A number of Zhuang Zi's main ideas are henceforth submitted here.

Zhuang Zi says that *Tao* is a kind of mysterious spirit separated from everything else. According to him, there is nothing in the world. It is empty of any "have" or "have not", thus leading to a fall into void, illusion and mystery.

Zhuang Zi denies that gods have any will or function, and emphasizes the features of *Tao* in its nature without actions as a way to fight against religion, but at the same time he shows determinism in talking about nature's *wu-wei* (non-action) by *Tao*. Therefore Zhuang Zi excludes gods but admits Fate that could not be comprehended or controlled in its role in natural and social phenomena.

Epistemology as one of the basic concerns in human intellectual development is initially presented at the hand of Zhuang Zi. The character of object for cognition is relatively limited to certain areas, therefore it is unable to be known by more people. The subjective competence for cognition is also relative, therefore it is impossible to make a complete cognition of more things in the universe. The criterion for truth is also confusing without a clear distinction between genuineness and falsehood or between right and wrong. Therefore Zhuang Zi has to adopt agnosticism as a world outlook.

Zhuang Zi regards the pursuit of spiritual freedom as a lifelong and endless target. He claims that all kinds of so-called freedom must have objective preconditions which restrict freedom in a way. Thus freedom is opposed to preconditions as required by traditional rules and circumstances. He proposes the reasons below for the deprivation of freedom.

According to Zhuang Zi, the ordinary people have the "self" while the saint loses his "self" without considering contribution or reputation in their meditations. He analyses natural phenomena, which gives rise to the loss of freedom and he takes a nihilist attitude towards it. He seeks unconditional and spiritual release to deal with social phenomena so that he could completely forget his own identity and immerse himself in a sea of worldly objects surrounded by void and mystery, thus completely giving up his subjective self and merging with everything in the world.

2.1.3 Legalism

1 A brief account

Represented by Shang Yang (about 390−338 BC) and Han Fei, the legalists were political realists who gave importance to a strict execution of the law in the political and economic development of the state. They challenged the viability of the Confucian model of a ritually constituted community with their call to law and order, but sidestepped the need to dispute the ritual-conduct-versus-law positions by claiming that different periods had different problems, and different problems required different solutions, as a justification for their innovations and reforms. Their advocacy of reform could be regarded as one of the early attempts to resort to political measures to adapt to social changes occurring in the transitional period from slavery to feudal society.

2 Han Fei (about 280−233 BC)

From an impoverished aristocratic family of the Han, a kingdom of the Warring States Period, Han Fei once studied under Xun Zi and then under Gui Gu-zi. He had a keen interest in the study of law and punishment. His ideas were spread and came to be appreciated by the king of the Qin Kingdom who read of his essays and wanted to meet him. But Han was imprisoned soon after he arrived at the capital of the Qin Kingdom due to Li Si's sowing discord. Han could not tolerate the insults in the prison and eventually committed suicide.

Han Fei's main ideas go as the following.

Becoming aware of the insufficiencies in the legalist thinking represented by Shang Yang, Shen Bu-hai and Shen Dao, Han Fei tried to put their ideas together in a combination of law (theoretical principles), tactics (ways of execution) and power (authority and an ability to carry things out), thus finalizing his legalist system and making himself representative of all legalist ideas. Han Fei was also critical of paradoxical ideas of Confucianism and other schools. He submitted the logical and rhetorical concept *contradiction*①, like the Confucian claim for great expenses for a funeral and Mo Zi's claim for little expense for a funeral.

Han Fei claims that history could not withdraw or repeat and had to go through changes. Therefore any return to the old days is impossible. Search for the causes for a social and historical development in economic life is what Han Fei tried to pursue throughout his life.

Han Fei argues that social and political reform, including ethical changes, ought to be decided by the amount of material support for living and the population. No legal rule was needed in ancient times due to the abundance of property and the small number of people. But clashes occurred later with the increase of population and reduction of property. He divides history into three periods, namely the upper period for morality competition, the middle period for intelligence competition and the present for force competition.

The relationship between monarchs and subjects is one of the major issues Han Fei attempts to handle in his observation and practice. A monarch's use of official posts and awards is to make his subjects serve him.

Opposed to the view of *jen* (humanity) and *yi* (righteousness), legalists argue that officials and non-officials could kill the monarch under certain conditions. The relationship among individuals is for him that of gains and losses, including the relationship between employers and employees, traders and customers, and landlords and tenants.

Han Fei's way of observation and judgment is basically that of materialist epistemology. For him, the world could be recognized by repeated observations and studies. One should try to be objective and get rid of subjective prejudice and follow the objective laws to know the world. One's knowledge and cognition

---

① The story came from a person from the Chu Kingdom, who boasted about both his spear and shield, which made his argument lose its logical ground. Later it is extended to refer to anything without a sound logical sense.

need to be tested by referring to practical factors, such as events occurring to the natural world or human society.

According to Han Fei, the general law of nature is *Tao* and the specific law in relation to everything in nature is *li* (reason). He was critical of the then popular superstitious ideas about ghosts and gods because he inherited Lao Zi's atheism and denied the will of heaven.

2.1.4 Mohism

1 A brief account

Mohism is another influential ideological school in the ancient period of Chinese philosophy. It was founded by Mo Zi (about 468 – 376 BC) and flourished throughout the Spring-Autumn and Warring States Periods. Towards the latter part of the Warring States Period, the Mohists split into three factions. Their influence dwindled as Confucianism was given more attention. But the essential ideas were absorbed by Xun Zi, the leading interpreter of Confucianism at the time, and through him left its influence on later generations.

2 Mo Zi's main ideas

Mo Zi is the first philosopher to criticize Confucius. Among the things he criticizes is Confucius' idea of *Heavenly Fate*. Mo Zi says that if we accept Confucius' fatalism, we would make no efforts to do anything, and the idea would further weaken our motivation to act rightly. Mo Zi's second objection is to Confucian depreciation of the importance of Heaven and the spirits. When Confucius is sceptical of the existence of spirits, Mo Zi argues that Heaven is describable and has a will and hence is able to delegate punishment and respond to sacrifice and petition. Hence he is paradoxical, both superstitious and opposed to human fate being determined by Heaven.

Mo Zi proclaims that the business of a moral person is to promote what is beneficial to the world and to eliminate what is harmful. He is opposed to ritual formulae and a luxurious lifestyle because such rites are a waste of time and money and are therefore impractical. He asserts that the yardstick for weighing the value of a certain theory resides principally in its conformity to the interests of the state and its people.

Mo Zi lived in a period of social turmoil and witnessed countless wars and killings brought on by the kings or aristocrats of various kingdoms. He holds that wars have given rise to many deaths of the ordinary people, damaged properties and stopped production. Hence he claims that wars should be opposed. But his opposition is not unconditional. He divides wars into the just and the unjust, and only opposes unjust wars.

Mo Zi attributes all worldly hatred and disasters to the lack of love and therefore proposes the idea of *jian-ai* (universal love). He advocates that one should care for another's country as one's own, another's family as one's own, another's body as one's own. If so, a favourable situation would occur in the world. There would be no wars, due to mutual love among the dukes and princes; there would be no usurpation of political power, due to mutual love among the ministers; there would be no personal damage, due to mutual love among individuals; there would be popular respect and benefit, due to universal love among the strong and the weak, the rich and the poor, and the wise and the foolish.

A survey of ancient Western philosophy

2.2.1 The inception of Western philosophy

Throughout the long and diverse history of the West, philosophy has had many different meanings. It could be an attempt to understand the universe as a whole, or an examination of man's moral responsibilities and social obligations; an effort to consider religious and scientific aspects of human faith and man's place in the universe, or an exploration of the values of truth, goodness, beauty, and so on. These are not all that philosophy involves and suggests, but they give some idea of philosophy's diversity and sophistication. The history of Western philosophy reveals in detail the concentrated activity of many philosophers' intelligent and solid work, which began in Greece where Socrates, Plato and Aristotle presented their ideas more systematically and established their schools of philosophy.

According to the ancient legend, the first important Greek philosopher is Thales of Miletus, who flourished in the first half of the 6th century BC. At that time the word "philosopher (lover of wisdom)" had not yet been coined. Thales was counted, however, among the Seven Wise Men (Sophoi), whose name derived from a term that then designated inventiveness and practical wisdom rather than speculative insight. Thales showed these qualities by trying to give the mathematical knowledge that he derived from the Babylonians a more exact foundation and by using it for the solution of practical problems, such as the determination of the distance of a ship as seen from the shore or of the height of the Pyramids. Though he was also credited with predicting an eclipse of the Sun, it is likely that he merely gave a natural explanation of one on the basis of Babylonian astronomical knowledge.

Thales' disciple and successor, Anaximander of Miletus (mid-6th century), tried to give a more elaborate account of the origin and development of the ordered world (the cosmos). Anaximander is the first to realize that upward and downward are not set absolutely. He believes that life is closely bound up with moisture, originated in the sea. All land animals, he holds, are from sea animals, because the first humans as newborn infants could not have survived without parents. Anaximander's successor, Anaximenes of Miletus teaches that air is the origin of all things. Like Thales, he places a special kind of matter at the beginning of the development of the world.

The first three Greek philosophers seem to believe in a kind of living matter. But this is hardly an adequate characterization. It is, rather, characteristic of them that they did not clearly distinguish between kinds of matter, forces and qualities nor between physical and emotional qualities. Contrary to the ideas of these Miletus materialist philosophers, idealist philosophers like Pythagoras believe the world is composed of numbers.

Nonetheless, the core of Greek philosophy did not come until the emergence of Socrates and his followers Plato and Aristotle. Their ideas represent the top achievements of philosophy at the time and have exerted a considerable and enduring influence upon later generations of Western philosophers.

2.2.2 The representative figures or schools

1 Socrates (469–399 BC)

As one of the most influential philosophers of Greek origin, Socrates did not leave any written record to posterity. His ideas and reputation were largely based on Plato's written accounts which disclosed Socrates' life and major contributions to philosophy. It seems that with his ideas and personality, Socrates won a devoted following among the young, but as well evoked suspicion from the authorities. He was charged with refusing to recognize the gods of the city and corrupting the youth. He was tried by the jury on a single day and found guilty by a small margin. Eventually he was sentenced to death self-administered by means of poison, probably hemlock.

Socrates' main ideas go as follows.

Socrates asserts that virtue is knowledge. No one is willingly wicked. If a man is wicked, it is due to his ignorance. The question of moral intention is secondary to him.

Socrates holds that an unreflective life is not worth living, that it is better to be treated unjustly than to do injustice, and that understanding of moral matters is the only unconditional good. He argues that death is not an evil and therefore a good person cannot be harmed by his death.

Socrates claims that the universe is organized and vivified by the divine spirit. Hence pious observances should be made to the gods, the popular personifications of the divine spirit. He asserts that the soul is immortal and will meet with judgment and retribution in the hereafter. There is a mystical side to his teaching, later developed by Plato and Neo-Platonists.

2 Plato (427 – 347 BC)

Born into a noble family in Athens, Plato first wrote some poetry before he met Socrates and turned his attention to the study of philosophy in the hope of a political career. He abandoned his desire, however, on the death of Socrates. He is said to have travelled extensively and met with some important people, such as Dion of Syracuse. He established the academy in Athens after he returned and started to teach philosophy to a group of students, among whom Aristotle was the best known.

Here are Plato's main ideas.

The idea or form of a thing is something of the nature of our abstract concept of that thing, but having a real existence outside the world of sense; it is unchanging reality behind the changing appearance. The knowledge of these is to be attained only by pure reason unaffected by sensation, and proceeding dialectic. The supreme idea is that of goodness, on which all the others are ultimately founded. To Plato as well as to Socrates virtue is knowledge of this supreme idea.

Physical love perpetuates the species and achieves a lower form of immortality. Best of all is the kind of love that eventually attaches itself to the form of beauty, since this is the most beautiful form (and perhaps the most important form as well) of all objects and provides the greatest happiness to the lover.

Beginning with an attraction to the beauty of one's body, one develops an appreciation of the beauty of other people which leads to a deeper attachment to the beauty of customs, laws and systems of knowledge and culminates in the discovery of the eternal and changeless idea of beauty itself.

Platonic love designates a purely spiritual relationship completely devoid of physical attraction. However, it is not exactly the case since what Plato desires is that physical contact should be restrained so as not to subvert the greater good that can be accomplished in human relationships.

Plato believes that justice is so great a good that it is worth any sacrifice. To achieve such justice, an ideal political community is proposed. Supposedly Plato's political ideas are best represented in his *Republic*.

Plato argues in *Republic* that an ideal city-state must make radical innovations. It should be ruled by specially trained philosophers. Their sexual lives are regulated by eugenic considerations not to know who their children are. They are forbidden to have private possessions. Positions of political power are open to women since they are equal. What makes this city-state ideally just is the dedication of each of its components (members) to one task for which that member is naturally suited and specially trained. The rulers are ideally equipped to rule; the soldiers are best able to enforce their commands; and the economic class, composed of farmers, craftsmen, builders, and so on, are content to do their work and to leave to others the task of making and enforcing laws.

3 Aristotle (384–322 BC)

Aristotle was born at Stageria in Chalcidice, the son of Nicomachus, physician to Amyntas II, king of Macedonia. In 367 BC he went to Athens to be a pupil of Plato till the latter's death 20 years afterwards. Then he left Athens and settled at Assos in the Troad together with a group of philosophers from the Athenian Academy, favoured by Hermeias, the enlightened prince of the neighbouring city of Atarneus. He remained there for three years, probably teaching and writing, and then went elsewhere to teach before he was invited by Philop of Macedon to be tutor to his son Alexander the Great. In 335 BC when Alexander started on his expedition to Asia, Aristotle returned to Athens and opened a school of philosophy known as the Peripatetic School from his habit of walking up and down while talking to his pupils. He also built up a considerable library there by collecting manuscripts as well as a museum of natural objects, with the help of Alexander. His academic and business efforts received assistance and protection from Antipater, the then governor of Greece and Macedon but provoked disputes and even attacks from other people in Athens. Aristotle left Athens in 323 BC after the death of Alexander and died at Chalcis the following year.

The following are Aristotle's main ideas.

Aristotle was probably the first philosopher in the West to explore the structure of reasoning, both formal and scientific, basing himself on the syllogism he discovered.

Aristotle tried to expose the nature of the real and essential substance of the universe. At the base of his doctrine is the distinction between matter and form. He tried to understand the universe by establishing a hierarchy of existence, each of which is the matter of that next above it and imparts form and change to that next below. At the lower end of the scale is primary formless matter, which has no real but logical existence. At the upper end is the "prime unmoved mover", an external activity of thought, free from matter, giving motion to the universe through an attraction akin to love; he identified this prime mover with God.

Aristotle examined the constituent elements of things that exist by nature. He dealt with such notions as matter and form, time and space, and movement and stagnation to expose the Four Causes, namely the material cause (out of which a thing comes to be), the moving cause (from which immediately originates the change), the formal cause (the change occurring to the form) and the final cause (the end or aim of the change).

Aristotle attempted to describe the movements of celestial and terrestrial bodies and regarded the Earth as a sphere but thought it was the centre of the universe. He collected quite a number of facts about animal life such as those about whales and other mammals, classifying animals into groups according to their ways of reproduction and adaptation to the environment and the evolution of organs.

Aristotle regards the good as the end of conduct, which leads to happiness but not to pleasure, honour or wealth, which are supposed to be the basis for happiness. He finds the highest happiness in a life of contemplation, in accordance with the virtue of the best part of his work (the rational principle) and manifests in a complete life. Happiness for ordinary people is to be sought in moral virtue and practical wisdom. He distinguishes between moral and intellectual virtues, defining moral virtues as dispositions, and lays stress on moral intentions.

In his eight books of politics, Aristotle discusses the science of politics from the point of view of the city-state. He argues the state is developed naturally by the grouping of families in villages for the purpose of securing to the citizens a good and self-sufficient life. Thus the essential characteristic of the state is not material but its moral purpose. The power of the state should rest with the good. He recognizes the advantages of democracy, but finds the highest form of government in the monarchy of a perfect ruler, if he is available.

Aristotle's *Rhetoric* deals with the methods of persuasion, divided into three parts, namely those by which the speaker produces on his audience a favourite view of his own character, those by which he produces emotion and lastly argument, by examples or by enthymeme (rhetorical form of syllogism). The work then discusses style and arrangement. In *Poetics*, Aristotle points out that poetry, like music, dancing, painting and sculpture, has imitation for its basis, but differs from the other arts in the means, objects and manner of imitation. He finds the origin of poetry in the instinctive love of imitation and traces the special origins and developments of tragedy and comedy. He divides "poetry" into tragedy and comedy, narrative (epic) and drama.

Aristotle then discusses the rules for metres of the epic, compares tragedy with epic drama and finally deals with problems, such as the censures of some commentators, like Zolius.

4 Epicurus (341–270 BC)

Epicurus is the founder of the Epicurean School (Epicureanism). Born in Samos of Athenian parents, he settled in Athens in 306 BC and set up an Epicurean community with his colleagues at Mytileme, Lampsacus and Athens. These groups set out to live the ideal Epicurean life detached from political society without actively opposing it and devoting themselves to philosophical discussions and the cult of friendship. Their correspondence was anthologized and studied as a model of the philosophical life by later Epicureans for whom the writings of Epicurus and his three cofounders known collectively as "the Men" held a virtually biblical status.

Here are Epicurus' major views.

Epicurus holds that philosophy consists in the wise conduct of life, to be attained by relying on the evidence of the senses and eliminating superstition and the belief in supernatural intervention. These ideas may be viewed in his great work *On Nature*, fragments of which still survive today.

Epicurus accepts in the main the atomistic theory of Democritus and asserts that every event has a natural cause. Atoms have only the primary properties of shape, size and weight. Atoms are in constant rapid motion at equal speed. Stability emerges as an overall property of compounds, which large groups of atoms form by settling into regular patterns of complex motion, governed by the three motive principles of weight, collision and "the swerve" — a minimal random movement, which initiates new patterns of movement and blocks the danger of determinism.

Epicurus claims that our world, like countless other worlds, is such a compound, accidentally generated and of finite duration. There is no divine mind behind it or behind the evolution of life and society. The gods are to be viewed as ideal beings, models of the Epicurean good life and therefore blissfully detached from our affairs.

Epicurus believes that pleasure (or absence of pain) is the only good, being the only good to the senses; and that the best pleasure, being accompanied by no painful want, is a perfect harmony of body and mind, to be sought in plain living and in virtue. The teaching of the school is concisely summed up in an inscription at a cloister in Lycia: "Nothing to fear in God. Nothing to feel in Death. Good can be attained. Evil can be endured."

Epicureanism enjoyed widespread popularity, but, unlike its great rival Stoicism, it never entered the intellectual mainstream of the ancient world. Its stances were dismissed by many as philistine, especially its rejection of all cultural activities not geared to the Epicurean good life. It was also viewed as atheistic and its ascetic hedonism was misinterpreted as crude sensualism (hence the modern use of "epicure").

5 Stoicism

One of the three leading movements constituting Hellenistic philosophy was Stoicism. Its founder was Zeno of Citium (334−262 BC), who was succeeded as head of this school by Cleanthes (331−232 BC). But the third head, Chrysippus (280−206 BC) was the greatest exponent and the most voluminous writer. These three people were the representatives of early Stoicism. Middle Stoicism developed largely at Rhodes under Panaetius and Posidonius, both of whom influenced the Roman politician Cicero's stoic ideas. Panaetius was more pragmatic and less concerned with the idealized sage. Posidonius made Stoicism more open to Platonic and Aristotelian ideas, especially reviving Plato's inclusion of irrational components in the soul.

The third period was called Roman Stoicism, the writings from which have survived in quantity, represented by Seneca (3 BC−65 AD), Epictetus (55−135 AD) and Marcus Aurelius (121−180 AD), with a strong primary focus on practical and personal ethics. Many prominent Romans were Stoics.

Following is a brief account of its main ideas.

Stoicism regards the world as an organic whole, animated and directed by intelligence, and consisting of an active principle (god) and that which is acted upon, a passive principle (matter). There are two inseparable aspects of reality: the universe absorbed into the divine fire and the universe starting on a fresh course exactly reproducing its predecessors.

The Stoic world is an ideally good organism, all of whose parts interact for the benefit of the whole. Only bodies "exist" and can interact. Body is infinitely divisible and contains no void. At the higher level of the universe are generated the four elements: air, fire, earth and water. Air and fire are active rational forces called breath while earth and water are passive. They interpenetrate each other thanks to the non-particulate structure of body and its capacity to be mixed through. A thing's quality is constituted by pneuma (breath, Greek), which has the additional role of giving it cohesion and thus an essential identity. In inanimate objects this unifying pneuma is called a hexis (state, Greek); in plants it is called physis (nature, Greek); and in animals "souls".

Stoic ethics is founded on the principle that only virtue is good, only vice bad. Health, wealth and honour are valuably preferred while their opposites are rejected. Justice and other virtues are found only in the sage, an idealized perfectly rational person totally in tune with the divine cosmic plan. The Stoics doubt whether any sages exist although they seem to have treated Socrates as one. To Stoics, sages act purely from "right reason", free from passion or morally wrong impulses. They are happy and truly free, living in harmony with the divine plan. All human lives are predetermined by the providentially designed, all-embracing causal nexus of fate; yet being the principal causes of their actions, the good and the bad alike are responsible for them; determinism and morality are fully compatible.

To Stoics, certainty comes through the cognitive impression, a self-certifying perceptual representation of external fact. Out of sets of such impressions we acquire generic conceptions and become rational. The highest intellectual state is knowledge in which all cognition becomes mutually supporting and hence "unshakable by reason" and this is the prerogative of the wise. Everyone else is in a state of mere opinion or ignorance. Nevertheless, the cognitive impression serves as a criterion of truth for all.

Stoic logic is propositional, in contrast with Aristotle's logic of terms. The basic unit is the simple proposition, the primary bearer of truth and falsehood. Syllogists also employ complex proposition — conditional, conjunctive and disjunctive.

6 Skepticism

In its most common sense, Skepticism means the refusal to grant that there is any knowledge or justification of knowledge. It could be either partial or total, either practical or theoretical, either academic or Pyrrhonian.

Academic Skepticism derived its name from the fact that it was formulated in Plato's Academy in the third century BC, starting from Socrates' statement that "All I know is that I know nothing." It was developed by Arcesilaus (316 − 241 BC) and Carneades (214 − 129 BC) into a series of arguments directed against Stoics, purporting to show that nothing can be known.

Below are its major views and developments.

Academic Skepticism dominated the philosophizing of Plato's Academy till the first century BC, when the Academy turned from Skepticism to a kind of eclectic philosophy.

Skeptical thinking found another home in the school of the Pyrrhonian Skeptics, which can be traced to its origin in Pyrrho of Elis (360 – 270 BC) and his student Timon (320 – 230 BC). Pyrrho was said to be not a theoretician but a practical doubter who would not make any judgments that went beyond immediate experience but aimed at a balanced imperturbability. The Pyrrhonists suspended judgments on all questions on which there was any conflicting evidence, including whether or not anything could be known. However they were not negative dogmatists like the Academic Skeptics for they said neither that knowledge is possible nor that it is impossible. They remained seekers while allowing the skeptical arguments and the state or quality of being the same or practically same in force or importance to act as a purge of dogmatic assertions. They tried to follow natural inclinations, immediate experience and the laws and customs of their society, without judging or committing themselves to any view about them. Thus they would have no worries and be able to function naturally according to law and custom.

The Pyrrhoman Movement disappeared during the third century AD for it was unable to replace the powerful religious movements of the time. It was not until the beginning of the Renaissance when the texts of Sextus and Cicero were rediscovered and used to formulate a modern skeptical view by Montaigne and Charron[①] that Pyrrhonian Skepticism was revalued and received more notice from the public.

Skepticism is instrumental in the birth of modern epistemology and modern philosophy at the hands of Descartes, whose Skepticism is methodological but sophisticated and well informed by that of the ancients. Skepticism is also a main force, perhaps the main force in the broad sweep of Western philosophy from Descartes through Hegel. However, since then it has suffered decades of neglect and only in recent years has it reclaimed much attention and even applause, like the assumption that "We do not know that we are not dreaming."

2.3 Comparative comments

Several points can be made by way of a comparative study of Chinese and Western ideological and philosophical systems in ancient times in spite of their basic diversities in historical and social developments.

---

① Charron, French moralist, famous for his skeptical treatise *de la Sagesse*, was Montaigne's friend.

2.3.1 Economic, political and intellectual circumstances

The tendency for political decentralization marked an important point of departure to denote the extent of certain social development if not exactly political maturity. Generally speaking, if we look at the socio-political situation during the ancient time in both China and the West, conditions were more similar than dissimilar. For example, when China was going through the Spring-Autumn and Warring States Periods, a transitional stage from separation to unification, the latter effected by the emperor of Qin Dynasty, decentralized rule allowed for more freedom to intellectual and academic development, even though China had to tolerate more civil wars and slower progress in agriculture and other economic areas. The same was true of Greece, the representative of the West at the time where intellectual freedom was available to all those involved in cultural and academic activities, like what happened in Athens. In the two cultures, political entity or more accurately, the leadership, was decided through different methods: one by inheritance procedure and the other generally by democratic process which meant, the ruler was approachable and prepared to adapt to different opinions. This was because decentralization limited the ruling power and made the established power more easily fall into the hands of the alien intruder.

Self-sufficiency was another interesting point in comparison. From a practical point of view, both sides had established independent economies based on self-sufficient private ownership of land. In China, the economy was centred on the land-owning feuds or plantations headed by slave owners or landlords while in the West it was shaped by the supply of slave and serf labour, supplemented by yeomen. The aristocracy was the core of the system. The lack of equality was commonly seen in every corner of the country in the form of privileges granted to only a few people. Such conditions remained unchanged throughout the whole Middle Ages of the Western civilization, with little intervention from the ruling class in spite of taxation or other forms of exploitation. To a large extent, the common people enjoyed certain freedom in choosing what they wanted in terms of farming or private business after the end of slavery. In China, the peasants' freedom was short-lived for the rulers after the Qin Dynasty soon tightened their autocratic rule by seizing more farmland and extracting more taxation from individual peasants. Such a situation used to deteriorate towards the end of each dynasty and hit peasantry both physically and spiritually.

At the same time, however, different forces arose from the long development of feudal or aristocratic society. The ruling class tried to relax the social contradictions by allowing limited freedom to its intellectual elite. The limitation varied between China and the West. Generally, China seemed to be harsher in her treatment of the intellectuals, particularly in the nationwide movement to build up the so-called ideological unification based on an interpretation of

Confucianism. Notorious actions against the intellectuals included such examples as the burning of books and the burial alive of hundreds of scholars at the hands of the Qin emperor. The West, in spite of some occasional violence to the intellectual like the execution of Socrates on the charge of infidelity, was generally more tolerant of different opinions. It could be seen in the dynamic performance of sophism, an event or function of public argument over certain social or cultural issues. But the difference was small considering the darkness of the long period of the so-called Middle Ages. The cultural development of both sides was closely associated with political development. For the early period when the political control was not so tight, there was more fruitful development in ideological and intellectual fields, such as the so-called flourishing of a hundred schools in their competitive struggle for academic ideas during the Spring-Autumn and Warring States Periods. This was almost in parallel with similar situation during the period of the city-states in Greece. As well the scholars in those days were all versatile and demonstrated talents in many areas. They were involved in a mixture of subjects without distinguishing between humanities and the sciences.

Among a variety of schools, materialism and idealism came to the foreground for their divided or even opposite interpretation of origins of ideas. Chinese materialist ideas, like those of Lao Zi, were close to Greek materialist ideas like those of Thales and Democritus from the School of Miletus. The interest in nature and ethics by both Chinese and Greek thinkers was another point in common. For instance, Lao Zi, Mo Zi and Xun Zi all devoted part of their time to the study of nature. Though they did not produce any specific results out of their research, they established a universal outlook on a material basis and became aware of the meaning of the material world for human beings. Comparatively Greek philosophers made more achievements in natural science. Aristotle, for example, studied the movements of fish and changes of weather. Other scientists, such as Euclid, Archimedes and Aristarchus, were even more famous for their remarkable accomplishments in such specific areas as geometry, physics and astronomy.

Ethics was another important discipline that both Chinese and Greek philosophers were concerned with. Chinese scholars, such as Confucius, Mencius and Xun Zi, all cared for self-cultivation by proposing a series of principles for people to improve their moral behaviour. For instance, how to follow a moral code to cultivate one's moral quality was a frequent practice among Confucius' followers. Their ideas derived from Confucius' humanitarianism and focused on offering strict control over human behaviours such as *du-shan-qi-shen* (care solely for self-interest) and *ri-san-xin-hu-ji* (frequent daily self-examination).

Greek thinkers also attached great value to ethical behaviour. Socrates, for instance, asserted a number of ethical tenets in his academic discussions, such as courage and virtues. Stoics and Epicurists also expressed their viewpoints on human behaviours. The Western philosophy, generally, emphasizes the importance of knowledge and reason as the core of virtue for the ordinary people to follow.

Both China and the West experienced a vigorous intellectual development due to loosely-dominated society and less intervention from politics. Despite a great distance in geography, culture and lack of mutual understanding, one could find some unusual similarities in the way of thinking among some philosophers. One example is probably the concept of the *happy mean* by Confucius and *mesotes* by Aristotle. Both imply the choice of mild way of handling affairs to avoid offence and radical means.

Dissimilarities are also quite obvious, such as the sense of unification and devision in politics and culture. The West appeared not so well balanced in terms of its economic and cultural developments. Earlier, only Greece and her neighbouring areas were at a more advanced stage and the rest of Europe were mostly in a barbarous condition. Comparatively, China, despite some differences, experienced a more balanced growth in economic and cultural conditions. This may be attributed to her almost uniform cultural background and racial origins after the first legendary unification in social and cultural development at the head of Huangdi, the legendary leader of Chinese ancient civilization.

In the West, economic development and cultural prosperity did not bring political stability and military advantage. There were the defeat of Greece by Macedonia and Rome and later the conquest of Rome by the German tribes. In China, the change-over of power seems to have been closely related to economic and cultural conditions, although there were also some exceptions, such as the Yuan and Qing Dynasties, which were set up by barbarous minor nationalities from the north. The general tendency of Western social development was less unified than that of China. China used to seek unification as a more important political target. All the Chinese historical books seem to regard periods of division as transitional or temporary, which was opposed to or different from the Western way of viewing similar periods. This is perhaps a key factor for China to keep its integration of such a large territory and population with a particularly long traditional continuity whereas Europe, the principal location of Western culture, which did not seem to disturb its later development, was divided into dozens of smaller countries.

Aside from the racial reason (95% or more of the Chinese population are composed of the Han nationality while the European population have no such dominant nationality), the Chinese were bound up by a cultural tradition of preferring unification as the highest form of national goal.

Cultural studies in the West were more preoccupied with that of the natural world and practical matters though occasionally some metaphysical topics also caught their attention. This is confirmed by the fact that quite a number of philosophers were inclined to handle natural subjects even in the early period. The best example is perhaps Aristotle who touched on quite a number of natural subjects, especially in physics and biology. Comparatively, Chinese scholars seemed in the main to be more preoccupied with purely academic humanities which were less practical and did not contribute much to material progress. Consequently, Western ancient philosophy would take more interests in practical and natural affairs or objects and would more easily develop into an enterprising spirit of adventure, invention and challenge, and was perhaps characteristic of harshness, liberalism, individualism and materialism while Chinese philosophy was restricted by its culture to be more concentrated on hierarchy, loyalty, discipline, centralization, nationalism, unification, book learning and personal relationships.

2.3.2 Philosophical and academic ideas

Here are a number of points on which Chinese and Western scholars were very close to each other. Scholars from both sides started to promote a certain perspective on social and world affairs and constituted an established world outlook, which ensured an intellectual tradition for both cultures. The diversities of the two cultures could be found in the traces of early developments.

1 Who creates the world?

For the Chinese scholar, Heaven has supreme control over nature and society. Heaven is the absolute authority and irresistible power so it is called "Heavenly Fate" with its own will according to Confucius. Another scholar, Lao Zi, says that *Tao* provides everything and there is no God while a third scholar, Xun Zi, claims that nature has its own laws, independent of man's desire. Generally Chinese scholars preferred a more objective view of the world, though some of them were inclined to deify nature and impose human will upon nature.

The principal Western scholar seems to be more subjective. For instance, Aristotle insisted that there is "the prime unmoved mover", by which he obviously referred to God. Socrates made it even clearer by saying that the universe is organized and vivified by divine spirit and God is the personification of that divine spirit. Many years later, Stoics tried to put more human elements into the argument when they asserted that all human lives are predetermined by a providentially-designed fate.

It is not difficult to see the similarity between the two sides at that time in spite of some diversity in their specific points of view. The Chinese appeared more scientific and more reasonable in terms of the way they treated the world and man himself. The major Chinese philosophers, such as Lao Zi and Xun Zi, started to take an objective world view and tried to build up an outlook based on the material constitution of the universe and confidently believed that man could triumph over nature. Confucius was perhaps a bit negative in his appeal to Heavenly Fate. But even so, he never had faith in ghosts or other superstition. Comparatively, the major Western philosophers seemed more god-haunted and chose to get reconciled with an unknown God, an almighty force that is able to control everything. The Western sense of God is a personified figure with a mysterious temperament. Aristotle might be a good example of that interpretation. He never really gave up his belief in almighty God while doing his scientific research of nature. His assertion about "the prime unmoved mover" was typical of this inclination. He seemed to advocate the contribution by both God and matter, which, to his mind, could work independently of each other and perform different duties. This inclination obviously affected many later scientists and continued in Western tradition.

2 How to view and handle the world?

Both sides seem to favour and benefit from practical experience, yet neither could draw a theoretical principle such as empiricism from their personal experiences. For instance, the Chinese scholar Xun Zi is opposed to the term "experience", but regards perceptual explanation as the start of acquiring knowledge. Another scholar, Han Fei, tries to be objective and claims that knowledge needs to be testified by referring to other factors, which is a wonderful achievement for that time.

Among the Western scholars of the ancient period, Aristotle is perhaps the closest to the practical approach due to his keen interest in the study of biology and other subjects of science. Stoics also take ideas about perceptual knowledge and realize the importance of how emotion contributes to the acquisition of knowledge. But unfortunately neither of them could deduce a theoretical canon out of these ideas. It was not until the 17th−18th century that empiricism was eventually brought forward as a theory.

The Chinese thinkers did not seemingly emphasize much about the value of intellectual development or rationalism in their works. Perhaps Confucius was the only one who made some remarks on this issue and talked about wisdom, which was still vague and was principally concerned with book knowledge limited to the ruling class and scholars whose career depended on working for the ruling class such as emperors and officials.

Comparatively, the Western thinkers appeared more positive on this issue. For example, Socrates argues that knowledge is virtue. Plato further developed his teacher's idea by adding that knowledge of ideas is to be attained by pure reason unaffected by sensation. Stoics went even farther by saying that sages all act from "right reason", free from passion. Skeptics indicated more suspicion over authenticity or justification of whatever they ever heard of or obtained.

Since the ancient Chinese and Western scholars were both inclined to be metaphysical and confined their studies to metaphysical exploration, most philosophical ideas were based on purely abstract meditation or examination or evaluation without making many a practical experiment or observation. Some of their achievements were marvellous, considering their simple and inadequate working conditions at the time. The concepts or ideas of materialism, idealism, dialectics, logic, rhetoric, atomism and God, for instances, showed fairly high accomplishments in academic and philosophical areas though they still needed to be perfected.

This was especially true of some Western philosophers who tried to establish their view of the world, such as Aristotle in his biological and physical work. Comparatively, Chinese philosophers were inadequate in the study of nature though perhaps they might make some observations of the sky for the sake of astrology, which was after all different from natural science.

In the early days of Greek civilization, some scientists, such as Euclid and Archimedes, appeared to focus on the study of nature with some extraordinary results, which led to the tradition favouring practice in natural subjects. China also had a few scholars who took interest in practical areas, like medicine, agriculture or mathematics, but their achievements were generally ignored and unable to shape a natural tradition as important as that of literary studies, which was later to develop into an official standard for enrolling official candidates. People doing natural studies were usually not expected to win favour or respect from society or government.

Consequently the different attitude towards natural studies determined the orientation of social and intellectual developments of the two cultures. China had to bear the monotony and depression of the intellectual climate attributable to its indifference to natural and practical studies based on a socially and intellectually biased environment. The West, in spite of long-term tortuous developments, tended to benefit from its practical and rationalist tradition based on practical values and a decentralized system. Generally, there was not much gap between China and the West in the ancient period in terms of freedom, encouragement or restrictions granted by the government as well as specific results from their work due to the decentralized system working simultaneously on both sides. The problem might have something to do with the focus of academic convention which was unfortunately dominated by some impractical tendency.

China had a long history in establishing systems of laws, as demonstrated in Lao Zi's assertions about *Tao* and Han Fei's legal ideas though Han's career as a politician was unfulfilled. The use of legal means, rather than deliberate tactics by autocratic rulers, should have led to a more tolerable state of private and public life controlled by the government. The failure of legal rule in China, like the Shang Yang Reform, suggested in many ways that legal institutions and execution required the development of certain social and intellectual conditions. After all, no rule of law could be expected in its real sense without an appropriate environment which could ensure impartiality in both the making and the execution of laws. This was perhaps the reason why China was slow in political reforms and unable to provide as sound a legal system as the West. Comparatively, the Western rule of law appeared more successful because of more open and democratic social conditions, such as the carrying through of a number of reforms by some tyrants among the city-states in Greek civilization.

    The term "harmony" came into use in the early history of philosophy on both sides. The earliest reference to harmony in ancient philosophical works, like those by Zhuang Zi, was perhaps the relation to the world which motivated one for theoretical speculation. As an ideal perspective of the scientist or philosopher, harmony serves to build up a sound relationship based on practical know-how. According to one Western philosopher, "It is, then, the concept of harmony which sets the parameters for Chinese philosophy — and not only for philosophy."①

    Harmony in Chinese culture has wide coverage, referring to many relations, such as those between the self, family and the society, or those between heaven, earth and man. Harmony could also suggest, as a cosmological principle, a balance between the "negative" and "positive" forces of *yin* and *yang*, or as a set of "correspondences" between the "five elements" of nature and their human analogues and so on. In a word, harmony is a necessary component of the Chinese philosophical system.

    While Chinese philosophy attached great importance to the concept of harmony, its Western counterpart also took into account the concept as a necessary element in its philosophical constitution. Pythagoras, the famous pre-Socrates philosopher and mathematician, tried to use numbers to explain the movement of the heavens. According to him, the heavens not only move around numbers but produce music.② Thus the state of harmony could be produced in the universe based on numbers.

    Comparatively, the Chinese seem to care more for the application of harmony as part of their essential cultural tradition and practically as a means to unite relationships of different kinds. This is perhaps one of the major differences between Chinese and Western philosophies or world views: the purpose of philosophical pursuits is unity or division. For the Chinese, it is unity or a happy get-together that brings together all efforts and struggles as a reward. For the

---

① See *World Philosophies: An Historical Introduction*, p. 61, David E. Cooper, Blackwell Publisher, 1996.
② See *The Cambridge Dictionary of Philosophy*, p. 761, Robert Audi (ed.), Cambridge University Press, 1999.

Westerners, however, it is doubtful that human beings can achieve such a purpose. Therefore Western culture would prefer to consider individual interests first in opposition to collectivism (national or community interests), which is usually the priority in Chinese culture. Maybe this is why the Chinese, both as a nation and as a culture, has survived the historical test of nearly five thousand years and remains as a single unit while Western civilization and culture comfortably settled down when falling into dozens of smaller parts after the Roman Empire collapsed. In contrast to Chinese claim for unification which is concerned with collectivism or even nationalism, Western civilization cares more for personal liberalism which seems to be away from Chinese idea about harmony.

When Epicurus and his followers believed that pleasure (or absence of pain) is the only good, and that the ordinary people should pursue a hedonist way of life, Mo Zi from Chinese philosophy held a totally different point of view in terms of attitude towards material life. For Mo Zi, life should be simple and economical and spirit is more important than material comfort. The difference between the two philosophers actually shows the gap between the two ways of living and judgment of world affairs. For Mo Zi, the evaluation of anything has to be made in the interest of the state and people. If it is in the interest of the state and people, then it should be adopted. But if not, it should be rejected. This is his attitude towards wars and some of Confucius' ideas. In a word, it is practical interest or utilitarianism that provides the theoretical basis for his principles and statements. Mo Zi is really a marvelous thinker and philosopher, given his time and his working and living environment. In spite of his insufficiencies, he is actually more than two thousand years earlier than the appearance of utilitarianism in the West.

It is not difficult to be aware that China and the West found much in common in the beginning of their civilizations. The ancient philosophers from the two cultures tried to use different perspectives and methods to explain and analyze the world they witnessed and lived in. From material to idealistic, from practical to metaphysical, from universal to specific, from mechanical to dialectical, philosophy and ideology have multiplied and diversified in their pluralist development and combinations and presented a vigorous evolution. What was characteristic of this period resided in the understanding and tolerance by each school of the other ideological schools. Though each of the schools persisted with its own claims, none of them could or even tried to establish a dominant position by extinguishing the others. This is because all these schools were in a way balanced in their influences and power of reaching ultimate dominance. It was the case with Confucianism in China when Confucius, together with his students, had to travel around in order to popularize his ideas among the local lords or aristocrats, the rulers of dozens of small kingdoms. It was also true of Plato and Aristotle who had to run schools in Athens to advocate their thoughts. Aristotle was even forced to leave Athens because of his accepting gift money from Alexandria the Great, his former student.

Such pluralist development continued a long while in the West until the appearance of Christianity, which was announced later as the only official religion and took over the mission of looking after Western intellectual and ideological developments. China did not have any formal religion, but Confucianism was authorized as the only officially recognized ideology, as Christianity was. These changes greatly affected the pace of development on both sides, which is to be discussed in the following chapter.

Both sides presented schools or figures who were unsatisfied with the then social or intellectual conditions and challenged them by offering their criticism. In China we had Mohism who criticized Confucian advocacy for luxurious funerals. In Western culture, Socrates and his followers, such as Cynics, were famous for their critical practice against the authorities. Comparatively speaking, Western philosophy was more skeptical and critical in terms of the spirit to hold on and defend what they thought of truthfulness and reveal what they regarded as wrongdoing.

2.4 A case study

In terms of initiating philosophical and intellectual development, Confucius and Socrates are probably the right examples as the most influential representative figures of both Chinese and Western cultural traditions. Their ideas and influences have made solid and enduring contributions to later generations to develop a full awareness of and systematic outlook on both humankind and nature. It is their courage and wisdom that dawned on human civilization and kindled the intellectual sparkle of more than two thousand years' development by a dark and tortuous journey towards the promised land. It is interesting and significant, though, to look into the details of these two giants' ideological repertoire for a comparison of their basic beliefs, personal views and philosophical contributions.

2.4.1 Setting for the birth of Confucius and Socrates' ideologies

National division and frequent armed conflicts were endemic in the period when Confucius and Socrates lived and worked. During the Spring-Autumn Period in China, the whole land was split into dozens of small kingdoms. Wars and clashes for territory and fortune gave rise to massive killings and damage to properties. Greece was also thrown into a haphazard or even a chaotic state marked by a division to over a hundred city-states. Apart from the conflicts among these states, Greece, had to make a terribly violent and merciless though eventually successful resistance to the Persian invasion, which brought great losses of human lives and material destruction.

Nevertheless, the two countries were granted a period of intellectual freedom partly because of the rulers' broadmindedness and partly because of ignorance of political and intellectual divergence. Spiritual gains were unconsciously therefore retained in the short interval between wars.

One of the interesting signs of social development on both sides at the time was the formation of a certain minor cultural class whose function had nothing to do with the established roles of the other classes, such as those of slaves and warriors, but related to the use of a certain culture. In China, it was a group of people called *ru* (儒) whose mission was to take charge of various kinds of ceremonies or business for the rich or well-to-do people, such as weddings or funerals. They were not rich but had to know different customs, rites and living styles required on public or private occasions. In Greece, there was a fashion for disputing in public over various issues, and hence a group of sophists or wise men appeared to meet the need for eloquent speakers in these arguments.

2.4.2 Personal and academic experiences

Confucius and Socrates both came from such a minor class. Both were involved in practical experiences, like working as a drummer in funeral processions or as a participant in a dispute. Their ideas were not acquired or inherited from other people, but obtained from their contact with these daily experiences. They arose out of social life and hence were found in common with daily essentials. This is why they attracted and were followed by a large number of disciples. Unlike the later masters of learning, they demonstrated their ideas and learning principally by lecturing or simply speaking, rather than by writing. Their ideas were recorded and disseminated by their students. They both had to live a mediocre or sometimes even a poor life during their lifetime, without being able to win favour from the then ruling class. Yet they never gave up their noble ideals, even towards the ends of their lives. To a large extent, they relied on their students to spread their ideas to more other people, and expand them into a more grandiose and powerful institution as an internationally influential ideology.

2.4.3 Religious faith

None of them had a strong sense of religious faith although they could not be said to reject the concepts like Heaven or God. Confucius said he would not talk about deity and ghosts, nor would deny their existence.① Socrates might have been stronger in his religious faith because he believed that man could not be separated from his soul and afterlife. But comparatively, he emphasized moral goodness more by regarding it "as the one thing that matters and he identified it with knowledge because to his straightforward nature it seemed inconceivable that anyone should see what is right without doing it."②

2.4.4　Political views

Before moving into the specific account of their major arguments, one has to be aware of the justification their theories try to build up. Confucius once said: "If without a right name, one could not make the right expression; if without a right expression, nothing succeeds consequently; if nothing succeeds, no rites or music could rise up; if without the rise of rite or music, no criminal punishment could work; if without criminal punishment, no civil rules are followed."③ Confucius' statement came from his worries about the political chaos and social turmoil occurring in his mother country during the Spring-Autumn Period on account of irreverent attitude towards the rites of the Zhou Dynasty. Therefore, he proposed to recover the social order by evoking respect for and operation of those ritual principles, thus initiating his philosophy as one of the major ideological schools of the period.

When Socrates started to engage himself with the heated arguments of those days, his situation was not exactly the same as that of Confucius. Athens has become a centre of political and cultural activities where science and philosophy achieved considerable progress. Though limited by material conditions, Greek thinkers were well on the way by simple observation and logical reasoning towards some important discoveries, such as the concepts of dialectics, logic and atomic theory. As a man of justice and honesty, Socrates belonged to the group of sophists who were basically professional itinerant teachers. They were eager to learn and teach, demonstrating learning and ability in their speaking and practice. They charged fees for their services, which earned them a reputation for both psychology and business. However, their influence and honour were thus also ill affected. Consequently, the voice of a prophet was in great need. Socrates' appearance filled up the vacancy.

The two philosophers, in spite of a huge gap in culture, had much in common. Both Confucius and Socrates showed heroic spirit by ignoring

---

① See *History of Chinese Philosophy* (2nd edition), p. 26, Chinese Philosophy Teaching Group, Beijing University, Beijing University Press, 2003.
② See *The Last Days of Socrates*, p. 8, Plato, translated by Hugh Tredennck, Penguin Books, 1971.
③ See *History of Chinese Philosophy* (2nd edition), p. 37, Chinese Philosophy Teaching Group, Beijing University, Beijing University Press, 2003.

prejudice and danger of the time and persisting in upholding justice and protecting the interest of the common people. Confucius risked his life to visit the kings and aristocrats to present his advice for reducing the suffering of the ordinary people. Socrates dared to criticize the authorities and air his political and ethical views. Their behaviours and opinions won the hearts of the people and proved to be of great significance though they suffered personal misfortune. In a sense, their status and influence were produced by their courage and wisdom.

2.4.5 Philosophical and cognitive issues

In their wide-range discussions of such topics as learning, the basis of knowledge, and various ethical, social, religious, political and intellectual issues, Confucius and Socrates touched on some important philosophical areas. In the case of Confucius, nothing could be more influential than his advocacy on *the doctrine of the Mean*, which was first submitted as a moral principle. Later scholars interpreted it as a way of thinking which chooses to be neutral and stable and avoid extreme actions. ① This principle worked as one of the core ideas in cognitive and intellectual development in China for thousands of years, guiding and perhaps also limiting Chinese ways of thinking in getting around to human relations and social development.

Socrates' contribution to epistemology lies in his concept of the Forms. For him, "The Forms or Ideas are not mere concepts, but are ultimate facts, intelligible to our minds yet quite independent of them. The things of our sensible world exist in a secondary sense, only in so far as they approximate to the corresponding Forms. They are effects of which the Forms are causes, although the precise relation is difficult to describe." ② This theory, further developed by his student Plato, grew into that of Ideas, serving as one of the early ways to explain human cognition and awareness of the exterior world. Just as what occurred to Confucius' *the doctrine of the Mean*, the theory of Ideas also received different comments and judgments from different groups of people. But as a theory of cognition, it has great merit of its own.

2.4.6 Ethical ideas

In ethics, both Confucius and Socrates have achieved a number of substantial results. Confucius derived his distinctive idea of *jen* (humanity), which refers to a human being taking a good attitude to his fellow people and then extends to the whole of society and nature, including the ruler's kind attitude to his subjects and

---

① See *History of Chinese Philosophy* (2nd edition), p. 23, Chinese Philosophy Teaching Group, Beijing University, Beijing University Press, 2003.
② See *The Last Days of Socrates*, p. 15, Plato, translated by Hugh Tredennck, Penguin Books, 1971.

the desirable human attribute of an emotional concern for all living things. This principle later developed into an all-encompassing ideal operating as a basic and dominant law for political, ethical and intellectual relations throughout all the feudal dynasties, exerting a tremendous influence.

Socrates' ethical view contains such ideas as virtue, courage, honesty and conscience, all of which were verified by his own behaviour. These ideas, separately manifested in his speeches recorded by Plato, pinpoint and highlight his quality of sainthood though he is never regarded as a martyr in the Christian sense. His views are revealing and original in his insistent concern for the significance of knowledge. "For Socrates, being virtuous is a purely intellectual matter: it simply involves knowing what is good for human beings; once we master this subject, we will act as we should, because he equates virtue with knowledge."[1] His sense of knowledge gives his ideas a rational force, which is proved by his own practical experiences. That explains why his ideas could survive the test of thousands of years of Western civilization.

In spite of the enormous honour and influence the two great philosophers share in history, they deserve to be carefully distinguished in their intellectual significance, which determined, in a way, the later difference between the two traditions. The rational and critical spirit in Socrates' ideology provides food for the Western intellectual tradition, while Confucius takes *jen* (humanity), *li* (rite) and the sense of hierarchy as the key ideas and heritage to pass down to later generations. There are certainly many reasons why Chinese and Western ideologies would be opposed to each other so fundamentally, such as different social and cultural structures and environments, personal temperaments of the rulers and so on, but the intellectual influence of these pioneering thinkers could never be ignored. This is their significance for this case study.

Questions for comprehension and discussion

1. Tell the developments and main ideas of the major schools of ancient Chinese philosophy and ideology, such as Confucianism, Taoism, Legalism and Mohism.
2. Describe the main ideas of the representative ideological figures or schools in the ancient West, such as Socrates, Plato, Aristotle, Epicurus and Stoicism.
3. What would you say about the intellectual and ideological differences and similarities which gave rise to the later divergences between the two sides? Give examples.

---

[1] See *The Cambridge Dictionary of Philosophy* (2nd edition), p. 860, Robert Audi, Cambridge University Press, 1999.

List of proposed books for further reading

1. 北京大学哲学系中国哲学教研室,2002,《中国哲学史》,北京:北京大学出版社。
2. 任继愈,1999,《中国哲学史》第一册,北京:人民出版社。
3. 冯友兰,2003,《中国哲学简史》(上),天津:天津社会科学出版社。
4. 复旦大学哲学系中国哲学教研室(编),2006,《中国古代哲学史》(上),上海:复旦大学出版社。
5. [美]斯东,1998,《苏格拉底的审判》,北京:生活·读书·新知三联书店。
6. 杨荣国,1954,《中国古代思想史》,北京:人民出版社。
7. 张再林,1997,《中西哲学比较论》,兰州:西北大学出版社。
8. Russell, Bertrand, *History of Western Philosophy*, vol. I, University of Notre Dame, 1963.
9. Soloman, Robert & K Higgins, Kathleen, *A Short History of Philosophy*, Oxford University Press, 1996.

Chapter 3

A Comparison of Middle-Age Chinese and Western Philosophies

The "Medieval Period" or the "Middle Ages" usually refers to the feudalistic period in Western history and roughly suggests a time between the end of the Western Roman Empire and the end of the Renaissance. Though China does not mark its feudalistic period with the term "medieval" or "middle age", we might still use this term to match the similar period from the end of the Warring States Period generally acknowledged as the beginning of the feudal society to the early years of the 20th century at the end of the last feudal dynasty as well for the sake of convenience of comparison. As is well known universally, this period is comparatively a dark period of time, notorious for autocracy, conquest, conspiracy, violence and slow social and intellectual development in both China and the West though one could still find some occasional remarkable achievements during this period and some scholars might still be positive about it. ① Yet at the same time, the middle period is an inseparable link between the ancient period and the modern age. To acquire a better understanding of the long process of human civilization, one can not leave out this period or ignore the intellectual contributions of the philosophers and scholars concerned. To inquire in a comparative way into the sources, performances and consequences of the intellectual forces during this period, therefore, may help us unveil some of the apparently mysterious factors underlying the sluggish process of prolonged historical development, both social and intellectual, in the long eons of human civilization.

 Social and intellectual background

Since Chinese history associates the rise of its feudalistic period with

---

① For instance, Professor Rod Home from Melbourne University wrote to me, saying: "Contemporary historians studying this period have shown that it was not nearly so dark as it has been portrayed."

unification under the centralized government, it is easier to open the middle period of Chinese civilization with the unification by the first emperor of the Qin Dynasty and finalize it at the end of the Qing Dynasty.

The Chinese middle age had to experience a dark period at the beginning. Qin Shihuang, the first emperor of the period was unfortunately notorious for his cruelty in his slaughtering of intellectuals and killings in the wars against other kingdoms, or in the legalist reign under the influence from Han Fei and Li Si, his prime minister. Li and Han were renowned for using heavy penalties against the innocent. The result was the burning of all the confiscated books and the burial of hundreds of scholars who dared to talk about current affairs of the day.

The Western medieval age began during the fifth century, about 700 years later than the Chinese one. The barbarous Germans who overthrew the Roman Empire almost knew nothing about cultured or noble ways of living and ruined large amounts of artistic works, including some magnificent buildings which were demolished in order to collect building material for their palaces at Aachen. A good example is the Frankish state, the Carolingian Empire[①]. However, the emperor Charlemagne the Great soon changed his ignorance of culture into respect for cultural affairs by inviting scholars to collect classical material and by running schools in the hope that his people's illiteracy or semi-literacy could be replaced by a cultural prosperity. Consequently, classical as well as Christian cultural traditions were generally inherited and preserved though some could have been spoiled and lost during the wars or chaos.

By contrast, the damage inflicted by Qin Shihuang on traditional culture, especially on the cultural heritage of Confucianism, was terribly great and irretrievable. The effect of the cultural disaster was not only indicated in a great loss of classical works, but extended to the neglect of and discrimination against knowledge in the years to come. It was not until about 70 years later that the Chinese cultural rehabilitation received official attention and was put into effect when Han Wudi, an emperor of the Han Dynasty, decided to adopt Confucianism as the only state orthodoxy as was proposed by Dong Zhongshu, a Confucianist scholar. However, that decision, apart from the advantages for the cultural affairs of the time, imposed a totalitarian dominance over and hence hindered later ideological development. A combination of feudalistic and autocratic rule with Confucianism pervaded since then the different stages of the feudal or medieval society in spite of changes of dynasties or governments in a span of over 2,000 years. The influence of Confucianism on the Chinese mentality could be compared with that of Christianity on the Westerner's mind in

---

① The Carolingian Empire was established by Pepin III whose son Charlemagne became the first Holy German Emperor. After the death of his son Louis I, the Treaty of Verdin divided in 843 the Carolingian into three parts which provided the bases for the boundaries of modern Western Europe.

a way, even though Confucianism is not, exactly speaking, a kind of religion. This is because its dominant role outpaced that of Buddhism, a religion introduced to China from India. The tight control over the intellectual and ideological development of the Chinese by Confucianism is obviously one of the reasons why Chinese society showed steady but not always positive enough sign of vigour and progress in its long history.

Meanwhile Western civilization also had to go through a long and sometimes even dark age when Christianity joined with aristocratic and feudalistic rule as an intellectual master or steward in the thousand-odd-year medieval period. It was characterized by political division as was indicated in the chaotic situations of several hundred small kingdoms or fiefdoms for most of time, and economic sluggishness and ideological depression. Nonetheless, except for the shortage of distinguished thinkers and scholars who made outstanding contributions, one could still perceive a number of representative figures and their influential ideas. To prepare for some more specific comparisons, we would take some three or four epitomizing schools or figures from each side for a more detailed account and comments.

3.2 Chinese representative philosophies

3.2.1 Fan Zhen

1 Life (450 − 515 AD)

Born into a humble and poor family, Fan Zhen achieved a career by hard working spirit in academic studies. He won his reputation by producing his famous work *On Divine Extinction*. The book acutely criticized the rampancy of Buddhism that had brought forward lots of economic, social and ideological problems as well as social turmoil. He once joined in a debate with a group of scholars in favour of Buddhism organized by the emperor, and established his reputation by refuting sharp-wittedly pro-Buddhist views in association with the chaotic situation due to the dissemination of Buddhism.

2 Major views

The Northern and Southern Dynasties had a fashion for Buddhist faith for a long while. The emperors and the aristocrats of the dynasty, like Xiao Yan (Liang Wudi) and his officials, not only cherished personal faith in Buddhism, but persuaded other people to do the same and finally erected Buddhism into the state religion.

Fan Zhen became aware of the danger of the fashion and exposed the damages it caused to social customs and stability by pointing out that Buddhism puzzled the people by uncertain lies, scared the people with pains of hell, seduced the people by absurd words and enticed the people by the happiness of paradise. Consequently many people gave up Confucian wear in favour of Buddhist gowns and threw away traditional ritual utensils for Buddhist mantle, to the degree that many families had to part from their children and were deprived of their heirs, soldiers suffered defeat in the battles, the vacancies in the government offices could not be filled up. Furthermore, food was consumed by the idle Buddhist monks and wealth exhausted in building up extravagant Buddhist monasteries.

Fan Zhen presents his theory of contingency by claiming that everything has its own natural causes of growth and development. Its occurrence and extinction depend on itself, and could neither be prevented nor necessarily missed. Whether or not one's life is happy, or one is born into a noble or rich family is entirely accidental, just as a falling flower could fall into a banquet in the hall or into a toilet. Therefore there is no basis for the theory of retribution for sin[①].

Fan Zhen asserts that body is primary while spirit is secondary in terms of priority. He adheres to a materialist monism[②], combining form and spirit and affirming that form cannot be separated from spirit, in opposition to the idealist assertion that spirit is indestructible.

Fan Zhen argues that the performance of thinking acts upon a material organ, the heart. In spite of imperfection, this agrees with the materialist principle and shows great progress by basing psychological performances on physiological performances to high significance in ensuring necessary command of human behaviours by right ideology.

The criticism of god's indestructibility also dealt a blow at the aristocratic landlord class by exposing their privilege and repudiating their die-hard insistence on the religious prejudice.

---

① The theory of retribution for sin, a term from Buddhism, meaning a meeting of punishment and evil behaviour according to one's deserts.

② Monism, a philosophical view which reduces all reality to a single principle of substance in contrast to dualism.

3.2.2 Zhu Xi

1 Life (1130－1200 AD)

Coming from Moyuan, Anhui(currently Jiangxi), but born and brought up in Fujian, Zhu Xi studied under Li Tong, a follower of Cheng Yi ① succeeding to Confucius' ideas. He lectured and wrote extensively on the interpretation of Confucianist ideas. His *si-shu-zhu-shi* (《四书注释》, Notations to The Four Books) was designated by the feudalist government as the compulsory textbook and the normalized standard key for all educated people at the time.

2 Major views

Zhu Xi believes *li* (理, reason) and *qi* (气, gas) are the two universally-existent beings. *Li* is the *Tao* (道, law or way) of metaphysics and the origin of animate beings. *Qi* is an instrument of physics and the form of animate beings. Therefore all human and animate beings would follow the principles of *li* and *qi* before they take their character and form.

In the relationship between *li* and *qi*, *li* is dominant while *qi* is to be dominated. *Qi* serves *li* which is of the same source but works in different positions, like that of being kind as monarchs, that of being respectful as subjects, that of being benevolent as fathers, or that of being filial as sons, etc.

Zhu states that *li* in charge of everything in the world is called *taiji* (太极). He regards *li* as the source of everything in the universe. According to him, *taiji* is a permanent existence, static and endless. But the movement and the end of everything is a result of *taiji*. He also trusts that *taiji* is of moral integrity and shows its supreme virtue in everything involved all over the world.

Zhu argues that knowledge is prior to action in terms of their relationship. He compares the relationship to one's walking that is conducted or directed by one's knowledge about the road. Only by knowing the reason or justification for something, could one expect to take actions for its fulfilment.

Action is more important than knowledge in terms of their priority. One's knowledge has to be acquired by actions and Zhu is opposed to staying indoors to acquire knowledge. Knowledge and action have a mutually-dependent relationship, something like that of eyes and feet, which means eyes need feet for

---

① Cheng Yi (程颐), one of the Cheng Brothers who were famous for their idealist philosophy as so-called Neo-Confucianism during the Song Dynasty.

walking and feet need eyes for identifying directions.

According to Zhu, human nature falls into two kinds: innate nature and acquired nature. This view was presented by some Buddhist doctrine during the Northern and Southern Dynasties and then developed by the Cheng Brothers and Zhang Zhai. Zhu has a summary of their ideas and claims that everyone is characteristic of his natural fine quality, such as kindness, righteousness, loyalty and filiality soon after his or her birth. It is only because of postnatal hindrances that he or she could not manifest fully these qualities.

Zhu asserts that mind is the decisive factor for one's body: Everything related to man centres round mind. Relationship between *Tao*'s mind and human mind needs to be defined. *Tao*'s mind comes from the heavenly innate mind and is of supreme benevolence, while human mind comes from man's physical form and is produced from its specific postnatal quality, which could be good or bad.

One is not to extinguish one's human mind but to make human mind obey *Tao*'s mind to be guided into safety from danger in respect of human cultivation.

Zhu believes *Tao*'s mind is heavenly reason but human mind is not exactly the same as human desire. Human mind could be good or bad while human desire must be bad. Therefore heavenly reason could not coexist with human desire. He claims that it is necessary to extinguish human desire to keep heavenly reason for the sake of cultivation. Human cultivation is in the final analysis, he insists, to seek *jen* which should cover kindness, righteousness, rite and wisdom in the feudalist ethical moral code.

The decisive factor in history depended on the good or bad aspects of human nature, especially the good or bad nature of the emperor. Zhu insists that heavenly reason dominated the three dynasties of Xia, Shang and Zhou and therefore they were ruled by benevolence. Human desire was popular after the three dynasties and hence the hegemony of politics on a rampage. Zhu's ideas of the kingly politics come from Mencius but are modified in that Mencius' kingly rule is measured by the ruler's ideology while Zhu's kingly politics is based on heavenly reason which is more abstract and perhaps objective. Also, Mencius stresses the necessity of economic development for the sake of improving the life of the average person, while Zhu emphasizs the need to lower living standards to reduce or extinguish human desire, thus turning out to be reactionary and opposed to development.

3.2.3　Wang Shouren

1　Life (1472 – 1529 AD)

　　Coming from Yuyao, Zhejiang and brought up in an official family, Wang Shouren was also called Wang Yangming. His father was once the minister in charge of personnel and he himself was minister of defence. He joined in many battles, putting down peasants' uprisings and fighting for the Ming government in an attempt to save the Ming Dynasty from being destroyed. He learned from his warring experiences that "it is easy to defeat the enemy in the mountain but difficult to beat the enemy in the mind." He attributed social order or disorder to human moral conditions and worked positively for the so-called purpose of "keeping the heavenly reason and dispelling human desire".

2　Major views

　　Wang maintains that *li* is mind, which is different from Zhu Xi's objective idealism that claims *li* is external to the mind. He borrows Mencius' conscience and advocates that mind is conscience and is prenatal or innate moral views. He says that body is dominated by mind and *yi* (righteousness) comes from mind. The root of *yi* is knowledge and *yi* is located in matter.

　　He also claims that nothing exists outside mind. He illustrated this point to a friend by pointing to a flower tree in a mountain, saying that the flower was non-existent if he did not see it and when he saw it, it was already in his mind. He tries to establish his principle by clarifying moral principles to be close to the ordinary people. He says in his *da-xue* (《大学》, Great Learning) that noble people regard all worldly beings as one family, regard China as one person and make everyone follow the ethical code, behaving as kind-hearted fathers and filial sons, friendly and modest brothers, polite spouses and righteous monarchs and subjects.

　　Conscience is the root of worldly creatures. In terms of mind, conscience is the source of everything in ontology and the criterion for right and wrong in epistemology. Mind is not only the subject of cognition but the object of cognition. The practice of cultivation and to seek conscience and substance could be summarized in the following: No reason or substance is out of mind. The practice to seek conscience is the reason to seek mind and the substance to seek mind. To seek substance is not that of acquiring it outside mind but to make readjustment of one's mind because substance is numerous all over the world and one could never expect to come to an end of it if one's target is outside mind.

The so-called "seeking substance" is a means of fulfilling the feudalistic "heavenly means" and fortifying one's feudalistic moral cultivation.

Both knowledge and practice are produced by mind. Wang regards practice as a form of representation of knowledge. The combination of knowledge and practice takes as its criterion the seeking of conscience. Knowledge is to know about "the heavenly law" while practice is to execute "the heavenly law". Its final purpose is to seek or acquire conscience, i. e. the feudalistic ethical and moral ideas.

3.3 Western representative philosophies

With the establishment of Christianity since the first two centuries, Western intellectual situation took up a new phase of change as initiated by the emergence of some ideological schools. Neoplatonism, among these schools, was perhaps more influential in terms of its social and intellectual significance and academic contribution to the ideological connection between classical period and medieval times though its occurrence was largely before the end of the Roman Empire.

3.3.1 Neoplatonism

1 Origin

Neoplatonism, a school of philosophy, arose at Alexandria in the 3rd century, that revived and developed the metaphysical and mystic sides of the Platonic teachings. Its chief exponents were Plotinus, Porphyry and Iamblichus. One of the famous members of the school was Hypatia, murdered by the Alexandrian mob in 415. She commented on Plato and Aristotle and taught astronomy as well. Among her students was Syneseus, a versatile and learned scholar, both a Neoplatonist and a Christian bishop. The last remarkable writer was Proclus of Byzantium, who produced a vast and consistent system, embracing the philosophical traditions of antiquity in support of paganism against Christianity, which was exhibited in his *Elements of Theology* which had a significant influence on the thought of Hegel.

Many of the later Neoplatonists carried metaphysical speculations to fantastic lengths, with a mingling of magic and eastern superstitions. Demonology in particular was highly developed and a complete hierarchy of good and evil demons was devised, who were thought to people the universe and were the object of semi-religious and semi-magical rites. The Neoplatonic School at Athens was closed by Justinian, the emperor of Eastern Rome in 529, but survived at

Alexandria till the end of the 6th century. Neoplatonism proper may be divided into three main periods: that of Plotinus and his followers (the 3rd century in Alexandria); the Syrian School of Iamblichus and his followers (the 4th century in Damaschus) and the Athenian School begun by Plutarch of Athens and including Syrianus and Proclus and their successors down to Damascius (the 5th century).

2 Plotinus (205 – 270 AD)

Plotinus was born at Lycopolis in Egypt probably and settled in Rome in 244 after an expedition in company with Gordian to Mesopotamia in order to consult Magi. He was a man of an extremely spiritual and mystical character. The essence of his philosophy is the desire to escape from the material world. He explained the universe by a hierarchy rising from matter to soul, from soul to reason and from reason to god, the final abstraction without form or matter, pure existence. Reality is the spiritual world contemplated by reason. The phenomenal world is a creation of the soul and has no real existence, matter being a mere receptacle for forms imposed on it by the soul. He often spoke of matter as evil and of the soul as suffering from a fall, and saw the whole universe as an inevitable result of the superabundant productivity of God.

In ethics, Plotinus enjoined purification by self discipline with a view to ascent to the spiritual world and the pursuit, impelled by love and enthusiasm of the divine. His writings were edited by his pupil Porphyry in six books of nine chapters each, hence called *Enneads*. He himself was mystic but he arrived at his philosophical conclusions by perfect logical means. He had not much use of traditional religion or any superstitions.

3.3.2 Scholasticism

1 Origin and features

For many centuries since the intellectual dominance of Christianity in the West, few people dared to say or do anything offensive against the Christian church. But with more people educated and more dissemination of classicist writings and ideas, some suspicion of Christian doctrines arose and the church began to feel the intellectual threat and thought it necessary to benefit from the spread of classicist works. This was an attempt to reconcile the doctrines of the Christian church with Greek philosophical thought (particularly with that of Aristotle), which became prominent from the latter part of the 11th century, involving a revival of interest in Greek literature limited to the study of logic. At this time and until the latter part of the 12th century, Aristotle was known in the West only in the Latin translations of and commentaries on a few of his works by Boethius and others. And so was Plato.

A great increase in the knowledge of Aristotle was brought about when the

Arabic translations of his works by Avicenna and Averroes became known in Latin versions. Aristotle had long been studied by the Arabs and Avicenna and Averroes were respectively his eastern and western exponents. Latin versions were made chiefly at Toledo from about 1200. Quite a number of scholars, like Roger Bacon and John of Salisbury, were involved in the project.

Scholasticism was supposed to designate a doctrine whose core was that of substance and accidents. As portrayed by Descartes and Locke, the Scholastics accepted the view that among the components of a thing were a substantial form and a number of accidental forms, many of which corresponded to perceptible properties of the thing — its colour, shape, temperature. They were also supposed to accept a sharp distinction between natural and unnatural motion.

2 Thomas Aquinas (1225 – 1274 AD)

Born at Aqino castle in Roccasecca, Italy, Aquinas took his early schooling at the Benedictine Abbey of Monte Cassino. He then studied liberal arts and philosophy at the University of Naples (1239 – 1244) and joined the Dominican Order. Later he went to Cologne and Paris for further studies and lectures. In 1256, he began lecturing as master of theology at Paris. Then at different locations he wrote prodigiously till returning to Italy in 1272, where he lectured on theology at Naples and continued to write till December, 1273. He died three months later en route to the 2nd council of Lyons. He was both a philosopher and a theologian. Most of his works were theological though there were also many strictly philosophical writings, such as *On Being and Essence*, *On the Principles of Nature*, and *On the Eternity of the World*.

Here are his major views.

Aquinas clearly distinguishes between strictly philosophical investigations and theological investigations. He holds that the natural light of reason is insufficient to discover things that can be made known to human beings only through revelation. For instance, belief in the Trinity[①] is impossible for those who are not revealed by God through faith opposed to using human reason. For them one or the other would have to be false and since both come to us from God, God himself would be the author of falsity, something Aquinas rejects as abhorrent. Hence it is appropriate for the theologian to use philosophical reasoning in theologizing.

In theology one reasons from belief in God and his revelation for created reality. In philosophy one begins with an investigation of created reality in so far as this can be understood by human reason.

[①] Trinity, a term in Christian theology, means the union in one Godhead of three persons: Father, Son and Holy Spirit.

For Aquinas the highest part of philosophy is metaphysics, the science of being as being. The metaphysician does not enjoy a direct vision of God in this life, but can reason to knowledge of him by moving from created effects to awareness of him as their uncreated cause. God is therefore not the subject of metaphysics, but can be studied only indirectly as the cause of the finite beings that fall under being as being, the subject of the science.

On the level of finite being, Aquinas adopts and adapts Aristotle's theory of unity by reference to a first order of being by a supernatural force or almighty God. For Aquinas as for Aristotle this unity is guaranteed by the primary referent in our predication of being, namely substance. Other things are named being only because they are in some way ordered to and dependent on substance, the primary instance of being. In this sense being is analogous to substance.

Best known among Aquinas' argumentation for God's existence is his interpretation of Aristotle's theory of the first mover. He argues that whatever is moved is moved by something else. One must therefore conclude to the existence of a first mover which is moved by nothing else but that which "everyone understands to be God".

Aquinas holds that certain efficient causes cannot exercise their causal activity unless they are also caused by something else. But nothing can be the efficient cause of itself since it would then have to be prior to itself. If there were no first efficient cause, there would be no intermediary and no last cause. He concludes that one must acknowledge the existence of a first efficient cause, which everyone names God. If all things are capable of not existing, at some time there was nothing whatsoever. What does not exist can only begin to exist through something else that exists. Therefore not all beings are capable of existing and not existing. There must be some necessary being and being might still be caused by something else. Therefore there must be some being that is necessary of itself and that does not depend on another cause for its necessity, God.

Based on the varying degrees of perfection discovered among beings one experienced, Aquinas holds that those things that are tuned to the maximum degree also enjoy being to the maximum degree; in other words he appeals to the convertibility between being and truth.

Based on the way things in the universe are governed, Aquinas observes that certain things that lack the ability to know, i.e. natural bodies, act for an end. This implies that they are directed to their ends by some knowing and intelligent being. Hence some intelligent being exists that orders natural things to their ends. This argument rests on final causality and should not be confused with any based on order and design.

Aquinas argues that to believe is an act of the intellect that assents to divine truth as a result of a command on the part of the human will, a will that is moved by God through grace. For him, the theological virtues, having God as object, are prior to all other virtues whether natural or infused. This is because the ultimate end must be present in the intellect before it is presented in the will and because the ultimate end is present in the will by reason of hope and charity (the other two theological virtues). In this respect faith is prior to hope and charity.

3.3.3　The Christian Reformation and Martin Luther

1　Background

For a long period in the medieval era, Scholasticism had been the systematization of the Roman Catholic understanding of the relation between the claims of human reason and the authority of divine revelation. To that end it had made use of philosophy, particularly the works of Aristotle to describe the natural potentialities of human ways to truth in order to keep Christian theology as the queen of the sciences. However, the waning prestige of the Papacy in the coming years has been correlated by some historians with the shattering of the Scholastic synthesis. Because the followers of Bonaventura and Aquinas had improperly elevated the primacy of faith and the authority of scripture, and expanded the realm of what was knowable by natural means so that primacy of faith was threatened by an all-engulfing rationalism, all the varieties of Scholastic teaching were under attack from those devoted to Roman Catholicism who contended that the crisis of faith and of the church called for a return to the authentic religious experience of the primitive church as set forth in the *New Testament*, as opposed to what the Scholastics claimed and practised.

At the same time there was also evidence among the common people of a tide of anticlericalism, much of it in reaction to the corruption of the church and the clergy, and of a growing skepticism among the intellectuals and secular rulers even about fundamental Roman Catholic teachings.

In addition to the increasing problems within the Catholic church, the relation of church and state shaped much of the history of Roman Catholicism on the eve of the Reformation. In most of the states embracing Christendom the 15th century was the time of an awakening of national consciousness, whose particularity and regionalism could set it in opposition to the Roman church. The situation was aggravated by the fact that 15th-century France, as the seat of the

Avignon Papacy and the stronghold of Conciliarism① represented by Chancellor Jean de Gerson and Cardinal Pierre. The latter came out to support her clergy in what were taken to be the historical rights of the Gallic church to administer its own affairs independently of Rome while maintaining its ties of filial loyalty and doctrinal obedience to the Holy See②.

By the time Protestantism arose to challenge the spiritual authority of the Papacy, the medieval class structure had undergone fundamental and drastic changes with the rise of the bourgeoisie throughout western Europe. It is not a coincidence that in northern Europe and Britain, the middle class was to become the principal bulwark of the Protestant opposition to Roman Catholicism.

2 The occurrence of the Reformation

By the end of the 15th century, there was a widely-held view that the church authorities of Roman Catholicism had been challenged in its moral prestige and administrative capacities to maintain its huge body of theology. For instance, the Papacy refused to reform itself, the councils had not succeeded in bringing about lasting change and the professional theologians were more interested in Scholastic debates than in the nurture of genuine Christian faith and life. The financial corruption and pagan immorality within Roman Catholicism led inevitably to the Protestant Reformation, which was initiated by Martin Luther, a German theologian.

Luther first taught philosophy and subsequently scripture at Wittenberg University. His career as a church reformer began in October 1517 with his public denunciation, in 95 theses, of the sale of indulgences. He produced three incendiary tracts: *Appeal to the Nobility*, *The Babylonian Captivity of the Church*, and *The Freedom of a Christian Man* (1520), which prompted his excommunication. His major contributions, apart from the translation of the Bible into German which took up the form of modern language, included the establishment of a biblical-christo-centric, anti-philosophical theology, his assertion of justification by faith alone and the priesthood of all believers, his reformation of the Mass and acknowledgement of only two sacraments (baptism and the Eucharist), and his advocating consubstantiation and the two kingdoms theory in church-state relations.

3 Effect, influence and significance

---

① Conciliarism, a Christian school, claims for the power by the council which serves as an assembly of churchmen to consider doctrinal, moral and legal problems.

② Holy See refers to the office or authority of the pope.

Luther showed his unsparing spirit in his attacks on the moral, financial and administrative abuses within Roman Catholicism.

Luther expressed his attitude of reconciliation in his struggle by saying that the primary object of his critique was not the life but the doctrine of the church, not the corruption of the ecclesiastical structure but the distortion of the Gospel.

Many of the other Protestant Reformers who arose during the 16th century were considerably less conservative in their doctrinal stance, distancing themselves from Luther's position no less than from the Roman Catholic church, like Luther's Swiss opponent Ulrich Zwingli who compared Luther's sacramental teachings with the medieval ones. The Anglican Reformation tried to steer a middle course, liturgically and even doctrinally between Roman Catholicism and Continental Protestantism.

As the varieties of Protestantism proliferated, the apologists for Catholicism pointed to the Protestant principle of the right to private interpretation of Scripture as the source of the confusion, saying that Scripture and Church tradition were inseparable and had always been, and that the Protestant elevation of Scripture to the position of sole authority was unjustified. They denounced justification by faith alone and other cherished Protestant teachings as novelties without grounding in authentic Church tradition. And they warned that the doctrine of faith alone, without works, as taught by Luther, would sever the moral nerve and remove all incentive for holy living.

3.4 Comparative comments

The middle period was basically a phase of slow and impassive change, showing slight signs of progress. In many ways it preserved what was inherited from the previous period and dragged on sluggishly under a heavy load or even a yoke imposed by the ruling class and ideology. The two sides were not exactly the same in terms of the length of the period, yet certainly shared much in common, such as the guidance by a leading ideology, feudal society with the experience of upheaval, conflict and war, which served as a transitional stage from the ancient phase to the modern phase. This was true of the situations in both China and the West.

Chinese intellectual development was enormously tightened and restricted because of the reinterpretation of Confucianism by Dong Zhongshu during the

Han Dynasty. The so-called three key links (i. e. subjection to monarchs by subjects, subjection to fathers by sons, and subjection to husbands by wives) in the reinterpretation led to the establishment of Confucianism as the only orthodox doctrine which dominated the ideology of the ordinary Chinese for two-thousand-odd years and affected the way of thinking tremendously by checking social and intellectual developments.

Similarly, Western intellectual development suffered a great deal from Christianity which grew up rapidly in its cooperation with feudal aristocracy not long after its birth. Its control over spiritual life of both church goers and non-believers deprived the ordinary people of their intellectual freedom and thus hindered social progress.

With the slow pace of social and intellectual developments, more and more people, especially the educated or culturally enlightened, became aware of the insufficiencies of such ideological tendencies. It was almost inevitable for them to disclose a sense of dissatisfaction first and then come to the point of repudiation and reformation of the deadening ideology. However, this process of readjustment and modification took hundreds of years and did not achieve any substantial results until the bourgeoisie came to power in the West and the Chinese feudal system was abolished. Western countries spent about 1,000 years completing this process while China, due to its specific social and intellectual conditions, had to double the time before it finally came to the end of this period. There are several points in common between them which explain how the human race shared the cultural advantages and came together in spite of their racial and ethnic discrepancies. However, the different social and cultural traditions contributed to why Chinese and Western cultural and ideological developments embarked on such totally different roads.

3.4.1 The establishment and defence of the orthodox ideology

1 The erection of the only orthodox ideology

In China, Confucianism was formally erected as the only orthodox ideology in the 2nd century BC and the other schools were abolished as illegal ideas. All the scholarly research was, from then on, conducted around Confucianism though the other ideas were never extinct but only turned to secret or underground operations. This was true of such distinct schools as Taoism and Legalism. Taoism, for instance, developed in the direction of mysticism and became a religious doctrine by providing religious faiths in connection with nature and asceticism.

Similarly, in the West, Christianity was declared to be the only state religion in the 4th century (380 AD). From then on, it developed and started to control spiritual life of most of the Western countries. Other ideological schools were excluded or obscured in the long period of the medieval ages.

2 Difference in the attitude towards orthodox ideology

Though China produced a number of scholars who were famous for interpreting and developing Confucianism, such as Dong Zhongshu, Zhu Xi and Wang Yangming, none of them was critical or courageous enough to make any critical assessment of Confucian ideas. Apart from overpraise or flattery, they almost all tried to use it as a tool to fortify the autocratic rule of the emperor. One could cite many reasons for such a phenomenon, but the key factor might have something to do with Confucian influence which claims that loyalty should serve as a key link for all people no matter who they are. That is to say, once you say or do anything against the ruler or the ruling ideology, you would be regarded as disloyal or traitor, which is equivalent of treason, a terrible misconduct no one dares or wants to commit.

Western thinkers, for the first part or even most of the medieval period, also did a lot to praise and defend Christianity, which culminated during the period of Scholasticism. Scholasticism lasted about 300 years before it was challenged and led to the Reformation which, in a way, was another kind of interpretation since the Reformation did not intend to deny Christianity completely. One could say the Reformation prepared the way for the development of more varieties of theology and ideology as part of the Renaissance. It is noticeable that Martin Luther, himself a priest and professor of theology, had not intended to reject the Vatican Church and its doctrine before he was forced to respond to the harsh edict of punishment by the Papacy. Coincidentally or not, the Reformation occurred as a result of resistance to the folly of the church authority which was produced in the long period of intellectual obscurantism of the Middle Ages and indicated the need for intellectual and religious changes.

3.4.2 Historical reasons behind the faiths

In China, the revaluation of and attack on Confucianism never really occurred till the beginning of the 20th century, when some educated people who were informed of Western ideas rose up in opposition to Confucianism. Most scholars through the long lapse of time took it for granted that Confucianism was the only truth which could apply to both official and non-official areas as guidance to life and career. The blind faith of course came from the autocratic rule, no matter which dynasty they belonged to, for obviously it benefited the emperor's ideological dominance over the ordinary people whose sense of revolt or resistance was quenched at its early occurrence. While the rebellious spirit was suppressed, it was difficult for the average to suspect and resist the ruling ideology though few scholars once fell into a rational meditation over the justice of some key issues, like the loyalty to the monarch at the end of the Ming Dynasty.

In the West, the repudiation and reformation of Christianity was also slow to come. The long medieval age did not seem to give voice to any open complaints about the church till the Renaissance and the Reformation when the sale of Indulgences caused protests and complaints and Martin Luther called for reform, which was integrated with a popular demand for humanism.

The Chinese suffered a longer period of autocratic reign and Confucian influence which conspired to impose a particularly powerful and stubborn dominance over the ordinary people. Comparatively, the Western intellectual condition became more tolerable after the Reformation. In spite of a pretty long dark period of the Middle Ages, the separation of secular and theological rule allowed for more freedom on the part of the average Westerners both politically and intellectually while the ordinary Chinese had to wait much longer for more intellectual freedom.

3.4.3 The view of Confucianism and Christianity

1 Political involvement

Confucianism is a doctrine established more than two thousand years ago. It underwent historical changes to be adapted to the actual needs of various periods and was reestablished and reinterpreted by Confucius' followers later on to justify itself in safeguarding the feudalistic rule. It was therefore regarded as sacred and worshiped by the rulers of almost every dynasty since the Han. Its influence pervaded, permeated and perpetuated almost every aspect of social and intellectual life throughout the whole of the Chinese feudal period, which continued to the beginning of the 20th century. It was more consistent, changeless and stubborn in terms of adaptation to outside forces in a form of strong combination with politics. It was not a religion, yet its role went beyond the social and political arenas to that of faith and spiritual affairs to make it very close to if not exactly the same as religion.

2 Ideological role

Christianity is a religion which survived the social and political changes of the last thousand years and kept its control over the ideology of Westerners in alliance with secular autocratic rulers and aristocracy, but remained comparatively independent of worldly politics. The separation of religion and secular life indicated the early tendency to limit its power and reduce unnecessary conflicts with non-religious forces in spite of some occasional withdrawals in its history. The advantage of such separation was manifested in its neutral role in the conflicts of secular rulers, when the Pope often appeared as an arbitrator. Compared with the Chinese combination of Confucianism with feudal politics, such separation seems more workable.

3 Connection in ideological control

Christianity, nonetheless, experienced several reforms and became somewhat tolerant, flexible and open in its attitude towards opposition and divergence and more adapted to social change while Confucianism refused to admit any substantial changes in spite of a couple of attempts to make further reinterpretations to solidify its application by the ruling class. The latter stubbornness came from its privileged advantages and from its ideological dominance by the official people. Its decline and final collapse simply appeared as a reasonable consequence. The assertion "to preserve heavenly laws and extinguish human desires" is a good example to enforce ideological control by going to extremes and therefore shows the danger of such an ideological trend. Amelioration then is a possible response to the abrupt changes expected of any form of ideology or society.

3.4.4 Influence on the attitude towards nature and learning

1 Negative effects on the study of nature

Most scholars in China were not interested in research on nature but indulged in literary writing. The few who worked in this area were either ignored, or could not go on with their work because of external circumstances, or were only employed for the study of fate, such as astrology rather than astronomy. In spite of the difficulties they were faced with, some individuals still attained a number of marvellous results because no ideological hindrances were imposed on their specific engagement or the contribution of individual talents and will and stopped their research. For instance, Bi Sheng's moveable-type printing, Zhang Heng's instrument for astronomical observation, and Song Yingxing's *tiangong-kai-wu* (《天工开物》, The Application of Natural Objects), Zu Chongzhi's ratio of the circumference of a circle to its diametre, etc.

In the West, not only were the scientific researcher's achievements ignored and even discouraged, but scientists were persecuted, such as Bruno and Galileo. At the same time, metaphysical and meticulous ways of thinking stimulated and promoted a kind of impractical trend so that the ruling class seldom cared for the organization of any practical work and few individual scholars cared for any practical spirit or specific project. Scholasticism was presumably shaped in such intellectual climate. The emergence of Scholasticism was manoeuvred by the church authority to evade or dissolve its spiritual crisis in response to the then current of popular interest in natural science.

2 Intellectual impediment in the study of academic and literary affairs

In China, the impractical tendency was reflected in the system of the so-called Imperial Civil Service Examination which was officially set up to enroll officials by their literary or eight-part essay based on their reading and understanding of Confucian works, greatly restricting the scope of their thinking and actions as well as limiting the development of scientific research and material production. The fact that this long-existing tradition met with no challenge may be attributed partly to tight control by the ruling class and partly to unawareness of the potential contribution of natural science. This is perhaps the reason why no charge was brought against an offender who knew nothing about practical matters but the ability to recite or talk emptily about Confucius' works.

In the West, this tendency was witnessed in Scholastic research which also greatly restricted the scope of knowledge and narrowed the field of scholarly work. Later on during the Reformation, the establishment and operation of Inquisition by Roman Catholic church provided the legal means for the persecution of many dissidents, especially the learned men who dared to say or do something in opposition to their Christian faith. Faith thus became an excuse for religious persecution and symbolized a period of darkness and obscurantism.

But the Western development of natural science seemed to be less hindered and achieved a substantial headway with the emancipation of mind during the Renaissance and later the Enlightenment.

3.4.5 Mysterious and religious factors within the ideological tendency

Mysticism was related to certain levels of production as well as social and cultural conditions. It was quite popular in the early history of human civilization, which was witnessed in the myths or fairy tales and other kinds of literary pieces both in China and in the West. But with the progress of social and cultural developments, it was gradually reduced. Yet still one could find traces of ghosts or supernatural beings in the middle period either in China or in the West.

In China, such traces were located in large numbers of ghost stories and further developed into a wide-ranging religious trend with the introduction of Buddhism, which culminated in the Northern and Southern Dynasties when both the emperor and the subject were trying to make themselves Buddhist monk. Fan Zhen's objection to Buddhist growing rampancy showed his intellectual foresight and political judgment based on the social and cultural damage by Buddhist dissemination in the country. On the other hand, the damaging effect of Buddhism also indicated the dwindling function of feudal bureaucratic reign and orthodox ideology as was represented by Confucianism. It was a clear sign to suggest that Confucianism, in spite of its ruling position in China, did not work very well to solve spiritual problems, such as those of faith or class contradiction and consequently gave way to the entry of Buddhism which manifested its advantageous effect on human mind by offering spiritual comfort and hope for future life.

Comparatively, the West did not lack religious engagement with social life since Christianity had occupied an important part of the Westerners' daily life in the Middle Ages. What is more, classical ideas like those of Plato and Aristotle, started to be blended with other forms of ideology, including some religious influence and mysterious ideas. Neo-Platonism was the product of such a tendency. Dynamic changes occurred to the intellectual development of the Westerners in the later period of the Western Rome and the following centuries. Either Neo-Platonism or Scholasticism tried to benefit from classical ideas and work on a new trend, hued with some mystical means, to bring about a new way to interpret and guide spiritual and intellectual life. Whether successful or not, these two schools were pretty influential at the time regardless of their limitations. As a transitional mode of thinking, they helped pacify human mind by referring to a mixture of classicism and mysterious aspect drawn either from Christianity or from legend. Compared with Fan Zhen's single-handed struggle against Buddhist rampancy, their efforts might be less heroic yet more widespread and persistent.

3.5 A case study

Philosophical achievement of the medieval period is a decisive factor in the social and intellectual developments of the later period due to its position as a link between the ancient time and the modern age. Aside from what has been discussed in a general way above, it might be illustrative to focus on some more specific situations and individual figures for a better understanding of why both sides made such slow and obscure advances during this period. One of the reasons, doubtless, is related to the suffocating spiritual dominance of Confucianism and Christianity. However, the social and intellectual situation seemed still tolerable and kept going though a bit slowly, in spite of the fatal weakness. Therefore, it might be useful to unveil these social and ideological complexities by making investigations into some representative figures and their ideas.

The two chosen figures, Zhu Xi and Thomas Aquinas, are both famous for their efforts to reinterpret and even reestablish respectively the then shrinking dominant ideologies — Confucianism and Christianity — in a vain attempt to hold back religious and ideological decline. They might be tragic figures in their attempt to prevent intellectual advances to a more liberal and open stage and their failure to provide a successful solution to the social and intellectual crisis, but at the same time they also contributed to a certain cause for what they thought justified, though the justification is suspect to later generations.

3.5.1 Motivation for scholarly modifications

Before we come to the details of their scholarly reinterpretations, we had better make some inquiries into their motivation for their efforts. Apart from personal reasons, one certainly could not ignore the social and intellectual environment they were faced with at that time. To a certain extent, these environmental factors helped evoke much attention to and strong concern for the social and intellectual crux under scrutiny by more and more people. Zhu Xi and Thomas Aquinas could be seen as representatives who aired their views in an eagerness to defend their ideals.

Zhu Xi's life was spent during the end of the Northern Song Dynasty, a period of national crisis when Jin troops often came in large numbers intruding into the territories of the Song until they captured the two emperors.[①] Zhu shared with many patriotic intellectuals the view that the country was too weak both militarily and politically. Unlike those talking emptily about impractical ideas to save the country, he stressed the need to modify and improve Orthodox Confucianism when their enemy became more threatening than ever. His reinterpretation of Confucianism was based first on his personal understanding of *Mencius* and then on the explanation of classical Confucianism by the recent philosophers such as Zhang Zai and Cheng Hao and his brother Cheng Yi. The latter three philosophers were famous for their presentation of a number of new concepts such as *qi*, *li*, *taiji*, etc. He also benefited from Buddhism which had been influential in China since its introduction from India during the Northern and Southern Dynasties. Zhu realized that the crisis confronting Chinese society was *au fond* a crisis in relation to intellectual development. Therefore it was absolutely necessary to find solutions to intellectual issues before one could find a way out of the social crisis. Maybe this was the reason he decided to devote most of his time to the study of and reinterpretation of Confucianism as a spiritual framework for Chinese society and culture.

Overall, Zhu Xi made a systematic and integrated development of Confucianism by absorbing all the essential ingredients from different sources, which led to the eventual establishment of Neo-Confucianism. In order to secure his time for scholarship, he tried to evade political involvements. After the end of a local assignment, Zhu did not accept another official appointment until 1179. His persistent refusal to accept a substantive public office reflected his dissatisfaction with the men in power and their policies, his spurning of factional politics, and his preference for the life of a teacher and scholar, which was made possible by

---

[①] Jin, a newly-emerging kingdom in the north of the Song territories, had developed out of a number of nomadic tribes and become militarily powerful and often intruded into the territories of the Song, thus causing great damages and losses and constituting a serious threat to the Song.

his receipt of a series of government sinecures.

Thomas Aquinas was thrown into the heart of the doctrinal crisis that confronted Christendom when the discovery of Greek science, culture and thought seemed about to crush it. He raised new problems in his teaching, invented a new method and used new systems of proof. He provided a new light by the novelty of this inspiration, which gave him the courage and power to go on to teach, with new opinions and new knowledge.

As an Italian theologian and Scholastic philosopher, Thomas Aquinas wrote a number of books, such as *Summa contra Gentilesc*, to defend Christianity in the light of the attacks made by Averroes and his followers in their interpretations of Aristotle. His greatest work is *Summa Theologica* (Summary of Theology), which was intended to be a sum of all learning. He also wrote several commentaries on Aristotle, who greatly influenced his thinking. His work was presented as the integration into Christian thought of the recently discovered Aristotelian philosophy, in competition with the integration of Platonic thought effected by the Fathers of the Church during the first 12 centuries of the Christian Era. Aquinas' work also realized an evangelical awakening to the need for a cultural and spiritual renewal both in the lives of individual men and throughout the church. He should be understood in this context as a Christian scholar influenced by his predecessors, such as the evangelism of St. Francis of Assisi, founder of the Franciscan order, and by the devotion to scholarship of St. Dominic, founder of the Dominican order.

During Thomas Aquinas' lifetime, the influx of Arabian-Aristotelian idea of science was arousing a sharp reaction among many believers; and several times the church authorities tried to block the influx of naturalism and rationalism that were emanating from this philosophy and challenging the ideological inclinations of the younger generations. He came to realize that something must be done to save Christianity from its weakened position affected by internal contradictions and external conflicts. The way out, however, did not seem that easy since Christianity had to cope with many problems. Nontheless, he did not show any fear but studied the works of Aristotle and eventually lectured publicly on them. Under his influence, for the first time in history, Christian believers and theologians had the courage to confront the rigorous demands of scientific rationalism. At the same time, technical progress was on the way to move from the rudimentary economy of an agrarian society to an urban society, which seemed to threaten the traditional dominance of Christianity and affected both ways of thinking and ways of living of the ordinary people, including those of the church people.

It is clear that both Zhu Xi and Thomas Aquinas emerged as pioneering figures promoting ideological reform and change to confront and dissolve social and intellectual crises. In other words, they made inevitable appearances as a result of historical development to meet serious challenges. In face of the challenges, they showed courage, intellect and capacity. More important than that is their subservience to moderate and more traditional means, such as the use of classical thinking, to substitute for the outdated ideas embraced in the traditional doctrine they once worshiped as the only moral and ethical standard.

Both philosophers wanted to reinterpret, rather than to dismiss, the traditional theory which had contributed for centuries to social and cultural development. In other words, they chose compromise as a basic means to handle the new situation characterized by drastic changes and the introduction of new ideas as a response to the old form of established thinking like Confucianism and Christianity that seemed impotent to cope with emergent social and intellectual problems.

3.5.2 Epistemology and metaphysics

It is obvious that Zhu Xi and Thomas Aquinas were entirely different in both their profession and their ideological tendencies. Zhu Xi's official career affected and helped foster his choice of promoting and prophesying Confucianism as his lifelong pursuit, while Thomas Aquinas, driven by his mission, dedicated himself to the formation of his belief in God and Christianity. In spite of these diversities, however, both men tried to respond to the call for social and intellectual changes by adapting the traditional mode of ideology to the then increasingly intensified crises and changed circumstances when having troubles handling social and cultural problems.

Regarded as one of the greatest philosophers after Confucius and Mencius, Zhu Xi, the cofounder of the Cheng-Zhu School, promoted Cheng Yi's thinking into a comprehensive metaphysics of *li* and *qi*. For him, *li* means a principle or law working in every object or event outside the human mind. Those providing general guidance to the operation of everything in the universe, either in the heaven or on the earth, are called *taiji*, a term he borrowed from Cheng Yi and that gave the source or origin of everything. As to *qi*, he defines it as something physical in relation to material force, always changeable and mainly transitory. But for him, *li* and *qi* are not to be separated or mixed. Things are composed of both *li* and *qi*. Furthermore, Zhu identifies *xing* (human nature) as *li*, *qing* (emotion) as *qi*, *xin* (mind) as *li* of the subtlest kind. These new concepts, however, were rejected by some of his fellow philosophers like Lu Xiangshan and Wang Yangming, who argued that mind rather than these *li* or *qi* should be followed.

Zhu also established his theory of epistemology by presenting three theses, namely knowledge is prior to action in terms of occurrences, action is more important than knowledge in terms of significance and the effects of mutually dependent relationship in spite of their difference. These views of cognition indicate Zhu's general tendencies of idealism by reversing the objects of knowledge and research and hence cause theoretical disputes.

These ideas were basically derived from earlier philosophers such as the Cheng brothers, but were developed by Zhu Xi into more systematic concepts and achieved a sense of integration in their ability to interpret social and intellectual events and thus exert tremendous influences upon later generations. Apart from the objectiveness characteristic of his idealism, Zhu Xi also set up an epistemological theory. He regarded the target of epistemology as knowing about *li*. He said: "Everything in the universe has a *li* (principle or *Tao*) to follow."① The method to know about *li* is called *ge-wu* and the purpose *qiong-li* (explore principles beyond limit). Because his new concepts helped reinterpret Confucianism and promoted it to a different stage, his theory is later called Neo-Confucianism.

Though his ideas never went unchallenged, Zhu Xi's Neo-Confucianism long dominated Chinese intellectual life and his commentaries on *si-shu* (《四书》, The Four Books) became required reading for all who hoped to pass the Civil Service Examinations of the later period. His intellectual influence was also paramount in Korea, and his ideas won wide acceptance and official support in Tokugawa Japan as well. If Zhu Xi's thinking basically originated from Mencius' and the Cheng's interpretation of Confucianism, Aquinas' theological assertions were based on his borrowing from Aristotle's classical principles. For instance, Aristotle's philosophy is structurally composed of the primacy of intelligence, the use of technology as a means of access to truth and mechanical arts as powers for humanizing the cosmos.

At that time Aquinas, like many other Christian scholars, had to confront the challenges from and join in a dispute with Averroes and his followers. It was certainly a difficult mission for Aquinas because Averroes was the outstanding representative of Arabic philosophy in Spain and reputed as the great commentator on and interpreter of Aristotle. In the course of this dispute, the very method of theology was called into question. According to Aquinas, reason is able to operate within faith and yet according to its own laws not dependent on anything else. The mystery of God is conveyed and incarnate in human language. Hence, it is able to become the object of an active, conscious, and organized elaboration in which the rules and structures of rational activity are integrated in the light of faith. Aquinas was the first to view theology expressly in this way or at least to present it systematically, and in doing so he raised a storm of opposition in various quarters. Hence, the inclusion of Aristotle's physics in university programs was not just a matter of academic curiosity. Naturalism, as opposed to a sacral vision of the world, was penetrating all realms: spirituality, social customs, and political conduct. The literary form of Aquinas' works must be appreciated in the context

---

① See *Chinese Philosophy History*, p. 238, Ren Jiyu, Renmin Press, 1964.

of his methodology.

All in all, Aquinas tried to put into declining Christian theology some lively and workable forces by combining faith and reason in order to save Christianity from the verge of collapse, though it seems hard to say that he did it successfully. Such an attempt made him approach Zhu Xi in a number of points. They are not only similar to each other in that they both had courage to break through the strong bondage of traditional forces, who refused to change and persisted in their conservative stance, but also showed a good sense of tactics and methods in their specific operations to promote their ideals. What is most characteristic of their methods is certainly that of reconciliation, which made them able to pick out from the past archives some useful ideas such as the Confucian sense of benevolence and Aristotle's view of reason and sense of nature and science. Their attempt effected some results by evoking both positive and negative responses from authorities and the general public and their influences endured till the modern age.

But one has to become aware that their ideas were limited because dualism and idealism were after all unable to provide a truthful and scientific answer to people's queries about human values and the nature of the world as well as the prospect of human physical and intellectual conditions. Considering the fact that their ideas were developed in the 12th – 13th centuries, we have no reason to blame them for their insufficiencies, but should care more about their courage and the intellectual progress achieved in establishing a certain critical view of the dominant ideological trend, even though such criticism was still limited. More important than the quality of these critical remarks is perhaps the way of making such criticism. They chose a way of compromise rather than some radical or violent means to proceed with a rational and maybe a more justified anatomy of the object they thought necessary to handle.

Another reason why their ideas were insufficient relates to the lack of practical and theoretical support, which could otherwise convince more people of their justification. Metaphysical and ontological arguments, though sometimes very powerful in its own way, often got entangled in empty talk about invisible and ungraspable concepts or theories. Unfortunately, the two philosophers were often involved in such impractical arguments without caring much about the theoretical ground and substantial evidence. It appears that their frustration, both spiritual and academic, was inevitable as experimental means of pursuing their inquiries, which were not yet available at the time. However, the fact that science was taken up as evidence in favour of rationalist argument indicates human intellectual progress and helps clarify theoretical ambiguities. It is exactly on this point that a gap emerges between Chinese philosophy and Western ideological development. But one could hardly ascribe this deficiency to the individual factors that involved Zhu Xi or other Chinese philosophers of this period. Maybe the social and intellectual tradition has to bear more responsibilities. After all, no one could come forward with an advanced ideology ahead of his time, since basically ideology always reflects the general conditions of economic and intellectual developments of the day.

3.5.3 Ethical principles

Zhu Xi tried to follow and reinterpret the initial doctrine of Confucius and Mencius on human nature with some modifications. For instance, Mencius advocated the benevolence of human nature, which refers to moral behaviours. Zhu took over the benevolence of human nature from Mencius and put into it elements of Buddhist nature to give it an ontological significance. Zhu says that such human nature refers to that of heavenly fate. According to him, differences in human nature go with differences of material force, which is divided into clear and muddy, bright and dark, and therefore gives rise to good and evil, clever and stupid in human nature. Those living in a clear and bright environment would expect to make themselves good in nature while those living in a muddy and dark environment would be evil in nature. Hence changes in human nature could be achieved by rubbing away mud and darkness. These judgments are largely based on a metaphysical inference without either experimental support or empirical evidence.

In ethics, Zhu Xi claims an omnipotent role for mind which, according to him, belongs to consciousness and can make judgments of right and wrong, recognize *li* and respond properly to behaviours. It is mind that decides body in terms of the relationship between mind and body. Mind decides external objects in terms of the relationship between mind and objects. He later furthered his explanation of mind by presenting the concepts of *human mind* (人心) and *Tao's mind* (道心). In Zhu's interpretation, human mind is purely for individual self-interest while Tao's mind is for the sake of justice. There is a human mind with a prenatal evil factor in opposition to an inborn Tao's mind. Such a view is obviously influenced by religion, either by Christianity or by Buddhism, which seems close to Christian advocacy for human original sin. Based on the concepts of human mind and Tao's mind, *heavenly principle* (天理) and *human desire* (人欲) derived from Cheng's theory, Zhu developed into the distinction between the two pairs. He argues that the distinction between human mind and Tao's mind is the same as that between heavenly principle and human desire. He argues that human mind embraces the possibility of both good and evil while human desire embraces only the possibility of evil. Therefore, heavenly principle and human desire are absolutely opposed to each other and can not coexist.

Zhu Xi went to extremes in making the two concepts, heavenly principle and human desire, unable to tolerate each other so that one must defeat the other until heavenly principle is preserved and human desire is destroyed. Meanwhile, Zhu Xi and his followers stressed the "investigation of things", by which they meant primarily the study of ethical conduct and of the revered Five Classics. The study of ethical and metaphysical principles in turn constituted what is built as personal faith and advices for the emperor whose self-cultivation might help restore the world order. [1]

As an Aristotelian thinker, Thomas Aquinas firmly believes that he could defend himself against a heterodox interpretation of "the Philosopher". Aquinas holds that human liberty could be defended as a rational thesis while admitting that nature is fully determined. In his theology of Providence, he insists on a continuous creation, in which the dependence of the created on the creative wisdom guarantees the reality of the order of nature. God moves sovereignly all that he creates; but the supreme government that he exercises over the universe conforms to the laws of a creative Providence that wills each being to act according to its proper nature. This autonomy finds its highest realization in the rational creature: man is literally self-moving in his intellectual, volitional and physical existence. Man's freedom, far from being destroyed by his relationship to God, finds its foundation in this very relationship.

Apart from faith in God, the other divine virtues include hope and charity. Hope is the theological virtue by which one believes that with divine assistance he will attain infinite God, i.e., eternal enjoyment of God. In the order of generation, hope is prior to charity. But in the order of perfection, charity is prior both to hope and faith. It is a virtue of habitual form that is infused into the soul by God and that inclines the people to love him for his own sake. Comparatively, charity is more precious for the acts of all other virtues are ordered to God through charity. [2]

Zhu's ethical views succeed those of the Cheng's as an improved version of feudal ideology, aiming to further restrict human mind, especially human feelings and the desire for material comfort and sensual enjoyment. He opposes human desires to the so-called heavenly principle — the universal laws or principles guiding the movements of everything in the world as if they are not allowed to coexist or to be reconciled.

Aquinas' ethical view is also harsh in that he could not tolerate any deviation from theological faith in God although he argues strongly against the traditional Augustinian conception of man as fallen.

Generally, ethics is a theory or discipline to deal with the principles and practice of human moral affairs. In other words, ethics is used to improve moral behaviours by providing necessary rules to define and control the human mind and body in their various activities. Therefore ethics is one of the most significant

---

[1] For more details see *History of Chinese Philosophy*, pp. 245 – 250, Ren Jiyu, People's Publishing House, 1966.

[2] See *The Cambridge Dictionary of Philosophy*, p. 40, Robert Audi, Cambridge University Press, 1999.

areas by which to judge and measure human spiritual values.

Both Chinese and Western philosophers have long ago been aware of the importance of ethical contributions. Ethical statements and quotations were made in the ancient classical writings like *lun-yu* (《论语》, The Analects) and *meng-zi* (《孟子》, Mencius) as well as *li-ji* (《礼记》, The Book of Rites). The earliest book on ethics in the West is Aristotle's *Nicomachean and Eudemian Ethics*. However, the Chinese view of ethics is far less human and systematic than the Western one in terms of moral concern for human integral development. This could be seen in Zhu Xi's argument about ethical principles.

Zhu Xi's emphasis on the destruction of human desire is not only a violation of human nature but goes against Confucius' teaching on human nature. For instance, Confucius claims that sexual desire belongs to human nature. It sounds ridiculous to force humans to give up what is biologically characteristic of his nature. On the other hand, the so-called heavenly law should be able to tolerate all the regular movements and activities of living beings in the world, which incorporates human behaviours. In a sense, all human behaviours originate from human desires. Without desires or emotions, human beings could not achieve any motivation nor expect to do anything. This desire could be biological, a desire for food, housing, clothing or sex, or anything to satisfy his biological need. This desire could be social or cultural, a desire for a good career, good fortune or simply a happy time. No one could survive without desire. Of course every desire has to be limited. Any excessive or inflated desire could be misleading and would give rise to offences or even crimes. It is then not the opposition or conflict between heavenly law and human desire, but an opposition between heavenly law and uncontrolled human desire.

Zhu Xi's intention was to help the ruler control social and intellectual order by strict ethical measures. But the question at the time was not exactly that of moral decline, but one arising out of social turmoil due to the invasion of the Jin troops as a result of political corruption and social chaos.

Aquinas' ethical views were produced to help resist, along with other ideas of his Scholasticism, the widespread suspicion of Christianity. Like Zhu Xi, Aquinas also wanted to provide a set of principles as a moral standard for his people, both Christian and non-Christian, to follow in their daily life. The three-part ethical code works both as a mirror for self-examination and a critical tool, based on Aquinas' inheritance of the classical philosopher's theory and his understanding of social and intellectual changes at the time. Though some of his ideas are still narrow in their adherence to Christianity, they are supposed to follow up the then intellectual current to reduce the increasingly widening gap between Christianity and newly-emerging ideological trends, such as the interest in the study of nature represented by Averroes, the Arabian physician and philosopher. The introduction of rational ideas into his Scholastic philosophy thus expanded greatly the humanist value of his ideas so that Christianity, both as a spiritual faith and a way of thinking or a world outlook, passed over its crisis and merged into a new period without suffering a more destructive experience. Perhaps one could say that Aquinas' Scholasticism built up a way through to the operation of rationalism and science, which eventually prepared for the arrival of the intellectual dawn of the West, i. e., the Renaissance, when more and more people, especially the educated, became aware of the significance of intellectual freedom and emancipation.

Comparatively, Zhu Xi was not that lucky in the sense that he did not have a social and intellectual environment similar to that of Aquinas. He had not heard of, let alone read of, natural science like that of Averroes, nor could he find anything beneficial from his ancient predecessors, such as Aristotle. Such diversity obviously gave rise to their distinction in their ethic views.

3.5.4 Political, social and intellectual concerns

It appears that ideology is always applicable in the service of politics, either in China or in the West. China, in particular, had the need to fortify political control with the assistance of ideology due to its traditional pattern of social development. It was then only too natural for scholars, many of whom were also officials, to make use of history, past politics, to draw intellectual lessons or to work on ideology in the benefit of politics. Many intellectuals, in the shadow of such tendencies, indicated their motivation by choosing to reflect on current or historical events in their writings of this period. Zhu Xi also took a keen interest in history and directed a reinterpretation of Sima Guang's history, *zi-zhi-tong-jian* (《资治通鉴》, The History as a Mirror for Government), so that it could illustrate moral principles in government.

In 1188, Zhu Xi said in a report that the emperor's character was the basis for the well-being of the ordinary people. He argues in *da-xue* (《大学》, Great Learning), a book on moral government, that by cultivating his mind the emperor set off a chain reaction leading to the moral transformation of the entire world. Zhu Xi continued to work on *da-xue* for the rest of his life and similarly, he wrote a commentary on *zhong-yong* (《中庸》, Doctrine of the Mean). It was largely because of the influence of Zhu Xi that these two texts came to be accepted along with *lun-yu* and *meng-zi* as the components of *si-shu* basic to the Confucian educational curriculum.

Zhu Xi's official career did not seemingly match his academic talent and reputation. He suffered from a series of frustrations on account of his sense of justice and frankness in personal temperament. On several occasions during his later career Zhu Xi was invited to the imperial court and seemed destined for more influential positions, but his uncompromising attacks on corruption and political expediency each time prevented him from more promotions. Zhu's historical outlook is a result of applying his idealistic philosophy directly to social history. One is the emphasis on human nature, i.e., the major factor in deciding historical changes depends on the good or evil of human mind, especially the good or evil of the emperor. Another is his perspective on the tendency to regress. He argues that the heavenly principle prevailed over the Xia, Shang and Zhou Dynasties where a politics of kingly benevolence emerged. Human desire was flooded after the three dynasties and then was the politics of despotic reign.

As a professional teacher untouched by the social and political affairs of his day, Thomas Aquinas was disturbed by intellectual and religious conflicts, which seemed to undermine the Christian dominance over the secular world.

In Aquinas' period, contemporary with the challenges from spiritual crises, there was a fear on the part of many that the authentic values of nature would not be properly distinguished from the disorderly inclinations of mind and heart. Theologians of a traditional bent firmly resisted any form of a determinist philosophy in relation to Providence and the notion of a gratuitous act of creation. Maybe Aquinas' working environment was somewhat easier for him to bear, though he also had to tolerate complaints about and even attacks on his academic views. This is partly because his profession separated him from the secular world (at least partly) where worldly and material cares brought about many worries and individual clashes and hence intensified human relations. However, Aquinas also suffered from attacks on his views.

But Zhu Xi was different. He was disturbed by both political and social concerns and apprehensions so that he could hardly sit down to his academic studies. The chaotic situation perhaps had something to do with the complexities of the Chinese way of handling human relations and the conservative institution of imperial official appointments. Bribery, nepotism, corruption and rumours prevented the regular operation of laws and rules. This acted against justice and greatly hurt many innocent people, including Zhu Xi and other intellectuals. The only way out for intellectuals in those days was to get an official appointment or one had to be locked up in one's study. No one could think of any other alternative. Impractical ways of learning worked in accompaniment with the inflexible official system so that the choice for his career or way of thinking or learning was confined to the so-called orthodox conventional pattern: literary writing and an idealist way of thinking. Few, if any, in the midst of Chinese scholars, could attempt different modes or methods like rationalism or the choice of science as a career.

Although Aquinas' argument with the followers of Averroes had for years been matched by a controversy with the Christian masters who followed the traditional Augustinian conception of man as fallen, this latter dispute now became more pronounced. In a series of university conferences in 1273, Bonaventure, a Franciscan friar and a friendly colleague of Aquinas at Paris, renewed his criticism of the Aristotelian current of thought, including Aquinas' assertions. Aquinas noted the significance of the inclusion of the history of nature in the history of the spirit and vice versa. He claimed that man was situated ontologically (i.e., by his very existence) at the juncture of two universes. Furnished with Aristotle's necessary concepts like the soul as the "form" and the body as the "matter", Aquinas became more convincing and powerful in his argument. For Aristotle, form is that which makes a thing to be what it is; and matter — that out of which a thing is made. They are the two intrinsic causes that constitute every material thing. For Aquinas, then, the body is the matter and the soul is the form of man.

Like Zhu Xi, however, Thomas Aquinas recovered his reputation within a few decades by receiving a posthumous honour. He was canonized a saint in 1323, officially named doctor of the church in 1567, and proclaimed the protagonist of orthodoxy during the modernist crisis at the end of the 19th century. This continuous commendation, however, cannot obliterate the historical difficulties in which he was embroiled in the 13th century during a radical theological renewal — a renewal that was contested at the time and yet was brought about by the social, cultural and religious evolution of the West. Aquinas was at the centre of the doctrinal crisis that confronted Christendom when the discovery of Greek science, culture and thought seemed about to crush it.

In the final analysis, it might be difficult to judge whose contributions are more important to the later intellectual development though both of them could claim to be the leading thinkers of the middle period of the two civilizations and both exerted tremendous influence upon later generations. Nonetheless, it is obvious that Aquinas' ideas are more modern because of his tolerance of science and the rational function in the arena of theology even though he never gave up his theological stance. His scholastic advocacy, despite its intention to defend Christianity, prepared the way for the arrival of intellectual emancipation and freedom, which would open the initial stage of the modern period. In comparison, Zhu Xi did not get in touch with science, or take advantage of rationalism, though their lifetimes were close. Doubtless, Zhu made a great effort to work into metaphysical meditation and to build up an ideological framework to contain all the necessary ingredients of material and spiritual ideas. However, he could not expect to make a breakthrough in terms of providing a new way or direction in which later generations could be inspired and enlightened in social and intellectual developments, as occurred to the Westerners who started to challenge their ideological and spiritual authorities in the Renaissance.

Questions for comprehension and discussion

1. In what way did the Chinese and Western intellectual development share with each

other in the hindrance of social progress in the middle period?
2. What do you think of the effects of the medieval intellectual trend? What are the similarities and dissimilarities between China and the West of this period?
3. In what sense and to what extent do you say the social and cultural developments were checked in the medieval time as a result of conspiracies by both the secular and theological or intellectual forces? Give examples.

List of proposed books for further reading

1. 楼宇烈、张西平主编,1998,《中外哲学交流史》,长沙:湖南教育出版社。
2. 任继愈,1999,《中国哲学史》第二、三册,北京:人民出版社。
3. 冯友兰,2003,《中国哲学简史》(下),天津:天津社会科学出版社。
4. 李泽厚,1985,《中国古代思想史论》,北京:人民出版社。
5. Macklerras, Colin, *Western Images of China*, Oxford: Oxford University Press, 1989.
6. Russell, Bertrand, *History of Western Philosophy*, vol. I, Notre Dame, Indiana: University of Notre Dame, 1963.
7. Soloman, Robert C. & M. Higgins, Kathleen, *A Short History of Philosophy*, Oxford: Oxford University Press, 1996.

Chapter 4

A Comparison of Modern Chinese and Western Philosophies

Modern age, in our sense of intellectual development, roughly suggests a period from the end of the Middle Ages onwards, which varies with its particular references. Hence modern age usually starts from the 16th century in the West while China is said to enter its modern age in the middle of the 19th century although capitalism has budded much earlier as a sign of modern development. Intellectual and ideological development is somewhat independent of social development and we might not follow rigidly the fixed chronological order of history textbook.

The dawn of modern age not only means a farewell to the thousand-odd-year-long darkness of the middle period, but suggests the arrival of a totally new era. This age is marked, first and foremost, by intellectual and ideological emancipation gained out of a spiritual awakening and awareness of the darkness of the past feudal society or medieval age and the immensity of human intellectual potential that would lead to rapid growth of social, economic and ideological forces. Why and how intellectual and ideological developments contributed to the resurrection and renaissance of human civilization as a whole, both in China and in the West, calls for our attention to its historical significance, which has affected and changed our current way of life.

However, the process of attaining such an awareness took a long while and actions taken to put into effect the ideal of establishing democracy called for enormous prices, including bloodshed revolutions and the painstaking efforts to search for the essential theory and necessary compromise with autocracy, which characterized the major events and representative figures and general ideological trends of this period. The study of intellectual and ideological conditions of this period would not only supply an investigation into general intellectual situation as a whole, but would offer us the possibility to work out the basic causes of such problems in the due course of intellectual development.

4.1 Social and intellectual scene for modern philosophy

The medieval or feudal period achieved little progress in social and intellectual developments and at the same time provoked more meditation over a number of critical issues. Among these is the question of how man could break down spiritual barriers for a better motivation in his endeavour for both material and mental comfort. Consequently, spiritual emancipation attracted the attention of the leading thinkers and scholars of the West, who were required to sharpen their wits to guide their contemporaries and compatriots in fulfilling their historical missions. To know more about this trend, we must seek more understanding of what was set against change during that particular period in social, economic and intellectual fields.

There were signs of social change indicating feudal decline and budding capitalism in China in the years around the 16th century. Large amounts of farmland were occupied by aristocrats and royal families, officially assigned or illegally seized. The majority of the peasants had to bear a heavy burden of taxation, hence peasant riots occurred one after another and in company with the alien invasion, finally led to the end of the Ming Dynasty. Meanwhile commercial production and trading activities flourished as a result of social progress and brought prosperity and wealth to the country. Nonetheless, such a tendency was often hindered by the autocratic central government whose cruelty and ignorance was aggravated by its stubborn insistence on its narrow-minded policies and rejection of different voices from the ordinary people, especially the intellectuals who were often persecuted or even executed for their dissident ideas. The sharp class contradictions and social upheavals eventually gave rise to intensified conflicts and civil wars which caused the ultimate overthrow of the Ming Dynasty in the mid-17th century.

The Western countries as a whole were also thrown into chaos and division because of the clashes for power among such major nations as France, Germany, Italy and England. But with the development of the Industrial Revolution, the bourgeoisie seemed to emerge as a class by gradually acquiring more political power in the process of promoting economic development and shaping national identity, especially in their struggles against the feudalistic aristocracy, such as in the Lutheran Reformation and in England's Glorious Revolution. Political success for the bourgeoisie was followed by its claim for intellectual freedom which guaranteed more fruitful operations and development of a chain of ideological schools on the threshold of modern age.

In China, the inheritance of the study of Neo-Confucianism, focusing on the reinterpretation of *jen*, *yi* and the identification of knowledge with practice, was seen in Wang Yangming's application of Confucianism into social and ideological reality at the time. Western thinkers had a similar tendency though their claim for practical experience was more inclined to specific projects, like Bacon's experimental devices or Hobbes' concept of social agreement.

The persecution of intellectuals for their dissidence and political criticism was common on both sides, such as the famous Dong-lin-dang Case which led to the execution of hundreds of scholars for their critical remarks about the then political situation, and the severe punishment of heresy or infidelity by the Inquisition of the Roman Church in the West.

The appearance of the anti-autocratic forces was in sight and democratic ideas began to take shape both in China and in the West. In China, the burgeoning of democracy in opposition to cruel totalitarianism was confined to a few scholastic works, like those by Huang Zongxi and Wang Fuzhi, and had very limited influence. In the West, the critical spearhead was directed at both theology and monarchy, with its increasing influence and thought-provoking nature, as indicated in the dissemination of the ideas of Hobbes and Locke, gaining more acceptability and wide popularity among the newly-emerging bourgeoisie.

The Chinese representative thinkers

4.2.1 Wang Fuzhi

1 Life (1619 − 1692)

Wang's ancestors moved from Taiyuan to Gaoyou, Jiangsu, before they settled in Hunan. One of his early predecessors once joined Zhu Yuanzhang① as an army officer and was rewarded for his bravery. The honour was kept and passed down for a number of generations. Then his great-grandfather started to devote himself to the area of letters and thus changed the traditional course of the family from a military to a civilian career. However, his grandfather and father did not pass the official examination nor received any official appointment, though they read extensively and established their academic status by refuting the ideas of Taoism and Buddhism.

When the Qing troops intruded into the neighbourhood of his hometown, Wang Fuzhi joined in the resistance but had to give in because of his frustration over the disunity and disagreement within the group of resistance. He had to

---

① Zhu Yuanzhang, the founding emperor of the Ming Dynasty, was initially the leader of a peasant revolt.

retreat to seclusion for academic research after this failure. From then on he isolated himself, concentrating on his academic studies, free from any political and external disturbance, and made remarkable achievements by turning out more than 100 books with over 8 million. words, among which 72 books with 4.7 million words were passed down to posterity, covering classical scripture, metaphysics, history, Buddhism, poetry and literature. The most accomplished were his *Annotations for Zhang Zizheng's Works* and *An Observation of General Historical Assessment*.

2 Major views

Wang Fuzhi's academic research focuses on the reassessment of Neo-Confucianism. He offers a severe criticism of the ideas represented by Wang Yangming, the then most influential representative of Neo-Confucianism. His criticism covers a large area such as Wang Yangming's advocating mental investigation and his distortion and fragmentary quotation of Confucius and Mencius by pointing out that Wang's academic practice ignored the fundamentals of the six classics[①].

At the same time, he insists that one should carry out practical study by being specific and authentic, i.e., establishing a right attitude towards learning by a careful reading and true understanding of the original texts of the classical writers. He also advocates an observation and research into practical social affairs, like his concern for social development and the everyday life of the ordinary people.

Wang Fuzhi is critical of restricting human desires and preserving the heavenly principle as advocated by Wang Yangming and insists that the country does not belong to one person and that the survival or end of a family is only a private concern no matter whether that family is a royal family or a common family.

He also claims that all the saints are heroes, saying that people should dare to

---

① The six classics refer to *shi* (《诗》, Poetry), *shu* (《书》, Book), *li* (《礼》, Propriety), *yue* (《乐》, Music), *yi* (《易》, Change) and *chun-qiu* (《春秋》, Spring and Autumn). Because of the loss of *Music*, *The Analects* was added during the Eastern Han Dynasty. The six classics were further developed into the nine classics in the Tang Dynasty with *Propriety* divided into *Propriety of the Zhou Dynasty*, *Ceremonial Propriety* and *Record of Propriety* and *Spring and Autumn* divided into *Gongyang Biographical Spring and Autumn*, *Guliang Biographical Spring and Autumn* and *Zuoshi Biographical Spring and Autumn*. Then during the Song Dynasty, it was expanded into thirteen classics with the former nine classics plus *The Analects*, *Filial Tales*, *Supplementary Poems* (*Erya*) and *Mencius*.

bear responsibility and show no fear for the sake of the nation in the struggle against the Qing invaders.

4.2.2 Gong Zizhen

1 Life (1792 – 1841)

From Hangzhou, Zhejiang, Gong Zizhen was the grandson of a well-known classical scholar. Gong showed his precocious talent at the age of 12 when he started to acquire the knowledge of the Chinese classical works from his maternal grandfather (Duan Yucai) and other learned scholars and became a pretty influential figure in the field of modern Chinese classical works in Beijing. But his official career was not very even and successful. He did not pass the palace exam until he was 38 though he had passed the provincial exam at the age of 18. He had been appointed as a petty official in different posts of the Ministry of Ritual Affairs and other government departments before he resigned ten years afterwards for a teaching post in a school at Danyang, Jiangsu where he died shortly afterwards at the age of 49.

His academic achievements were principally located in his study of Confucian classics, combined with historical research. He predicted inevitable emergence of social crises based on his severe criticism of social darkness. Further to the harshness of his social criticism, he submitted some proposals to solve the problems, the core of which was the social reform, one of the key references to the later reform by Kang Youwei and his company.

2 Major inclinations and views

Gong initiated the scholastic effort to care for political tendencies. No one dared to comment on politics at the time lest he prepared himself to suffer from persecution, including the death penalty or exile. Most scholars immersed themselves in textual research of the works of Confucius and other classic writers. Gong was among the pioneering group of writers who worked against this tendency by combining his academic research with social reality and political affairs of the time, as in his criticism of the policy towards intellectuals and his prediction of social turmoil, as confirmed shortly by the Taiping Peasant Uprising.

Gong severely criticized the then impractical tendency of ignoring reality in academic research of Chinese classic works of Confucianism.

Gong called for reform, saying that the longest ruling dynasty could not survive 800 years, but the Tao's rule could last forever. Change was to be unchecked, no matter how long it took. The law from one dynasty's ancestors was likely to come to no avail and the opinions from a thousand commentators were not to be feared for they were to be silenced. The opportunity for reform should be taken rather than offered to newcomers. As his poem goes: China is vigorous with / its circumstances, but appears / sad by its total silence. / I would advise the Lord to revitalize the land, / and dispatch the talented with no prejudice.

Gong divided the social situation into three grades, the chaotic, the orderly and the weak. He called the then social situation the weak, which superficially resembled the orderly in many aspects, but was actually not far away from the chaotic. His estimation was verified by what happened ten years after his death when the Taiping Peasant Uprising broke out and greatly shocked the dynasty whose social stability and prosperity were thus torn away and never healed.

Towards the end of his life, Gong felt frustrated with the fact that his proposals were not accepted and that his offer of service to Lin Zexu was also refused, which is why he gave up his post as a petty official in the capital.

4.2.3 Kang Youwei

1 Life (1858 – 1927)

Born into a bureaucratic-landlord family in Nanhai, Guangdong, Kang received a strictly feudalistic formal education in reading classic Confucian writings. At the same time, he was affected by what came from the development of capitalism and its ideological representations, especially those in Hong Kong which he witnessed in its colonial order. From then on, he started to pick up what was advantageous to Chinese social development from western Europe. Stimulated and provoked by Chinese failures in the wars staged by the French and other imperialist invaders and by the corruption involved in the government officials of the Qing despotism, he presented with other candidates of the Civil Service Examination in 1888 his first petition for the amelioration of politics to save the country. He was later provoked by the idea of Liao Ping, another reformer who advocated the modern classic Confucian view. Then he submitted a co-occurrence of reformist thinking and modern classical Confucian scripture so that he could elucidate Confucianism with reformist ideas and pave the way for the formation of reformist theory and the organization of the reform movement.

Kang presented his second petition, together with a group of other candidates for the Civil Service Examination after the Chinese-Japanese War in 1895. Not long after the appeal, he was received and authorized by Emperor Guangxu in 1897 with full power to deal with the new policies and projects of the reform. But unfortunately, this reform lasted merely 100 days or so before being quenched by Dowager Cixi, the old lady behind the scene who held the actual power.

Kang exiled himself abroad to escape the following arrest and execution which occurred to his comrades. He subsequently led a group of royalists and tried to restore the monarchy of the Qing Dynasty in opposition to the revolutionary group headed by Dr Sun Yatsen. He was also engaged in an unsuccessful restoration coup and persisted stubbornly in his stance till his death.

2 Main ideas

Identifying a number of old classics like *Tale of Art and Culture* and *Scholars' Biography* in *Han Shu Annal* as false Confucian works was part of Kang Youwei's research. Based on this part of his initial work, he went on to set right the errors. He criticized the books which were affected by old classical Confucianism, such as *Scholars' Biography* in *Latter Han Annals* (《后汉书·学士传》) and *Tale of Economics* in *Sui Shu Annal* (《隋书·经济》).

In order to supply more evidence, Kang often quoted Sima Qian and Liu Xin's statements and thesis to confirm his viewpoint by discerning falsehood or truth in old classical Confucian works. As well he offered an account of how classical Confucianism was passed on and how modern classical Confucianism came to clash with the old classical Confucianism.

These ideas all came from Kang Youwei's book *xin-ru-jia-jing-dian-wei-shu-kao-zheng* (《新儒家经典伪书考证》, A Textual Study of False Documents of New Classical Confucianism) and exerted great influence upon the historical points of view of the later generation, like those of Liang Qichao and other scholars of the May 4th Movement. The book was a breakthrough from the traditional and out-moded textual reading method popular since the Qianlong period. Soon after its publication, it was reprinted in Shanghai and many provinces and spread all over the country, receiving both positive and negative responses. But it was soon banned and destroyed by the Qing government. The book was actually based on Liao Ping's ideas, which had been revealed to Kang before the latter established his view. Since the book was involved in a controversial issue set off in the Han Dynasty, many people held different views about its reliability.

Kang attributes the origin of sorrow to several boundaries. They include the national boundary which divides territories and tribes; the class boundaries which divide the noble and the wretched, the clean and the dirty; the racial boundaries which divide yellow, white, brown and black people based on their skin colour; the sexual boundary which divides male and female; the family boundary which divides father and son, husband and wife, elder and younger brothers; the trade boundary which divides peasants, workers and merchants; the disorder boundary which divides the laws of unfairness, difference, impassability and unjustness; the species boundary which divides man, birds, beasts, insects and fish; the pain boundary which divides various kinds and endless sufferings.

He points out the ways to get rid of pains, saying no state exists and the whole world is under the rule of a general administration by several divisions. All governments, either central or local, should be elected by the people. No family or male-female cohabitation should go beyond a year. A pregnant woman should enter an educational institute for unborn children and a born child should be admitted into a baby-raising house. The sick should be admitted into hospital and the old into the nursing house. All the grown-up men and women should serve in the institutes for children, the old or the sick which are to be founded by the elected government as they do in the army. All dormitories and dining-rooms should be run publicly and used freely by the people who contribute with their services at different posts. Those who make academic inventions or special contributions at the state-run institutions should be awarded special prizes. A warning for indolence at work should be the highest form of punishment. All the dead should be cremated and the crematorium should be close to the chemical plants.

These ideas have been proved to come from Mo Zi and Buddhism and illustrate Kang's dream of an ideal way of life and political blueprint though they are not practical at the time.

In addition, Tan Sitong's *ren-xue* (《仁学》, Study of Jen) is more typical of the practical intellectual advance in the early years of Chinese democratic awareness and awakening. Tan Sitong is one of the martyrs killed at the Wuxu Reform[①] and his ideas are very rebellious against the traditional culture and society. This is principally reflected in his book *ren-xue* which severely criticizes the so-called three key links (monarch-subject, husband-wife and father-son), and claims that these relations should be treated as those among friends like the Westerners.

Faced with the critical situation in which the Qing Dynasty lost wars to French and Japanese invaders one after another, Kang Youwei pressed the urgent need for reform in his appeal to Emperor Guangxu, saying that the survival of the country depended on this. Only by carrying out sweeping reforms, could the country survive; otherwise it would be destroyed. According to him, no law remains unchanged in the span of 100 years. If reform is only confined to some

---

① Wuxu Reform, a political reform launched in 1898 by Emperor Guangxu of the Qing Dynasty, with the assistance from Kang Youwei and others. It lasted only about 100 days and then was suppressed by Dowager Cixi, the old mother queen who held actual power behind the scene.

specific matters, like railways, schools or business, it only amounts to some changes related to business rather than the whole-scale reformation that is needed.

But after he came back from his long exile abroad Kang changed his view, saying that reform should not be precipitate, but ought to be slow and gradual. He stressed more of the difference between China and the Western countries and became more conservative and stubborn as a royalist politician and propagandist.

Kang Youwei claims that if Confucianism is dropped or set aside, all the Chinese customs and conventions would be extinguished, and hence all the Chinese land and races would be extinguished. He asserts strongly that a constitutional monarchy needs to be established.

4.2.4 Sun Yatsen

1 Early life (1866 – 1925)

Born into a farmer's family, Sun Yatsen was able to go to Hawaii to receive a Western education in his youth thanks to his brother's assistance. Sun's determination to change the old China came from his worry about the way the country, which had clung to its traditional ways under the conservative Qing Dynasty, suffered humiliation at the hands of more technologically advanced nations. Forsaking his medical practice in Canton, he went north in 1894 to seek his political fortune. In a long letter to Li Hongzhang, governor general of Zhili at the time, he set forth his ideas on how China could gain strength, but was frustrated by the response, which referred him to a scheme of agricultural association. From then on, he embarked on a tortuous road leading to a baleful change for both the country and himself.

In 1904 he established several revolutionary groups in Europe, and in 1905 he succeeded in forming a revolutionary coalition called *tong-meng-hui* (同盟会, the United League) in Tokyo. For the next three years the society was propagandized effectively through its mouthpiece, *min-bao* (《民报》, People's Journal). The United League was very loosely organized and Sun met with a series of setbacks, from the failure of armed revolts to unwelcome treatment by foreign governments. In such circumstances, Sun spent a year in 1909 – 1910 touring Europe and the United States before he raised more money in Canada and the United States, which led to a number of unsuccessful uprisings. On October 10, 1911, a local revolutionary group in Wuhan, one of many in China by that time, began another uprising which, in spite of its lack of coordination, unexpectedly managed to overthrow the provincial government. Its success inspired other provincial secessions and led to the overthrow of the Qing Dynasty.

Sun Yatsen learned of the Wuhan Revolution from the newspapers while he was in Denver, Colorado, in the United States. He returned to Shanghai in

December and was elected provisional president by delegates meeting in Nanjing. Knowing that his regime was weak, Sun made a deal with Yuan Shikai, a military warlord who had been the military leader of the Qing Dynasty entrusted with full power by the court. On February 12, 1912, the emperor abdicated; the next day Sun resigned, and on the 14th Yuan was elected his successor after a negotiation among the parties concerned where a compromised agreement was reached.

2 Main ideas

Sun Yatsen's ideas were formed during his years of exile, in opposition to the conservative ideas represented by Kang Youwei, centring on the way of how to build up and promote a new China. These ideas gradually developed into a doctrine called *san-min-zhu-yi* （三民主义, Three Great Principles） as the ideological basis of the political program of the Chinese nationalist forces, championing the principles of nationalism, democracy and socialism.

The principles were originally formulated as slogans for the United League, one of the early organizations prior to the 1911 Republican Revolution. After the failure of this revolution to establish democracy in China, Sun formed a new party, the Kuomintang or Nationalist Party, utilizing his principles as fundamental doctrine. In 1922 the Kuomintang formed an alliance with the Chinese Communist Party. Sun Yatsen, in response to Communist demands for a more formal party ideology, gave a series of lectures which interpreted and expanded his three principles.

The first principle is nationalism which had meant in the early days opposition to the Qing (Manchu) Dynasty and to foreign imperialism; and later was reinterpreted by Sun as denoting self-determination for the Chinese people as a whole and also for the minority ethnic groups within China. The second principle, the "rights of the people", or "democracy" was interpreted by Sun as allowing the Chinese people to control their own government through such means as election, initiative, referendum, and recall. The last principle, the people's livelihood or socialism, was interpreted by Sun as the idea of equalization of land ownership through a just system of taxation.

After the Kuomindang-Communist split in 1927, both the communists and the nationalists claimed to be carrying on the true spirit of the Three Great Principles. The disputes eventually led to civil wars and long-term turmoil till the communist victory and taking over state power in 1949.

Sun's views about the need for the support of foreign powers for Chinese revolution militated against the anti-imperialist trend of the young left-wing intellectuals whose later departure and suppression led to the failure of the first civil war. Only half-heartedly accepted was the principle of the people's livelihood, or socialism, one of his Three Great Principles. Though various evaluations are given to his socialism, it seems certain that it did not bring much hope or confidence to the ordinary people who could not detect any sense of happiness but sinking deep and helpless into the turmoils and sufferings of the following succession of warring events.

4.3 The development of modern Western philosophy and its representative figures

4.3.1 The Renaissance: F. Bacon and T. Hobbes

1 Background

The Renaissance suggested the rebirth of Western civilization, with a new emphasis on the classics — the ideas about the art and literature of the ancient Greeks and Romans. The watchword of the Renaissance was humanism, a conception of dignity of the individual, which had developed since the 14th century. And it was described as the discovery of the world and the discovery of man by an 18th-century historian. This emphasis on rebirth and discovery suggested a dismissal of the entire millennium before the Renaissance, the medieval epoch, which started to be called the Dark Ages. Renaissance humanism can be seen as a recoil and a relief from those awful medieval years. Feudalism had all but collapsed and a new mercantilism and sense of exploration dominated Europe.

A new secular ideal of a sophisticated and cultured urban class was coming into prominence, whose name was the bourgeoisie and whose mission was to make more fortune and to win more freedom and build up democracy by capitalist mode.

However, the bourgeoisie had to be patient and needed a pretty long period to get ready for her historical mission, which was the Renaissance. The Renaissance remained in many ways medieval and sometimes mystical. It is important to remember that the new emphasis on the dignity of the individual was born and nourished within the embrace of the Judeo-Christian tradition. The Renaissance transition lasted from the mid-14th century to at least the 16th century and was initially a literary and artistic movement before being later defined as the most spectacular scientific revolution.

Aristotle was both a central concern and the most problematic figure for the Renaissance, both in science like his belief that the earth was stationary at the centre of the universe, and in politics like his celebration of the gradually disappearing city-states and his defence of slavery. Among Aristotle's most illustrious critics were Francis Bacon and Thomas Hobbes who were both his antagonists and at the same time owed him a lot.

2 Francis Bacon (1561 – 1626)

Francis Bacon is usually recognized as the founder of the modern scientific tradition, which means particularly that he broke with Aristotle and insisted on a purely empirical and experimental method. Bacon is not famous for his specific theories or discoveries in the way that Copernicus, Kepler, Galileo and Newton are known. Rather he theorized about science and knowledge in general. In particular, he developed the experimental method that would have much influence on the later scientific tradition, which involved careful observation and controlled, methodical experiment.

Bacon, like Aristotle, still trusted knowledge over experience. He attempted to justify the pursuit of knowledge by saying that "knowledge is power" and defended science as the ultimate dominion of humanity over nature and as the study of God's work.

One of the most powerful aspects of his philosophy is the critique of various idols of human nature, which block or distort proper scientific inquiry. For Bacon, all the previously established images or ideas were inappropriate or even harmful to the acquisition of authentic information because they would hinder the initiative for more cognitive investigation.

3 Thomas Hobbes (1588 – 1679)

Thomas Hobbes was not a scientist but a metaphysician and developed a purely materialist and mechanistic model of the world, in his best-known book *Leviathan*, regarding the world as mere matter in motion. He spent half his career defending a cosmology that did not exclude theology. In *Leviathan*, he offered a harsh vision of human life by describing selfishness as the reigning principle for the human race and life as a war of each against all, which was typically "nasty, brutish and short".

In this mutually dangerous and combative context, men and women got together and formed a social compact for their mutual safety and advantage. They gave over some of their modest power to the sovereign — the king who would rule over them not by divine right but by common agreement. And with this agreement humanity would further be protected by the idea of justice. Justice itself was the product of contractual society and not its presupposition.

4.3.2 Empiricism and J. Locke

1 Background

With the rise of science and its emerging victory over the authority of the church, Europe entered into a celebration of the rediscovery of an old faith, faith in reason. The so-called Enlightenment first came up in England, following fast the scientific achievements by Isaac Newton and the swift and relatively bloodless political changes of the Glorious Revolution towards the end of the 17th century. It then moved to France and other European countries in the following century. In company with the rapid social alterations of the period, the Enlightenment thinkers put great trust in their own experiences and their own intellectual autonomy, which was bound to result in opposition to the church and its authoritative teachings. In place of the sectarian battles that had blooded the past for several centuries, they insisted on being cosmopolitan-citizens of the world, ignoring national boundaries and rejecting sectarian affiliation. Consequently their truths had to be testified universally, not imposed on others but to be discovered independently by them.

The new ways of thinking obviously promoted tremendously the capitalist development both at home and abroad though there was a dark side to such an expansion, like the trading of slaves and exploitation of workers and forced seizure of farmland. Yet the adventuring spirit encouraged by these ideas won them gains unprecedented in any previous historical period. By the late 16th century, the European superpowers had launched a series of wars to seize more wealth and colonies.

These remarkable changes in turn provided the possibility and necessity for Western thinkers to present a new theory for the sake of promoting social and economic developments in the interest of the bourgeoisie. Empiricism came into being naturally as a result of such a demand, in opposition to abstract reason and speculation.

2 John Locke (1632 – 1704)

John Locke initiated the British empirical tradition by jettisoning the long-standing suspicion of the senses that had persisted in the West since before Plato. Locke suggested that all knowledge comes from the senses.

Locke was a physician, a practical man who had little time for the obscure terms and tedious arguments of the Scholastic tradition. He was also a political man and had been so involved in British politics that he was forced into exile in Holland, where he befriended William and Mary of Orange[①] who would soon take over the throne of England. He subsequently wrote two influential treatises on government which had not been dealt with so elaborately since Plato's *Republic*. Furthermore, he submitted a relatively new notion of human rights, in particular, the right to private property, which brought him both reputation and contribution to the theory of the bourgeoisie.

In addition to his contribution to politics, Locke established a theory for the justification of the newly-emerging bourgeoisie by focusing on the principle that all knowledge begins with experience, which he claims as a matter of common sense in opposition to the obscurity of the Scholastics and the complex schemes of the rationalists. The latter contains Descartes, Spinoza and Leibniz, who argues for a number of inborn or innate ideas. Locke argues that the mind is more like an empty closet, illuminated only by the light that comes from the outside.

He also asserts that experience gives sensations and from these sensations our understanding comes to derive various new and more complex ideas. All our knowledge is derived from sensations.

However, Locke made two compromises in his empiricism. First he yields to metaphysics in accepting the idea that one finds it necessary to talk about things-in-themselves apart from one's experience of them. In this, he accepts Aristotle's notion of substance.

Locke's second compromise is his distinction between two kinds of properties or qualities: those which we perceive as inherent in an object itself, such as its shape or mass, and those which depend on our perception of it, i.e. the effects that a thing has on us, like colour. Locke is a pioneer in the psychology of perception and he is one of those who found out the effects of light on the eyes by concluding that what the light does is to stimulate the eye and the mind in certain ways before one is able to "see" colours. However, one might argue that everything one experiences is in the mind and there is neither a need nor a justification for talking about the world "out there".

Locke's insufficiency lies in his religious faith. In order to defend his belief in

---

① Here William refers to William III, king of England, Scotland and Ireland, who emerged as the leader of European resistance to Louis XIV's aggression and married Mary, the Protestant daughter of the future James II of England. Invited by a group of political leaders to intervene in England in 1688, he was later proclaimed joint sovereign with his wife, Mary II.

God, he fell back on traditional Scholastic arguments, like the argument that nothing comes from nothing and since one exists, one can be certain of the existence of God, the Creator.

4.3.3 J. Rousseau and the French Revolution

1 Background

The American and French Revolutions were both momentous and magnificent spectacles and both were revolutions of ideas, upheavals provoked not only by bad government but by the clash of ideas of justice and injustice, ideas about the nature of society and about human nature. These ideas were directly drawn from the French thinkers represented by Rousseau and Voltaire (1694−1778).

Rousseau and Voltaire were both self-styled philosophers of the Enlightenment, but neither had any patience with metaphysics and epistemology. They confined their attention to less abstract and more practical matters such as politics and education. Consequently they had enormous influence on their tumultuous times.

Voltaire admired the English Enlightenment and Locke's political philosophy in particular. He imported both back to France to attack the French government and the Catholic church. Meanwhile he defended reason and individual autonomy and took delight to prick the hot-air balloons of metaphysics and theology in his day, thus setting in motion the middle class (or bourgeois) demands for reform and preparing the stage for the French Revolution.

Rousseau was a more subtle and complete thinker and did not shy away from grand theories of human nature and society, which provided the guiding principles and fighting spirit for the bourgeois revolution which came shortly after his death.

2 Jean-Jacques Rousseau (1712−1778)

Jean-Jacques Rousseau, unlike Voltaire, came from the working class, and his father was a horologist. To a large extent he was a self-made success, famous for his daring spirit and original talents which were manifested specially in *Emile* and *The Social Contract*.

Rousseau's early essays, in which he challenged the alleged benefits of civilization and defended the life of contentment in an affluent and very competitive state of nature, shook up the staid and self-satisfied aristocracy of Europe and brought him a reputation as a young scholar of critical courage. He furthered his exploration of human society and nature by elaborating his theory of man who, according to him, is basically good, and his conception of human society, in which human beings are not bound together out of mutual insecurity (as Hobbes suggests) but rather realized together their higher "moral" natures.

The state of nature is not, as Hobbes once said, "nasty, brutish and short", but instead "the pre-societal creatures are happy and content", indifferent if not sympathetic to others. As citizens and as participants in "the general will" of society, human beings are free to impose the law on ourselves, even in the context of society, remain independent as they once were in nature.

However, the state of nature is no place to cultivate and exercise the human virtues, though it could have been happy. Accordingly, Rousseau finds no contradiction in his attempt to retain both the natural sense of independence and our mutual commitment to make and to obey the laws of society. Nevertheless, the original entry into society is neither wilful nor happy. Humanity took a fall from our independence and contentment in the state of nature. No greater crime has ever been committed in human history than the possession of private property, which has brought about the whole litany① of inequalities and injustices that have ruled human life.

Rousseau and Locke were opposed to each other in their attitudes towards private property, supported respectively by the French and American Revolutions. However in both revolutions the Enlightenment assumption was the reality and importance of natural rights and independence.

Rousseau's view on the development of the social contract was a great contribution to the bourgeois revolution. The social contract was not an actual historical event, but a philosophical fiction or metaphor as a certain way of looking at society as a voluntary collection of agreeable individuals. The terms of the social contract consequently define the ideal society as one in which we willingly impose the law on ourselves. We are self-governing and, as in the state of nature, we remain free and independent. Therefore the central Western ideal of individual autonomy is rendered compatible with the legitimacy of the state, and the ideal of the natural goodness of humanity replaces the age-old notion of original human sin. Then came the American and French Revolutions.

4.3.4   J. Mill, F. Nietzsche and the dawn of the new era

1   Background

The American and French Revolutions brought shock and horror to European monarchs and aristocrats and other conservative forces. The Enlightenment was not viewed as a universal and cosmopolitan philosophy, but as a profession of the reigning ideas in London and Paris, a bit of intellectual imperialism. It was especially so in Germany which was still scattered and disunited, and whose language and culture had too long been treated as barbarian and second-rate. Even the king of Prussia spoke mainly in French. In general,

---

① Litany, ceremonial form for prayer.

the new ideals born of science and universal rationality played a secondary role.

However, Germany had her own philosophical exponent, Leibniz, who was a spectacular example of the new Enlightenment spirit, a pioneer of the new mathematics and new rationality. But the ultimate champion of the Enlightenment within Germany was Immanuel Kant (1724 – 1804), a student of Leibniz. He was an enthusiastic follower of Newton's physics and a sympathetic onlooker of Rousseau's new radical theory of society and education.

Kant believes that the ordinariness of nature and the harmony of nature with our faculties guide us towards an ever more profound religious perspective, a sense of the world not limited to knowledge and freedom or even to faith in the ordinary sense of the term. It is a sense of cosmic harmony, perhaps not reminiscent of Aristotle and his divine interpreters but looking forward to some of the most dramatic and philosophic visions of the 19th century.

Apart from some wars that haunted the Europeans, quite a number of significant occurrences during the 19th century brought about changes that had a great impact on the lives of many people and the development of many countries. Among the philosophical discoveries and doctrines were Hegel's objective idealism, Kierkegaard's existentialism, Marxism, Darwinism, Comte's positivism, political economics by Adam Smith and David Richartus.

In England the Industrial Revolution produced a boom in commerce which, accompanied by colonial expansion, was changing the world's economic and social developments. With the development of social and economic conditions and structures, people's attitude towards life, personal and social, underwent drastic and profound transformations, such was the new emphasis on personal satisfaction that naturally suggested a new philosophy, asserting that the maximization of personal happiness would become the ultimate end. This philosophy was called utilitarianism whose most eloquent spokesmen were Jeremy Bentham (1748 – 1832) and John Stuart Mill. Another important philosophy in the last 20 – 30 years of the 19th century is that of will of power initiated by Friedrich Nietzsche, one of the most outstanding figures and geniuses in Western philosophy, who suggests that human beings are nothing but a bridge between the ape and the *Übermensche* (superman) thus questioning the future of the human being.

2 John Mill (1806 – 1873)

Jeremy Bentham gave the utilitarian movement its first and official statement and its name, but John Mill gave utilitarianism its brilliant defence, presentation and formulation.

Bentham argues that the essential principle of utility is to maximize pleasure and minimize pain and proposed a serious reform of the English penal system on this basis. Mill adds the quality of pleasure in respect of spiritual gains and emphasizes the importance of poetry and philosophy. In conjunction with his utilitarianism elaborating on the virtues of the enterprise philosophy, Mill also defends a powerful theory of individual rights. His view is a classic statement of what is traditionally called liberalism, a position he clearly inherited from Locke. He claims that the only reason to limit anyone's freedom is to protect the freedom of somebody else. Especially important is the freedom of speech.

Mill also renovated British empiricism from the overwhelming influence of German idealism by insisting that all knowledge comes from experience, to such an extent that he even regarded mathematics as a matter of experience, a high-level set of generalizations and abstractions from our experience of counting, shapes and so on.

3 Friedrich Nietzsche (1844 – 1900)

Nietzsche's contribution to Western civilization is versatile, including his reassessment of the Western tradition, his conception of the superman and his judgment of human nature.

In tracing the evolution of Western thought, he looked back to early Christianity, to the ancient Greek philosopher Socratic, and even earlier to Homer and the pre-Socratic dramatists. He saw the Western Greek heritage to be in conflict with its Judeo-Christian background. He utterly rejected the synthesis of the two that had developed throughout the history of Christianity. He was struck by what occurred in history. He claims that God is dead. While the Judeo-Christian tradition sought the explanation of misfortune in sin, the ancient Greeks took profound sufferings to be an indication of the fundamentally tragic nature of human life.

In *The Birth of Tragedy*, he speculates that the Greek view of tragedy reflects two different perspectives, which the Athenians associated with the gods Apollo and Dionysus. Dionysus is the god of wine, sexuality and revelry, representing the dynamic flux of being, the acceptance of fate and the chaos of creativity. The individual is dispensable from this perspective, but the individual can find profound satisfaction in being part of the wild, unfolding rush of life. From the Dionysian perspective, individual existence is but an illusion and our true reality is our participation in the life of the whole. Apollo, as the sun-god, reflects by contrast the Athenian fascination with beauty and order. From the Apollonian perspective, individual existence is undeniably real and human vulnerability is genuinely horrible. Yet the Apollonian perspective makes this reality appear beautiful and enables us to forget our vulnerability for a time and simply love our finite lives in the world. Nietzsche applauds the ancient Greeks for their ethical outlook which stressed the development of excellence and nobility in the face of fate, in contrast to what he saw as the gloomy Judeo-Christian obsession with sin and guilt.

Plato and Aristotle also displayed some vestiges of that more ancient outlook, yet Nietzsche regarded them as "decadent". The Greeks he admired were the pre-Socratic playwrights and the warrior heroes they described. He praised them by saying "they know how to live".

Nietzsche contends that human beings and other beings in nature are essentially wilful, and further suggests that we are willed to power, i. e. driven by the desire to keep expanding our vitality and strength. To him, survival is secondary. Against Schopenhauer's pessimism about the meaning of life, Nietzsche insists that vitality itself is the meaning of life. It is the affirmation of life that should be the conclusion of philosophy, not its rejection or resignation.

According to Nietzsche, many if not all of the prohibitions of Judeo-Christian ethics are levelling devices that favour the weak and mediocre and put more talented and stronger spirits at a disadvantage. Therefore Nietzsche defends a view in his *Beyond Good and Evil* to pass moralistic judgments on our own and others' behaviours towards a more creative psychological and naturalistic perspective.

He calls for the direction of human energies back into the life of this world. As opposed to the Christian world view, which treats human life as a mere beeline to the afterlife and celebrates an eternal world outside time as more important to this one, Nietzsche advocates a revival of the ancient view of eternal recurrence, the view that time repeats itself cyclically. For him, it is life and life alone that counts for anything. Philosophical thought, he insists, should always be subordinate to our efforts to live well, not the other way around.

4.4 Comparative comments

4.4.1 Social and intellectual conditions

Both China and the West were at a crossroad, faced with a choice, either to continue the original journey which would have no hope or good end, or to take a new road open to more possibilities and perspectives though their intellectual awakening occurred during different periods of time. The opportunities were equal to seek new lifestyles, more material wealth and greater spiritual freedom, considering the similar conditions in retarded social and economic developments on both sides after a long period of medieval darkness. Nonetheless, a series of diversities appeared along with economic and social developments in the long years of transition from the medieval period to modern age.

1) Economically speaking, some new signs came up in the latter part of the Middle Ages. Towards the latter half of the Ming Dynasty in China, agricultural production was greatly promoted while much farmland was seized by big landlords and aristocrats. The majority of peasants had to work as tenants and social polarity was aggravated rapidly. Meanwhile quite a number of merchants at the same time were active in the cities as mediators between the small and middle-sized

businesses and workshops and the consumers, most of whom were city-dwellers. A small amount of goods were sent discontinuously abroad as foreign trade with the southeast Asian countries had started. But generally, the production was self-contained and still self-sufficient, strictly controlled and restricted by the then centralized totalitarian government.

The Western economy at large, had started to embark on a path of rapid growth long before Chinese economy gained speed. It was marked by large-scale production of textile and woollen goods and the expansion of colonial aggression and settlement overseas as was characteristic of the Industrial Revolution which occurred first in England and Italy, then in France and other European countries. Obviously the West had broken down the barriers to a new era and was well prepared for rapid development in the economic field as a result of the Reformation and the Renaissance which helped remove political, social and religious barriers and supplied social and intellectual motivation for a more energetic concern for and participation in capitalist development which greatly changed the old world of feudalism and theology.

2) Politically speaking, some important changes occurred. The increasingly sharpened contradictions and conflicts, as a result of seizing by top-ranking officials and royal family vast tracts of farmland from the ordinary peasants in China, gave rise to peasant riots which led ultimately to the downfall of the Ming Dynasty and hindered further economic development. The change of regime, however, did not solve the social crisis which could not be avoided under autocracy with its closed-door policy. The weakness, therefore, of the Qing Dynasty was exposed about a hundred years and half after its establishment when Western warships began to bombard Chinese soil during the Opium War. The social chaos in China was intensified and social security was thus brought to an unprecedented state of crisis and danger, on the brink of destruction.

The West, on the other hand, despite its turns and twists as was witnessed in the acute contradictions between classes and nations, was set on a route of solid achievements and steady progress. An important feature of this period was the formation and growth of the bourgeoisie which arose as a result of the economic and social development and bore the responsibility of putting an end to the feudalistic autocracy and promoting social progress. However, the road to power for the bourgeoisie was not even. The ruling class of feudal autocracy refused to give up its power unless it was put under great pressure or defeated in the battlefield. It was true of both sides when violence had to be used as the only solution.

3) Intellectually speaking, the two sides began to manifest more diversities. China showed some signs of calling for more democracy and freedom of speech with occasional condemnation of totalitarianism. But generally such voice was very weak and sometimes even unheard due to the tightened control of feudal autocracy shaped and aggravated in the two-thousand-odd-year period in tune with the dominance by Confucianism. Therefore, such an intellectual tendency

was unable to evoke any substantial progress to benefit further intellectual and social developments. The intellectual development was merely confined to a few scholars such as Wang Fuzhi, Huang Zongxi and Gong Zizhen, who were either rejected and repressed by the autocratic rulers or had little effect on social reality because of their separation from the ordinary people.

The Western intellectuals suffered from a lack of intellectual freedom as well, especially from the restriction on the study of natural science, as shown in the persecution of Bruno and Galileo by the Inquisition. But as time moved on, such repression gradually relaxed and gave way to more tolerance of different views of and attitudes towards the world, with the unfolding of the Renaissance including the Reformation and the Enlightenment. Intellectual freedom was reaching the educated and the ordinary people with their faith and in ordinary life during this period. Human rights became a universally accepted measurement of behaviour for individuals, organizations and governments.

A number of Western thinkers were famous for their ideas about seeking individual freedom and equality of the relationship between individuals and the society. From Thomas Hobbes and John Locke to Jeremy Bentham, John Mill and Jean-Jacques Rousseau, just to name a few. They were founders of a series of theories in defence of the capitalist behaviours and bourgeois patterns or systems, laying a solid foundation for its later development. Compared with their Chinese counterparts, Western ideas were more systematic, effective, practical, scientific and democratic in spite of their limitations and insufficiencies.

4.4.2 Contribution to social progress

1 An estimation of Chinese contribution

Generally, the Chinese intellectual influence was largely inadequate during a pretty long period after the West moved into the modern age. It was partly because Chinese social status was quite obscure and minor, and partly because China was economically self-sufficient. It was basically characterized by a politically-oriented autocracy with a poorly-educated majority of the population, and the rulers would seldom tolerate any different ideas which were deemed unorthodox or heretic, like those of Wang Fuzhi or Huang Zongxi and even Gong Zizhen and Kang Youwei.

However, their ideas certainly helped to shape the ideals for a better social framework and to pinpoint the weakness of the society of the time. Many of their views were practical in the sense that they lived among the ordinary people they were familiar with and hence knew well Chinese historical and social developments. Gong Zizhen's claim for change and reform in the prime of the reign of the Qing Dynasty and Kang Youwei's plea for and plan of reform should be considered as an important development of Chinese sociological and philosophical thinking though it was not a success on account of the limit of the age, especially without the necessary support of a powerful political force.

2 An estimation of Western contribution

The Western ideas were produced at a time when the bourgeoisie was coming to or was actually in power. It was much easier for their ideas to be close to social reality and to be accepted in the form of law. For instance, the ideas of social contract and human rights were not only the academic concept presented by Hobbes, Locke and Rousseau but were written into the bourgeois laws or political declarations such as the American *Declaration of Independence* (1776) and the French *Declaration of Human Rights* (1793). Their success was not just a result of the talent of a few intellectuals, but a result of combined circumstances of social development like the emergence of capitalist mode of production. It is a good example to show how heroes are produced by situation. The Chinese failure, on the other hand, was not due to the imperfection of the theory concerned, but to the shortage of certain social conditions in which such a theory could take root and spread out before it could be eventually recognized, familiarized and successfully applied.

4.4.3 Philosophical and social significances in theoretical exploration

1 Theoretical inheritance and exploration

Chinese philosophers and thinkers, like Wang Fuzhi, Huang Zongxi, Gu Yanwu and Kang Youwei, worked deeper and further into the interpretation of Confucianism, expanding its practical and external aspects by emphasizing the importance of integration with social reality, clarifying the relationship between research and social reality with such concepts as *tao* and *qi*, *ti* and *yong*, essence and vacancy. The latter was manifested in the arguments of Wang Fuzhi, Gong Zizhen and Kang Youwei. These ideas seemed less metaphysical and less transcendental, but were still related to the tradition of Chinese classical ideology and lack of academic and intellectual courage, originality and systematism.

Western philosophers, such as Kant and Hegel, cared for the ontological issues and tried to make rational investigations of the nature of physical and spiritual existence by either monistic or dualistic ways of thinking. Their theoretical principles were more strict, metaphysical and systematic.

2 Difference in national temperament and intellectual inclination

The Western thinkers were comparatively more practical. During this period they helped establish a more comprehensive and systematic range of ideas to justify and defend the capitalist expansion, like the ideas of the social contract, human rights, empiricism, the division of state power, utilitarianism, positivism and pragmatism. They were the positive and fruitful results by the bourgeois thinkers of the changing social reality at the time.

Comparatively, the Chinese thinkers did not and could not do much in this respect due to the social and economic circumstances in their times, though some of them touched on the issue of political power and social system such as in Huang Zongxi and Wang Fuzhi's repudiation of the monarchy, Gong Zizhen's claim for reform and Kang Youwei's concept of the universal harmony and his appeal to the emperor for reform. But generally these ideas were limited in their function and the gap with the West was evident. The best appraisal that could be made of the Chinese thinkers, is that their contribution worked as a kind of preparation or warm-up drill for the would-be reform or revolution. The basic reason for the difference was the slowness in social and economic developments due to the hindrance of the feudalistic monarchy which refused stubbornly to make any change as shown in the Wuxu Reform. The Chinese thinkers in the meantime could not have expected powerful support from the ordinary people who were not intellectually advanced enough to be aware of their danger and weakness, as their Western counterparts did from the ordinary people during the Enlightenment. The lack of sufficient and efficient contact between the few prophetic figures and the majority of the population in that society contributed to the belated awakening of the Chinese people, who had to pay a pretty high price in the following years, through the civil wars and the Anti-Japanese War.

4.4.4 Critical spirit

Chinese philosophy and social ideology did not lack critical spirit if that spirit referred to dissatisfaction with the status quo or the social, intellectual or political tendencies of a certain period, figure or school. In this sense most figures covered in this period were characteristic of such a spirit. But the spirit was insufficient in two aspects. First it was not directed to the right point, i. e. towards the obstacles to social and economic development. Second it was often hastily shaped by assuming a radical or alien form so that it was short of a theoretical foundation and could not be accepted by the majority and hence often developed into an antagonism towards its critical objects. For the first point, almost all of the philosophical and ideological explorations in this period were formulated within the framework of traditional Chinese philosophy or ideology. What was criticized therefore served basically to protect or perfect rather than to modify or replace the traditional ideology, thus limiting its significance. For instance, their ideas had nothing to do with the poverty of the peasants or restrictions on commercial production or intellectual freedom, all of which were obviously central issues to the social, economic and intellectual developments of the time. For the second point, the spirit could not be encapsulated in a theoretical framework which would have offered a deep-going and substantial inquiry into its objects of criticism and have adopted a step-by-step and moderate persuasive method to enable the majority of people and the rulers to take it easy first and then to accept it. Of course its antagonism also concerned the attitude of the ruling class which was often unfortunately quite stubborn and even hostile to reformers, such as the Wuxu Reform pursued by Kang Youwei. For the first point, all the figures mentioned in this section could be taken as lessons.

Comparatively, the Western critical spirit was more direct, practical, thorough and enduring. For instance, their critical spearhead was always directed to the corruption of theology and feudalistic aristocracy, from Luther to Hobbes and from Locke to Voltaire and Rousseau. At the same time they always tried to provide a theoretical framework to arm the bourgeoisie with sufficient rational or other forms of theoretical interpretation, such as Locke's empiricism or Mill's utilitarianism which helped soon to win the powerful support from the broad masses of people and strengthened its position to fight against its enemy. Although they had to resort to violence occasionally, they preferred to take more moderate and reasonable measures by making reconciliations to defend the bourgeois interests and seize state power. This is a process — as long as about two centuries — to the final completion of the bourgeois revolution in the West. Notice quite a number of countries underwent the change by making compromises in spite of the fact that there were frequent bloodshed cases.

4.4.5 The range and depth of intellectual influence

The major schools and figures of the last couple of centuries imposed their enduring influence on social, economic and intellectual developments of modern age on both sides. However, these influences differed a lot in terms of their popularity, actual effects and significance they produced.

The philosophical effects promoted by the Chinese representatives helped to complete Confucianism as a discipline in its practical application and fortified its position in China's academic circles. Such study and interpretation of Confucianism did not appear closely relevant to social development, partly because it was not favoured and supported officially and partly because the majority of Chinese were illiterate or semi-literate and did not care much about such scholarship as the ideas advanced by Wang Fuzhi, Huang Zongxi and Gong Zizhen. Even Kang Youwei's reformist ideas were not popular, being confined to a small circle of intellectuals. Therefore their influence was limited and they could not expect any essential support from the average person.

Comparatively, Western philosophical ideas could spread more rapidly, widely and efficiently, partly because Western society was less tightly controlled and partly because the average were better educated and offered more positive responses. This could be detected by the depth and width of the Renaissance and the Enlightenment movements, both of which attracted large groups of average people over a long space of time and aroused or heightened their social and intellectual consciousness. In this sense one could never leave out the contribution of these two intellectual movements in considering the social and intellectual advances of Western civilization. In addition the ideas were more concerned with the public interest, i. e. the bourgeois interest which dominated the society and concerned the majority of the population. The general hostility of the ruling class to the new ideas did not last too long and relaxed after the Reformation as a result of emerging reconciliation in general public so that the society could tolerate different kinds of ideology, including those of opposition and criticism.

4.5 A case study

In both China and the West, some new ideas had to be produced when society was undergoing drastic changes. Huang Zongxi (1610 – 1695) and Jean-Jacques Rousseau presumably rose to prominence in such circumstances on account of their remarkably original ideas intended to change established political and intellectual traditions.

4.5.1 A reflection on social change

Huang Zongxi lived through the social turmoil and personal frustrations of the period between the end of the Ming Dynasty and the beginning of the Qing Dynasty. Armed conflicts and the use of violence caused large stretches of land to lie waste, large amount of property to be destroyed, and large numbers of people to be killed or wounded. No wonder Huang and a few other thinkers of his day were motivated to dig out the roots of the disastrous outcome hidden behind these terrifying phenomena.

In France, the 18th century witnessed frequent wars, starvation and natural disasters, which weighed on ordinary people and brought about great losses to their lives and wealth. The social crisis provoked serious meditations over social, political, religious and intellectual issues. The philosophical ideas proposed by the Englishman John Locke and other philosophers like David Hume provided the theoretical basis for a rational reflection by French thinkers on the then social and intellectual conditions.

Additionally behind this intellectual musing was the Industrial Revolution which had begun producing huge amounts of cheap products through a combination of mass production and scientific research. Fuelled by the economic power released out of industrial development, intellectual requirements kept growing and gradually evolved into a wide-ranging intellectual movement, the

Enlightenment, which was unfolded as a necessary continuation of the Renaissance and a spiritual preparation for the French Revolution. As one of the most remarkable figures of ideology, Jean-Jacques Rousseau had undoubtedly every right to speak for the modern Western intellectual development.

The opening scenes for the birth of the two philosophers were not exactly the same though they were relevant to one another in a certain sense. Obviously French soil was more fertile and nourishing for an open mind due to its contact with and reception of a rationalist tradition from the outside. Comparatively speaking, China was far more conservative and inadequate in terms of intellectual preparation for the advent of social and intellectual changes, due to the tightened control over intellectual and ideological conditions of over 2000 years from the national unification by Qin Shihuang till the end of the Ming Dynasty. Perhaps this is the reason why Huang's early sense of democracy is of great significance.

4.5.2　Strong sense of critical spirit

Huang Zongxi, born in an intellectual's family, went through a life of personal tortuousness and complexities as well as national crises in the period of the change of dynasties. Motivated by his intention to sum up the bitter experiences of national disasters of this period, he devoted all his life to a deliberate study of the hidden factors working for the collapse of the Ming regime. His concluding tenets, mainly drawn from his *ming-yi-dai-fang-lu* (《明夷待访录》, The Destruction of the Ming Dynasty: An Assessment to Be Made), offered a critical review of feudal totalitarianism and some proposals for the administration of political affairs.

Though Huang's achievements were not confined to these two respects, his major contributions were largely concerned with them and also won him an unparallelled high reputation in sharply repudiating autocracy.

Opposite to Confucius' advocacy of loyalty of the subjects to the monarch, Huang asserts that the relationship between monarch and subject has changed in the long period since the Qin and Han Dynasties. He gives a detailed account of the development of that relationship, beginning from the ancient time. He argues that the ancient monarchy was established, due to the fact that someone could work to promote his people's interests and remove his people's disinterest. In other words, in ancient times the monarch regarded himself as a guest instead of a master of the world and his work as in the service of his people, not of himself. But later on, things were reversed. The monarch took all interests to himself and all disadvantageous or unfavourable things to his people. Thus the monarch worked as the master of the whole world and his people as guests in the world. This is why the monarch, since the Qin and Han Dynasties, was regarded as a mortal enemy. His so-called great unselfishness actually meant his great selfishness. ①

The bitter and harsh tone of Huang's critical remarks is echoed by Rousseau's severe condemnation of human vices. He blames human societies by saying that human vices came from the time when human societies started to be formed and men and women began cohabitation, which suggests the establishment of a family and human relations and neighbourhood. For him, these signs suggest the beginning of society, that replaced the state of nature and put an end to peace and stability of human conditions. Thereafter human beings were thrown into a state of competition and instability because of the emergence of property and inequality. He believes that human beings could not get rid of the dilemma unless they achieve social and intellectual freedom. He says in *The Social Contract*: "Man was born free, but he is everywhere in chains." ②

4.5.3　Social and intellectual analyses

In his series of essays and books, such as *Discours sur les sciences et les arts* and *Discours sur l'origine de l'inégalité*, Rousseau argues that the growth of civilization corrupts natural goodness, and that the growth of society has led to the growth of inequality. ③

These ideas have distinguished Rousseau remarkably as a great thinker of the Enlightenment, through his penetrating insight into the essence of society and of inequality. Consequently his theory contributed a great deal to the theoretical constitution for a bourgeois revolution.

Comparatively speaking, Huang's analysis of Chinese social development, especially that of the monarchy, seems inadequate in that there is a lack of a necessary association with social development rather than an attribution to individual performance or moral judgment.

In spite of his evident theoretical insufficiencies, Huang does reveal his awareness of intellectual system and foresight in his proposals about the solution to political problems. He assumes that the autocratic laws about the emperor's ownership of state should be abolished while the universally operating law should be retained. He also suggests legal government should come before the man with legal reign because no legal reign could be expected without a legal system and no one could offer a legal rule without a justified legal system. Furthermore, he proposes the use of the academic institute to accomodate the discussion of political affairs and for political purposes. He argues that what the emperor approves of is not necessarily right and what the emperor rejects is not necessarily wrong. Hence

---

① See *History of Chinese Philosophy* (2nd edition), p. 368, Chinese Philosophy Teaching Group, Beijing University, Beijing University Press, 2003.
② See *Encyclopaedia Britannica Library: Rousseau, Jean-Jacques*, p. 2.
③ See *The Penguin Companion to Literature*, 2, p. 669, Anthony Thorlby (ed.), Penguin Books, 1969.

no emperor would be daring enough to present his judgment as the only justification, but a public judgment by the academic institute would be more preferable. ①

He suggests that the academic institute should be established at different levels such as the central, provincial and local. The post of chief of each institute should be held by an important scholar of each level. The chief of the central academy would be equal in status to a prime minister and this position should be taken up by the most prestigious scholar with nationwide influence. He could offer classes to the emperor, who should join in a group of students attending the class.

Moreover, the academic institute would be authorized to prepare public opinions to decide important issues, to supervise the government's work and to make or withdraw appointments of officials. ②

4.5.4 Political significance in academic study

Considering the time he lived in, Huang's ideas were really marvellous though they were never put into effect. To some extent they were also similar to the representative system of legislation of the West. The essential point of his proposal was his awareness of the need to restrict autocratic power. Despite the imperfections of his design for political power, it was the early attempt to challenge the Chinese monarchy and to promote Chinese political reform. Its significance can never be overestimated. It could have contributed more to the development of democracy if the idea had been accepted by a certain monarch as what was to happen in Britain. But unfortunately China was not prepared for such a drastic political change. Its autocracy and dictatorship came to its final stage and became more stubborn and merciless in terms of concentrated power and political dominance over the ordinary people, especially the intellectuals who were confronted with more persecutions and even death penalty for any intolerance of or disrespect towards the rulers.

In contrast to Huang's unhappy experience, Rousseau was lucky although he also suffered a lot both in his personal life and in his relationship with the society. At least his ideas were after all presented in his favour to the public through the publication of a number of his books, both fiction and theory, and cherished enormous influence among the rank and file, in a more tolerable intellectual environment. This was especially true of his posthumous influence which culminated in the French Revolution where Rousseau was universally acknowledged and regarded as the hero and master who had laid the foundation

---

① See *History of Chinese Philosophy* (2nd edition), p. 370, Chinese Philosophy Teaching Group, Beijing University, Beijing University Press, 2003.
② See *History of Chinese Philosophy* (2nd edition), p. 370, Chinese Philosophy Teaching Group, Beijing University, Beijing University Press, 2003.

for the revolution with his social theory.

Rousseau's theory, especially that of the social contract, was more complete and thorough-going and therefore more easily acceptable to the bourgeoisie when the latter rose up in revolution against autocracy. But more important was the tremendous force which Rousseau's theory evoked and which dwarfed Huang's by comparison. This was not just because Huang had hidden himself far away from the centre of Chinese political and intellectual life and did not realize the significance of building up more communications with the outside world. It was also because the majority of the Chinese population at the time still lived in a state of national terror and poverty, worried about security and the daily necessity of feeding and sheltering themselves, unable to think of intellectual needs as their Western contemporaries would do. It was impossible in these circumstances to expect ordinary people to acquire any knowledge or even to cherish any desire to learn what Huang had written about. This was indeed the tragedy of China as an old civilization and with a long history.

The distinction between Huang and Rousseau is not strange at all for a number of reasons.

Firstly, the social setting they were confronted with was different. The average Chinese still lived in feudal society tightly controlled and reigned by autocracy and had no idea about democracy and freedom while the majority of the European population had started to show early signs of intellectual awakening and awareness.

Secondly, the intellectual and cultural tradition Huang and Rousseau inherited was different. The knowledge Huang acquired at the time was basically that of Confucianism which he might be suspicious or even critical of, but could never expect to reject totally. Consequently he was limited by Confucian ideas such as focusing on book knowledge, especially that of humanities while neglecting that of natural science, caring for national or collective contribution but ignoring individual merit, etc.

As a successor to the ideas of social progress of the previous generation, Rousseau developed social contract and claimed for the right of the people to overthrow totalitarian reign, thus bringing modern age a new theory based on democratic politics and people's right and approaching the modern sense of a totally different concept of bourgeois state.

Thirdly, the critical spirit they manifested and represented was different. Huang's criticism was serious in a sense, but appeared inadequate in a way. He was harsh and even satirical against the feudal monarchy and emperor, but he never came to the point of putting an end to the system of feudalism. Maybe it was what a Chinese scholar was afraid of inwardly because it would be regarded as an offence against heaven as was forbidden.

But Rousseau was different. He had no such pre-destined fear for the so-called forbidden area. His criticism of the society, history and current affairs of his day had no limit. He went to such depths that he would even claim for the change of power, change of a political system and an upturn of social classes.

Questions for comprehension and discussion

1. What was the general social and intellectual climate during the period from the 16th century to the end of the 19th century in both China and the West?
2. What are the major intellectual contributions the Chinese thinkers made in the modern age? What are the contributions their Western counterparts made in the same period?
3. What are the principal similarities and dissimilarities between the two sides in terms of intellectual and ideological developments? Give examples.

List of proposed books for further reading

1. 朱谦之,1983,《中国哲学对欧洲的影响》,福州:福建人民出版社。
2. 张国刚、吴莉苇,2006,《启蒙时代欧洲的中国观——一个历史的巡礼与反思》,上海:上海古籍出版社。
3. 张西平,2001,《中国与欧洲早期宗教和哲学交流史》,北京:东方出版社。
4. 严建强,2002,《十八世纪中国文化在西欧的传播及其反应》,杭州:中国美术学院出版社。
5. Donald, Lach, *Asia in the Making of Europe*, Vol. III, Chicago & London: The University of Chicago Press,1993.
6. Kenny, Anthony, *The Rise of Modern Philosophy: A New History of Western Philosophy*, Volume 3, Oxford: Oxford University Press, 2008.

Chapter 5

A Comparison of the Chinese and English Languages

In many ways, Chinese and Western languages are quite different from each other. It is not just a matter of speaking different tongues, but rather a kind of manifestation of cultural oppositions and systematic divergence as well as different ways of thinking, as demonstrated in vocabulary, pronunciation and grammar. The resultant huge gap or diversity is a product of long years of social and intellectual developments in association with diverse geographical and historical conditions. However, they could also be seen as being connected in a way since the speakers of both languages share much of the same human value, which provides the sources and means of communication aside from the separate foundation of language. For the sake of convenience, we will focus on English as an epitome of the Western language since it is the most popularly spoken Western tongue in the world at present time and embodies all the necessary elements for discussion.

5.1 The origin and development of the Chinese and English languages

Both Chinese and English (languages) have a long history though their origins derive from different linguistic families. They are regarded as the world's most important languages in terms of the number of speakers and their popular use in world affairs. A brief account and review of their development might help offer some rough ideas of the historical importance of these two languages.

5.1.1 The development of the Chinese language

Chinese belongs to the Sino-Tibetan language family. It was initiated about 5000 years ago, based on pictographic and ideographic form that has been reshaped and improved in different stages. The archaeological finds made in the ruins of a number of pre-historical cultural centres like those at Zhoukoudian (周口店), Dingcun (丁村), Yangshao (仰韶), Longshan (龙山) and Liangzhu (良渚), indicate that our ancestors started to communicate with each other in a language limited to some simple sounds though its range and scope might have been, long ago, the company with their physical labour. However, written language emerged much later. The invention and development of written language progressed through a number of phases before it was ultimately established in its current form we use every day.

The first stage dated from the earliest period when Cangjie (仓颉), an official in charge of history during the Huangdi (黄帝, the Yellow Emperor) period, is said to have produced and recorded Chinese characters based on the original inventions and implements of the ordinary people at the time. The created language was used popularly and continuously till it was passed to the Qin Dynasty when Qin Shihuang (秦始皇, the First Emperor) unified into seal characters the Chinese written dialects and languages used in different places before the national unification. Consequently the Chinese language moved into the second stage. The important events during this period included the invention of *ba-gua* [1] (八卦, the Eight Diagrams) by Fuxi (伏羲), a legendary figure at the time, the discoveries of the ruined characters at Dawenkou (大汶口) and Banpocun (半坡村), and the formation of *ya-yan* [2] (雅言) based on the popular dialects of the Huangdi time during the Spring-Autumn Period. The second stage of the development of the Chinese language did not come to an end till the beginning of the 20th century when the Qing Dynasty was overthrown. At that time a group of educated people tried to popularize and disseminate the new ideas by simplifying the Chinese language into the so-called *bai-hua-wen* form (白话文, plain spoken language) instead of the sophisticated classical Chinese language by borrowing the Western Latin letters. From then on, the Chinese language moved into the third stage by both adopting a simplified form and identifying itself with everyday life. Eventually the Chinese language has taken on a new lease of life and made more considerable and effective contribution and commitment to Chinese modern advance.

5.1.2 The development of the English language

English belongs to the Indo-European language family, which includes such subdivisions as Latin, German and Slav. English is a member of German branch. Like other Western languages, English has gone through a number of phases of

---

[1] *Ba-gua*, a set of signs with symbolic meanings. It is said to be created by Fuxi, a legendary figure in the ancient times, and be used to tell fortune. A detailed interpretation about it is presented in *yi-jing* (《易经》), a book produced in the Zhou Dynasty.

[2] *Ya-yan*, a term of Chinese language, means elegant language.

historical development. In a way, one could say English is an output of a mixture of different languages used by diverse peoples. The first people in England about whose language we have definite knowledge are the Celts. The arrival of the Celts in England coincided with the introduction of bronze into the island, which occurred long before any other later language was used.

The other source language, which was practised in England, refers to Latin. It was spoken rather extensively for about four centuries before the use of English. Latin was introduced when Britain became a province of the Roman Empire in the first century, even before Caesar took his army and temporarily occupied part of Britain. With the introduction of Roman lifestyle, such as Roman houses and baths, heating apparatus and water supply, dresses and ornaments, pottery and glassware, temples and even theatres, Latin came into formal application by the majority from the military and official affairs to religious and public occasions. However, it did not indicate a widespread use of Latin by the indigenous population. On a whole, the use of Latin was not sufficiently widespread to allow it to survive though many people in Roman Britain habitually spoke or even wrote it. The use of Latin started to decline after the 5th century when the Roman troops were forced to leave the island, yet some traces remained in English.

The most decisive impact on the formation of the English language as we know it is a product of the invasion by Germanic tribes, which eventuated in the years of the Roman withdrawal from Britain. For more than a hundred years, bands of conquerors and settlers migrated from their continental homelands in the region of Denmark and other low countries such as Friesland, and established themselves in the south and east of the island, gradually extending into occupied areas of the highlands in the west and north. According to the ancient *Ecclesiastical History of the English People* by Bede[1], the Germanic tribes that conquered England were mainly the Jutes, Saxons and Angles. Anglo-Saxon civilization was eventually established after many years' fighting with the Celts who had driven away the Jutes but failed in their clashes against the Saxons and Angles.

The English language is the one which has resulted from the mixture of the dialects of the Anglo-Saxon people who had moved to the British Isles and then joined the Celts before the 10th century. English was further expanded into a multi-national language with a growing vocabulary added by the languages of the Scandinavian, like the Danish and the Swedish, and finally by the French. The latter came to the islands as the official language after the Norman Conquest in 1066. Though English remained an independent language, it admitted quite a

---

[1] Bede was a theologian historian in England between the 7th and 8th centuries and his reputation was based mainly on his scriptural commentaries. The book was a source vital to the early days of the conversion to Christianity of the Anglo-Saxon tribes.

large number of French words. This influx did not stop till the end of the 17th century when French was still an official language at court. Owing to the inflow of French and other European languages (Italian contributed a fairly large number of musical terms, for example) as well as other factors arising out of social and cultural developments, the changes in the English language were never finished and continued well beyond the end of the Middle Ages. This was especially true of the words from the British colonies, like India, America and Africa. Consequently, English became simpler and less inflected laying its foundation as an internationally used language, gaining its importance with the growing power and status of the British Empire in political, military and economic fields. The modern age of English is usually considered to have started from Shakespeare, whose oeuvre in the Elizabethan period marked an important break from the ancient and medieval English with his marvellous plays. From then on, English has developed a great deal and became more acceptable and popularized by getting more adapted to the different needs and contacts with different circumstances, such as the establishment and expansions of overseas colonies in the 18th and 19th centuries, which brought the language to more and more places in the world and created more accents and dialects. Ultimately, it is established as an international or global language with quite a number of varieties, such as American, Australian, New Zealand, South African, Indian, Canadian and even Singaporean Englishes.

5.2 The main features of the Chinese language

5.2.1 The ideographic language in general

Before anything else, Chinese is an ideographic language and most of its characters originate from an imitation of the shape of certain objects or things. It is principally form, rather than sound, that decides meaning, though sound has occasionally contributed to the constitution and identification of some characters. The ideographic and sound features are identified in the excavated artefacts inscribed with early language symbols, such as those on tortoise shells, animal bones, bamboo files or bronze articles. Therefore, Chinese is often called hieroglyph or pictograph language in the Western world.

When we say Chinese is a form-based language, we mean the Chinese unit of language or character morpheme is founded on a variety of basic strokes that provide the constituents of several thousand characters. Though the earliest forms of many of these characters were possibly derived out of certain objects or creatures, they are transformed into more abstract shape through gradual changes over a long period of historical development. It is not so easy to discern any specific meaning out of the first glance at most of the characters though some still retain identifiable elements. At the same time, we should not take for granted that the Chinese character has totally rejected phonetic function. As a matter of fact, one could depend on some cues or hints from or assistance in pronunciation, such as the side part of a character that would not necessarily give a right pronunciation but could offer a clue. For instance, "妈" is composed of "女" and "马". We could easily detect its pronunciation by its side part "马". The same is true of "铜" because of "同"; and then "城" and "成"; "忠" and "中"; "媳" and "息"; "伟" and "韦"; "停" and "亭"; "澎" and "彭"; "滨", "缤", "槟", "镔" and "宾"; "捞", "涝", "唠" and "劳". But be careful of these side parts. Some of them could be misleading. For instance, the right pronunciation for "著" is "zhu", not "zhe" as its side part "者" indicates. Other examples include "祝" and "兄", "滞" and "带", "小" and "尖", etc.

5.2.2 Flexibility in sentence structure

There are no fixed rules for making sentences in terms of word order and parts of speech, though generally, subjects are put at the beginning of a sentence and the predicate verbs follow closely the subject. The core of Chinese is meaning which takes command of structure and other forms. For instance:

1) 我吃饭了。
   SVO (I have taken my meal.)
2) 我饭吃了。
   SOV (I my meal have taken.)
3) 我关门了。
   SVO (I have shut the door.)
4) 我门关了。
   SOV (I the door have shut.)
5) 他们去观看球赛了。
   SOV (They have gone to watch a ball game.)
6) 观看球赛的人都走了。
   ASV (To watch a ball game the people are gone.)
7) 观看球赛必须得到批准。
   SV (To watch a ball game must get the permission.)
8) 山不山,水不水;男不男,女不女;人不人,鬼不鬼。
   (ellipsis of the link verb and repetition of the key characters)
9) 坛坛罐罐,山山水水,生生世世,沸沸扬扬,风风雨雨。
   (overlapping of the word could work as a predicate or emphasis)

5.2.3 Sense of tense and inflection

No tense or inflection occurs to verbs in the Chinese language. Differentiations are made only by some adverbial signifiers, such as "将","要","已经","了","过","曾经","正在","打算","准备", etc. Chinese do not care much about the grammatical rules because they did not have any formal or authoritative grammar till the end of the 19th century.

1) 他(已经)看过电影了。
2) 他正在打球。
3) 我们准备明天动身。
4) 他们曾经去过那里。

5.2.4 Elliptical elements

There always exist quite a lot of elliptical elements in a sentence or daily conversations where no strict restrictions are found in grammar.

1) （天）下雨了。（我）吃饭了。（他）上课了。（我们）开车了。
   (Subjects are omitted.)
2) 孩子小,瓜很甜,衣服薄。
   (No verb appears in these fragments.)
3) 枯藤老树昏鸦,小桥流水人家。
   古道西风瘦马,夕阳西下,断肠人在天涯。
   (Nominal sense groups with omitted predicates.)

5.2.5 Chinese as a tonal language

The Chinese language is characterized by tone which dates back to the Wei and Jin Dynasties on account of the use of *fan-qie*[①] (反切), an approach of pronunciation. But since the Southern Dynasties, a criterion has stuck to the scene and kept working on four tones. By employing different tones in reading or uttering a word, one could detect different meanings. Therefore tone has become an important means to identify and differentiate words in Chinese.

For instance, choosing different tones suggests entirely diverse meanings through the reading of the following characters:

同,铜,桶,痛;开,凯,楷,慨;是,时,石,市;邹,走,奏,揍;央,扬,养,样。

The reason for the criterion of four tones was proposed by Chen Yinke (陈寅恪), a distinguished scholar of linguistics: "The introduction of Buddhism from India brought Sanskrit to the attention of Chinese scholars at the time, to be a model in building up the four tones in Chinese."[②]

---

① *Fan-qie* refers to a traditional way of Chinese pronunciation. It is used by borrowing separately part of sound from two characters and thus producing the pronunciation for a new character. It is said to start from the Han Dynasty and have continued till the introduction of Latin letters as the phonetic symbol.
② See *The History of Chinese Linguistics*, p.200, Pu Zhizhen, Shulin Publishing House, Taipei, 1990.

5.2.6 Chinese pronunciation

Chinese phonetic symbols were not designed throughout the long history of Chinese language development till the early years of the 20th century, when some scholars of Chinese studies proposed to import the Romanized pronunciation for the Chinese characters. However, the Chinese pronunciation had received some assistance from such devices like *du-ruo*(读若, read like), *zhi-yan*(直言, direct pronunciation), *huan-yan*(缓言, slow pronunciation), *chang-yan*(长言, prolonged pronunciation) and *duan-yan*(短言, shortened pronunciation) as well as diphthong or overlapping till Bernhard Karlgren[①](高本汉, Gao Benhan) introduced Romanized phonetic symbols after the May 4th Movement.

Most of Chinese characters are monosyllabic and lack of variety and even limited in the range of presenting vowels or consonants in pronunciation. For instance, the Chinese language does not have certain sounds like [θ], [v] and [ʌ]. Instead the Chinese language has a lot of characters which have repetitions in pronunciation but vary in meaning, which is called homonym. The Chinese language is insufficient in terms of the shortage of phonetic symbols. One could hardly detect the differences between a longer sound and a shorter one in earlier times and hence the ancient scholars tried to indicate this by such expressions as "长言" (prolonged pronunciation) or "短言" (shortened pronunciation). These problems remained unsolved until Romanized letters were borrowed at the turn of the 20th century.

5.2.7 Chinese vocabulary

As to the vocabulary of the Chinese language, a number of features are worth mentioning, including character formation, meaning and pronunciation.

In addition to the pronunciation discussed earlier, Chinese character formation is certainly quite characteristic of Chinese national culture. Rather than following the sound pattern, Chinese character formation focuses on visual frame or structure. They are composed of basic units which provide the essential constitution combined with other elements to make a character. According to *Modern Dictionary of Chinese Language*, there are altogether 188 radicals or basic units for the constitution of Chinese characters.[②] There could be some exceptions, but most of Chinese characters are inseparable from these radicals. These radicals might make different contributions to the formation of Chinese characters. Most of them offer clues to either sources or meaning.

---

① Bernhard Karlgren, a Swedish Sinologist.
② See *Modern Dictionary of Chinese Language*, p. 16, Dictionary Section (ed.), Institute of Chinese Linguistic Research, Chinese Social Academy, Commercial Press, 1985.

For instance, "氵" usually suggests the relevance to water; "金" has much to do with metal; "扌" relates to a kind of movement or action; "女" represents female; "木" originates from plants; "气" indicates a connection with gas or air; "火" symbolizes fire or burning action; "石" stands for natural solid, stones or mineral objects; "言" means speaking and extends to any behaviours or states relevant to speaking or mental work.

Although the radical is important to character formation, the most fundamental element is the strokes such as "丶", "丿", "一", "丨". All kinds of constituents of Chinese characters, even radicals, have to be made up of strokes. These basic components, either strokes or radicals, are both characterized by visual rather than sound cues. Without identifying exactly the meaning of a particular character, the reader could achieve the basic understanding of its rough sense. This is because the changeable composition of a character, none of which presents exactly the same form, offers a variety of basic ingredients to provide pleasing visual stimulus, which is similar to the principle of aesthetic appreciation.

Furthermore, the Chinese language has also considerable numbers of homophones and synonyms, which provide more colourful and vivid imagery. As well Chinese vocabulary was expanded by the introduction of quite a few foreign words. The trend of assimilating more words from foreign sources has accelerated Chinese cultural and social communication with the outside world and benefited its advance towards a more open and civilized state.

After a heated dispute over the future of the Chinese language at the turn of the 20th century, more and more scholars, both Chinese researchers and Western Sinologists, became aware of its advantages which were typically advocated by the Swedish Sinologist Bernhard Karlgren: "Chinese language is really produced by Chinese creative spirit, unlike the Western language borrowed from the distant alien people of the ancient time. No one in the West could understand the special respect for the language by the local Chinese. Rich in abundance of eye-pleasing form, the Chinese language could give rise to endless imagination. The Chinese language resembles a beautiful and lovely lady while the Western language seems like a humble servant maid who appears helpful but unattractive."①

With the introduction of Romanized phonetic symbols for the pronunciation of Chinese characters, the Chinese language gained remarkable headway, promoted by the surge of social changes and cultural promotion as well as academic research after breaking down the fetters and yokes of feudalistic autocracy.

5.2.8 Chinese grammar

Though the Chinese language did have some grammatical performances in

---

① See *History of Chinese Modern Linguistics*, p. 449, He Jiuying, Guangdong Education Press, 1995.

the ancient classics, such as the use of passive voice in *chun-qiu* (《春秋》, Spring and Autumn), the modern Chinese language grammar was not established until the end of the 19th century when Ma Jianzhong published his *ma-shi-wen-tong* (《马氏文通》, Ma's Grammar) in 1898.[①] About ninety or so grammar books were brought forward in the first half of the 20th century, excluding those submitted by the foreigners or produced abroad. Generally speaking, these grammar books fall into two categories. One category, as represented by *ma-shi-wen-tong*, belongs to the group of imitation of the Western pattern. After a short period of following the available models of Western grammar, the Chinese grammarians tried to re-orientate their research on a collection and analysis of raw material by establishing a new perspective and methodology of deduction and induction characterized by the sense of modern science, which includes classification and comparison. Consequently the second category emerged with a number of theoretical systems and approaches that came into being with respect to the research of the Chinese language. However, none of these theories is mature or authoritative enough to be adopted as the theoretical foundation of the Chinese language.

5.3 The main features of the English language

The English language is totally different from Chinese because of its vast diversity of origins and specialized features. Compared with Chinese, English is a fairly recent language considering the fact that its birth occurred only 1500 years ago, as a mixture of three or four national languages. Its pronunciation and vocabulary, based on phonetic alphabet, also show tremendous differences from Chinese and demonstrate how a sound foundation in the long historical development leads to an established language with its own independent features.

5.3.1 Shape-and-inflection structure

English as a whole is manoeuvred and manipulated by various linguistic forms, such as the changes in spelling to show grammatical functions, the rules for structure and pronunciation such as verb tense, the *-ing* and *-ed* forms for present and past participles, suffixes, prefixes, past tense with *-ed* for regular verbs, etc. Generally, the change of word form takes control of meaning which derives from structural modifications.

In spite of the limited number of grammatical inflections, English is perhaps easier to master than most of other European languages due to its inflectional

---

[①] See *The History of Chinese Linguistics*, p. 457, Pu Zhizhen, Shulin Publishing House, Taipei, 1990.

simplicity. In comparison with those classical languages like Sanskrit, Greek, Latin and even modern languages like Russian, French and German, English has been deprived of the complicated rules for the inflections of the noun, the adjective, the verb, and to some extent the pronoun. In the process of simplifying and reducing inflectional complexities, English doubtless has gone farther than most European languages. The noun inflection is reduced to only the plural form and possessive case while the original elaborate Germanic inflection of the adjective has been completely removed except for the comparative and the superlative degrees. The verb has been simplified by the loss of practically all the personal endings, the almost complete abandonment of distinctions between the singular and the plural (except for the verb *to be*), and the gradual discarding of the subjunctive mood. Nonetheless, the tendency for the simplification of English inflection does not mean a decay of grammar, but contributes to the efficiency in learning the language. Practical experience of first language acquisition has exhibited and confirmed the fact that a child in learning his native language by simplified inflections, could hardly feel the advantage an adult does in learning his second or foreign language by simplified inflections. Therefore, the inflectional simplicity benefits the acquisition of English by adults or those who would take English as a second or foreign language and thus contributes to the widespread adoption of English as an international language.

Additionally, English distinguishes itself from other European languages in having adopted natural gender rather than grammatical gender. Nouns in most European languages are either masculine or feminine, and some languages, like German, even have three genders with an additional neuter. English has abandoned almost all these complexities during the Middle English period. It was assumed that one could decide the gender from the context and overall meaning. All nouns naming common living creatures in English are masculine or feminine according to the sex of the individual creature, and all other nouns are neuter.

5.3.2 Sound-identified language

English and other Western languages are identified principally by sound. One can basically discern and even spell out a word as soon as one catches its pronunciation. Therefore sound patterns contribute much to the meaning and form of a certain word or a cluster of words. There is an agreement between physical constitution and sound patterns in English and other Western languages.

The formation of English pronunciation phonemes, apart from those of the Celtic and Germanic languages, could not ignore Latin influence that is certainly obvious. They include some accented vowels and diphthongs (*oe*, *a*, *o*, *u*, *ea*, *eo* and *io*), suggesting they were once followed in the next syllable by an *i* or *j*. Under such circumstances *oe* and *a* became *e*, and *o* became *e*, *a* became *oe*, and *u* became *y*. The diphthongs *ea*, *eo* and *io* became *ie*, later *i*, *y*. Thus *bankiz* >

benc (bench), *musiz* > *mys* [*plural of mus* (mouse)], etc. The chance occurred in English in the course of the 7th century, and when we find it taking place in a word borrowed from Latin, it indicates that the Latin word moved into English long before that time.

Towards the end of the Old English period, English underwent the third foreign influence, the result of contact with another important language, namely the Scandinavian. From the 8th century onward, the Scandinavians began a series of attacks upon all the lands close to the North Sea and the Baltic Sea, both for plunder and conquest. One example was the Swedes establishing a kingdom in Russia. The other examples included Norway colonizing parts of the British Isles and Iceland, the Danes establishing the Dukedom of Normandy and the Norman conquest of England. These events certainly exerted considerable influences on the development of the English language. For instance, one of the simplest cases to recognize is the development of the sound *sk*. In Old English this was early palatalized to *sh*. But in Scandinavian countries it retained its hard *sk* sound. Consequently native words like *ship*, *shall*, *fish* have *sh* in Modern English, while words borrowed from the Scandinavians are generally still pronounced with *sk* like *sky*, *skin*, *skill*, *scrape*, *scrub*, *bask*, *whisk*.

5.3.3 Accent as the sign for differentiation in meaning or part of speech

Accent contributes much to English pronunciation and identification of word meanings. For instance:

1) con´tent, *n*., conten´t, *a*. & *v*.; con´test, *n*., contes´t, *v*.
2) row [raʊ], *n*., row [rəʊ], *v*.; bow [bəʊ], a weapon for shooting arrows, *n*., bow [baʊ], bend, *v*.
3) sub´ject, *n*., subjec´t, *v*.; ob´ject, *n*., objec´t, *v*.

The function of accent in English has much to do with the understanding of English. Its role is similar to that of tone in the Chinese language. If tone in Chinese helps identify different meaning of Chinese characters, accent in the English language could also do the same as is indicated in the above examples though such function is still fairly limited in English. Sometimes a slight change of pronunciation would have the same effect as is shown above.

5.3.4 The constitution of a variety of rhyme and rhythm

Rhyming scheme is principally applied in verse and consists of a number of principles.

1 Classification of rhymes

Generally the rhyming scheme is composed of single, double, treble, broken, internal and half rhymes. These rhymes are determined by the number of vowels in rhyming and the position in a poetic line. Single rhyme means one vowel plus one or two consonants. Double rhyme means two vowels plus the consonants concerned. Treble rhyme means three vowels plus the consonants concerned. Broken rhyme suggests the rhyme has to depend on more than one word, such as estate / their gate. Internal rhyme means the rhyme within rather than at the end of a poetic line. Here's an example from Coleridge: "The Sun came up upon the left, / Out of the *sea* came *he*; / And he shone *bright* and on the *right* / Went down into the sea."

The rhyming scheme is guided by the following rules:

1) Usually rhyming demands the repetition of the vowel(s) and the consonant(s) at the end of a line, or grouping of the same or similar vowel(s) or consonants in the middle of a poetic line.

2) Accented on the first syllable and unaccented on the second syllable in double rhymes.

3) Accented on the first of the three syllables in treble rhymes.

2 Rhythm

Classical English poetry has altogether 6 metres or measures forming metrical units of a poetic line, namely iambus, trochee, anapaest, dactyl, amphibrach and spondee. These metres were borrowed from Latin and Greek and applied to English poetry during the classical period. They supposedly decide how the metrical units are formed and consequently how many feet occur in a particular line of a poem. It should be noted that modern poets largely disregard these artificial constraints and that various kinds of free verse now dominate poetry in English today. Even Shakespeare preferred blank verse as the medium for most of his writing.

5.3.5 The expansion of vocabulary by borrowing from other languages

In a way English is a result of long-term interaction of quite a number of diverse languages based on the Anglo-Saxon dialect. Its vocabulary is composed of a mixture of source languages. It includes the borrowing of a large number of words from different origins, like those from Latin, Greek, native American, French, Russian, Persian, Scandinavian and Asian languages as well as combined words either formed of its own or in association with science or other fields of study. Following are some examples of such loan words.

Latin is perhaps the first important language that the Anglo-Saxon borrowed from in their daily life, on account of the Roman intrusion and the introduction of Christianity. The words that were borrowed in the early period are only a partial indication of the extent to which the introduction of Christianity affected the lives and thoughts of the English people. The English did not always take a foreign word to express a new concept. They would prefer to use an old one. For instance, they did not borrow *deus* because they had the word *God*. So were the words *heaven* and *hell*. However they have introduced about 450 Latin words as a result of the Christianizing of Britain before the close of the Old English period, such as *pope*, *bishop*, *priest*, *monk* and *abbot*.

In addition to the words borrowed from Latin, the English vocabulary has also been affected by Scandinavian languages. It is especially demonstrated in the earlier literary works passing down from the ballads or classical writers like those of Chaucer. For instance, *lythe* means "listen", *wight* means "strong", *busk* and *bowne* mean "prepare", *gar* means "to cause someone to do something", *may* means "maid", etc.

Apart from Scandinavian influences, English has also taken many words from other languages. Here are some examples to indicate the borrowings from other languages:

1) Native American: chipmunk, hominy, moose, raccoon, skunk, tepee, wigwam;

2) Dutch: brandy, cruller, landscape, measles, uproar, wagon;

3) Italian: balcony, canto, duet, granite, opera, piano, umbrella, volcano, pizza, spaghetti;

4) Spanish: alligator, cargo, contraband, cork, hammock, mosquito, herry, stampede, tornado, vanilla;

5) Greek: acme, acrobat, anthology, barometer, catarrh, catastrophe, chronology, elastic, magic, tactics, tantalize;

6) Russian: steppe, vodka, ruble, troika, glasnost, perestroika;

7) Persian: caravan, dervish, divan, khaki, mogul, shawl, sherbet, jasmine, paradise, check, chess, lemon, lilac, turban, borax, spinach;

8) Indian: khaki, curry, tiffin, juggernaut, jungle, chutney;

9) Australian aboriginal: kangaroo, koala, emu, bilabong, boomerang.

5.3.6 Varieties of English established in the modern age

With the development of colonization and industrialization in the years after the Renaissance, the use of English is no longer confined to the British Isles, but spread to the other continents, such as America, Asia, Africa and Australia. A variety of English dialects have been shaped out of long years of development away from the native country. The larger groups of the modified English include American English, Australian English, New Zealand English, Canadian English, South African English and Indian English. These types of English indicate certain kinds of diversities though they keep the basic patterns of their mother tongue. In pronunciation, [eɪ] turns to [aɪ] in Australian English, such as "day" becoming "dai", "pay" becoming "pai". More differences in American English could be detected, such as retroflexion of [ə(r)], or / and [ɑː] to [æ], like path, calm, father; [ɒ] turning to [ɔː], such as log, long, law, cause.

In vocabulary, apart from dialects with special spelling, also some significant divergences occurred to certain words in non-British English, such as labour > labor, colour > color, neighbour > neighbor, behaviour > behavior, programme > program, dialogue > dialog, catalogue > catalog in American English. Some special words in Australian English such as *paddock* meaning "field", *crook* meaning "ill", *bowyang* meaning "a trouser strap", *waddy* meaning "bludgeon (heavy club with one end thicker or heavier than the other)". There is not too much difference in grammar though some diverse uses fall within non-British English, such as have got > have (acquire, receive, possess). Subjunctive mood is another category to indicate differences. Subjunctive mood seems to make more appearances nowadays in non-British English after the verbs like *demand*, *require* or *request*, *suggest*, *insist* and *move*.

Comparative comments

In spite of the vast differences between the two languages, some similar traces could still be found in the principles for establishing systems of pronunciation, vocabulary, sentence construction and semantic structures for communication, such as the common proprieties or etiquettes on both sides for handling the complicated relationships between human beings and their environment. It could be suggested that human languages are linked by some common guiding principles or values, which originate out of the similar human experience and awareness of the historical development of the human civilization.

5.4.1 The origin of the two languages

Both Chinese and English were initially derived from the pictograph. The Chinese language has kept to the tradition of written symbols by improving a great deal the way of communication through sticking to the form of pictograph while the English and other Western languages turned to the sound-based alphabetical language system in the long process of social and cultural developments.

The English and other Western languages started at the inception of their development from the pictograph, such as the one established by the Cretan during the Minoan period, which could be traced to the Carthaginian language. Another example is runes or matchstick signs which provide the basis of an alphabet used by the Vikings, known as "Futhark". Runes fell into two groups: Common or Danish Futhark, and Swede-Norwegian, each with sixteen basic signs. They were found in great numbers in Central Sweden and Denmark, recording voyages, legal agreements and deaths, sometimes in skaldic verse. The

16-sign Futhark of the Vikings had been condensed from a more complicated "Rune Hoard" used from the Bronze Age onwards for the occult divination, with more resemblance to natural objects. Archaeologists found later on more variants of runes, such as the 33-sign series in Anglo-Saxon England and the 18-sign series of Armenian Runes.

The discoveries of these ideographic symbols not only offered a picture of the mysterious and beautiful world of the Vikings, but supplied a clue to understand the origin of the writing system of the English and other Western languages. Moreover, the English and other Western languages are thus linked to the Chinese language in its historical origin by drawing on the pictographic form, consequently providing the basis for further comparison though their orientation might be inclined to different focuses.

1 The social aspect of the two languages

Overall, the linguistic evolvement is more inclined towards easier access and simpler approach to perform its social commitment. Different from the phonetic-oriented tendency of the Western languages, the Chinese language grew into a more sophisticated system by focusing on a form-centred written language. But Chinese has become more colloquial and inclined to social reality of daily needs from the early 20th century onwards, though such development had to be divided between oral and written forms. Meanwhile, the English and other Western languages were also modified a great deal to adapt to daily usage by the ordinary people and the rapid development of social and economic affairs.

Among the motive forces for the change in language, no one could underestimate the contribution of social factors, which work together with other forces to drive forward language evolution. This is true of what happened both in China and in Britain. Drastic social and political changes towards the end of the Warring States Period in China brought about the need to put an end to social chaos and meanwhile provided a rare opportunity to reform and unify a variety of local dialects into a national language. It was the same case with the development of English. The ultimate form of English emerged during a period of a few centuries after the Anglo-Saxon intrusion into the British Isles and the following conflicts with the Celts, the French and the Scandinavians. It was this social turmoil and political instability that contributed to the emergence of a new language.

For the same reason, English has gained a considerable development since the end of the Renaissance on account of the Industrial Revolution and colonial expansion. The rapid social change associated with industrial and financial growth, colonial migration and settlement, promoted a demand for more effective communication and thus greatly intensified the escalation and expansion of the English language.

On the other hand, the Chinese society entered a long-term phase of sluggish development following the country's unification, because of strictly controlled and repressive regime imposed by a centralized autocratic government. The Chinese language exhibited little change in the two-thousand-odd-year development, losing its vigour and vitality and labouring under the severe dominance of the feudalistic monarchy, which refused to open China to the outside world. In fact, the ruling class tolerated little social and economic reformation and resorted to the severe punishment and depressed lifestyle to deal with many intellectuals and their practice of language and literacy.

The positive and negative experiences of both languages testified to the significance and necessity of social changes for the development of language. Armed with a sense of social obligation since entering the modern age, the two languages have both admitted more elements from and reflected various aspects of a growing amount of latter day social phenomena and events as an increasingly dynamic vehicle of accommodation and for communication between human beings across national boundaries.

2 More contact between China and the West by mutual borrowing

China was once a very conservative country by virtue of keeping its door tightly closed and refusing to admit anything foreign. But with the rapid change in economic and intellectual developments in the 19th century, the Chinese attitude towards foreign languages and Western culture was somewhat modified and gradually began to absorb into Chinese the elements of English and other Western languages. The best example is the formation of a Chinese grammar, which was a result of following foreign models and adopting foreign principles to build up and expand the new concept of the Chinese language. As well a large number of words have been taken into Chinese out of the English vocabulary, such as OK, TV, VCD, "的士" (taxi), "派对" (party), etc. Western languages, particularly English, also picked up quite some Chinese terms, especially those in social life, such as *kowtow*, *sampan*, *mahjong*, *ginkgo*, etc.

5.4.2 Diverse linguistic applications and features

1 Different orientations

The Chinese language is basically ideographical in form and conveys ideas directly by the visual medium in writing and by tone in speaking, while the English and other Western languages are based on phonological composition of sound and accent both in speaking and writing to convey meaning. All of the distinctions between Chinese and Western languages start from this juncture and proceed in diverse directions for the sake of communication, working independently of each other in terms of pronunciation, construction of ideas and the structure of the two languages.

2 Difference in conveying sound

The Chinese written character is based on one syllable and therefore is simple and tends to be rich in tone for the sake of making subtle distinctions to suggest varieties of meaning. A Western language such as English relies on the change of pronunciation and intonation to convey different ideas and therefore appears more complicated and sound-based in terms of communicating information.

3 Intelligibility of literal form and ease of pronunciation

The English language is neutral, abstract and rational because no internal links exist between its form of letters and the message it intends to convey, other than syllabic stress and intonation pattern in sentences, and hence the English language is not easily comprehended at its first sight. In contrast, the Chinese language is more discernible and easily comprehensible because its characters are formed by specific images combined with meaning.

Such difference shows the advantage of pictorial language. For instance, "日" comes from the image of the sun, which makes sense at the first sight and therefore it is easy to grasp its meaning through the reader's imagination whereas *sun* in English does not offer any special difference from other words in its appearance because they are all composed of the same letters from the same alphabet. Therefore it is not so easy to detect its meaning at the first sight in comparison with Chinese. At the same time one could not pronounce "日" in Chinese without being given phonetic symbols while *sun* in English could be pronounced easily at the first glance.

4 Access to computer devices

The Chinese language shows its advantage of easier and rapider access to computer systems than the Western languages, thus could be expected to be a more efficient and effective tool for future developments. Some statistics show that Chinese characters could be entered into computer more rapidly than Western letters.

5 Storage of documents

The Chinese language is easy to archive in records because the visually-oriented feature helps it to remain little changed while the Western languages seem to be more changeable in an historical process. This is because the speech-oriented characteristics make them more subject to change. The English language has a larger vocabulary, which is also less efficient for the preservation and storage of documents.

5.4.3 Historical changes in language form

The Western languages, including English, have been affected by more external influences and introduced more new rules and underwent more changes than Chinese. For instance, ancient English had many more inflections for verbs, nouns, pronouns and adjectives. But modern English has dropped most of these inflections and tended to be simpler and easier to learn and use. Chinese, comparatively speaking, has kept most of its traditional form and suffered little influence from the outside world in terms of the number of characters or grammatical rules. For instance, the sentence order has remained unchanged though drastic changes occurred to vocabulary and society throughout the 20th century. The written form of the Chinese language was then changed into a much simpler version, with subsequent effect on both vocabulary and sentence length.

The production and development of human language is closely related to certain historical conditions which entail the application of language to enhance the physical and spiritual progress of the human race. The level of discourse and forms of the language depend to a certain extent on the specific social circumstances in which language is used. Therefore Chinese and English, no matter what divergences exist between them, are both affected by the social developments that would define their specific character.

Chinese society, beginning from an early stage, has been characterized by its politically focused orientation, its role in the centralization of power and its control by an officially-dominated system of administration. Its culture, language included, as part of fundamental instruments subject to this general social tendency, has had to adapt its form and usage to the special nature of the Chinese social temperament.

One of the most important occurrences in Chinese political life is perhaps the unification of the country. The two major unifications in China both had something to do with the language change. The first unification took place during the period of Huangdi (黄帝, the Yellow Emperor) when he vanquished Yandi (炎帝) and other tribal leaders and settled down in the Central Land (中原) for the first time in Chinese history. The diverse local dialects were then replaced by a newly created Chinese language, in the hands of Cangjie (仓颉), based on the dialect used by the Huangdi tribe. The second unification occurred during the period of Qin Shihuang who defeated all the other warring states and established his centralized dynasty. One of his merits was to enshrine the authoritative status of *xiao-zhuan* (小篆) as an official language for all formal documents and business letters over his unified territory.

Another important social factor in the development of the Chinese language is the system of administration dominated by the monarch. If political unification laid the foundation for the evolution of Chinese culture, the centralized system also put official administration headed by the emperor, above all other vocations and in a way affected or even impeded the social progress and economic prosperity. Consequently the language, as a product and tool of social development, had to be limited in the prevailing narrow and prejudicial circumstances. These imposed restrictions on its popularity and academic study. For instance, classical Chinese served basically as the only criterion for official enrollment and appointment, constituting an impassable and insurmountable barrier for the average person, considering its special linguistic difficulties. Chinese society seemed to be controlled by a relatively small group of people who were fortunately admitted after passing the Civil Service Examination, which required a good command of the difficult classical Chinese language. Consequently the majority of the Chinese people were excluded out of the mainstream of this hierarchical society which was making a hard struggle for its survival and development. Meanwhile the language was deliberately maintained in an outmoded, erudite, intricate, puzzling and impractical position, unable to contribute much to the acquisition of practical knowledge or technologies, since it was distinct from spoken language and remote from social reality.

Rather than established by an order from above as Chinese was, English came into being in a more vigorous and natural manner as a result of the living environment and its practical requirements. In comparison with Chinese, English was much younger and was created by assimilating all the necessary elements and ingredients from a number of established languages, such as the Celtic, Latin, French and Scandinavian languages before it was ultimately formed into the Anglo-Saxon based language. English, soon after its birth, has been open to the introduction of other languages, which has occurred time and again with various foreign intrusions. Roman occupation left traces of Latin as an heritage in the British Isles. The Anglo-Saxon people took both Latin and Celtic into their Germanic dialects before they developed and established English as a mixture of several languages. Following this was the French Conquest which enriched the English vocabulary, and finally the Scandinavian intrusions leading to the embodiment of Danish, Swedish and Norwegian influences on English.

The French influence upon the vocabulary was much more direct and observable. As happened generally, the interchange was to some extent mutual. A good many English words found their way into the French spoken community in England. Nonetheless, their number was not so large as that of the French words introduced into English. English, representing a culture that was regarded as politically inferior, had more to gain from French, and there were other factors involved. There were so many French words pouring into English in those years that there was nothing comparable to it in the previous or subsequent history of the English language. In changing from French as an official language to English for daily use of the ordinary people, they transferred much of their governmental and administrative vocabulary, their ecclesiastical, legal and military terms, their familiar words of fashion, food and social life, and the vocabulary of art, learning and medicine. In the long historical development many old English words were replaced by French, such as *eam* by *uncle*, *anda* by *envy*, *oepele* by *noble*, *oepeling* by *nobleman*, *Dryhten* and *frea* by *prince*, etc.

English has also adopted quite a few words from Latin, such as *climax*, *appendix*, *epitome*, *exterior*, *delirium* and *axis*, which still keep their original Latin forms. Some of the Latin words were adapted or simply had their endings removed after their introduction, such as *conjectural* from *conjecturalis*, *consult* from *consultare*, *exclusion* from *exclusionem*, *exotic* from *exoticus*, *conspicuous* from *conspicuus*, *external* from *externus*, *brevity* from *brevitas*, etc.

The vigorous growth of English is not only ascribed to the influence from foreign invaders, but also to the religious and economic developments. For example, Christianity brought to England not just a new belief, but a new culture that was found in the use of religious terms of Latin as well as different styles of life. With this spiritual awakening, more people became skeptical of divinity and sought individual spiritual emancipation and a happy life based on physical enjoyment. The spread of the Renaissance ideas brought about the demand for religious reform and rapid growth of productivity. English then embarked on a phase of rapid expansion to meet increasing social needs. More and more scientific and technological achievements added to the power and popularity of the language as a result of the Industrial Revolution, an enduring drive initiated by the bourgeoisie who came to power after the Glorious Revolution.

5.4.4 Psychological and aesthetic effects of the two languages

It goes without saying that the development of language contributes much to both social development and psychological revelation which serve to expose the hidden side of what is presented. The psychological function, as an important part of linguistic features, commits itself to the representation of extensive internal areas. People need to handle different kinds of problems by engaging themselves with thinking processes. However, human ways of thinking are greatly affected by culture. The Chinese would pay more careful attention to the complexities of human relations, such as the influences on a person of his superiors and inferiors at his work and of his career prospect and family considerations in his private life. Psychological implications of a language are determined by one's social circumstances as well as by one's human value and aesthetic sense. These factors constitute one's psychological pressures which work through language to offer necessary messages or instructions, as witnessed in the diversity of daily life, academic work, literature or art.

The Westerner, especially the English-speaker, might choose to be more practical and ego-centric. He would not care so much about what other people think of in the respect of human relations, but care more about his own actual interests and persist in his own opinions. He would not normally hesitate to express his feelings and even ignore the voice of intervention from outside. Many Westerners are straightforward, open-minded and inclined to democracy as a way of living and thinking. Of course there are exceptions, for even the English are considered rather cold and class conscious by southern Europeans.

The Chinese language demonstrates psychological qualities coming from its hidden cultural heritage. This is revealed by their concern for human relations, book knowledge, official career, loyalty and filiality, dominance and discipline, etc. The English language, on the other hand, is noted by its concern for reason and freedom of expression, love of wealth and interest in religion and faith, science and nature, practical matters and adventure, etc. However, with the development of globalization, these differences are greatly reduced in the process of more cultural contact and communication as people have more access to the understanding and exposure of different cultures and languages.

The Chinese traditional language is therefore full of such idioms or expressions as:

- 人情大于债,头顶锅盖卖。
  (Human emotion is more important than debt. One has to sell one's last belongings to pay back his emotional debt.)
- 书中自有黄金屋,书中自有万钟粟,书中自有颜如玉。
  (One could find in books a house of gold, countless grain and charming ladies.)
- 读书做官。
  (Study for an official career.)
- 忠孝两全。
  (Loyal to the state and filial to the parents.)
- 遵法守纪。
  (Abide by both laws and working discipline.)
- 克己奉公。
  (Consider little of one's own interest and devote to the public.)

The Chinese idioms are featured with succinct form without saying they are marked by strong sense of moral principles typical of Chinese traditional culture. Either with four or six characters, they are all neat in structure and eloquent in sound. They are all linked by logic, such as cause and effect or emphasis like parallel or repetition. They are also featured with brevity and vitality of Chinese traditional culture, embodying loyalty, discipline and diligence as well as a strong desire to seek an official career.

In English there are also quite a number of set expressions and idioms indicating their cultural tendencies. Following are some examples:

- Think with the wise but talk with the vulgar. Zeal without knowledge is

- fire without light.
- Virtue and happiness are mother and daughter.
- Wise men propose and fools determine. Wise men learn by other men's mistakes, fools by their own.
- Wit once bought is worth twice taught. A hedge between keeps friendship green.
- Business is business. Cheat me in the price but not in the goods. Actions speak louder than words. Envy never enriched any man.
- He that lives well is learned enough.
- Divide and rule. Happy is the country that has no history.

One could see these English idioms or proverbs are also rich in their implications with a universally philosophical wisdom though they are a bit old-fashioned. It is easy to discern wit, fun, sense of humour and desire for pleasure and happiness, which indicates cultural difference between the West and China. Comparatively Chinese idioms care more for human relations which involve those between monarch and subjects, father and son, in addition to Confucian influence on the average Chinese. Meanwhile the Chinese idioms seem more concise and neat with respect to aesthetic form though the English and other Western idioms are more carefree and open-minded.

5.4.5 External influences

Both languages have been subject to much influence from outside. For Chinese, it was first Sanskrit and then the Western language that offered influences. For English, it was the Celtic, Latin, French and Scandinavian languages. However, the degree to which the two were influenced varied a lot.

The Chinese language, as we have discussed earlier, has kept long a closed-door social and cultural convention and practice, partly because with a long-term tradition inherited from the past, she used to indulge herself in the central status in the East, and partly because her autocratic rulers could not get rid of narrow-mindedness and self-conceitedness. Chinese history witnessed two changes of political power from the hand of the Han people to the hand of two minor nationalities, one being Mongols and the other Manchurians. In addition to the factors mentioned above, another important reason for linguistic continuity and unity was related to the barbarity of these two newly emerged ruling groups, which motivated their willingness to emulate and benefit from Chinese culture and language. It explains why they had to use the Chinese language, together with their own dialect, as the official languages to help calm down the newly conquered land and population in the benefit of their reign. Such a policy, in turn, provided powerful support to the continuation of Chinese culture and language in spite of her political frustration.

At the same time, the Chinese language benefited from foreign culture. We could at least offer two examples. One is the term *fan-qie* (反切), an example cited previously. It was supposed to originate from the influence of Sanskrit associated with Buddhism some time during or even earlier than the Southern Dynasties.① The other is *yin-biao* (音标, phonetic symbols) introduced from the Western language with the recommendation of some Western Sinologists, like Bernhard Karlgren in the early 20th century. But generally Chinese was closed to the introduction of other languages in comparison with English.

The English language, nonetheless, took a different attitude towards foreign intrusions. English certainly underwent many changes in pronunciation, vocabulary and grammar in the period of foreign occupation. One of the reasons was of course the advanced and sophisticated culture from the intruders in many cases and the strong demand for linguistic nourishment from external cultures. As well the English were basically less conservative and even open to the importation of other languages. Their national identity was built up in a long process of taking in and mixing more ingredients from other linguistic and cultural sources, like Latin, French and Scandinavian languages. The opening process was further sped up and expanded after the Renaissance with more overseas colonies established and more English-speaking people moving out of their native country as mentioned earlier. Subsequently a variety of English dialects were practised in the former British colonies like the United States, Canada, Australia, New Zealand, South Africa, India and even quite a number of other smaller countries where English has been spoken and written as a semi-indigenous or official language. Thus the English language has been greatly enriched by local languages and cultures.

In grammar, the two languages have both borrowed something from outside as additional tenets or reference for the improvement of the original rules of their own. In China we have Ma Jianzhong who helped establish Chinese grammar based on a Western model. The English have also assimilated some nourishments from outside in building up their own grammatical system, such as the inflections from Scandinavian and Germanic languages, like the *-s* of the third person singular, present indicative of verbs and the participial ending *-and*, corresponding to *-end* and *-ind* now replaced by *-ing*. However English grammar appears to be restricted in her development by her attempt to simplify the rules and get rid of all redundancies. The great changes that reduced the inflections of Old English to their modern proportions had already taken place before 1550. In the few parts of speech that retain some of their original inflections, the reader of Shakespeare or the Authorized Version Bible is conscious of minor differences of form. In the framing of sentences one may note differences of syntax and idiom that, although they attract attention, are not sufficient to interfere seriously with understanding.

---

① See *The History of Chinese Linguistics*, p. 195, Pu Zhizhen, Shulin Publishing House, Taipei, 1990.

Nevertheless, English grammar is still in a process of modification although such change is limited. For instance, the substitution of *you were* for *you was* in the singular occurred about 1820 and *it is I* is now less popular than *it is me*. What was left of the subjunctive mood in occasional use is reduced to a few exceptional cases like *if I were you*. Some tendency towards loss of inflection in the nonstandard English is one of the possible changes in the current development of English, such as *he don't* or *who do you want*.

5.4.6 Academic study

Academic study of language was initiated in China much earlier than that in Britain though perhaps the Chinese language study was quite different from the situation for Western linguistics. The Chinese language study focused more on literature or historical records rather than on spoken language, as has been the case with most modern Western linguists. The Chinese scholars started their language studies as early as in the Han Dynasty after the pioneering statement on language issued by Xun Zi during the Warring States Period. The representative figures and works of the early period included *er-ya* (《尔雅》) by an anonymous author, Yang Xiong and his *fang-yan* (《方言》, Dialects), Xu Shen and his *shuo-wen-jie-zi* (《说文解字》, Interpretation of Texts and Characters), Liu Xi and his *shi-ming* (《释名》, Explanation of Names). Their achievements marked the founding of Chinese linguistics of the ancient times. However, the Chinese ancient linguistics was different in a way from modern linguistics by focusing on philological aspects. Compared with the modern Western linguistics, the Chinese ancient language study might be diversified in the range of their material but did not seem too faraway removed from the objective of language study when it took up the use of characters and pronunciation as the target for research. The earliest linguistic study was the classic work of the ancient language, which chose to interpret the meaning of ancient literary texts by focusing on the language itself unlike the study of classic work of modern language which tends to focus on meticulous textual research by working out the unevidenced implications.

The later studies of Chinese language tended generally to proceed in two directions. One went on with the interpretation of characters and linguistic theory, such as Kong Yingda's *wu-jing-zheng-yi* (《五经正义》, Revised Interpretation of Five Classics), and Duan Yucai's *shuo-wen-jie-zi-zhu* (《说文解字注》, Annotation to Interpretation of Texts and Characters).

The other emphasized pronunciation in association with semantic interpretation, such as Gu Yewang's *yu-pian* (《玉篇》, Jade Text) and Gu Yanwu's *yin-xue-wu-shu* (《音学五书》, Five Books on Phonetics). Such grammar research was comparatively inadequate though it started as early as in the

Spring-Autumn Period. ①

One of the important results of linguistic study is the production of *fan-que* which was supposed to be created towards the end of the Eastern Han Dynasty, possibly under the influence of the language of the kingdoms in the west of China. The emergence and popularity of *fan-qie* contributed a lot to the pronunciation of Chinese characters. *Fan-qie* is said to have been produced in the light of Sanskrit of the Western Land (西域). In spite of some arguments about the origin of *fan-qie*, its use is of much practical significance to the development of Chinese phonetics and pronunciation. The books concerned with *fan-qie* and phonetics included Lu Deming's *Textual Interpretation of Classics* and Lu Fayan's *Rhyming Devices*.

For various reasons, English did not gain the social status in England that it deserved till long after the Norman Conquest when French had found its way into English as a necessary and beneficial supplement. English became a polyglot language used popularly by the majority of the English. The formal study of English was not started till well into the 16th century when the Society of Antiquaries was founded by an archbishop to hold meetings to study antiquity and history. The meetings might have spent some time discussing the improvement of the language in connection with a similar move by the French Academy concerned with the reform of French spelling.

The publication of *A Dictionary of the English Language* in 1755 by Samuel Johnson in two folio volumes was hailed as a great achievement, though a number of smaller dictionaries had been published before him. In spite of its inadequacies, like its ludicrous etymologies, prejudicial caprices and discriminatory definitions, Johnson's dictionary included a host of words with a very large coverage, much more fully than what had ever been done before, providing thousands of quotations and illustrations of the use of words.

After Johnson, more English scholars have been engaged in language studies, focusing on the practical usage or other language skills, including George Campbell with his *Philosophy of Rhetoric* and Robert Baker with his *Reflections on the English Language*. Among the works of linguistic scholarship was a coherent prescriptive tradition, namely to systematize the facts of English grammar and draw up rules by which all grammatical questions could be viewed and decided. Many of the conventions accepted up to the present day were first formulated by grammarians in the 18th century, such as the prescriptive distinction between the two verbs *lie* and *lay*, the use of *shall* and *will*, was apparently first made in the second half of the 18th century.

---

① The Chinese traditional language study used to focus on social, historical and literary aspects mixed with language rather than on linguistic features. Hence it is not exactly the modern sense of language study and has undergone radical change under the Western academic influence since the introduction of Western linguistic methodology.

The linguistic scholars at the time considered that appropriate methodologies were largely those of logic, etymology and the examples set by classical Latin and Greek. In the latter half of the 18th century, the study of language was shifted to actual usage as the beginning of the modern era of linguistic study. The representative figure of the new doctrine was Joseph Priestley, whose *Rudiments of English Grammar* insisted on the importance of usage. Despite the early achievements by the 18th-century linguists in language research, one must be aware of their limitations, which halted application of language doctrines.

The success of the British on the sea in the 19th century left England in a position of undisputed naval supremacy and gave it control over most of the world's commerce. The political and economic achievements helped lead to academic attention to the study of language. The last two centuries offered an excellent opportunity to observe the relation between a civilization and the language which is an expression of it. The most striking aspect of the English language is probably the part that science has played in bringing it to its current form. Such areas as bacteriology, biochemistry, electricity, physics, chemistry, astronomy, psychology have provided an extraordinarily large number of new words and expressions to the English vocabulary which, together with entertainment and human spiritual and material pursuits, constitute the raw material of language study. The English linguists seemed to care more for the use of language in social and psychological areas, intending to inquire into the specific applications of language in the areas relevant to human interest or values or the relationships between language and other activities.

The academic study of the two languages within the two cultures took different directions, though they may have started with similar elements. The Chinese linguists appeared to be keener on the study of the origin of characters and the explanation of the implications emerging from the form of the characters concerned. They were particularly concerned about identifying the historical factor in the structures of language and thus built up a reputation for their textual research. They did seem to care much for the grammatical rules or roles in language development. This gave rise to the shortage of a systematic grammar for the Chinese language. Also they seldom referred to the social circumstances or other practical situations in their language study.

The English scholars also had some interest in the meaning and origin of words, as in the case of compiling dictionaries, which focused on the interpretation of the meaning of common words. But as time moved on, they seemed to shift their attention to language usage and other practical areas. The study of grammar is one example and the expansion of linguistic areas is another. This tendency shows the English scholars had less concern about political uncertainties and were more keen to combine academic and practical conditions.

Questions for comprehension and discussion

1. What is characteristic of the Chinese language?
2. What is characteristic of the English language?
3. What are the major similarities and dissimilarities between Chinese and English? Give examples from your own experience.

List of proposed books for further reading

1. 王力,1958,《汉语史稿》,北京:科学出版社。
2. 濮之珍,1990,《中国语言学史》,台北:书林出版有限公司。
3. 何九盈,1995,《中国现代语言学史》,广州:广东教育出版社。
4. McArthur, Tom, *The English Language*, Cambridge: Cambridge University Press, 1998.
5. Jeremy Smith, *A Historical Study of English Function, Form and Change*, Oxford: Routledge, 1996.
6. Albert Bauth, Thomas Cable, *A History of the English Language* (the 5th edition), Upper Saddle River, NJ: Pearson Education, Inc., as Pentice Hall Inc., 2002.
7. Mark Robson, Peter Stockwell, *Language in Theory: A Resource Book for Students*, Oxford: Routledge, 2005.

Chapter 6

A Comparison of Chinese and Western Poetry

Written poetry, as one of the earliest literary forms, dates back over three thousand years in both China and the West. Different from other literary genres, particularly prose writing, poetry is traditionally characterized by its formal and musical elements like rhythm and rhyme as well as the abundant use of figures of speech. Chinese and Western poems, in spite of different cultural traditions and temperaments, find much in common in both poetic form, and the feelings and ideas they express over their long historical development. These features take root in their respective social and cultural environments in addition to the political, religious and aesthetic values which we human beings inherit from our ancestors and which provide the common ground for a comparative study.

6.1 An account of the development of Chinese and Western poetry

6.1.1 The story of Chinese poetry

In China what has survived of the earliest poems is *shi-jing* (《诗经》, The Book of Songs) supposedly collected and edited by Confucius. The book contains about three hundred poems, covering a wide range of subjects, in either narrative or lyrical form. These poems dated from the beginning of the Zhou Dynasty and continued to the end of the Zhou, including the life story of Houji (后稷), a legendary god-like figure creating crops, the heroic deeds of the ancestors, like Gong Liu and Zhou Wenwang's grandfather, and the military manoeuvres against the Shang's rulers led by the Zhou's leaders. Another kind of poetry is the record of agricultural production and farmers' lives in the Zhou society. The third kind of poetry in *shi-jing* belongs to the category of powerful and severe criticism of the exploiters of long-term forced labour or satire directed at the exploiters. In addition, there are quite a number of poems about love, marriage and family life. Finally there are poems of vivid description of patriotic feelings, those praising beauty of some ladies and those extolling courage and skill in men's hunting experience.

Following the tradition of *shi-jing*, subsequent Chinese poetry demonstrates a rich tendency towards realism in later generations, exposing the dark side of society and providing images of all aspects of social life. For instance, the extravagance of the rich and the corruption of the upper class, complaints about and hatred for exploitation and oppression by tyrants and conquerors in addition to the poems about worries, protests and nostalgic feelings of the lower class people or soldiers who were forced into long military expeditions. All of these topics could be seen in the poems from different periods, with their various styles and lengths.

Aside from a real portrayal of life during the different periods, many of the Chinese poems are well-known for their fantastic use of imagination. Starting from the ancient time, this trend has displayed the romantic spirit by focusing on creating visionary situations, beautiful fantasies, or presenting magic powers and eerie images based on legendary stories, fairy tales, religious beliefs, or simply the products of poets' own imagination.

In the long years of its development, Chinese traditional poetry has established a set of strict disciplines and rules such as the fixed form for poets to follow, as in *ya-yun* (押韵, rhyming devices), *ping-ze* (平仄, tonic measurement) and *dui-zhang* (对仗, contrastive couplet). Chinese classical poetry, apart from the basic poetic patterns, has produced another special group of poems called *ci* (词). This form is even more restricted in the choice of characters in terms of tonic variety and number of characters or length of a sentence. Although the ancient Chinese poets did make a great effort to improve the poetic form by taking nourishment from folk songs and other diverse sources of culture, Chinese classical poetry still found itself sometimes in an embarrassing and even awkward position. This is because its form could not be learned easily nor used by the ordinary writer, especially those who were not well educated. It is perhaps for this reason that Chinese classical poetry was solely limited to a small number of readers and writers. The new form of Chinese poetry eventually failed to come into being till the beginning of the 20th century at the expense of all its traditional forms, with the influence coming from Western poetry.

Chinese new poetry is totally different from the old form in its use of plain spoken language without any restriction on the number and tone of the characters. Not long after its appearance, it was recognized and accepted by more and more poets and readers and soon replaced the old form as the major vehicle for Chinese poetry. However, the dismissal of the poetic rules gave rise to some problems as well, especially how to present some suitable structural form as a substitution for what was removed, such as the traditional rhythm and rhyme. It might not be entirely unreasonable for some people to complain about what they regard as flavourless and tasteless new poems as were particularly exposed in the light of the advantages of classical Chinese poetry.

The closest successor to *shi-jing* in China is probably Qu Yuan, a patriotic poet whose work is tinted with a tragic colour due to his frustration over both his own career and the fate of his native land. Qu Yuan's contribution to the development of Chinese poetry derives from romanticism, which refers to his rich imagination based on myths and to his love of the landscape of his native country thanks to his bitter experiences.

The combination of mythological figures with legendary tales could also be witnessed in Homer's epic and in the Roman poet Virgil's *Aeneid*. Virgil's work is viewed as a succession to and even an imitation of Homer's epic for the hero is supposed to have survived the siege of Troy before becoming the founder of the Roman Empire. The striking feature of the poem is its representation of Italy as a nation and of Roman history as a continuation from the founding of the city of Rome to its later expansion. Obviously it is a work in praise of national feelings and patriotic spirit, which resembles Qu Yuan's work, such as *li-sao* (《离骚》, Worrying Experiences). *Li-sao* is basically an account of the poet's feelings, life experience, ideals and complaints, rather than a story. But its strong sense of patriotic emotion and self-sacrificing spirit in combination with wild imagination and the use of mystical images, served as a powerful inspiration to the Chinese people throughout the long process of historical development.

The second stage in China saw the climax of poetic development in two respects. The first was the composition of folk songs and folklore, which were found among the group of folk songs collected by the Musical Institute of the Han Dynasty (汉乐府). The best example is *kong-que-dong-nan-fei* (《孔雀东南飞》, The Southeast-Bound Peacock), a long poem of love describing the persecution of a young lady by her mother-in-law, a symbol of feudalistic morality on one hand and devoted love on the other.

The second direction is taken by some talented poets whose works have contributed a great deal to the development of both the realistic and romantic traditions. They include the Caos (father and sons), Tao Yuanming, Wang Wei, Li Bai, Du Fu, Bai Juyi, Wang Anshi, Su Shi, Lu You, Xin Qiji, Li Qingzhao, etc. Most of them tried to indicate their concerns for state affairs and their love of beautiful landscapes. Their poems keenly evoked a variety of feelings and stimulated the reader's mind by offering both sensuous and rational perceptions or impulses. At the same time, poetic forms like *wu-yan* (五言), *wu-lü* (五律), *qi-yan* (七言) and *qi-lü* (七律), were improved and perfected by virtue of a series of literary designs and inventions, such as more accurate, strict and sonorous rhythms and a more precise choice of words.

The final stage of Chinese poetic development was also marked by plain language. It started in the early 20th century. The pioneering modern poets opened a new era by giving up the formal written classical language and picking up instead a plain vernacular language in poems, stories and other literary forms.

Among the best-known poets are Guo Moruo, Xu Zhimo and Dai Wangshu. Some famous scholars and writers like Lu Xun, Hu Shi and Zhou Zuoren also got involved in the new poetry movement. They tried in their writing to get rid of the restrictions of traditional rules, like the strict rhyme, rhythm and formal diction, and advocated a kind of free verse style to pursue a new and more relaxed mode of poetry. Some of them were also enlightened by new techniques borrowed from Western modernist poetry, especially from the Symbolists.

6.1.2 The story of Western poetry

Western poetry originated probably from folk tales and ballads that culminated in the creation of such epics as *The Odyssey* and *The Iliad* by the blind Greek poet Homer. Unlike China's short poems in *shi-jing*, these two epics are long narrative verses about the Greek military conquest of Troy. One is about the last ten days' siege and final seizure of the city while the other deals with the adventuring experience of the hero Odysseus, king of Ithaca, on his way home from the conquest and the eventual arrival on his home island and reunion with his wife Penelope and son Talemachus. The poetic achievement made by Homer and other Greek poets was followed by Roman poets represented by Virgil, Horace and Ovid. Virgil's *Aeneid* was hailed as the great masterpiece glorifying a legend of the Roman ancestor who showed the hero's dauntless spirit after departing from Troy in a style of Homeric epic.

Their followers could hardly match them in this respect with any works of substantial significance. More popular poetic fashion during the later ancient and earlier medieval period was the heroic epic which followed the tradition initiated by Homer's epic. Among the best-known epics are the Germanic *The Song of Hild-Brandt*, the Anglo-Saxon *Beowulf*, *Edda* from Iceland, the French *The Song of Rolland* and the Celtic *Tristan and Isolde*. These epic poems are usually very long, more than 3,000 lines or so, taking a rhythm of hexameters in praise of the heroic deeds and adventures of the nobility.

The Middle Ages did not produce any reputable poet or poetic work until the emergence of Dante and his masterpiece *The Divine Comedy*. The poem, composed of three parts, centring respectively around Infernal, Purgatory and Paradise, handles the sophisticated theme of human destiny based on his own life experience, particularly his political career and religious faith against a corrupted and evil world.

Western poetry came to its highpoint after the Renaissance. The poetic achievements were represented first by John Milton's *Paradise Lost* and *Paradise Regained* and then by the Elizabethans and the 17th-century Metaphysical poets. After a period of classicism in the 18th century we had 19th-century Romanticism which included poets like Wordsworth, Coleridge, Byron, Shelley and Keats. If we go back to Milton's poems, we would find them in line of succession from classical poetry, which he utilized in response to complaints about and criticism of the political conditions in his day. He tried to advance these objections by embodying his views in Biblical tales. The much later Romantic poetry, how-ever, tended to be more individualized and more concerned about appreciating nature. In spite of holding a range of differing views on social affairs, the focus of Romantic writing was more towards an exposure of the poet's inner world and pouring out of emotions. The inclination towards aesthetic pursuit kept them mostly well away from close contact with social conditions. Nonetheless, some of them, like Byron and Shelley, were still socially-oriented even at the end of their brief lives. But the majority of the Romantic poets were more passive, introverted and tended to be more emotionally bound. Perhaps we could not say they were anti-social, but certainly they were frequently pessimistic about human society. It is in this sense that we might say these Romantics paved the way for the birth of modernist poetry.

Modernist poetry was initiated by the French Symbolists whose early signs were indicated in Baudelaire's *Les Fleurs du Mal* (1857) which led to the appearance and development of symbolist and imagist poetry about 30 years afterwards, represented in the work of such famous poets as Mallarme, Valery, Rimbaud, W. B. Yeats, Ezra Pound and T. S. Eliot.

It is modernist poetry of course that led both China and the West to come together and shift their attention from their external and physical concerns to the representation of the inner mind of the modern man. Generally, China has received more modernist influences obtained from Western poetry in terms of free style with less restrictions than vice versa. These influences were recorded in the early new poems during the May 4th Movement. The dissatisfaction with social darkness and the use of the weird imagery, the bursts of irrational emotion — all were found in the poems characteristic of symbolism written by Guo Moruo and his fellow poets from the Creation Society (创造社) as well as those of such famous poets as Dai Wangshu, Aiqing, Bian Zhiling, Feng Zhi, etc. At the same time, some Western poets, like Ezra Pound and Amy Lowell and a few imagist poets, also tried to benefit in some ways from Chinese ideology and culture by adopting some Chinese characters in their works or translating and transcribing a lot of Chinese classical poems into English in the early years of the 20th century.

6.2 Central concerns in Chinese and Western poetry

All significant poems are almost without exception noted for their embodiment of serious concerns about human life and political or social issues of the day. Poetic form in a way contributes to the reader's appreciation of poetry, but it is not always a major factor, since, after all, he has to be fed with ideas rather than just pleased by visual imagery or sonorous enjoyment. One could find lots of interesting things in the tastes of readers, which could help explain both the similarities and dissimilarities between China and the West. Perhaps it is worth noting that Chinese and Western poetry both used more or less aesthetic form or formal features of poetry to distinguish it from prose (or ordinary speech) and to make it simple to memorize, in the same way as musical tune helps us to memorize songs. In spite of the formal aspect, however, poetry on both sides focuses on its concerns about political, social and emotional representations.

6.2.1　Political issues

　　Chinese poetry is characterized by political aspiration and ambition. No matter whether they were politicians or scholars, classical poets were mostly concerned with state affairs and constantly displayed a spirit of devotion to political or religious faith and their mother country in their pursuit of ideals. Examples could be found in the works of such figures as Qu Yuan, the Caos, Du Fu, Li Bai, Bai Juyi, Wang Wei and many others. Such a trend was summed up by Bai Juyi in his famous statement: "Essays are composed for current affairs while poems are written for specific matters."（文章合为时而著,歌诗合为事而作。）China has a tradition that poems should serve to expose social reality and help to express personal feelings. A large number of poems indicate individual political frustrations, longing for the opportunities to carry out political ambitions: "I've a great ambition but feel merely wronged, I'm much talented but have to tolerate a low position."（徒志远而心屈,遂才高而位下。）by Wang Bo; "I'll help the emperor to hold sway/As that of Yao and Shun, a recovery /of purified social custom."（致君尧舜上,再使风俗淳。）and "Worry for the average in times of poverty, / With sighs stirring me up warmly."（穷年忧黎元,叹息肠内热。）by Du Fu.

　　The link to political and social reality also has its manifestations in Western poetry. For instance, Byron expresses his strong desire for the liberation of Greece: "And musing there an hour alone, / I dreamed that Greece might still be free; / For standing on the Persians' grave, / I could not deem myself a slave." Byron's contemporary, Shelley, also conveys his emotional care for his political ideal: "Ashes and sparks, my words among mankind! / Be through my lips to unawakened earth / The trumpet of a prophecy! O, Wind, / If Winter comes, can Spring be far behind?"

　　It is not difficult to see the high priority of concern for political issues on the part of the Chinese. Beginning perhaps from the day the Chinese child (usually from a wealthy family) was assigned to study under a certain scholar, he knew very well that the best prospect for him was to seek an official career. If such a situation was not forthcoming for all, doubtless it worked for the majority.

Therefore political consciousness was deeply rooted in the mind of all those scholars, suggesting that they had to develop in that direction or they would be taken as failures. No wonder Du Fu and his fellow poets devoted so much space to deal with political affairs. Comparatively speaking, the Western scholars seemed to have more career choices. For instance, many of them might choose to be priests, another attractive career in those days since the church was no less inferior than other official positions either in terms of social status or in terms of income. That is perhaps the reason why Western poetry does not have too much emphasis on political aspect though a few exceptions, like Milton, Byron and Shelley, could be excessively enthusiastic about political affairs.

6.2.2 Social concerns

Exposing social darkness and expressing sympathy for the weak and wretched are often seen in many poems, both in China and the West.

Chinese poetry has a tradition to show social darkness, which was shaped in the early stage. Many poets were involved in such a tradition. Among them are Du Fu and Bai Juyi who are famous for exposing the cruelty and violence of the ruling class. Their poems, like *san-li* (《三吏》, The Three Officials), *san-bie* (《三别》, Three Departures), *mai-tan-weng* (《卖炭翁》, The Old Charcoal-Seller) and *xin-feng-zhe-bi-weng* (《新丰折臂翁》, The Broken-Armed Man from Xinfeng), portray the terrible experiences of the ordinary people in those days of warring turmoil. In the West, similar descriptions appear in the writings of many poets. Dante's revelation and repudiation of church corruption in *The Divine Comedy*, Milton's satirical remarks and rejection of the theological authority in *Paradise Lost*, and T. S. Eliot's portrayal of spiritual barrenness in *The Waste Land*, are all typical examples of longer poems either in structure or story development.

Such a tendency is of course not confined to a few distinguished poets as mentioned above. For instance, one could locate the expressions of strong dissatisfaction with the ruling class by the poor serfs or tenants in *shi-jing*, the earliest collection of poems in ancient China. Such poems as *fa-tan* (《伐檀》, Lumbering) and *shuo-shu* (《硕鼠》, Big Rat) are all typical of satirizing and critiquing the exploiters and oppressors. *Fa-tan* says: "You did not sow nor barrow and then, / why should you obtain so much?" *Shuo-shu* says: "You big rat, do not feed on my corn! / You big rat, do not feed on my wheat! / You big rat, do not feed on my wheat-shoots!" Obviously big rat here refers to the merciless landlord and ruling class people. The value of these two poems consists in the assertion of the right of the lower class people, which is of great significance for social progress. Later historical developments of the material and intellectual conditions appear to be tortuous in seeking the way to an improved future.

Chinese poems, especially the scholarly poems, compared with their

Western counterparts, appear to manifest more care for social and political issues. This is perhaps because the Chinese upper class and the rulers seemed less concerned with the well-beings of their subjects and the ordinary people which consequently heightened the significance of social issues and political tension. But of course it does not mean the Westerners did not have such problems. As a matter of fact, we could time and again detect similar oppositional signs within their works. Maybe Chinese poets and men of letters were more socially-oriented and found their observations or experiences in their poetic expressions.

Before the Roman Empire was eventually established in Europe, there had been a period of chaos and uncertainty which gave rise to social and intellectual disorder as to what was to be done for the poets as well as for the ordinary people. There had been no constitutional safeguards in the republic, under Sulla, Pompey, the triumvirs, or even Julius Caesar. Augustus improved police service which probably made lower-class Romans at least feel safer under him.

Emphasizing conservatism by precept and his own example, Augustus encouraged the simpler virtues of a less sophisticated age, and his success made this sedate but rather static outlook fashionable. People accepted the routine of his continuing rule, at the cost, however, of some loss of intellectual energy and moral fervour. People's imaginations still fostered rich visions of Roman victory which in turn helped evoke a national spirit of heroism or patriotism and build up a more rational atmosphere. This helped to produce Virgil's grand poem of historical narrative and acclaim for Roman heroism as well as generating the light-hearted observations by Ovid and other poets whose work reflected on varieties of social life at the time.

In spite of certain similarities between the histories of China and the West, the different cultures and social circumstances contributed to diversities in the modes of expressions and even attitudes towards the supreme ruler.

6.2.3 Personal concerns

When one says that many Chinese classical poems are politically and socially oriented, we do not mean that they do not express any other concerns. Personal concerns always occur as major themes for every poet. Such themes as love, private affairs or business interests have preoccupied time and again many poets who produced their reflections, observations and judgments.

Love poems have been especially popular with both Chinese and Western poets. One of the ancient Chinese poets famous for choosing love as a subject is perhaps Li Shangyin, best known for the so-called untitled poems. Here is one of them: "You offered an empty promise for coming / and made no appearance after your departure, / Though it struck five at the moon slanting tower. / A dream for the long separation was hard / to wake by crying while a letter remained yet / to be dried up when hastily written."(来是空言去绝踪,月斜

楼上五更钟。梦为远别啼难唤,书被催成墨未浓。)

Quite a lot of poets have expressed the feelings of love. Li Bai's *chang-gan-xing* (《长干行》, Changgan Tune) is a famous love poem with a pretended voice of a young lady: "With my forehead just covered / with hair, I broke a flower twig for a game. / At the gate. You came riding a bamboo horse / running round the bed / and playing the green plum."(妾发初覆额,折花门前剧。郎骑竹马来,绕床弄青梅。)

The Westerners showed the same kind, if not exactly the same amount of interest in love poetry. Blake, Wordsworth, Byron, Keats, Browning and Yeats, all have left a large number of poems of this kind. Here is one by W. B. Yeats called *Words*:

'My darling cannot understand
What I have done or what would do
In this blind bitter land.'

And I grew weary of the sun
Until my thoughts cleared up again,
Remembering that the best I have done not goe
Was done to make it plain

That every year I have cried, 'At length
My darling understands it all,
Because I have come into my strength,
And words obey my call';

That had she done so who can say
What would have shaken from the sieve?
I might have thrown poor words away
And been content to live.①

Yeats' poem is both strongly emotional and a bit despondent, based on a well-chosen scene of spiritual depression, which evokes the poet's imagination on how he could expect his lover's understanding. Compared with the plain and direct wording of Yeats' poem, the Scottish poet Robert Burns' *A Red Red Rose* is more enthusiastic and open-minded in terms of the way to show loving feelings:

O, my luve's like a red, red rose
   That's newly sprung in June.
O, my luve's like the melodie,

---

① See *W. B. Yeats Selected Poetry*, Jeffares, A. Norman (ed.), Macmillan and Company Limited, 1962.

That's sweetly played in tune.

So fair art thou, my bonnie lass,
    So deep in luve am I:
And I will luve thee still, my dear,
Till the seas gang dry.

Till a' the seas gang dry, my dear,
    And the rocks melt wi' the sun:
And I will luve thee still, my dear,
While the sands o' life shall run.

And fare thee weel, my only luve,
And fare thee weel awhile!
And I will come again, my luve,
Tho' it were ten thousand mile![1]

    These poems all handle the subject of love, but obviously different in their focuses. The two Chinese poems seem more relevant to social life and cultural tradition of the past. The poets choose to offer more specific descriptions of love scenes, such as the time and place for appointment or happy memories of funny games expressing innocent love in childhood. One of them works indirectly in the viewpoint of an observer and the other directly plays the role of a lady preoccupied with nostalgic feeling. The Western love poems use similar methods to handle the topic. The first indicates a lover's unhappy mood due to his lady's being unable to understand him. It could be drawn from the poet's real experience and feeling and hence appear touching. It is perhaps similar to the first Chinese poem that both share a sense of despondence provoked by a lack of understanding. But obviously the Chinese poem is more than just depressed, but imbued with frustration and complaints with such words as "empty promise for coming and made no appearance after your departure". The pretended tone as a lady could arouse much imagination about the identity of the narrator: a wife, a lover or a prostitute. Yeats' poem also contains imagination as a device to seek for the lover's understanding which is more directly conveyed.

    The second pair is targeted with love itself. The Chinese poem handles the innocence and purity of budding love in childhood. The vivid images such as "ride a bamboo horse" and "play the green plum" are properly selected to adapt to nostalgic meditation over one's adolescent age so that they are established into part of Chinese idioms to represent innocent love before they move into adulthood. Robert Burns' poem is famous for taking red rose as the symbol of love which has summed up and opened up a new route for expressing love which

---

[1] See *The Progress of Poetry*, Horne, Colin, O'Briene, Maurice (ed.), Heinemann, Melbourne, 1969.

is also regarded pure and priceless. Thus the images like green plum and bamboo horse from Chinese poem and red rose from Scottish poem are endowed with permanent significance symbolizing enduring love which goes beyond poem boundary. All these poems are emotionally provoked as if engaged in a dialogue. Despite the different background, one could find easily the use of understatement and strong desire of love typical of their own culture. Attractive, provocative and meditative, these poems strike a powerful chord in the reader by their specific technical means. The result is that the reader's spiritual responses and rewards are drawn from these love poems.

6.3 Aesthetic sense in poetic production

One of the obvious gains expected in reading and understanding poems is the poet's desire to approach or evoke the aesthetic sense. Human beings share so much in their aesthetic perceptions, such as the sense of beauty, and the feelings in response to similar observations or ideas or events, no matter what cultural background one comes from. Let us try to focus on some aspects to gain more specific awareness of these aesthetic senses.

6.3.1 Emotional touches on various occasions

One of the major evidences indicating aesthetic perception certainly has much to do with human emotion released with the company of natural scene. The Chinese poets, like Li Bai, Su Shi, Li He and Dai Wangshu, are all famous for their emotional richness on different occasions and subtle reflections on various events, personal experiences and lyrical perceptions about nature. Following are some examples:

1) Li Bai's love of landscape, like his lifestyle as a travelling knight or swagman, is conveyed as: "I fear no distant travel searching / angels amidst the five top mounts / for I enjoy the visit to / the famous ranges all my life."(五岳寻仙不辞远,一生好入名山游。)
2) Li He's preference for absurdity or the sickly or deathly beauty is expressed in his wild imagination: "Distant China looks like nine points of smoke / while a torrent of sea water pours from a cup."(遥望齐州九点烟,一泓海水杯中泻。)
3) Su Shi demonstrates his nostalgic feelings and exclamations over bygone days and the tortuous nature of human life, such as: "When is the bright moon coming out? I ask the sky, holding a cup of wine."(明月几时有,把酒问青天。);"The great river runs eastward, / heroes passing by waves / of thousands of years."(大江东去,浪淘尽,千古风流人物。)

4) Wang Wei manifests his peace of mind in his Buddhist and metaphysical reflection on landscape: "A river flows beyond the sky and earth / with a query of the existence of the scenic mountains."（江流天地外,山色有无中。）; "The bright moon lights up pine woods, cobbles overflowing with crystal fountain."（明月松间照,清泉石上流。）

5) Dai Wangshu's desolation and bewilderment are perceived in his *yu-xiang* (《雨巷》, Rainy Lane): "Holding an oil-paper umbrella, I wander / Lonely in a lengthy, lengthy and quiet rainy / Lane. Hopefully I could meet a lilac-like girl / With a worried and complaining look."（撑着油纸伞,独自/彷徨在悠长,悠长/又寂寞的雨巷,/我希望逢着/一个丁香一样地/结着愁怨的姑娘。①)

Westerner's emotional exuberance is mostly reflected in some poems of the Romantic period, like those of Byron and Wordsworth. Romantic poets also had certain political enthusiasm yet sometimes had to pay highly, even at a price of their lives, as in the case of Byron. But generally they would mostly employ reason to control their political fervour and chose a more peaceful way of living and eventually adopted a rational view of the world. This is the case with Wordsworth, who retreated from his passion for the French Revolution to the world of nature. He abandoned liberalism to concentrate on a meditation on human life and nature with their harmony and beauty. One of his representative poems is *The Prelude*. His shorter poems also indicate similar meditations, as in *I Wandered Lonely as a Cloud*: "I wandered lonely as a cloud / That floats on high o'er vales and hills, / When all at once I saw a crowd, / A host, of golden daffodils; / … / Continuous as the stars that shine / And twinkle on the milky way."

6.3.2 Awareness of natural charm

Another poetic subject that attracts the attention of both Chinese and Western poets is that of nature. Chinese nature poems started as early as the days of the birth of poetry itself with subjects taken from the land, farming and crops. However the special kind exclusively describing nature did not come on the scene till perhaps Qu Yuan and even later times when more landscapes and natural objects became the poetic fashion. Qu Yuan employed many images of nature in his poems, such as birds, flowers, mountains and rivers to express his care for the fate of his country and different moods of joy, anger, suffering and frustration. But the poems containing natural objects as their central concerns arrived perhaps only in the Tang Dynasty. Li Bai and Wang Wei are both famous for their narrative and lyrical account of natural objects. Li Bai's *wang-tian-men-shan* (《望天门山》, A View of Mount Tianmen), *guan-shan-yue* (《关山月》, The Moon at Guanshan) and *tian-mu-shan-meng-bie* (《天目山梦别》, A Farewell to the

---

① 详见《戴望舒诗集》,四川人民出版社,1981。

Dream Journey to Mount Tianmu). Wang Wei's poems are more delicate in conveying his personal observations and perceptions of natural objects. His poetry of landscape is both an admiration of beautiful scenery and a display of his aesthetic sense of nature. Most of his nature poems are quite short, yet with much undertone, such as his *shan-ju-qiu-ming* (《山居秋暝》, Mountain Living at an Autumn Dusk), *gui-song-shan-zuo* (《归嵩山作》, Writing after a Return Journey to Mount Song), *zhong-nan-shan* (《终南山》, Mount Zhongnan), *han-jiang-lin-tiao* (《汉江临眺》, An Overview at Hanjiang River), etc. Following lines are taken from his *guo-xiang-ji-si* (《过香积寺》, Passing Xiangji Monastery): "No path for entry cuts through ancient forest for humans, but where does the bell ring in the depth of mountains? Fountain bubbles are heard out of steep stones when green pines saturated coldly in the sunshine."(古木无人径,深山何处钟。泉水咽危石,日色冷青松。[1])

  Nature poetry in the West also has a long history and probably culminated initially at the time of Romanticism. Over the centuries many of the poems in this category describe rivers, mountains, trees, plants, the sky, the wind, night and day, the seasons, animals and the ocean. However the earlier poetry can give no clear idea of the peculiarly 19th-century ways of handling nature. In the past two centuries or so, among the Western nations the most striking social change has been the movement of people away from the country to the city as industrialization increased and drew the population more and more into the urban vortex. It is therefore understandable that much popular nature poetry has associated the country, the village, and childhood with nostalgia for early youth. Along with feelings about nature and early youth in the poems of the Romantic period is a further conception of external nature as an environment in close, deep and harmonious affinity with man. Without such a conception, much of the 19th-century fine poetry could not have been written. The variety of nature poems suggests the completeness of this relationship between man and nature and certainly no phase or feature of the outer natural world dealt with in the poetry is without its appropriate counterpart in the inner world of human personality. Nature, then, can be all things to all men. To the revolutionary Shelley, the rough wind wails, like the poet himself, for the world's wrongs. For Keats, beset by longing and heartache, the happiness of the nightingale's song intensifies an unbearable consciousness of unattainable pleasures. For Tennyson, the transient glow-worms of the graveyard yew-tree correspond to the transience of his own relief from sorrow. He allows dawn to remain dawn, but his human protagonist describes how he "... felt my blood / Glow with the glow that slowly crimsoned all / Thy presence and thy portals, while I lay, / Mouth,

---

[1] See *Companion to the Poems of the Tang Dynasty*, p. 53, Xiao Difei et al (ed.), Shanghai Dictionary Press, 1983.

forehead, eyelids growing dewy-warm / with kisses balmier than half-opening buds / of April, and could hear the lips that kissed / Whispering I knew not what of wild and sweet ... ".

Many similarities between Chinese and Western poets are evident in their love of nature and employment of images taken from nature. Such a harmonious relationship has never been so intimate between man and nature as appears in the poems mentioned above. However, a closer examination of the poems could help us discern the subtle difference in the valuing of nature and the way to treat nature. The Westerner's traditional view of nature seems more focused on a rationalist tendency as indicated in the objective observation and description of natural scenery though some Romantics would be inclined to nature worship and emotional colouring, such as those nature poems by Coleridge and Keats. The Chinese poets are more often than not lost in a kind of emotional bewilderment related to their official career or other secular or ideological considerations, when writing about natural observations or meditations, which would reduce greatly rationalist and objective quality in their work. The typical examples include the poems by Li Bai, Du Fu, Wang Wei and Su Shi. Apparently these poems picked natural objects as a foil or symbol to their different moods, especially those of political frustration, emotional displeasure, spiritual loss or intellectual bewilderment. In contrast, the Westerner's treatment of natural objects seems more integral, introverted and less politically-minded. It is demonstrated in the Romantic's handling of natural things, such as Keats' *Ode to a Nightingale* and *To Autumn*, Shelley's *Ode to the West Wind* and *To a Skylark*, Wordsworth's *I Wandered Lonely as a Cloud*, etc. No matter what they wrote about, they all tried to devote themselves to an intense integration and harmony with nature's beauty, purity and nobility, such as Tennyson's *Choric Song*. It is more than a matter of praise or admiration. Nowadays this tradition draws on and is even expanded by some modernist or post-modernist poets like Ted Hughes who depicts eagles, leopards, foxes and other natural objects as part of a single universe in which man lives.

6.3.3 Philosophical meditations

Many poems in this category convey philosophical or metaphysical ideas. For the poets, nature or whatever organic links humans are shown in their poems only serves as symbols or metaphors. The true intention of the poet seems to go beyond material level into a transcendental level higher than the secular world of everyday life. For the sake of convenience, we may just call them philosophical poems. Let us first look at Chinese poems of this kind with Tao Yuanming as the first example. Here are some lines from his famous *gui-yuan-tian-ju* (《归园田居五首(其一)》, Return to Farming Life (1)):

A cage bird misses its old forest,

> A pond fish thinks of its original water.
> I dig up wild land in the south
> after going back to keep to my old belief.
> …
> Dim is the distant village
> and tender the smoke from the chimney.
> Barking comes from the bottom of the lane
> while a cock crows from the top of the mulberry.
> No dust is visible in the yard while
> leisure is confirmed by the open door.
> I stayed long in the cage and
> regained my entry into nature.
>
> (羁鸟恋旧林,池鱼思故渊。开荒南野际,守拙归园田。……暧暧远人村,依依墟里烟。狗吠深巷中,鸡鸣桑树巅。户庭无尘埃,虚室有余闲。久在樊笼里,复得返自然。[①])

Tao's poem expresses a strong sense of self-satisfaction with and spiritual enjoyment of nature, which culminates in the last line "regained my entry into nature", to suggest the integration of man and nature, a philosophical assertion by Chinese Taoism. Tao is not the only Chinese poet whose work shows philosophical meditations. Fan Zhongyan, a well-known politician and essayist of the Northern Song Dynasty, has also left a few poetic lines with philosophical implications. His poem is a reflection on history after reading a historical book. "I laugh at Cao Cao, Sun Quan and Liu Bei / For their making every effort in vain only to have seized one third of the territory, / … No one could survive longer than a hundred, / Ignorant while young and worn out while old, / Only those in between care for their empty fame. / Top rank and large fortune, ask the white-haired, how to get rid of."(昨夜因看蜀志,笑曹操孙权刘备。用尽机关,徒劳心力,只得三分天地。……人世都无百岁。少痴呆、老成悴。只有中间,些子少年,忍把浮名牵系。一品与千金,问白发,如何回避?[②])Wang Anshi, also a distinguished politician during the Song Dynasty, produced his meditation on the same topic: "Yi and Lü, the two weakening veterans, well experienced through historical changes / had fished or ploughed. / The heroes would have aged obscurely if not the opportunity. / But they met by chance with Tang and Wu, the two kings, / and easily helped them rise up / as if lost in laughing and talking. / Who would compete for merits with them until a thousand years later?"(伊吕两衰翁,历遍穷通。一为钓叟一耕佣。若使当时身不遇,老了英雄。汤武偶相遇,风虎云龙。兴王只在笑谈中。直至如今千

---

① See *Dictionary of Annotated Chinese Ancient Poetry*, Ho Xinhui (ed.), Chinese Woman Press, 1988.
② See *Dictionary of Annotated Ci-Poems of the Tang and Song Dynasties*, Zhou Rucan et al, Shanghai Dictionary Press, 1988.

载后,谁与争功!①)

The two politicians might not strike the same chord in political aspirations, but certainly they both presented some universally accepted viewpoints. Worthwhile or not, political careers would provide different tastes and choices for Chinese politicians. But this is not the case with most of the Western thinkers or poets. Alexander Pope once wrote: "Nature and Nature's Laws lay hid in Night. / God said, Let Newton be! And All was Light. / Oh be thou blest with all that Heav'n can send, / Long Health, long Youth, long Pleasure, and a Friend: / Not with those Toys the female world admire, / Riches that vex, and Vanities that tire. / With added years if Life bring nothing new, / But like a Sieve let ev'ry blessing thro',..." Pope refers to some common occurrences in daily writings, involving skill and judgment. His wit is his ability to see beyond the error itself the danger of misleading, which is generalized into a philosophical statement and produces a meaningful idea.

Another English poet, Thomas Nashe, is famous for his awareness of some simple yet universally confirmed truths, included in the advice he offered. "Rich men, trust not in wealth, / Gold cannot buy you health, / Phisick himself must fade. / ...Beauty is but a flowre, / Which wrinckles will devoure / Brightness falls from the ayre, / Queenes have died yong, and faire, / Dust hath closed *Helen's* eye."②

Both Pope and Nashe attempted to seek something eternal and more valuable than those physical and visible, a spiritual or moral value that could be kept. Newton's Nature's Laws or Nashe's advice on fortune and beauty certainly go against the conventional ideas at the time when they wrote these poems. Whatever topic they handled, such poets certainly grasped something essential as occurred also to Chinese poets when they made a comment on politics. The point is, they chose different issues as their themes and subject matter because they had to write about what they were familiar with and wanted to discuss as determined by their given social or cultural circumstances.

Generally the Chinese poets seem more politically-oriented and socially-minded, less metaphysical and somewhat introverted while the Westerners are more individualistic, independent and care less for political affairs, sometimes more metaphysical.

6.3.4 Imagination

Poets are naturally imaginative and like to compose their poems to achieve a good aesthetic dimension by thinking far and wide and making close associations

---

① See *Dictionary of Annotated Ci-Poems of the Tang and Song Dynasties*, Zhou Rucan et al, Shanghai Dictionary Press, 1988.
② For the poems of Pope and Nashe, see *The Penguin Book of English Verse*, p. 37 and p. 203, John Hayward (ed.), Penguin Books Ltd, 1956.

with legends and myths. This tendency seems to apply to both Chinese and Western poets.

Among the ancient Chinese classical poets are a number of figures well known for their colourful imagination. Qu Yuan, Li Bai and perhaps Su Shi are the most influential. Let us take some examples from Li Bai and Su Shi. Here is Li Bai's description of Yang Yuhuang, a concubine of the Emperor Tang Xuanzong: "One thinks of clothing at the sight of cloud and misses a charming lady at the sight of flowers, / The spring breeze gently touches the rails where dew thickens on flowers. / If not at the top of Mount of Jades, / It could be at the moon-lit fairyland that we meet."(云想衣裳花想容,春风拂槛露华浓。若非群玉山头见,会向瑶台月下逢。①) The deft mix of the beauty, flower and the emperor is marvellously realized. But the poet's imagination has to journey still further on when the myth about The Mother Queen Wang Mu and fairyland is used as a contrast to bring about the climatic delicate depiction of the concubine's charm.

Li Bai's imaginative picture is that of a human figure while Su Shi's is of an ode on nature. The latter's *shui-diao-ge-tou* (《水调歌头》②) is an imaginative account of the poet's nostalgic feelings on the evening of the Mid-Autumn Festival, a traditional occasion for Chinese families to get together for a reunion. "When to have the bright moon? I ask the blue sky, / without knowing which year should this night belong to in the heaven. / I want to go back by wind, but fears being unable / to tolerate coldness at a height / where magnificent buildings are located. / Rising to dance singly with my shadow / I prefer to live in the human world."(明月几时有?把酒问青天。不知天上宫阙,今夕是何年。我欲乘风归去,又恐琼楼玉宇,高处不胜寒。起舞弄清影,何似在人间!③) The poem is a natural and imaginative mixture of human life and the widespread legend about the heavenly world around the moon. Based on the myths, the poet brings into full play his imaginative power and builds up a marvellous blend of human experience and supernatural existence to beautifully picture a vision of the imaginary world.

Comparatively speaking, Keats' imagination in *Ode to a Nightingale* is just as well demonstrated in the lines such as "Though the dull brain perplexes and retards; / Already with thee! Tender is the night, / And haply the Queen-Moon is on her throne, / Cluster'd around by all her starry Fays; / But here there is no light, / Save what from heaven is with the breezes blown / Through verdurous

---

① For Li Bai's poem and the details of Yang Yuhuan, please refer to *Companion to the Poems of the Tang Dynasty*, Xiao Difei et al (ed.), Shanghai Dictionary Press, 1983.

② A tune of classical *ci* in ancient Chinese poetry, which is used for the singing of *ci* in its circulation as cultural amusement among the ordinary people.

③ See *Dictionary of Annotated Ci-Poems of the Tang and Song Dynasties*, Zhou Rucan et al, Shanghai Dictionary Press, 1988.

glooms and winding mossy ways. " The pure description of a natural scene is beautifully combined with the myth of the moon and builds up a noble picture of the poet, flowers and the moon. It almost has the same effect as the image of Su Shi's moon. But Su's moon seems more human since he shows his concern for every Chinese family, while Keats' moon sits there like a majestic ruler for the ordinary to worship. However, both the poems show vigorous power by relying on the images drawn from their distinctive traditions and adapting them to a circumstance they hope for as an ideal to evoke and provoke more spiritual inspirations.

6.3.5 Cultural taste

The use of symbols to create images in poetry over its long development has contributed much to the variety and enrichment of literary language in both cultures. The poems are marked by a series of distinct features and have gradually evolved the distinguished styles which now constitute part of national identities and help enhance their aesthetic awareness on both sides.

Chinese poetry is unique in the sense that it is essentially written in ideographical form and could give lots of associations. Therefore, Chinese poetry is usually concise and neat with richer implications from a comparatively more limited number of characters but indicates through its visual medium the significant advantages over Western poetry. Besides, the visual perception elicited by the Chinese characters could offer some more aesthetic pleasure than that by Western languages. This is the reason why some Western poets, such as Ezra Pound, incorporate in their poems some Chinese characters to build up an extra aesthetic sense. At the same time, the non-phonetic pronunciation and spelling of these words give rise to more difficulties for the ordinary people and have limited the number of learners of Chinese by the people outside China over a long period. This has served as a major barrier to social and cultural development of China and its influence on the West.

But these diversities are just surface observations. Diversities that are more profound have to be perceived through a series of investigations of cultural and literary assertions. We have chosen a number of issues for more detailed analyses.

Most Chinese poets seem to focus on a low-spirited mood, as demonstrated in poems of separation, frustration and suffering. Many of these feelings are passed on through subtle and indirect expressions. Yue Fei, a patriotic general during the Southern Song Dynasty, wrote about his depression when unable to carry out his strong aspiration to take back the lost territory: "Crickets kept murmuring last night and broke me awake from a dream, / in which I had travelled a thousand miles. / Late into the night, I rose and walked lonely round the steps. / It was quiet, a bright moon hanging beyond the curtains. / ... / I intended to express my mind at a musical instrument, / but few bosom friends are around who could catch it after breaking a string. "（昨夜寒蛩不住鸣，惊回千里梦，已三更。起

来独自绕阶行,人悄悄,帘外月胧明。……欲将心事付瑶琴,知音少,弦断有谁听?①) The sad and solitary tone is easy to detect from the environment associated with the night, the moon and silence as well as the poet's lonely monologue. If this piece is politically inclined and motivated, the following one by Xin Qiji, a famous poet a bit later than Yue Fei, is more about his aging life: "I am declining terribly, / worried about the passing life, / in which few friends have survived. / My white hair hangs endlessly long, / laughing at countless worldly affairs, / Which of them could please you? / Green hills are charming in my eyes and so am I to them hopefully. / My current situation is roughly like my appearance. / Casually I take a cup of wine at the eastern window / of my house when I recall Tao Yuanming / who composed a poem immediately at a pause. / Those who are lost in pursuing fame on the other bank, / could expect to detect the good flavour of pure wine? / I turned round and shouted, cloud flying and wind rising. / I rail against the ancients not because / I could not meet them / but because / they could not endure my craziness. / It is the two or three youngsters who know about me." (甚矣吾衰矣!怅平生／交游零落,只今余几。白发空垂三千丈,一笑人间万事,问何物、能令公喜?我见青山多妩媚,料青山见我应如是。情与貌,略相似。一尊搔首东窗里,想渊明、停云诗就,此时风味。江左沉酣求名者,岂识浊醪妙理?回首叫,云飞风起。不恨古人吾不见,恨古人不见吾狂耳?知吾者,二三子。②)

　　Xin's poem discloses a mood similar to that of Yue Fei. His taste for wine and emphasis on his joy are greatly reduced by his nostalgic feelings and mention of those seeking fame. Nothing is mentioned of solitude in the poem, but that lonely feeling pervades the whole poem with no friends or other people sharing his ideals, which frustrates his spiritual pursuit. It is in this lack of spiritual comfort and assistance that these two poems find something in common. They appear powerfully conveyed also because they are written in the first person, which brings more subjectivity and personal feelings and commitments.

　　It is not so easy to find similar poems in the West because of the difference in subject preferences. Rather than protest against the monarch or evil ministers or dirty politics, the Westerners might choose injustice, God, morality or anything personal, as the subject to appeal to. Here is a poem by Gerard M. Hopkins, a poet whose recognition came after he died: "Thou art indeed just, Lord, if I contend / With thee; but, sir, so what I plead is just. / Why do sinners' ways prosper? And why must / Disappointment all I endeavour end? / Wert thou my enemy, or thou my friend, / How couldst thou worse, I wonder, than thou dost / Defeat, thwart me? Oh, the sots and thralls of lust / Do in spare hours more thrive than I that spend, / Sir, life upon thy cause. See, banks and brakes

---

① See *A Hundred Ci-Poems of the Tang and Song Dynasties*, Hu Yunyi (ed.), Zhonghua Press, 1961.
② 详见《辛弃疾诗集》,王冶主编,济南出版社,1995。

/ Now, leaved how thick! Laced they are again / With fretty chervil, look, and fresh wind shakes / Them; birds build- but not I build; no, but strain, / Time's eunuch, and not breed one work that wakes. / Mine, O thou loud of life, sends my roots rain."

We do not know exactly what happened to the poet before he produced this poem. But certainly there was something torturing his sense of justice so that he decided to write it to make complaints. He is arguing with a powerful opponent, but is seemingly confident in his ability to challenge the divine justice, with the obvious injustice of his own situation. With the end of the first couple of lines of contention, the poem is shifted to a more personal pleading as he points to the ironic paradoxes of alleged divine love and his own unmerited failure, to the easy success of the lazy and the sensual in the face of his own honest, patient and frustrated service. In spite of his despairing sense of failure, Hopkins' faith remains alive with the hope of spiritual rebirth.

Similarly, Shakespeare's *Sonnet 29* also handles the theme of self-doubt: "When in disgrace with fortune and men's eyes / I all alone beweep my outcast state, / And trouble deaf heaven with my bootless cries, / And look upon myself, and curse my fate, / Wishing me like to one more rich in hope, / Featured like him, like him with friends possess'd, / Desiring this man's art, and that man's scope, / With what I most enjoy contented least; / Yet in these thoughts myself almost despising, / Haply I think on thee, — and then my state, / Like to the lark at break of day arising / From sullen earth, sings hymns at the heaven's gate; / For thy sweet love remember'd such wealth brings / That then I scorn to change my state with kings."

The difference between the two poems is clear enough in spite of the similar subject matter. If Hopkins' poem targets the unfair conditions by challenging God, Shakespeare's is directed against the poet himself with a strong sense of irony. The sense of restless frustration and barrenness of spirit could be detected in the first few lines while the following lines convey more of satirical tone though the lark's image in relation to the heaven's gate seems more positive at the end of the poem.

Perhaps it is not difficult to realize that different cultures could bring out differing products of their aesthetic taste. The reader's appreciation of the Chinese poet's concern is mainly effected by virtue of his sympathy for the personal frustration arising from the unjust environment marked by political persecution or other kind of deteriorating spiritual state. However, the reader's judgment of the Western poem is placed more on a politically neutral or objective basis because the two poets did not refer to specific social factors or events that were responsible. Rather more clearly expressed in the poems is a claim for justice that is represented by God or conscience. It is not just determined by faith, but by culture in association with lifestyles and ways of thinking, which helps interpret the differences detected in these poems.

6.3.6 Social satire

Aesthetics concerns culture and different cultures can provide different understanding of poetic themes. As well, the satirical sense can sharpen aesthetic awareness and enable the reader to take pleasure in a scornful, critical or sarcastic remark.

Western poets like to adopt a satirical tone in their works. Few, if any, seem to be worried about revenge or retaliation as a result of their sharp satires. Comparatively speaking, Chinese poets seldom use satires because of the undesirable or even negative results that would occur after its use. However, occasionally one could read of some satirical lines, which could supply different perceptions. Let us look at some examples. Here is a lyrical poem by Lu You, a well-known poet during the Southern Song Dynasty: "Fifteen years have elapsed since the announcement of the peace edict, / and the general is free from warring, futile at the border. / Singing and dancing is heard out of the depth of the heavy red gates, / The stabled horses die out of overweight and the unused bow broken. / ... / The abandoned people are expecting to be liberated despite their humiliating experiences, / How many places present tonight's hateful tears?"(和戎诏下十五年,将军不战空临边。朱门沉沉按歌舞,厩马肥死弓断弦。……遗民忍死望恢复,几处今宵垂泪恨。①) The poem was written against the social turmoil of the Southern Song Dynasty when half the Chinese territory was occupied by the Jin troops. The corrupted royal government did nothing to retrieve the lost land but indulge itself in material luxury and hedonist pursuits, without caring for the ordinary people who had been abandoned and suffered from the occupation. The poet's sense of frustration and discontent are expressed through his satirical remarks as he points to the emperor and general by "peace edict" and "free from warring, futile at the border". His tolerance is simply uncontrolled through the satirical tone in the words like "singing and dancing", "out of the depth of the heavy red gates", "horses die out of overweight" and "the unused bow broken" which are set against "the abandoned people" and "their humiliating experiences". The poet's temperament simply turns to anger and rises into sharp tone of satire and attack as he presents the scene the clear contrast between luxury of the upper class and of "hateful tears" of the deserted people, which suggests the disgust and even hatred for both the aggressors and those corrupted officials and so-called peace-advocating ruling class.

If Lu You's satire is politically-oriented, Su Shi's work dwells on agricultural production: "Silkworm is well grown up / while wheat is half yellow. / Heavy rain patters before and behind the mountains. / Farming men and weaving women are busy with their work / but the white-clothed angel sits high at the

---

① 详见《陆游诗选》,陆应南(编),广东人民出版社,1984。

hall."(蚕欲老,麦半黄。山前山后水浪浪！农夫辍耒女废筐,白衣仙人在高堂！①) One could instantly catch the satirical sense by reading of the busy scene of the working people in opposition to the highly-throned angel, which reflected on the true situation in the rural area of the Song Dynasty where few local officials showed much concern for peasants' life.

Western poems seem more capable of using satirical means to deal with moral or social issues. This is because many Western poets regard satire as a necessary function because all individuals, all societies and all eras are full of vices and follies, and the poet would not be human if he did not sometimes use his art to protest. The poet might believe he is taking a God's eye and is heaven-directed, by choosing to use satire as a mundane form of poetry and comes closest to replicating our common judgments as a social being. A good satire expresses with wit and force, and sometimes with deep feeling, our own disapproval of the human race in general and the specific voices of particular persons. Here is part of an example by the 17th-century aristocratic poet John Wilmot, titled *A Satyr against Mankind*:

> Which is the basest creature, man or beast?
> Birds feed on birds, beasts on each other prey;
> But savage man alone does man betray.
> Press'd by necessity, they kill for food;
> Man undoes man, to do himself no good.
> With teeth and claws, by nature arm'd they hunt
> Nature's allowance, to supply their want;
> But man with smiles, embraces, friendship, praise,
> Inhumanly his fellow's life betrays,
> With voluntary pains, works his distress;
> Not through necessity, but wantonness.
> For hunger, or for love, they bite or tear,
> Whilst wretched man is still in arms for fear;
> For fear he arms, and is of arms afraid;
> From fear, to fear, successively betray'd. ②

This is obviously a satire directed at human wickedness. It is a dark picture of human weakness which seems hard to evade or escape. Similarly, Jonathan Swift's satire on human values from the following century appears no less harsh in

---

① See *Dictionary of Annotated Ci-Poems of the Tang and Song Dynasties*, Zhou Rucan et al, Shanghai Dictionary Press, 1988.
② John Wilmot (1647 – 1680), English poet, wrote a number of light and graceful poems, many of them extremely gross. His work includes *A Satyr against Mankind*, and *Valentinian*, a tragedy adapted from Beaumont and Fletcher.

terms of tone and invective:

> Beauties, like tyrants, old and friendless grown,
> Yet hate repose, and dread to be alone...
> As hags hold Sabbathes, less for joy than spite,
> So these their merry, miserable night;
> Still round and round the ghosts of beauty glide,
> And haunt the places where their honour died.
> See how the world its veterans rewards!
> A youth of frolics, an old age of cards;
> Fair to no purpose, artful to no end,
> Young without lovers, old without a friend;
> A fop their passion, but their prize a sot;
> Alive ridiculous and dead, forgot![①]

It is a description of the horrid old society and its values, characters often presented in Restoration drama. Their gatherings are likened to the orgies of the medieval Witches' Sabbath, but without any of the positive evil that gave the Walpurgis Night its terror. Instead it is the negative aimlessness and emptiness of the "mercy, miserable night" that provokes the poet's contempt. These women have made the world of fashion their only existence, and the epithet "veterans" is heavily ironic.

One might identify a vast gulf between the Western tradition of satire and Chinese satire though they are not exactly on the same basis of comparison since they are drawn from different periods. But more important is the subject matter which indicates different concerns for the two cultures. It is quite clear that Chinese poets care more about social and political affairs while Western poets are more interested in individual experiences and the observation of human nature. However, they both have something unpleasant to pick up from their observations, either from social or political aspect or from daily conventions. The event or figures as the objects of their observation are perceived and judged by certain ideological perspectives which are tinted with strong senses of satire and criticism.

Poetic form

Chinese and Western poems are related through the use of sound patterns

---

① Jonathan Swift (1667 – 1745), English writer, is famous for his satire. His best-known work is *Gulliver's Travels*.

and figures of speech, which are among the most substantial features of poetic form working respectively in the two languages. In the meantime, each form of poetry has its own technical feature or prosody as with its unique sound patterns and textures. Let us look at them separately.

6.4.1 Sound pattern

Whether in Chinese poetry or in Western poetry, sound patterns and specific devices are the most important and striking features peculiar to the genre, and therefore different from other literary forms, such as prose and drama.

The Chinese classical poetry is very strict with its sound pattern composed of rhyme and the choice of characters. It falls basically into two categories, namely the ancient style and the modern style. The ancient style refers to the one established before the Tang Dynasty and the modern one refers to that established during the Tang Dynasty. The ancient style, comparatively speaking, does not offer very strict requirement except some regulations for the end rhymes. A poem could have any kind of length in terms of the number of characters in a line and the number of lines. A line could have three to seven or even more characters, but mostly would have four, five or seven characters. The modern style imposes stricter rules. For instance, it requires that a line should have either five or seven characters, each poem should have either four or eight lines. The rhyming characters should not go beyond those listed in a special group. Besides, the non-rhyming words should agree with the specified tone, either level or non-level in pronunciation.

Western poetry has also its own rules regarding sound controlling devices. To make things easier, let us take English poetry as our focus for comparison. The measure of English poetry is called metre or scansion and the unit of measurement in English traditional verse is the foot. There are two measurements involved in a metre, one being the kind of foot and the other being the number of feet in the line.

The English have borrowed from Latin the classical names for describing the number and order and character of the syllables that form "feet". Feet may be either disyllabic or trisyllabic, including iamb (an unaccented syllable followed by an accented one), trochee (an accented syllable followed by an unaccented one), spondee (two accented syllables together), dactyl (an accented syllable followed by two unaccented ones) and anapaest (two unaccented syllables followed by an accented one). Among all these types of feet, the most popular one is iambic in English verse. It suits the nature of the language better than any other, and probably nine tenths of formal English poetry uses this foot as its basic metrical unit.

A line of verse contains one foot or more. Again the classical names are offered, namely monometre for one foot, dimetre for two feet, trimetre for three feet, tetrametre for four feet (also called octosyllablics), pentametre for five feet, hexametre for six feet (also called alexandrines) and heptametre for seven feet. It should be noted that these principles were imposed on the natural Germanic-based English language during the Renaissance. Today they are rarely considered as anything other than a highly artificial method for the composition or analysis of poetry derived from French or Latin influences.

English poetry in its classical form may be either rhymed or unrhymed. Rhyme is matching of sounds at the end of lines. This may be the last syllable of the line and is called single or masculine rhyme, such as "And hears the Muses in a *ring* / Aye round about Jove's altar *sing*." Sometimes it may be the last two syllables which is called double or feminine rhyme, such as "And add to these retired leisure, / That in trim gardens takes his pleasure." For dactylic verse the rhyme has to be triple, such as "Touch her not scornfully, / Think of her mournfully." But in serious verse the rhyme is seldom more than double.

Rhymes can be internal, within the line as well as at the end, such as "And a good south *wind* spring up *behind*; / The Albatross did followed every *day*, for food or *play* / Came to the mariner's hollo!" Sometimes the sound could be just similar rather than exactly the same, and then it is called half- or slant-rhyme, such as "Little Tommy *Tucker* / Sang for his *supper*. / What did he have? Brown bread and *butter*."

Some English poems seek to be more modern by using "assonance", a chiming of the vowel while the consonant plays no real part in sound pattern. In the following line the poet uses "i", "o" and "a": "numbered sleepers *groaned*".

Other sound devices include alliteration (sometimes called alliterative scheming or rhyming), onomatopoeia (the imitation of natural sound in words), cacophony (a succession of harsh, slow-moving syllables), euphony (light and harmonious sound), and special rhyme schemes such as the couplet (any rhymed pattern of two lines), the triplet or tercet (three-rhymed pattern), etc.

Generally both Chinese and Western classical poetry has established strict rules for rhyme and choice of vocabulary. The Chinese poetry seems to cares more for rhyming while the English poetry, because of its accented language, cares more for rhythm. The Chinese classical poetry continued for more than two thousand years and perfected its form by supplying more and more complex principles until the new form of poetry was introduced and created during the May 4th Movement under the Western influence. This new form of poetry certainly provided more freedom for the poets by getting rid of all the established rules for choosing the right characters for rhyme and tone. In terms of understanding and popularization, the new form of Chinese poetry certainly made due contribution. But at the same time every poetic form has its own aesthetic principles for composition and appreciation. To break down the old form is much easier than to establish the new one. It is nearly a century since the initial years of the new poetry. Nonetheless, it is still hard to say if the Chinese new poetry has produced any established and sufficiently mature principles for the younger poets to follow. In some of the poems, in spite of their fluency and powerful expression, one has difficulty finding harmony or aesthetic experience which a reader desires and appreciates as in reading Chinese classical poetry.

Comparatively speaking, Western poetry has introduced both mild and more profound changes while keeping most of its traditional features in the hands of certain poets. However, classical scansion rules have been largely replaced by variants such as the "sprung rhythms" of Gerard M. Hopkins or the abstract forms of modernist and post-modernist poets. Except for the rhyming devices, the rhythmical pattern is still at work as the most striking force in English poetic writing. Even for rhyming, some poets may still take liberty to employ it if they like. A review of English poetry as a whole and one could find out that most of traditional poetic forms are still in use, for instance, the measurements of feet and the counting of poetic lines, the arrangement of rhyming words and other devices. Almost all the major principles still work well even if some are perhaps out of date and are no longer chosen so often as they were. Comparatively, Chinese poetry is influenced too much by political factors. It is certainly justified to substitute a republic for a monarchy and substitute new culture for old culture. The crux for poetry, however, is not so definite as to whether all the old elements of traditional form should be completely abolished in the process of pushing forward poetic reform.

6.4.2　Imagery

If poetry does not count without the use of sound pattern, it could hardly survive without the device of imagery. The American poet Robert Frost once said: "Saying one thing and meaning another", which perhaps gives a good interpretation of imagery. One could say rhythm and imagery run together in poetic harness, as the two indivisible horses for poetic carriage riding on the journey.

Language at large is characteristically metaphorical in both China and the West, which serves as the basis for employing poetic imagery. It is true of both Chinese and Western poems. Imagery is frequently though not necessarily always composed of figures of speech, which basically refers to either simile or metaphor. This tendency works in both Chinese and Western poems. For Chinese poetry, Li Bai's *wang-lu-shan-pu-bu* (《望庐山瀑布》, View of Waterfall at Mount Lu) is typical of its metaphorical application:

Smoke rises out of the incense-burner under the sun,
I sit watching the waterfall hanging from the front river;
The torrent is cascading down at a length of three thousand yards,
as if the Milk Way falls down from the heaven.
（日照香炉生紫烟，遥看瀑布挂前川；飞流直下三千尺，疑是银河落九天。）

Doubtless "the Milk Way falls down from the heaven" is most successfully selected and suited to the context on account of the agreement between waterfall and the heavenly river suggested by the Milk Way so that the poem is passed down from generation to generation up to the present.

Many Western poets also like to take nourishment from nature or ordinary life. Here is William Blake's *The Sick Rose*:

O Rose, thou art sick!
The invisible worm,
That flies in the night,
The howling storm,

Has found out thy bed
Of crimson joy;
And his dark secret love
Does thy life destroy. [①]

At the surface level of this poem, one could get a fable-like story through the images of rose and worm which provides the insight into a fairy tale concerning an innocent figure in her sad experience from the attack of an evil demon. The poem creates a feeling of some sinister and violent passion behind the simple but ominous words. The language of the poem implies at once that the real intent is symbolic; the rose and the worm and the situation between them are an inner drama that has nothing to do with a flower garden.

The further interpretation, however, depends on the interrelations suggested by the words that have been charged with sensations and the possibility of extended significance. The oppositions of rose and worm, of "joy" and "destroy" suggest the presence of corrupting evil in the moral and emotional order as in the natural order. Although it is not easy to define exactly the relations between the image and its hidden implication, one could roughly regard rose to stand for joy and worm for destroyer on behalf of evil. Since the secret lover is "he", it would mean that beauty in any form always seems threatened by potential destruction. It indicates that it is either womanhood or a specific woman who is ruined in this context.

In contrast to the symbolic implication and sophistication of Blake's poem, Li Bai's poem seems more direct due to the use of a simile. Among the Chinese classical poems one could find many famous pieces for the use of difficult allusions as a way to convey the author's hidden implication. Such kind of poems usually

---

① William Blake (1757 – 1827), English poet and painter, was from earliest youth a seer of visions and a dreamer of dreams. His work is tinted with mystery as well as an exquisite simplicity arising from directness and intensity of feeling.

require some wide-range knowledge on the reader's part and could easily lead to misunderstanding. This is true of both sides, which could be verified by the two classical poems in the following case study, though the use of figures of speech herein is not necessarily very difficult or goes beyond our understanding. In spite of the difference, however, it is evident that figures of speech, either open or hidden, either simile or metaphor, have been valued and applied widely as one of the most important ways for poetic creation.

The tolerance of different ways of thinking and writing and diverse literary forms is something Chinese poets could learn and benefit from their Western counterparts. It is generally acknowledged that Chinese classical poetry has its inadequacies, especially its strict requirements for choosing the right words to match the rhyme and tone. Consequently these rules may affect strongly the way poets seek to express themselves. After all, whatever form of language poetry assumes, it has to meet with the spiritual needs of the ordinary people. Hence the simplification and modification of the sophisticated form of Chinese classical poetry is necessary and inevitable. Yet it does not mean any poetic reform or modification has to adopt radical means and to be executed on the basis of removing all the old modes and styles. How to establish a new and acceptable form of poetry to satisfy spiritual needs of the majority of people by taking up nourishments from both Chinese classical poetry and Western poetry remains a problem for the readers and writers of Chinese poetry. Presumably it is not easy to find the final established form within a predictable period but certainly it is worthwhile to make continuous efforts towards the target.

6.5 A case study

For a deeper and more comprehensive understanding of the connections between Chinese and Western poetry, it might be helpful to focus on two sample poems. Qu Yuan's *li-sao* and Dante's *The Divine Comedy*, as the widely accepted representatives respectively from each side, might serve as the targets of our study by comparison.

Both Qu Yuan and Dante are doubtless among the greatest poets of their own cultures, with their immortal works *li-sao* and *The Divine Comedy*. These constitute a lasting influence with far-reaching significance within world literature. In spite of the wide gap of over a thousand years between the two poems, their central concerns, spiritual pursuits and imaginative power have supplied the possibility for later generations to benefit from and follow as an inspiration and a source to draw on either for spiritual guidance or as a classical sample for writing poems.

It might appear somewhat strange when we notice that each of the two works was set against some similar circumstances at its inception. Perhaps it is worthwhile to provide some rough ideas about the motivation of the two poets.

Qu Yuan was an important minister in the Chu Kingdom before he wrote the poem. He had won the trust of the king and had been assigned with heavy responsibilities to draft political documents and deal with external affairs. He was then filled with high expectations of his land to become strong and prosperous. Unfortunately, he suffered from frustrations before long since the king took bad advice from some conservative ministers with evil designs and changed his attitude towards Qu Yuan who was later forced to move out of the capital. Finally he was sent into exile and took his own life in a river on hearing that the country was invaded and ruined by the Qin troops. It was his extreme care for his native land and his strong opposition to evil forces that drove him to pick up his pen and set to write about his emotions and ideals before his death.

Dante's life was shaped by the long history of conflict between the imperial and papal forces called, respectively, the Ghibellines and the Guelfs. ①

The hegemony of the Guelfs had been restored in Florence in 1266 by an alliance forged between the forces of France and the papacy. By 1300, however, Dante had come to oppose the territorial ambitions of the Pope, which in turn propelled Dante into further opposition to papal policies. A new alliance was formed between the papacy, the French and the exiled Black Guelfs. The Pope dismissed the other two legates and detained Dante. On March 10, 1302, Dante and 14 other Whites were condemned to be burned to death. Thus Dante suffered the most decisive crisis of his life, which led to his long exile and eventual death in Ravenna②, a foreign province far from his native Florence. *The Divine Comedy* is produced in such circumstances and powerfully handles this spiritual crisis. Indeed, he makes it the central dramatic act through which a long string of prophecies are manifested. However, it is also Dante's purpose to show the means by which, he triumphed over his personal disaster, thus making his poem into a true "divine comedy".

Dante's poem was composed at a time when he was threatened with the death penalty by the papacy yet he was not reconciled to the frustration of his political ideals. Qu Yuan chose to meditate over the nature of his ambition and the possible ways of saving his motherland from the destruction by the aggressors, the Qin troops, who started to make intrusions at the time. His *li-sao* reflected his

---

① The Ghibellines and the Guelfs refer to the two politically opposed groups in Florence. As it had been during the time of the Guelf, the party supporting the Pope, and its rival Ghibelline were engaged in a civil strife in the 1290s. Florence once again became a divided city. The ruling Guelf class of Florence became divided into a party of "Blacks", led by Corso Donati, and a party of "Whites", to which Dante belonged.

② Ravenna, a city in Italy, is famous for its long history, especially its glorious past as the capital of the Western Roman Empire.

mental state as a struggle to sketch a map for his people to become aware of the danger as well as the necessity to take urgent measures to prevent the decline of the country.

The vernacular form of poetry did not come to public notice in Western culture for any remarkable achievements till Dante's *The Divine Comedy* was published in 1320 or so. Dante's poetic reputation lies in his perfect combination in this great work of history, realism, religious enthusiasm and life experiences, patriotic feelings and political perspectives, spiritual admiration and moral judgment. It is a very long work, made up of three parts and consisting of a total of 14,233 lines based on the *terza rima* scheme[①].

Qu Yuan's *li-sao* falls into eight sections. The first three sections tell of his own origin and family as well as his political ambitions, experiences and determination to carry forward his grand ideals. These descriptions are generally more realistic and personal, endowed with a strong sense of touching emotion and strong will. Beginning from the fourth section, the poem turns to a spiritual representation and narrative based on a combination of myths and allusions. These mythological figures and stories include the legendary emperors Yao, Shun and Yu, the solar god and moon goddess, his entry into hell and admission into the heaven.

The central concerns of the poem rest on his praise of the wise rulers and his negative comments on the dark and evil forces: "The sun and the moon are both overshadowed, with the spring and autumn in their place./Grass and trees are on the decline, added by the worry for aging beauty./Where the three queens showed their charm./The large amounts of flowers made their appearances./Poisonous herbs and wild weeds are mixed with high plants of pretty blossoms which are not the only existences./The upright ancient rulers Yao and Shun were justified in following the Tao principles, / in contrast to Jie and Zhou who were rampant with their cruel reign…"(日月忽其不淹兮,春与秋其代序。惟草木之零落兮,恐美人之迟暮……昔三后之纯粹兮,固众芳之所在。杂申椒与菌桂兮,岂唯纫夫蕙茝。彼尧舜之耿介兮,既遵道而得路。何桀纣之猖披兮……[②])

As well, the poem is full of distressed and solitary emotions expressing the strains and frustrations he suffered from in his political career in addition to his worries and resolve: "Look forward and backward to observe the situations of the ordinary people. / Is it the unjust applicable and the unkind tolerable? / I do not regret what I did though danger and death threat approaches me. / I hold a fragrant plant to shield my tears falling down my coat. / I kneel down, fully dressed, to present an appeal, hoping my justice could deserve a just response."

---

① A verse form consisting of hendecasyllable tercets, rhyming aba, bcb, cdc and so on. It was used by Dante in *The Divine Comedy*.

② See *Dictionary of Annotated Chinese Ancient Poetry*, Ho Xinhui (ed.), Chinese Woman Press, 1988.

(瞻前而顾后兮,相观民之计极。夫孰非义而可用兮,孰非善而可服？阽余身而危死兮,览余初其犹未悔。揽茹蕙以掩涕兮,沾余襟之浪浪。跪敷衽以陈辞兮,耿吾既得此中正。①)

A claim for justice and condemnation of evil and darkness was naturally understandable at the time, but unfortunately difficult to be executed due to the limited vision and moral judgment. Such inadequacies are also reflected in Dante's poem. Dante's great work is constructed in three parts that describe respectively the poet's journey into Hell, Purgatory and Paradise. According to the poetic design, the poet is respectively led by Virgil, the Roman poet, and Beatrice, Dante's former lover, into Hell and Purgatory. *The Divine Comedy* is a glorification of God, but it is also a sharp and profound protest against the insufficiencies of theology and an exposure of the evils and darkness of Christianity at the time. Hell is "a vale of tears, a place to undergo a period of trial and suffering, an unpleasant but necessary preparation for the after-life where alone man could expect to enjoy happiness". The whole poem is pervaded by Dante's conviction that man should seek earthly immortality by his worthy actions here, as well as prepare to merit the life everlasting. In the poem the protagonist Dante himself witnesses the terrible scene where the sinners, whatever misbehaviours they have ever committed, are thrown into various places of punishment. "Below them they see the River of Blood, which marks the First Round of the Seventh Circle as detailed in the previous Canto. Here are punished the Violent Against Their Neighbours; great war-makers, cruel tyrants, highwaymen — all who shed the blood of their fellowmen. As they wallowed in blood during their lives, so they are immersed in the boiling blood forever, each according to the degree of his guilt, while fierce Centaurs patrol the banks, ready to shoot with their arrows any sinner who raises himself out of the boiling blood beyond the limits permitted him."

The touching spirit of *The Divine Comedy* is such that few in literary history could match, due to its power of revelation. It is similar to that of *li-sao*, the Chinese classical poem, which also provides powerful inspiration, though according to certain ideological or religious criterion, perhaps it lacks the details and specific classification of human behaviours demonstrated within *The Divine Comedy*.

In spite of its limitations, *li-sao*, as one of the longest works of ancient Chinese poetry, is highly regarded for its patriotic feelings and reflection of personal ideals full of romantic imaginations based on a mixture of ancient myths and figures and ideologies such as Confucianism and Taoism. The latter is perhaps even more significant in terms of its intellectual contribution, though it is just the beginning and its budding has to be developed into some more mature form. As a poet, Qu Yuan has never been granted a more secure status than what he achieved in *li-sao*, by manifesting his talent for imagination in his grouping

---

① See *Dictionary of Annotated Chinese Ancient Poetry*, Ho Xinhui (ed.), Chinese Woman Press, 1988.

together such a variety of historical and mythological figures. Maybe those ideals are still visionary and impractical in terms of a system of ideology, yet the structure and prospect are so magnificently interwoven and deftly composed as to impart an everlasting impact as an everglowing pearl in the crown on the intellectual development of Chinese civilization.

Apart from the exposure of the horror of the Hell, Dante in his poem also shows the grace of God and the change of heart of the sinners through the descriptions of Purgatory. Thus, the poem is endowed with the great significance of an epoch-making classic like the epics of ancient times. In fact, his great poem enjoys the kind of power peculiar to a classic: successive epochs have been able to find reflected in it their own intellectual concerns. Even in the early 20th century, readers found the poem to possess an aesthetic and linguistic power that far transcended its structure and argument. Dante created a remarkable repertoire of character types in a work of vivid mimetic presentation, as well as a poem of great stylistic artistry in its pre-figurations and allusions. Moreover, he incorporated all of these important political, philosophical and theological themes to add to moral wisdom and lofty ethical vision. Most important of all, this long poem is the first great Italian literary work ever written in vernacular Italian rather than Latin.

Basically, *li-sao* is a lyrical poem with occasional narration as a necessary additional device for expressing the poet's feelings and viewpoints. An example is the part accounting for his journey from the morning departure through a number of meetings and appointments till the end of the trip. It is generally not a systematic survey of social or intellectual conditions in China at the time, even though it covers extensive subjects and conveys strong emotions along with personal judgments. Compared with *The Divine Comedy*, *li-sao* is perhaps more personal and limited in its social and intellectual importance considering the fact that there is a gap of a thousand and half years as well as the tremendous environmental disparity between the two works and their cultures.

In spite of all these, the connections between the two poems are also quite evident. The political motivation, the intention to deal with spiritual targets, the means to convey emotional frustrations and complaints about various issues, the vivid imagery as a way to display the authors' wide-ranging knowledge and sensible judgments based on mythological and historical awareness, all work together to contribute to the form, themes and profundity of the poems. Either in structural form, imagery or theme, these two poems, as literary works of such long endurance, are both regarded as having an unparalleled influence upon later generations, either on readers or writers.

Like Cao Xueqin from China or Shakespeare from England, Qu Yuan and Dante have created universal types of work based on social reality and historical foresight, and in so doing considerably enhanced and expanded the treasury of contemporary literary productions.

Questions for comprehension and discussion

1. Give an account of the development of Chinese and Western poetry.
2. Say something about the similarities and dissimilarities in the major concerns of Chinese and Western poems.
3. Make a comparison between Chinese and Western poetry in terms of poetic forms and concerns by referring to one or two specific examples from sound patterns, imagery, subject matters or themes.

List of proposed books for further reading

1. 蘅塘退士,2003,《唐诗三百首》,北京:中华书局。
2. 孙多吉编著,2005,《中国诗歌史》,西安:陕西人民出版社。
3. 曹顺庆,1988,《中西比较诗学》,北京:北京出版社。
4. Dante, Alighieri (translated by John Ciardi), *The Divine Comedy (The Inferno, The Purgatorio and The Paradiso)* , Washington: The New American Library, 2003.
5. Hamburger, Michael, *The Truth of Poetry: Tensions in Modern Poetry from Baudelaire to the 1960s* ,London: Anvil Press Poetry, 1996.
6. Woodring, Carl, Shapiro, James, *The Columbia History of British Poetry*, New York: Columbia University Press, 1994.
7. Deane, Patrick, *British Poetry since 1950: Recent Criticism and the Laureateship*, New York: Contemporary Literature Press, 1999.

Chapter 7

A Comparison of Chinese and Western Fictions

Both Chinese and Western narrative literatures have a long historical tradition in that the earliest form of narration was born at the very beginning of the two civilizations. Nevertheless, fiction as an independent genre, compared with poetry and drama, was much later in its eventual establishment. It is perhaps necessary to give a brief account of the historical development of Chinese and Western fictions before we could acquire a better understanding of how fiction came into being as an established form of literature and finally won the favour of more and more people. It is also necessary to inquire into a variety of similarities and dissimilarities in subject matter, central concerns, writing techniques as well as general features and cultural implications peculiar to each of the two civilizations. All these are to be explored comprehensively, consistent with the brevity of this chapter.

7.1 Historical development of Chinese and Western fictions

History often makes one wise with the real experience our ancestors have ever undergone. Therefore historical development of fiction in both China and the West gives us both knowledge of narrative literature and appreciation of the true merit of this form of art in its conveying social and cultural information as well as aesthetic sense.

7.1.1 An account of fiction development in China

Chinese fiction is a by-product of Chinese social and cultural developments as part of Chinese civilization. Almost from the very beginning of its development, Chinese fiction was closely associated with a variety of influences coming from economic, social, political, military and cultural evolvements and in turn fiction provides subtle artistic touching forces into human mind. These mutual influences explain why Chinese fiction takes realism as its principal trend through most of its development.

1 The early period of Chinese narrative literature

Chinese narrative literature, the forerunner of fiction, dates back to a period as early as before the Qin and Han Dynasties over two thousand years ago when *shan-hai-jing*(《山海经》, The Tales of Mountains and Seas) and *mu-tian-zi-zhuan* (《穆天子传》, Mu Tianzi's Biography) were produced. Some fables and myths were included in the two books as the earliest budding of fiction. Some historical annals like *han-shu*(《汉书》, The Annals of the Han Dynasty), *wu-yue-chun-qiu* (《吴越春秋》, The History of the Wu and Yue Kingdoms), *sui-shu*(《隋书》, The Annals of the Sui Dynasty) also had some narrative passages that read like fiction. But the real sense of fiction had to wait long after a fashion for composing stories during the Northern and Southern Dynasties. These may be classified as ghost tales and anecdotes. The former included some fairy tales and legends, characteristic of mythologies (ghosts and other unreal elements). The best-known work is *sou-shen-ji* (《搜神记》, The Tales in Search of Gods) which collected together such stories as *Ganjiang and Moye*, *Han Ping the Couple*, *Li Ji Killing the Snake*, etc.

The anecdotes comprised the personal behaviours and words of some distinguished literary people collected into various anthologies. The most reputed and earliest of the kind is *xi-jing-za-ji* (《西京杂记》, The Miscellaneous Tales of the Western Capital), which featured the famous story *Wang Qiang*. The story tells about how Wang Zhaojun, one of the best-known beauties in Chinese legend, was selected as a princess to be married off to a Hu prince, at the instigation of Mao Yanshou, the painter who had failed to show her true beauty in his drawing for presentation to the emperor. The emperor was so annoyed that he immediately had Mao executed after Wang was gone.

Another book is Liu Yiqing's *shi-shuo-xin-yu* (《世说新语》, New Tales out of Conventional Affairs), which established a moral criterion for the judgment of different kinds of behaviours by the literati. For instance, there were those about Xie An's composure of mind in such circumstances as of being either cheerful or risky.

2 The second period of Chinese fiction development

The second period started with the birth of ghost stories and tales of chivalrous swordsmen produced during the Jin and Northern and Southern Dynasties, which culminated in the Tang Dynasty. In spite of the achievements, such as the improvements of characterization and plot design, the Tang fiction confined itself to the short story type. The basic form of fiction came into being during the Tang Dynasty when legendary stories were produced. These had to traverse three stages before the fictional form was eventually shaped. The initial stage derived influence from ghost stories of the Northern and Southern Dynasties and focused on the strange feudalistic descriptions of man's contact with fairies, ghosts or beastly creatures, as in *gu-jing-ji* (《古镜记》, The Tales of the Old Mirror), *bai-yuan-zhuan* (《补江总白猿传》, Biography of a White Ape), and *you-xian-yao* (《游仙窟》, A Visit to a Fairy Cave). The second stage was marked by the combining of fantasy with social reality, such as *zhen-zhong-ji* (《枕中记》, A Recollection of Dreams), *nan-ke-tai-shou-zhuan* (《南柯太守传》, The Life Story of the Magistrate Nanke), *liu-yi-zhuan* (《柳毅传》, Liu Yi's Biography) and *li-wa-zhuan* (《李娃传》, Li Wa's Story), etc.

3 The third period of Chinese fiction development

The modern sense of extended narrative, especially the form of novel, was not clarified until the third period between the Ming Dynasty and the beginning of the Qing Dynasty when the mature form of fiction was manifested in the emergence of a number of well-reputed literary works.

These novels or story collections were brought to public readership and exerted much impact on social life. They include such novels as *san-guo-yan-yi* (《三国演义》, The Historical Romances of the Three Kingdoms), *shui-hu* (《水浒》, The Water Margin), *xi-you-ji* (《西游记》, The Western Pilgrimage) and *jin-ping-mei* (《金瓶梅》, The Romance of the Three Ladies). The climax, however, was reached only when *hong-lou-meng* (《红楼梦》, The Dream of Red Mansions), *ru-lin-wai-shi* (《儒林外史》, The Scholars) and *liao-zhai* (《聊斋》, The Ghost Stories of Liao Zhai) came out. One could say the Chinese traditional fiction achieved its perfection and maturity during those years when its creative ideas and techniques were further developed to the extent that it could match the other forms of Chinese literature and gradually social acclaim by its popularity among the ordinary people.

Hong-lou-meng could be said to represent the highest level achievement of Chinese classical fiction. In respect of plot structure and development, characterization, variety of language and realistic representation of society, this novel could hardly be matched by any of its contemporaries. *Ru-lin-wai-shi* also had an extraordinary quality in its exposure of social darkness, especially represented by its strong satirical tone.

Modern fiction appeared in China at about the same time as modern poetry when plain language began to be adopted in literary works. It was only a matter of time before the new ideas or techniques such as symbolism, the stream of consciousness and other modernist terms were borrowed from Western literature by Chinese writers. The new trends were soon shaped into an influential drive opposed to the traditional literature. At the forefront was realism, a theoretical term only introduced into China at the turn of the 20th century though its idea was not unfamiliar in this country with a long cultural tradition.

The Chinese modernist trend could be broken into two phases. The first phase was shaped not long after the May 4th Movement and operated principally before 1949. The second phase refers to the rebirth of modernist writing from the 1980s on-wards. The first phase involved the achievements in both fiction and poetry. It was particularly demonstrated in the writing of short fiction which benefited from new techniques borrowed from their Western counterparts. The typical example is the neo-perceptional group composed of a number of young writers, intending to manoeuvre sensuous or sensual perceptions, especially the libido in the daily life of the urban residents. One of their representative works is Liu Naou's anthology *du-shi-feng-jing-xian* (《都市风景线》, The Urban Landscape), containing a number of stories imbued with detailed portrayal of the subtle changes in the mood of the characters.

The second phase has produced a fairly large number of writers who have brought about a variety of experimental novelettes or stories of different styles, especially the psychologically-oriented writers. Among them, Wang Meng, Chen Rong, Han Shaogong, Mo Yan and many others have distinguished themselves with their own productions, which attempt to use the new methods taken from Western literature to work on Chinese society and culture as subject matter or thematic concerns. Such works as Wang Meng's *hu-die* (《蝴蝶》, Butterfly) and *hai-de-meng* (《海的梦》, Love at Sea), Chen Rong's *jian-qu-shi-sui* (《减去十岁》, Ten Years Reduced), Mo Yan's *hong-gao-liang* (《红高粱》, The Red Sorghum), etc. have become widely popular in China for their successful combination of Western technique, especially psychological approach and traditional Chinese culture with the help of mass media, particularly cinema.

Comparatively, China's literary development, fiction included, appeared slow and retarded by its social turmoil and cultural barriers in certain stages of the 20th century, and had to tolerate a period of wandering and slow development till the country opened its door to the rest of the world towards the end of the 1970s when she started to reassess and reestablish her relations with the outside world, especially the West.

7.1.2 An account of Western fiction development

The Western narrative literature and fiction has traveled down a long way with tremendous changes and remarkable achievements, which not only produced quite a number of world-reputed masters of literature, but helped promote the advance of human spirit and civilization.

1 The beginning of Western narrative literature

Western fiction originated from narrative tales whose early traces were found in Aesop's fables or narrative poems, such as Homer's epics *The Odyssey* and *The Iliad*. However, a more complete form of fiction had to wait for several centuries until the appearance of *The Golden Ass* by the Roman writer Lucius Apuleius and *Metamorphoses* by the Roman poet Ovid. *The Golden Ass* is an excellent narrative work, telling how a Greek youth Lucius was changed into an ass due to his mistakenly taking a dose of magic powder prepared by a sorceress. The ass was then set upon by a band of robbers and went through a series of adventures and hardships before he was finally rescued by a goddess and changed back to a man. *Metamorphoses* is a lengthy collection of Greek and Roman myths and legends, focusing on miraculous transformations, some stories being concerned with notables of Greek and Roman social and cultural life, such as Pythagoras and Caesar.

The early period of Western fiction mostly consisted of myths and fables and only a few relate to real-life episodes of love or adventure. Overall they are short and simple and reflect the social conditions at the time. There was not much development in fiction during the Middle Ages except the legends about knights, once popular in France and Britain. Unlike the epics, these legends usually represent some romances or adventure stories composed without much historical ground, such as those about Beowulf, Tristan and Iseult, or the Knights of the Round-Table and King Arthur.

2 The development of Western fiction

Western fiction made steady progress and established a well developed form during the Renaissance. Among the early successful novelists were Francois Rabelais (1494 – 1553), the French writer famous for his *Gargantua and Pantagruel*, and the Spaniard Miguel de Cervantes (1547 – 1616) with his *Don Quixote*. In a sense the two novels inherited and developed the realistic tradition by showing and satirizing the dark and malign forces of the day. At the same time they provided an example of how to build up a framework for a longer narrative in prose. These two works were followed by more novels whose authors continued the creative development of characters and events based on their imaginative insight into social reality. Examples could be identified among a group of English writers like Daniel Defoe (1660 – 1731) with *Robinson Crusoe*, Jonathan Swift (1667 – 1745) with *Gulliver's Travels*, Samuel Richardson (1689 – 1761) with *Clarissa Harlowe* and *Pamela*, and Henry Fielding (1707 – 1754) with *Tom Jones*. The publication of these novels, either realistic or romantic, laid a foundation for the whole edifice of traditional Western fiction. The development of fiction came to its culmination in the 19th century — the boom in more significant and grandiose forms of novels. They include such novels as Dickens' *Bleak House*, Thackery's *Vanity Fair*, George Eliot's *Middlemarch*, Manzonis' *The Betrothed*, Stendhal's *Red and Black*, Gustave Flaubert's *Madame Bovary*, Victor Hugo's *Notre Dame de Paris* and *Les Misérables*, Balzac's *Comedie Humaine* which included about 90 novels and stories, Dostoevsky's *Crime and Punishment*, Gogol's *Dead Souls*, Turgenev's *Fathers and Children*, Leo Tolstoy's *Anna Karenina*, *War* and *Peace* and *Resurrection*, Mark Twain's *The Adventures of Huckleberry Finn* , and Melville's *Moby Dick*.

3 Modernist fiction in the West

The third stage in the Western novel's development is marked by drastic changes in the form and technique introduced by modernist fiction.

Western fiction underwent a series of transformations by the experimental novelists or pioneering writers in the phase of modernism, like Henry James who initiated the character's psychological perspective as a narrator in his *The Ambassadors*. Then he was followed by more avant-garde schools and a large number of distinguished writers and their representative works. They include the stream of consciousness, expressionism, surrealism, existentialism, angry young men, lost generation, black humour, magical realism, which contributed, one after another, a lot to the development of Western fiction both in form and in thematic exploration. Among the best-known novelists and their oeuvre are James Joyce and his *Ulysses* and *Finnegans Wake*, Marcel Proust and his *A la recherché du temps perdu*, Virginia Woolf and her *To the Lighthouse*, Franz Kafka and his *Metamorphosis*, Thomas Mann and his *The Magic Mountain*, William Faulkner and his *The Sound and the Fury*, D. H. Lawrence and his *Women in Love*, William Golding and his *Lord of the Flies*, Kinsley Amis and his *Lucky Jim*, Norman Mailer and his *The Naked and the Dead*, Vladimir Nabokov and his *Pnin*, and Patrick White and his *Twyborn Affair*.

Their achievements had widespread and lasting influence on the development of Western fiction and other forms of literature all over the world, including China. These influences have helped shape a continuous drive through various means of experiment of literary representation, dissemination and appreciation in combination with popular culture such as cinema, sports and pop music and moved into part of current globalization as an important participant. At the same time, fiction still keeps its traditional form and works independently of other literary and cultural genres in a way to look after itself in terms of self-improvement and adapting itself to social and intellectual and artistic needs.

7.2 General sense of fiction as a literary genre

Chinese and Western writers manifest great similarity and diversity in their understanding of fiction as an artistic form, in spite of the fact that their differences have been narrowed in the recent past due to frequent contact with and better understanding of each other. The differences are greatly reduced in the individual works as well as in the writing principles following generations of cultural communication and understanding between two sides, which could be traced back to the early days of Chinese and Western fictions. It is interesting, though, to get down to some differences which could be summarized into three points for the sake of how to understand fiction as a literary genre taking shape against certain social, historical and cultural conditions. The first is its focus on story development, the second is its historical concern, and the third is its inherent moral function. These three points might serve as the ground for our discussion of the distinction of the two sides.

7.2.1 Story development in early fiction

Either the earlier tales in Chinese myths and ghost anecdotes or the later novels, are almost all characteristic of providing a strong sense of a good story on the part of Chinese fiction: interesting and attractive in terms of its plot and tension well organized and highlighted by some risky, yet tightly controlled events. One could find many examples to support this point: the legendary tales about love affairs or romantic conventions in ordinary life have shown frequent occurrences in classical fiction. For example, a young and learned scholar of lowly origin meets with a young and pretty lady from a rich family. Another typical scene is an official working for his promotions by corruption and bribery, who is very vividly presented to satisfy the ordinary people's sensuous and sensual needs to experience curiosity and enjoyment. One has to admit these kinds of story developments have their own charm in their ability to provoke strong desires and excitements, in contrast to the lack of other amusements in those days. For instance, many tales in *tang-dai-chuan-qi* (《唐代传奇》, Legends of the Tang Dynasty) belong to some touching love affairs and emotionally touching human relations, which met with a demand of pleasure and amusement among the ordinary people and passed down to later generations. Many of them were drawn from historical sources and equipped with moral principles based on Confucian ideas, such as care for official career, scholars' life and fortune's contribution as well as respect and sympathy for love and family relations.

One could also find the same kind of narrative in the early period of fiction in the West. The proper examples might be Ovid's *Metamorphoses* and Giovanni Boccaccio's *Decameron*.

Ovid's *Metamorphoses* is composed of dozens of myths and legends drawn from Greek and Roman sources. The book starts with the transformation of Chaos into the ordered universe, and after a succession of tales, comes to an end with the death and deification of Julius Caesar. Ovid goes beyond the range of the Graeco-Roman legend in the tale of Pyramus and Thisbe, the lovers of Babylon. Though all the stories are loosely organized and indicate no guiding thought, they supply some interesting individual stories and show Ovid's talent for composing narratives.

In spite of unevenness in the midst of over a hundred stories in *Decameron*, the best stories are interwoven with the circumstances and details of the contemporary society, for example, the conflicts between fortune and human nature with its concern for earthly self-reservation or self-indulgence rather than abstract concepts of morality or religion. Such conflicts produce a dynamic type of novella full of memorably dramatic scenes.

In terms of attractiveness in story development, both Chinese and Western early fictions have demonstrated quite a lot in common. Many of them were not originally created by the authors concerned, but were adapted or recomposed out of the myths, legends or fairy tales scattered elsewhere. These similarities were determined by the unchanged or slowly-changed social circumstances and thus such storytelling continued a long while until the eve of modern age.

7.2.2 Historical aspect of fiction

Asto historical concerns, the earlier Chinese fiction is usually said to be part of history that was always used to serve as a lesson for the rulers in applying his tactics to rule the country. Fiction was regarded as something related to history while history also contained some vivid and touching descriptions of historical figures or events, which made historical records resemble literary works. The best example of the latter is *shi-ji* (《史记》, The Historical Annals) by Sima Qian, in which many records are presented in literary language, demonstrating the fine qualities of some historical images. Some literary works, at the same time, were produced out of the raw material of historical records, such as *san-guo-yan-yi*. In parallel with the historical book *san-guo-zhi* (《三国志》, The Annals of the Three Kingdoms), *san-guo-yan-yi* could be regarded as an unofficial supplement to *san-guo-zhi*. This example indicates the close relation between fiction and history.

Western fiction also has some connections with history, but would not be so close as those in China. For the Westerners, perhaps history is history and could hardly if ever expect to adopt the form or structure of fiction, such as the case in *san-guo-yan-yi* versus *san-guo-zhi*. Maybe the Chinese author has cared too much for history and would not give up the function of history even in times of leisure. The Western author certainly chooses to enjoy himself by writing fiction and prefers to write something lighter and entertaining or amusing rather than serious historical events. For many Westerners, history seems a bit too heavy for relaxation though there could be some sorts of history with significant literary value such as Gibbon's *The History of the Decline and Fall of the Roman Empire* or Lytton's *The Last Days of Pompeii*. The former of the above, altogether six volumes, could be one of the greatest historical works in English language. Yet after all it is based on historical facts and would not claim to be a work of fiction. Another example is perhaps Leo Tolstoy's *War and Peace*, which is composed on the basis of Napoleon's war against Russia. Tolstoy's novel certainly shows great differences from *san-guo-yan-yi* in both focus and style. It will be handled comparatively in the later section as a case study.

The Western sense of historical fiction is not exactly the same as the Chinese one. One kind of Western fiction close to Chinese historical fiction might be picaresque or travelogue tales. The early European novels, such as *Don Quixote* by Miguel de Cervantes or *Gargantua and Pantagruel* by Francois Rabelais or even *Robinson Crusoe* by Daniel Defoe or *Tom Jones* by Henry Fielding, all have something to do with certain current or past social events of the time and are strongly suggestive of contemporary types of social life. But again, this sort of fiction is surely different from the Chinese sense of historical fiction as the latter is perhaps a kind of record of history with almost every event and figure coming from historical reality. The other kind that deserves the title of historical fiction is probably Walter Scott's novels, that are mostly based on historical reality, such as *Rob Roy*, *The Heart of Midlothian* and *Ivanhoe*. In these novels he chose to depict historical events and characters and hence achieved a sense of genuineness and truthfulness which greatly provoked the curiosity and interest of many people to read the books and discuss the connection and similarity between the novel and history concerned. The response to Scott's historical fiction resembles what has happened to *san-guo-yan-yi* and *shui-hu* though the former is somewhat dwarfed by the latter in terms of continuous influence.

7.2.3 Moral value of fiction

Moral function is perhaps one of the controversial issues in both Chinese and Western fictions. It does not mean either side neglects or belittles or devalues the role that a moral sense can play in fiction, but suggests the divergence in understanding what moral role one should play in his or her own culture. This is perhaps the reason why both cultures have produced a number of books with different evaluations of this aspect of society at different historical stages. The most striking examples might be *jin-ping-mei* in China and *Lady Chatterley's Lover* in the West. Both novels established their influences and reputations with the portrayal of sexual behaviour. They were targets of severe criticism and suffered from condemnation by the public. Therefore, the authors and their works had experienced long-term suppression before their eventual release from censorship.

The complicated and tortuous experience of the two books manifested the human intellectual changes in moral awareness and view of sexual descriptions. It is a pity that human beings have to spend such a long time improving themselves morally and intellectually, but certainly it is a relief to overcome the barriers set by intellectual obscurity and folly and indicates the huge progress made by the human race. However, it also brings a challenge to the moral code. Moral values occur every now and then in the judgment of literary work. Sometimes it is not so easy to tell moral problems from its ideological or aesthetic values.

In the West, official standards of public taste also dominated a long while over publication of literary works. Not only were certain novels by D. H. Lawrence taken as pornography and forbidden for sale within Britain, but other great writers were deprived of the right to publish domestically. James Joyce, for example, had to publish his *Ulysses* outside of Britain for overemphasis on sex. Even Shakespeare was bowdlerized in the Victorian Age. But of course such harshness in executing morally-oriented censorship has greatly reduced in the later years, due to the promotion of intellectual freedom and human rights in the West. Regard for intellectual choices and multicultural possibilities has evoked more moderate attitudes towards and even tolerance of different trends and themes and techniques in fiction as well as other literary genres. Nonetheless, the dominant conservatively-oriented views within the mainstream of fiction have rarely given way to radical or leftist tendencies in literary production. The so-called new right ideological trend represented by Ronald Reagan and Margaret Thatcher in the late 1970s and 1980s, is actually a continuation of the middle-class or bourgeois moral advocacy in their claim for the polished, cultured and cultivated taste and faith as well as criteria in life and judgment. It was initiated perhaps by Henry James in his literary criticism and then further developed by F. R. Leavis in his practical criticism and cultural studies. No one could totally deny the political effect on the establishment of this theoretical framework, yet meanwhile one could perceive the crucial function of non-political factors which were independent of political influences and contributed to the eventual shaping of the cultural and literary values and norms. In a way intellectual development helps expand non-political influences and benefits a better understanding of moral sense and standards to apply to literary and cultural reading and studies.

7.2.4 Social significance of fiction

Though Chinese fiction has had a long history and attracted a large audience, yet it could hardly find itself capable of fostering literary works in a more independent, objective and fair manner because of political preoccupation. No one could really get rid of political influence on literature, but excessive consideration of politics could affect one's independent stance in making his judgment. Politics needs to locate its proper position in the altar of literary criticism, which should be more neutral and independent of external voices.

In China, fiction used to be downgraded to the low rank along with a body of folk tales or legends unofficially composed or collected. It was associated with textual composition of ungrounded, legendary, fragmentary and miscellaneous material, such as myths, anecdotes, fairy tales and ghost stories. Most of these stories were based on a kind of imagination, rather than on social reality or verisimilitude. Some of them were of wide circulation and to a certain extent, represented social tendencies or ways of life of selected people at the time. This kind of writing occurred very early in the history of fiction writing and later imposed strong influences. As time moved on, people were more aware of the importance of depicting social affairs. Fiction came to adapt itself to the mode of realist representation. Chinese narrative writing in the form of prose fiction could not be separated from its particular cultural background, especially the strong bondage with superstitious ideas. Thus many stories in the early period of prose writing had involved ghost legends. Though one could find traces of real life in these stories, generally they were based on superstitious imagination and richly peopled with ghosts, and retaliation cycles or intervention of divine power, which was very characteristic of Chinese Buddhism. Almost all the pieces in *sou-shen-ji*, a collection of short stories during the Northern and Southern Dynasties, belong to this category, such as *Han Ping the Couple*, *The Youngest Daughter of King Wu*, etc. The later stories from the Tang Dynasty seem to relate more to social reality though still having much to do with ghost legends, like *Huo Xiaoyu's Story*.

In contrast to the emphasis on positive didacticism by traditional Chinese fiction, Western fiction seems to care more for amusing and entertaining effect though social significance is also placed in its due position. The two earlier novels, *Gulliver's Travels* and *Robinson Crusoe*, contain humorous remarks and funny actions, which not only provoke laughter and amusement, but also evoke serious meditation over social corruption and violent capitalist accumulation of original capital.

7.2.5 Preparation for modern fiction

Fiction gained rapid progress not long after its birth because of its close connection with social reality either in China or in the West.

In China, the early narrative story was principally used to reflect social life of merchants and young intellectuals and consequently became a fashion in the cities as main topics of storytelling, a kind of entertainment popular in public life during the Song Dynasty. In the West, the significant story appeared as early as in the Roman period when *The Golden Ass* and Ovid's *Metamorphoses* began to present a growing though still limited number of stories based on legendary tales or myths.

However, the real sense of creative writing of fiction did not come until around the 15th — 17th centuries when the novel as an essential form of fiction was brought into being with the publication of such Chinese novels as *san-guo-yan-yi* and *shui-hu*, and such Western novels as *Gargantua and Pantagruel* and *Don Quixote*. Fiction was formally recognized by the society as one of the major forms of literature after the Renaissance in the West and around the end of the Ming Dynasty in China. From then on, fiction has undergone a series of rapid and radical changes and developed into an unprecedentedly and vigorously prosperous period with an unpredictedly large readership. Armed with literary theories of different kinds, fiction subsequently moved into the ensuing stages of realism, naturalism, romanticism and modernism.

Each group is marked by some special features and indicates different focuses and priorities of the two sides. For instance, realism is dominant in traditional fiction and witnesses such representative works as *san-guo-yan-yi*, *shui-hu*, *jin-ping-mei* and *ru-lin-wai-shi* in China in line with Defoe's *Robinson Crusoe*, Dickens' *Bleak House*, Stendhal's *Red and Black* and Tolstoy's *War and Peace*. Either in China or in the West, romanticism seems less influential in fiction than in poetry. Maybe Chinese novels like *xi-you-ji*, *jing-hua-yuan*(《镜花缘》, The Tales of Visionary Land) and *liao-zhai-zhi-yi* (《聊斋志异》, The Odd Stories of Liao Zhai) could be counted as romantic works, also Western novels such as Hugo's *Notre Dame de Paris*, A. Manzonis' *The Betrothed* and Aleksandre Pushkin's *Yeygeny Ornegin*. But if we make further exploration, we might find the basic difference between them. Chinese romance is more relevant to fantasy and myth though social implication is perceived while the Western fiction is more directly related to social reality no matter whether it is romantically-oriented or realistically-oriented as these examples demonstrate.

With the eventual accomplishment of the traditional form of fiction, more and more people began to heighten fiction as one of the most popular and hence most important genres of literature. Its contribution to the embodiment of sophisticated human spiritual life and the uplifted animation of human energy is tremendously amazing. At the time, however, some writers of original creation started to make further exploration of both theme and form in fiction at an attempt to promote narrative literature to a new height.

7.3 Central concern and subject matter

Subjectmatter and thematic concerns of fiction take root in social soil and national identity of the countries concerned. However, human nature is the decisive factor in the motivation and concerns of the writer in his composition of fiction. Therefore, one could find similar traces in the tendencies' constitutions and characterization of any kind of fiction. Most of the novels and stories are related to each other in one way or the other. Either Chinese or Western fiction could be classified, for instance, into such subjects as political and historical inclination, social convention, love romance and myth or supernatural stories.

A general survey of fiction could find much in common between China and the West in respect of their interest in historical and political subject matter. For instance, they share many interests in though not necessarily the same view of material improvement and enjoyment, spiritual pursuit and intellectual awareness, emotional affection and impulse, moral priority and justification, social justice and development, economic wealth and prosperity, military operation and victory, political strategy and power seizure, etc. These subjects are universally acceptable to the writers as writing concerns both in China and the West, modern or ancient. Therefore, the human race could claim those great works of lasting value which have survived the test of time and space and are recognized universally by both the writer and reader, because these writings embrace those common qualities. Either *hong-lou-meng* or *Anna Karenina* is viewed as a novel of universal significance since it embodies such invaluable topics as eternal love, emotional sensitivity, philosophical penetration, social exposure and tragic spirit, as is conveyed in polished language, psychological depth and unified structure.

7.3.1 Historical and political concerns

Among the variety of subject matter and concerns of fiction, it is history and politics that occupy a very important position. This is because these two areas have more direct relevance to the people's desire of acquiring more fundamental knowledge about historical and political issues in addition to satisfying the curiosity of general public.

Perhaps it is the reason why Chinese historical and political novels *san-guo-yan-yi* and *shui-hu* could become so popular and have remained unchanged in attracting the taste of a large readership in the space of over five hundred years. In the centuries after the publication of these two novels, few Chinese have not read of them, due to the fascinating story development and the moral provocation one could gain from the reading. The strong sense of justification and heroism has deeply touched the hearts of the ordinary readers and kept inspiring generation upon generation of the Chinese. The fundamental issues, like life and death, war and peace, justice and corruption, loyalty and disloyalty, heroism and cowardice, wisdom and stupidity, benevolence and cruelty, all these are well represented and balanced in the two novels as well as in other books of similar topics.

Generally, Chinese and Western novels are related by common social concerns and ethical values. Though the Chinese are inclined to prefer more subject matter of historical or political concerns in the earlier classical novels, such as *san-guo-yan-yi* and *shui-hu*, it does not mean Westerners do not care to deal with social and historical subjects. As a matter of fact, the great novel has often much to do with important events in the social and historical developments of their nations. Comparatively speaking, however, Westerners seem to lack epic-sized structures and detailed descriptions of important historical events to the extent of *san-guo-yan-yi* and *shui-hu*, though one could cite as an exception

Tolstoy's *War and Peace*. This novel certainly unfolds an unprecedented breadth of scene in depicting Napoleon's war against Russia. But the above-mentioned Chinese novels appeared in the main between the 16th and 17th centuries, about two centuries earlier than the major Western examples.

Another feature is the strong sense of moral didacticism asserted in the Chinese historical and political novels. For example, the advocacy of loyalty, benevolence, righteousness and credibility is very popular among the Chinese novels. The three sworn brothers Liu Bei, Guan Yu and Zhang Fei in *san-guo-yan-yi*, Song Jiang's brother-like treatment of his friends in *shui-hu*, Yue Fei's whole-hearted devotion to the monarch and his country, and the brotherhood relationship at Wagang Fort, are widely spread and established as part of Chinese classical cultural tradition because of the novels disseminated across the land.

However, most of Western writers, in the early period of the 17th and 18th centuries in Europe, could hardly break away from the influence of chivalry and picaresque writing in terms of structure and subject matter. Their works would represent some historical and political descriptions, such as the portrayal of knight's idle lifestyle and showy air of heroism in their behaviours, as shown in the image of *Don Quixote*. The real sense of history in Western fiction was only confined to a few writers in those days like Walter Scott from Scotland. Many of his novels are devoted to historical fiction, but their concern is quite distinct from that of Chinese historical fiction. *Ivanhoe* as one of his best-known works, for instance, centres round a kind of triangular love affair though its historical settings are drawn from historical record based on the hostility and enmity between the Saxon and the Norman during the period of Norman Conquest. Compared with Chinese historical fiction like *san-guo-yan-yi* or *shui-hu*, both of which are designed to depict an enormously grand scale of social, political and military events and representative figures of the time based on a broad perspective and profound insights, the Western fiction seems limited in its exploration of the historical dimension. It was not so often during and before the 19th century to locate such depictions as the historical scenes related to the French Revolution in Charles Dickens' *A Tale of Two Cities*. But later on, historical fiction of the West has received more attention. For instance, there appeared a large body of historical fiction after the two world wars. Among the best-known writers of historical fiction, Herman Wouk's name should not be forgotten. His two-volume historical novel set in the World War II, *The Winds of War* and *War and Remembrance* have brought his name to the households of millions of people all over the world. The concerns of both horror and heroism are well represented in these books, though controversial, and could in a way stand for historical fiction which views historical reality in realist mode.

7.3.2 Social convention

Social concern refers to the issues of social life which involve a wide range of subject matter, from family life to social relations, from public service to individual business, from social satire to eulogy of certain positive deeds or quality.

In China, more and more writers are concerned with the daily life of the ordinary people as time moves on since the beginning of the Qing Dynasty. One of the earlier books of such kind is probably Wu Jingzi's *ru-lin-wai-shi* dealing with intellectual life of the ordinary scholars in the Chinese feudal society. Various qualities and personalities of the intellectuals in those days are presented vividly and ironically, focusing on the paradoxical nature of their temperament and performance, such as erudition and incapability, arrogance and humbleness, ambition and impracticability, courageousness and timidity, sense of justice and submissiveness. Many of his intellectual characters, such as Fan Jin and Wang Mian, are poor or inferior in social position in opposition to the wealthiness and arrogance of the rich and officials, either as a result of unjust treatment by the then society or due to the misguided intellectual mission based on impractical tendency. In addition, the novel is a critique of the Civil Service Examination System, which comes from the author's personal experience and observation and demonstrates the pernicious influence of the system on the intellectuals.

Western fiction has a longer tradition caring for social convention. At the very beginning of modern fiction, social life was regarded as a focus of creative writing. For instance, *Gargantua and Pantagruel* and *Don Quixote* alike are both informed by the social conditions of the time, reflecting chivalry lifestyle and conflicts between the Christian church or aristocracy and the ordinary people, especially the lower class people. *Gargantua and Pantagruel* centres round the two giants who represent the humanist pursuit of ideal life set against the Christian church. *Don Quixote*, on the other hand, shows more fun and satire of a Spanish gentleman who imagines himself to be a knight. Together with his partner Sancho Panzo, Quixote meets with countless events or objects which are all regarded as enemies and therefore give rise to many jokes and misunderstandings.

The specific concerns of the two sides could be diverse, but they are all drawn from social reality of the time. A realistic tendency is evidently characteristic of the early novels on both sides. Such tendency became the mainstream of writing and remained dominant on both sides for a long time until its climax in the West in the 19th century when realistic masterpieces such as those by Dickens, Thackeray, Eliot, Stendhal, Balzac, Tolstoy, Chekov and others came out to wide acclaim of the world. Chinese fiction also developed in the direction of further exposing social reality. Novels like *lao-can-you-ji* (《老残

游记》, The Tale of Lao Can's Travels), *er-shi-nian-mu-du-zhi-guai-xian-zhuang* (《二十年目睹之怪现状》, Twenty Years' Witness of Strange Phenomena) and *nie-hai-hua* (《孽海花》, Flowers of the Adverse Sea) all provided a picture of different kinds of social conditions in old China and hence left noticeable traces in the development of Chinese fiction. But obviously fiction of social convention does not exclude other types of writing which are handled in the following section.

7.3.3 Love romance

Both Chinese and Western fictions contain a large number of romance works famous for their description of sexual relations between men and women. In China, such a tradition could be dated to the early years of fiction during the Tang Dynasty, where the story of Cui Yingying and others were produced to represent sexual love between a young scholar and a young lady, which was developed into a pattern for the later romances and proliferated as a fashionable genre.

Western romances came much later. The early form might be that of the picaresque with some interlude of love affairs to add to the main story development. The first real love story is perhaps Henry Fielding's *Tom Jones* which centres around the sexual relation between Tom Jones and his girlfriend Sophia.

Love is not always happy and sometimes would bring sorrow and distress as Charlotte Bronte's *Jane Eyre* and her sister Emily Bronte's *Wuthering Heights* have demonstrated. Stendhal's *Red and Black* shows the misuse of love for personal career and fate. Thomas Hardy's *Tess of the d'Urbervilles* is even tragic when the heroine is put on the gallows due to her murder of Alec, her seducer, for the sake of revenge and in releasing her instant fury at losing her virginity. Modern love stories seem to care more for the psychological impulse rather than social issues in respect of sexual love. D. H. Lawrence's fiction might serve as an example. His *Sons and Lovers* and *Women in Love*, both show this tendency. The former gives an account of how Paul the son could not part from his mother's shadow and fails as a lover for the two young ladies based on a kind of Oedipus complex while the latter handles the issue of sexual relationship between the two couples centring around the significance of marriage and homosexual relation.

Chinese fiction writers, on the other hand, are evidently positioned unfavourably at this stage in comparison to their Western contemporaries. Nonetheless, it does not mean one is unable to find any significant works during this period, which could match the values of the great novels of the West. Take for instance the two famous novels the Chinese writers produced during the 1920s and 1930s. One is Ba Jin's *jia* (《家》, Family) and the other is Lao She's *luo-tuo-xiang-zi* (《骆驼祥子》, The Rickshaw Rider). Both the novels are set against the decline of old China where the ordinary people from all walks of life struggled and staggered for making a living. Either the national capitalists or poor workers had to build up their fortune by riding over social and economic barriers as what happens in *luo-tuo-xiang-zi* while the young in Ba Jin's *jia* have to tolerate great pressure from both the society and the feudal family and work hard to live a happy life and pursue their ideal and love by getting rid of feudalistic ideas and influences. If Mingfeng's death is a sign of cold-blooded and inhuman attitude towards and treatment of a maid by the feudal family, who disallows the love between the young master and the humble maid-girl from an obscure origin, Juehui's eventual departure from his family marks the eruption of a rebellion against that family as well as the feudal hierarchy and ideology. *Luo-tuo-xiang-zi* might be different in that the hero's love is more practical and successful in spite of the differences between Xiangzi and Huniu. Their happiness is shortly maintained before Huniu is killed due to dystocia.

Sex is certainly the central term and one of the most sensitive words in love stories. In the West one could not forget Lawrence's name when coming to the topic of sexual descriptions. His *Lady Chatterley's Lover* is widely renowned for its overexposure of sex, which is supposed to represent the opposition of vitality of life force and decline of industrialization. In China, a similar topic could be found nowhere but in the classical novel *jin-ping-mei*, which deals with the sexual relations between Ximen Qing, a rich rogue and dissolute playboy, and his three concubines. Both the novels focus on the portrayal of sex and provide details to the sexual occurrences based on an elaborate design symbolic of social and intellectual circumstances of the period in which the protagonists lived despite the gap of about three centuries between them.

Love fiction usually has great expectation of happiness in its theme, but sometimes it could also be tinted with a tragic sense. The tragic sense in many Chinese and Western love novels is not isolated or accidental. It has something to do with the social circumstances of that particular society. Either Christian or aristocratic factors, or feudalistic and other backward forces, are shown to be barriers to the development of pure and mature love relations.

It would be meaningless to compare the thematic concerns of such a diverse background, which derived from a different national identity and different cultural tradition. The point, in the way the central ideas or concerns are worked out by the above-mentioned writers, represents entirely divergent or even opposite artistic temperaments and styles. The Chinese novels, no matter how different they are in their own central themes, basically depend for their acceptance on the attractive story development. All the major figures and events are related to each other by cause and effect, while ignoring the psychological movements or communication within the mind. In a sense, Chinese fiction is subdued in its revelation of the mental development of human figures, despite its focus on social and historical representations.

7.3.4 Myth and supernatural tales

Aside from love affairs working as an important part of fiction concerns and subject matter, myth and supernatural writings have also contributed considerably to the constitution of fiction.

In China, ghost story has a long tradition which could be traced to the Wei, one of the Three Kingdoms after the Eastern Han Dynasty as well as the Jin Dynasty and the Northern and Southern Dynasties. *Sou-shen-ji*, for instance, is an anthology of such kind produced during the period. However, the most famous of the kind is *liao-zhai-zhi-yi* by Pu Songling, a scholar who failed at the Civil Service Examination of the Qing Dynasty and devoted himself subsequently to the collection and recomposition of the ghost stories in the anthology. These stories are beautifully recreated and are mostly based on human experiences and temperaments like love, study travel and social relations. Therefore they have been widely disseminated and won the favour of many people in China.

Another famous myth is doubtless *xi-you-ji* which combines Buddhist legend with Chinese social life and invents a number of lifelike and fascinating supernatural figures. Among them are Monkey and Piggy who, semi-human and semi-animal as they are, have achieved omnipotent capacity to handle and overwhelm various kinds of demons and ghosts on their way to escort Tang the Monk to collect the Buddhist scripts from the Western Heaven where they are eventually deified alongside the Monk on account of their merits.

The third example is Li Ruzhen's *jing-hua-yuan*. It tells of many odd and interesting travels and encounters of three Chinese tourists, such as visits to the Woman Kingdom and Gentleman Kingdom with a strong sense of irony against social reality in China.

The Western tradition of myth is also just as strong as that of China. *The Golden Ass*, for instance, picks up an ass as the image for the protagonist to change into. Then Ovid's *Metamorphoses* also contains many supernatural beings who are imbued with human nature and superman's power.

Such mythological tales and supernatural descriptions have au fait pervaded the whole process of Western fiction development. Giants in *Gargantua and Partagruel*, or haunted images in some of Edgar Allen Poe and Henry James' ghost stories. Its culmination, however, did not come till the modernist period. Supernatural images are used frequently in the works of those expressionist writers, including Kafka's *Metamorphosis* where the hero turns into a beetle unable to endure pressure from both work and life of modern society.

Another famous modern novel *The Lord of the Flies* is a fable-like novel which employs the mythological idol Lord of flies to suggest the theme of fear set against the crisis of human civilization due to the opposition between democracy and autocracy. Other novels, such as George Orwell's *Animal Farm*, and those of the more recent magical realist mode from Latin America are also pertinent to this area, giving a large variety of representations, which depart from social realism.

Chinese myth is, generally speaking, limited to early fiction and has not gained further headway after moving into the 20th century. Probably this is because a ghost legend alongside ghost ideology is regarded as part of superstition and excluded out of the mainstream writing though the taboo is not very harsh and did not affect the use of myths or ghosts in creative writing. Even so, the ghost image is not positively regarded in regular Chinese culture. But with the revival of modernist writing, some younger writers, such as Can Xue and Han Shaogong, have consciously adopted the odd imagery, like ghosts and demons and other supernatural beings. This tendency indicates the narrowing gap between Chinese and Western novelists in terms of seeking traditional culture in company with transplanting international successful practice onto national soil in the fresh wind of so-called postmodernism.

7.4 Writing methods

Fiction started generally from the demand of the ordinary people, particularly the lower class people, as a popular, inexpensive and interesting way of entertainment, like hearing and enjoying their ideas and feelings to be passed around. Therefore, fiction, almost from its origin, was motivated by its realist need, though the term "realism" was not used in its initial stage. For a long period of time, the method of fiction creation was confined to storytelling and the amusing effect was based on external description, rather than other considerations. Such a method and awareness need to be modified obviously with the development of social and intellectual circumstances, especially after moving into the modern stage. More and more fiction writers became aware of the necessity of readjustment of the writing techniques arising from differences between the external and internal focuses, physical and psychological depictions, omnipotent perspective and perspective of an individual character, formal language and informal language, surface meaning and connotative implication, etc. Hereafter are presented some of the major points concerning the methods of fiction writing.

7.4.1 Language features

The use of language as an important feature contributed much to the quality of fiction. Most of Chinese classical literary works, including poetry and drama, were composed in the classical written language which was not so easy to understand for the ordinary people. Such a tendency had lasted many years and remained unchanged until the Song Dynasty when spoken-language tales appeared. In comparison with the tales of the Tang Dynasty, these spoken-language stories represented more widely the lives of broad masses of the ordinary people, especially those with inadequate education, such as merchants, handicraft workers and housewives. The stock characters of such kinds of social groups entered fiction and received favourable responses as positive figures, which had been rare in Chinese fiction. These stories certainly became more popular and enlarged fiction readership, marking a new phase for Chinese popular fiction. It was the outcome of China's middle period of prosperous development of agriculture, handicraft production and commerce on the one hand and vigorous growth in urban culture on the other.

Rather than focusing on the characters from the upper and wealthy classes, as in the previous period, *hua-ben* (话本, the spoken-language tales) of the Song Dynasty handled mostly everyday life topics of the ordinary people. The authors were not necessarily scholars or officials or other members from the upper class, but would come from ordinary city dwellers or even from poor origin. Love affairs among the average people, women's initiative in pursuing their true love or struggle against tyranny and corruption of the officials on the part of the rank and file were portrayed vividly in these stories. Overall, Chinese fiction thus in its development was confined to the short story form and a narrow range of subject matter, such as love affairs or conflicts between officials and the ordinary people. The real sense of fiction was not established until the emergence of classical novels, which had to wait for a couple of centuries.

Chinese plain and spoken language made its early appearance in the classical novels long before it was adopted formally in fiction and other literary forms at the turn of the 20th century as a milestone in Chinese modern literature. Compared with the language in poetry, fiction adopted spoken language as early as in the Southern Song Dynasty when *hua-ben*, an early form of fiction was produced, which greatly helped enlarge the readership and popularize fiction to meet daily spiritual need. From then on, more and more classical written language was gradually removed and fiction as part of popular literary culture was recognized as a major literary genre.

Western fiction was somewhat different in its later development and in terms of the use of language though it had shared a lot with Chinese fiction in respect of form and popularity. Its early form had also focused on story development and the use of magical means, like that of *The Golden Ass* during the period of Roman Empire. But later on, tales like the verse narratives in the Middle Ages had much to do with the ordinary people (mostly city and rural dwellers and lower class people) and reflected their joys and sufferings, often marked with rich imagination and realistic tendencies. Instances are such as those from Chaucer's

The Canterbury Tales and Boccaccio's *Decameron*. These stories, however, were still difficult to read though they were based on oral legends spread widely and passed from generation to generation. They were largely the outcome of the English language which developed from old English through many changes yet still presented a large number of slangs and old forms of English which brought difficulties to the readers, most of whom moved from outside and built up a considerably large population as the mainstay of the city. Hence like Chinese fiction, some basic features, such as minimal characterization, simple but interesting story development and plain language were budding in the early works of this period. However, it was only in the genre of novel that both cultures eventually found their most representative way of writing. Quite a lot of writings were originally drawn from oral stories offered by storytellers in China or from plays staged by travelling troupes in the West.

One thing worth mentioning is the use of slang, as manifested in Mark Twain's *The Adventures of Huckleberry Finn* where American slang entered as part of fiction language, violating the routine forbidding slang, colloquialism and other form of dialect in literature. Similar use of vernacular English can be seen in colonial literature as in Henry Lawson's bush tales and Joseph Furphy's novel *Such Is Life* in Australian fiction. Earlier than that was the appearance of large numbers of colloquialism in the realist works in England and other European countries. Maybe this tendency opened a new page in the creation of fiction though Western modern languages, English included, had served as the vehicle of fiction and literature since the Renaissance, which preceded and prescribed the pioneering reform of Chinese culture and literature bringing forward the plain and spoken language into Chinese new fiction.

7.4.2 Narrative structure and perspective

Novel writing requires a careful and deliberate consideration of structure, which is usually chronologically ordered. The typical arrangements in Chinese classical novels, such as *san-guo-yan-yi*, *shui-hu* and many other historical novels, almost all follow such a pattern without any flashback or variation in narrative sequence. The early Western novels, such as *Gargantua and Pantagruel*, *Don Quixote* and *Robinson Crusoe*, are also structured chronologically. Considering their close relation with social documentation peculiar to narrative realism, this feature seems natural and had to continue well into the 19th – 20th centuries when the use of flashback was developed.

Apart from time order, another common narrative feature with fiction on both sides is narrative perspective. Omnipotent and omniscient methods had been prevailing for quite a long time before the 20th century. The narrator's voice at the time suggested the author's stance and control of the whole novel, which was pervasive and omnipotent. The narrator's control was irresistible and obligatory in a sense, since it came from the author's point of view. Such a tendency remained unchanged in Chinese fiction till very late into the 20th century. Comparatively speaking, Western fiction showed earlier signs of perspective innovation, as represented by Strether, the protagonist and narrator in Henry James' novel *The Ambassadors* (1903), which marked a demarcation line for fiction in terms of narrative viewpoint. From then on, fiction has evolved into more realistic modes, in that characters no longer seem tools controlled by authors, but appear to be shaped by the sophisticated interactions taking place in the midst of the real situation of human relations and viewed by characters themselves. Such narrative perspective is certainly more lifelike and closer to real life, and therefore acceptable to both readers and writers. The technique has hence become fashionable and popular within a short space of time. Unfortunately, Chinese fiction did not catch the fashion in good time and had to wait several decades due to certain reasons before modernist techniques and narrative perspectives were introduced.

7.4.3 Characterization and psychological writing

Among the techniques of fiction, characterization is perhaps the earliest and most developed since it appeared almost with the production of fiction. Since fiction focuses on the portrayal of characters, we might say fiction could hardly survive without characters. Therefore focus on characters has become the first and most important mission for all fiction writers. Careful observation, vivid description, subtle representation and penetrating or universal insights are all aspects of characterization. Many images, based on these descriptions, therefore, are produced simultaneously with an exploration of deep thematic concerns set against certain social backgrounds or based on a selected philosophical or religious or cultural framework. One could find a multitude of examples among the novels of each culture. Such characteristics indicate that Chinese and Western writers are united by their human nature and social and cultural awareness as well as by their ability to demonstrate intellectual perception.

However, characterization is also an area where both Chinese and Western fictions show their distinctiveness. Usually Chinese characters in traditional fiction are inclined to be divided into the positive and the negative, such as loyal or treacherous, good or evil, mild or violent, courageous or cowardly, intelligent or stupid — the so-called linear characters. In Western fiction, characterization is also divided into different kinds, but not always based on the criterion of being positive or negative. Rather, these characters would be more diversified and colourful and objective in terms of presentation, such as the simple-minded and the complicated as indicated in E. M. Forster's term, flat or round characters. ①

Classical fiction, either Chinese or Western, cares much for a division of positive and negative characters, but the individual characters are generally endowed with more than a simple or stereotypical temperament, rather, a mixture of different or even opposite elements of sophisticated human nature. In Chinese fiction, typical characters include Cao Cao, Liu Bei and Zhuge Liang in *san-guo-yan-yi*, and Song Jiang, Wu Song and Gao Qiu in *shui-hu* while in Western fiction one could list Don Quixote, Robinson Crusoe, Heathcliff, Anna Karenina, Vronsky, etc.

If social concerns are dominant among the earlier Chinese and Western novels, psychological concerns become very popular in modern Western fiction from the end of the 19th century after a long period of silence since Samuel Richardson's psychological novel *Clarissa Harlowe* made its first appearance in the 18th century. It is doubtless true of Western fiction where changes started from the late 19th century when Henry James came into his later period of writing by producing *The Wings of the Dove*, *The Ambassadors* and *The Golden Bowl*, pioneering an entirely new mode called psychological realism, with a focus on mental or psychological exploration of his characters' inner world in relation to social reality. Henry James is then followed by a whole new generation of writers who turned their perspectives from the external and conventional concern for social reform or superficial characterization to those of internal and psychological depth. Modernism, as it is called, marks a drastic change as well as a thoroughgoing penetration into human mind, leading to a completely radical and totally new direction in fiction writing.

In spite of the tremendous divergence modernism has brought to literature, most Western writers have tried to choose a middle line of writing by intermingling different kinds of ideas and methods, hoping such a compromise would not offend the conventional reader while picking up some new ideas to follow and even appearing to merely please the fashion for modernism. However, the experimental novelists never give up their ambition and have been recognized universally to be the most accomplished with their modernist works of fiction.

---

① According to E. M. Forster, characters in fiction are either flat or round, depending upon whether the writer sketches or sculptures them. A flat character generally has only one ostensible trait or feature, or at most a few distinct marks. A flat character seldom surprises the reader, is immediately recognizable, and can usually be represented by a single sentence while a round character presents us with many facets and is generally drawn with sufficient complexity to be able to surprise the reader without losing credibility. Such a round character may appear to the reader as he / she appears to the other characters in the story. If their views of him / her differ, the reader will see him / her from different angles. This is not to say that a flat character is an inferior work of art. In most fiction — even the greatest — minor characters tend to be flat rather than round. Flat characters reflect a writer's different observations of human life. For more details, see *The Aspects of Novels*, E. M. Forster, Gale, 2002.

One of the best examples is perhaps the development of the stream of consciousness technique, which worked on a totally new narrative perspective and employed skills that initially confined their works to the needs and tastes of a small circle of readers at the turn of the 20th century when Dorothy Richardson presented her novel *The Pointed Roof*. With the persistent efforts of such writers as Marcel Proust (1871 − 1922), James Joyce (1882 − 1941), Virginia Woolf (1882 − 1941) and William Faulkner (1897 − 1962), the stream of consciousness shortly became one of the most established and favourite techniques of the new school of modern literature. The novels of the stream of consciousness like *A la recherché du temps perdu* by Marcel Proust, *Ulysses* and *Finnegans Wake* by James Joyce, *To the Lighthouse* and *The Waves* by Virginia Woolf, and *The Sound and the Fury*, *As I Lay Dying* and *Light in August* by William Faulkner, have become master-pieces acknowledged by the majority of today's literary readers and critics.

If we look over the major achievements in Chinese fiction, we would find out that psychological writing, comparatively speaking, was obviously limited and less known in the rest of the world in the same period. Not only was Chinese fiction short of works as influential as those modernist writings in the West, or even as those classical works in the earlier period of China, like *hong-lou-meng* or even *shui-hu*. It is not just a matter of technique or style, but an awareness of the nature of the social and intellectual issues faced with the country at the time. Joyce's *Ulysses*, for instance, is highly reputed largely because of its exposure of the major modern crisis occurring to the Irish people. Instances are such as Catholic influence on the average Irish, the corruption and incapability of the citizens of Dublin, and discrimination against the Jew and the women. In addition, its use of a symbolic structure based on Homer's *The Odyssey* and its psychological and vivid description of the chief protagonists' inner minds provided contemporary readers with a totally new reading experience from a novel. Of course, Joycean artistic exploration, especially language experiment, is of vital importance to appreciating Joyce's literary achievement as a whole. But one could hardly offer such a positive comment without considering his thematic concerns. It is exactly the deepening of social themes that Joyce's novel could make a successful presentation, rather than merely offering a kind of language modification or revision of normal narrative style. In a word, perhaps, one could say Joyce's prestige as a master novelist is established on an organic combination and unity of both justified social realist perspectives and perfect artistic inventiveness based, first of all, on his intensely psychological approach to characterization.

7.4.4 The use of imagery and other rhetorical devices

The fourth characteristic of writing technique common to both sides of fiction is that of imagination, in terms of the way to use imagery and atmosphere in fiction. For Chinese fiction, it was the apparition of supernatural images interacting with human characters in a world full of injustice and darkness as well as emotion and temptation. Such a tradition began with the early period of Chinese fiction and developed in the later ghost stories, culminating in *xi-you-ji*.

In this novel, Monkey not only seized by force the elixir[①], but also played havoc with and greatly disturbed through his rebellious spirit both the Heavenly Emperor and the Hell King[②]. Monkey's image and temperament supposedly originated not merely from Indian myth, but was a result of further development of the Chinese mystery tradition in early monster and ghost stories.

At the surface level, the novel is structured as a mythical tale set against Buddhist legend. Nonetheless, the tale itself is also a modified version of the true story of Xuan Zang, a Buddhist monk from the Tang Dynasty, who was dispatched by Tang Taizong, the emperor, as a missionary to fetch Sanskrit scripts from India. Tang the Monk, with his disciples, the legendary figures Monkey, Piggy and Monk Sha, worked together as the protagonists of the novel. The author imbued the characters with his feelings and viewpoints of social reality at the time, especially his views of social justice, his caricature of falsehood and malice, his rebellious demonstration of the orthodox establishment and his attack on the ruling class. The reader could easily relate Monkey to the embodiment of the wronged, the deceived, the oppressed and the rebellious. Also Monkey stands for the smart operator and seeker of justice, which are of great appeal to the reading public.

In contrast, Western fiction was not so popularly associated with ghosts and monsters, though one may also find such images as those by Edgar Allen Poe and Henry James, or in Gothic novel by Monk Lewis and Mary Shelley. More popular were the images of exaggeration, such as Rabelais' giant-like characters Gargantua and Pantagruel, or Jonathan Swift's description of either Lilliput where the inhabitants are six inches high or Brobbingnag where the inhabitants are as tall as steeples. Such imagination probably came from the Western literary tradition of using monsters or supernatural images in its early literature, such as English epic *Beowulf*, French epic *Chanson de Roland* and German fragmentary epic *Hildebrandslied*.

This kind of exaggeration and imagination also appeared in Chinese fiction in addition to the use of ghost images. The best-known novel of the kind is perhaps Li Ruzhen's *jing-hua-yuan*. The tale *Woman Kingdom* from this novel is widely told and remains one of the favourite items in the repertoire of some local entertainment troupes. The attractiveness of the tale is of course not just the reversed order in the

---

[①] Elixir, a word from medieval alchemy, means eternal-life medicine.
[②] The Heavenly Emperor and the Hell King, the two legendary rulers respectively of Heaven and Hell in Chinese myth, originated probably from Buddhist culture.

social roles played by men and women, but its hidden advocacy for sexual equity and its satirical tone employed to poke fun at a male-controlled hierarchical system.

7.4.5 Satirical and critical tone

The sense of satire is not confined to *jing-hua-yuan*, but is quite a popular feature common to a number of novels in both literatures. It is especially true of the Chinese novels towards the end of the Qing Dynasty. They include *nie-hai-hua*, *lao-can-you-ji*, *guan-chang-xian-xing-ji* (《官场现形记》, The Tale of Exposing the Official World) and *er-shi-nian-mu-du-zhi-guai-xian-zhuang*. All of them focus on an exposure of social darkness with bitter ironies and sarcasm, so penetratingly commenting on corruption, nepotism, snobbishness and moral decline which haunted human nature and retarded social development. *Er-shi-nian-mu-du-zhi-guai-xian-zhuang* covers widely various dark corners of society towards the end of the Qing Dynasty. The events and characters presented in the novel involve official, commercial and foreign business occasions. In this sense the novel has really achieved a good reputation on account of its wide-ranging influence and social exposure of some negative aspects at the time. Lu Xun once put it: "It is a pity that its description is inadequately offered by either over-exposure of evil or going beyond authenticity. Hence it only serves as talking stuff or laughing stock for leisure conversations."①

Western fiction often seems more preoccupied with such satirical descriptions. The early Chinese novels may have been principally concerned with documentary record and preferred to describe historical events and characters, but early Western fiction seemed to care more about a corrective and satirical portrayal of human nature and political corruption. For instance, Swift's character Gulliver obviously took a satirical attitude towards the empty talk of politicians when describing the heated dispute over which end of the egg should be broken. In Cervantes' depictions, Don Quixote's addiction to reading romances of chivalry led to his adventures and his errant search of wrongs to set right. Cervantes presented an ironical and multi-dimensional integration of enigmatic relationships of the ideal and the real, the true and the illusory, madness and sanity, art and life as the themes in the context of human experience.

Satirical portrayal doubtless has much to do with a profoundly critical spirit. One could hardly imagine any satirical way of writing without the author's taking a critical view of the characters or events he or she is to write about. Comparatively speaking, Western fiction is imbued with more critical spirit and satirical tone, though Chinese fiction might also show such traces occasionally.

Li Boyuan's *guan-chang-xian-xing-ji* is another novel to reveal and repudiate social darkness by focusing on the corruption of the government officials. It has

---

① 详见《中国小说史略》,鲁迅,上海古籍出版社,2006。

achieved an astonishing effect due to its sharp tongue and insightful penetration into the depth and bottom of the then society. It is meaningful to note that many figures of the novel could find similar prototypes in social reality. For instance, the Prime Minister in the novel in many ways resembles Rong Lu, the Prime Minister at the time. The petty officials like Zhao Wen and Qian Dianshi are typical of those petty officials of the Qing monarchy, featured with such qualities as being greedy, deft, secret and selfish, and even shameless. As Hu Shi once mentioned in his preface to the book: "We have to admit that most of the materials in the novel have epitomized the actual situation in the official world of the time."①

To some extent Hu's words sound reasonable. For instance, in addition to the similarity between Mr Hua the Prime Minister and Rong Lu the real Prime Minister at the time, the Black Uncle refers to Li Lianying the Head Eunuch. But as occurs to most of fiction, one could hardly expect a created figure to be exactly equivalent of a real figure. As a matter of fact, all the fictitious characters are grounded on a recreation of the qualities composed of a number of real characters. Take Mr Hua the Prime Minister as an example. His image is typical of the bureaucratic temperament popular at that time. One of his famous utterances is: "More kowtow and less talk." No one could exactly confirm if it was drawn from Rong Lu the Prime Minister, but one could cite a list of VIPs of the time in relation to it, which includes even Zeng Guofan, one of the most distinguished politicians and scholars in the 19th-century China. In this sense one could say this novel has presented some typical characters as the symbol of universal significance and hence has achieved a good effect by means of symbolism in exposing and repudiating the negative aspect of the official world towards the end of the Qing Dynasty.

Symbolic representation has also applied to Western fiction. We could cite similar devices of symbolic representation in a number of novels in the 18th and 19th centuries, even if we do not enthuse over the use of many symbols in modernist fiction. In addition to the previously mentioned instances, such as the dwarf people of Lilliput, the giants of Brobbingnag, Yahoos and horses of Houyhnhnms in Swift's *Gulliver's Travels*, and the three giants in Rabelais' *Gargantua and Pantagruel*, another arresting novel famous for its symbolic description certainly is the American novelist Herman Melville's *Moby Dick*. The novel is set against a symbolic account of the conflict between man and his fate, based on a story of how the one-legged captain Ahab and his sailors fight with Moby Dick the white whale in a life and death voyage. The doom and violence of the novel, conveyed through the coarse and vivid details of the struggle between men and the animal, manifests the author's tragic sense and satire of human fate and highlights the merit of symbolic representation as an artistic

---

① 详见《官场现形记》，李伯元，上海古籍出版社，2005。

technique. More novels of this category include Thomas More's *Utopia*, John Bunyan's *The Pilgrim's Progress* and Samuel Butler's *Erewhon* as well as a number of modern novels as represented by E. Hemingway's *The Old Man and the Sea*.

7.5 Case studies

Fiction, as one of the most popular though perhaps one of the youngest literary genres, shows its advantages in giving accounts of vernacular stories in natural, comprehensible and vivid ways. It is more than just a matter of knowing its general features and form according to some theoretical or literary introduction, but one needs to be acquainted with its specific components and categories by getting in touch with individual works as case studies of fiction. We need to take into account the criteria for our selection of these examples since the novels selected should be suited for the sake of comparison.

Aside from subject matter, our major consideration is the central concern of a novel, which seems more appropriate for intercultural comparison. It does not mean of course that we will not consider writing techniques. In fact, writing method nowadays contributes much to our assessment of a literary work. In a scale of comparison, there are several criteria, namely subject matter, background, structure, general concerns, characterization and major techniques. But on account of limited space, we have to focus on the central concerns while other aspects of fiction will be considered as well when necessary.

Probably we could concentrate on two groups of novels. First is a comparative study of *san-guo-yan-yi* by Luo Guanzhong and *War and Peace* by Leo Tolstoy as a category of political and military affairs. The second group is a study of social transformation and love relationships represented respectively by Cao Xueqin's *hong-lou-meng* and William Faulkner's *The Sound and the Fury*.

7.5.1 A comparative study of *san-guo-yan-yi* and *War and Peace*

The first category for comparison is of military affairs. The two wars concerned in these two novels are well known in each country. One is the notorious Napoleonic invasion of Russia and the other is the civil war lasting several decades in ancient China. In spite of the great temporal gap between the two wars and the difference in their nature, one could detect similarities in the social and economic influences, and these should be our focus of attention.

In China, civil wars were frequent, either at the beginning or the end of a dynasty, and brought about tremendous damage and disastrous impacts on the innocent civilians and society. Neither side in the war could assert any sense of justice, though both sides tried to. Yet in *san-guo-yan-yi*, the author appears more positive to Liu Bei and his gang though it is doubtful if he deserves it. Napoleon's war is certainly aggressive and therefore unjust and Tolstoy's stance is clear and justified in defence of his motherland.

However, the two novels are not just reputed for their political concerns but rather for their reflections on social and military ramifications. *San-guo-yan-yi* focuses more on military strategies and tactics of a number of operations directed by the political leaders and their major advisers, with some historically famous battles, such as *The Chibi Battle*, *The Arrows Borrowed by Straw Boats*, *Borrowing Eastern Wind* and *The Empty City Trap*. In these touching and revealing stories, Zhuge Liang's wisdom, Zhou Yu's narrow-mindedness, Cao Cao's sinister ambition and Liu Bei's humanness and humility are all discernible. They present vividly a picture of general social and cultural conditions of ancient China at that time, through showing the ways to handle complicated human relations and what to do to build up a military superiority by making use of the strength of the friend and the weakness of the enemy.

The popularity and success of the novel of course lies in the author's able representation of the traditional or dominant idea: longing for stability provided by a wise politician who is able to pull the ordinary Chinese people out of chaos and suffering. The central idea is conveyed through the descriptions of various battles and different characters. Liu Bei, Zhuge Liang and their group have thus received more favour and sympathy either in their time of victory or in their time of failure. The positive portrayal of this group constitutes a great contrast to the author's negative attitude towards Cao Cao. In the author's judgment, Liu Bei is of royal origin in addition to his love for the ordinary people as demonstrated in his protection of the civilians when pursued by the military troops of other warlords. Liu's behaviour is praiseworthy according to the author, because they comply with a consistent assertion of benevolence in Confucianism as part of Chinese traditional thought. The same is true with Zhuge Liang whose foresight and ability in handling political, military and economic affairs is combined with his devotion to Liu Bei and his son. This has won him much honour as a wise and devoted national hero. In contrast, Cao Cao's poor image as a wicked politician is almost known to everybody in China because of the popularity of *san-guo-yan-yi*.

War and Peace by Leo Tolstoy came out much later than *san-guo-yan-yi*. The latter was issued in the 14th century and the former in the 19th century. The two wars involved have an even greater gap than the time of writing: one targets a civil war occurring about eleven centuries earlier and the other less than one century earlier. In spite of these divergences, the concerns for social changes and the recording of the mental influences on historical development and the human spirit, seem to work similarly in the two novels. Tolstoy remarked this way in the epilogue of the novel:

History is the life of nations and of humanity.... The ancient historians all employed one and the same method to describe and seize the apparently elusive — the life of a people. They described the activity of individuals who ruled the people, and regarded the activity of those men as representing the activity of the whole nation.

The question: how did individuals make nations act as they wished and by what was the will of these individuals themselves guided? The ancients met by recognizing a divinity which subjected the nations to the will of a chosen man, and guided the will of that chosen man so as to accomplish ends that were predestined. For the ancients these questions were solved by a belief in the direct participation of the Deity in human affairs. Modern history, in theory, rejects both these principles. It would seem that having rejected the belief of the ancients in man's subjection to the Deity and in a re-determined aim toward which nations are led, modern history should study not the manifestations of power but the causes that produce it. But modern history has not done this. Having in theory rejected the view held by the ancients, it still follows them in practice. [1]

Tolstoy probably tries to find some justification in his description of the characters who, to him, should be of more general significance in terms of social development. The war with Napoleon, to his mind, is more than a war, which leads to killing and destruction, but a means to survey social changes and human mind. Rather than a focus on the specific strategies and tactics of military field as *san-guo-yan-yi* attempts, Tolstoy tries to mix up military depictions with the ordinary life of the civilians, epitomized by the aristocratic families, such as love affairs and other social business peculiar to the Bezukhovs, the Bolkonskys, the Rostovs and the Kuragins, including their luxurious way of life and their points of view of current affairs. Under his keen observation and delicate descriptions, the major figures, such as Andrew Bolkonsky, Pierre Bezukhov and Natasha Rostov, are endowed with some noble qualities against those negative characters like the Kuragins.

The war, in a sense, serves as a testimony for both men and women in their attitudes and in their temperament. Andrew Bolkonsky's patriotism and bravery, Pierre Bezukhov's pursuit of social progress and ideal way of living are no doubt an embodiment of some positive images against the performances of degeneration and voluptuousness represented by the latter's wife Helene. The author's interest in delicately exposing innermost feelings and motive forces of his characters provides insight into both human nature and social complexities.

---

[1] See *War and Peace*, epilogue 2, Leo Tolstoy, FONTANA / Collins, 2007.

The description of these figures and their conflicts are signs of individual roles in promoting social development and this marks Tolstoy's fundamental difference from Luo Guanzhong whose care is limited by his world view and values as a Chinese scholar in the middle period of Chinese feudal society. This difference, however, does not necessarily suggest Tolstoy's superiority over Luo, but rather a diversity in relation to the cultural difference and characteristic of time. On the other hand, Luo's macrocosmic structure of the story plus his true representation of Chinese cultural tradition (although not good or advanced enough by the current moral standard) is no less positive than Tolstoy's ideas, considering the five centuries' gap between their lifetimes.

One could find quite some similarities between the two novels despite the disparities mentioned above. A grandiose and wide-ranging picture of wholesale social, military and cultural or intellectual developments, for instance, certainly supplies an elaborate investigation into general conditions of each society at its own time though each side shows different social and intellectual developments. On the part of China, one could get a glimpse of how an intellectual worked typically in his own way, either away from the centre of power, choosing a hermit's way of life, or seeking to serve a political ruler for an opportunity to carry out his political ambition. On Russia's part, the established aristocracy seemingly had more access to political power and could more easily seize opportunities to take up a political career. Hence, the author chose to present more of cultural events, such as various kinds of gatherings and other social occasions to show off cultural interactions as a conventional way of self-introduction to social circles. The latter mode perhaps also indicates the switch of focus from the limitation of closed form of intellectual lifestyle to the more open, modern, intellectual and cultural mode of life as a sign of social and intellectual progress, which naturally suggests the different levels of social and intellectual developments peculiar to the two countries where the distance of time added to the difference of culture.

7.5.2 A comparative study of *hong-lou-meng* and *The Sound and the Fury*

Hong-lou-meng and *The Sound and the Fury* could be matched in that they both belong to the group of saga, or family history. Saga refers to a large area of fiction, which extensively covers a variety of origins, temperaments and consequences. *Hong-lou-meng* as one of the best-known classical literary works in China, is associated with its social and historical revelations, especially the profound knowledge and criticism of feudal society which was in a process of deterioration. Also it is a vivid account of a great romantic love story.

The Sound and the Fury presents the decline of the southern aristocracy in the United States and reveals some sophisticated love and other emotions involving the main characters and their relationships. Both the novels are an attempt to expose and condemn the decadence and corruption of old aristocracy. Neither novel is autobiographical, but both have included traces of a glorious past of the authors' family. As well, the love stories serve as a main thread if not the only dominant event in the plot development of these novels.

Hong-lou-meng focuses on the deterioration and downfall of a noble family, the Jia brothers who are conferred jointly the titles of Lord Ningguo and Lord Rongguo. However, due to the mismanagement, excessive luxury, decadence, corruption (such as incest, embezzlement, bribery, adultery and even murderous disregard for human lives) and lack of education as well as the inadequacy of the feudal system itself, the Jias seem inevitably doomed to decline. The depth of the novel of course is not confined to the repudiation of the evil of the Ning-Rong families, but implies bitter criticism of the emperor. When Jia Yuanchun, the emperor's concubine, comes back after a separation of a couple of years, she says sadly to her grandmother and mother: "Why do we have to keep crying without speaking or laughing since you sent me to that forbidden place where I could see none of you, nor do I know when on earth I could expect to meet you again."①

The central story of the novel develops around Jia Baoyu and Lin Daiyu, both of whom are rebellious and tragically bound in love. As the most indulged grandson of the family, Baoyu cherishes strong love for his cousin Daiyu who, in turn, loves Baoyu in the same vein. Out of her ignoring of social convention and over-sensitiveness, Daiyu could not be accepted by Baoyu's family, including her maternal grandmother. On the other hand, the snobbish Xue Baochai, another cousin of Baoyu, is chosen to marry Baoyu who has no freedom to decide his marriage and has to reluctantly accept her. The tragedy not only occurs to Daiyu who dies as a result of the event, but to Baoyu who eventually chooses to leave Baochai to make himself a monk. More than a personal tragedy, the failure of their marriage symbolizes the lack of sympathy and understanding of human right and feeling, which symbolizes the doom and decline of the feudal society and its institutions.

The Sound and the Fury, on the other hand, points to similar signs of self-destruction embodying the fatal sickness of aristocracy which provokes a series of alienations or malign events emerging from social changes affecting the Compson family. Very much like the noble origin of the Jia family in *hong-lou-meng*, the Compson family was once the genteel southern patricians. But that glory is gone with the passage of time, and the family has to tolerate a degenerate, perverted life on their shrunken plantation. The disintegration of the family is first revealed by the dispirited lifestyle of the Compson couple. Mr Compson is an alcoholic

---

① See *The Dream of Red Mansions*, p. 206, Cao Xueqin, People's Literature Press, 1962.

while Mrs Compson is a proud, snivelling, hypochondriacal mother. The fatal weaknesses apparently also fall on the children: Benjy being an idiot, Caddy involved in an adultery, Quentin unable to pull himself out of his incestuous love for his sister and taking suicide, Jason being dishonest and mean. The family seems unable to avoid the approaching doom and tends to grow even more dissipated in contrast to the strength of the Negro servants who are inclined to be both physically strong and financially prosperous.

In spite of the tragic atmosphere of the two novels, they share in showing the inevitable tendency of the aristocracy or feudal bureaucracy for fatal ruin. Obviously, they have distinct features in writing techniques and thus specific concerns.

Hong-lou-meng is much longer and grander in its size and structure, in the sense that it aims to give a comprehensive and integral representation of a typical feudalistic and bureaucratic family based on both political network and family relation. The encyclopaedic detail and description of the novel could hardly be matched by any writer, including Faulkner. As a realistic story, the Chinese novel has a style which inquires into different aspects of social reality, such as drinking, food, clothes, housing, medicine, etiquette, decoration and literary scholarship. This makes it unique in its range of subject matter and way of expression, conveying a very wide range of subjects of knowledge, customs, lifestyles and groups of people.

Comparatively speaking, *The Sound and the Fury* is simpler and narrower in terms of subject matter and themes, with little to give it more amplitude apart from a simple presentation of the life story of the Compsons. This is because the novel limits its focus to the relatively simple relations within and between the family members, especially the children of the Compsons. Obviously, the limited focus of the novel determines its restricted dimension, its length and its depth, which do not parallel those of its Chinese counterpart.

The Sound and the Fury, nevertheless, has its own strengths. The novel is inventive in its technique of using four different narrators to provide a more objective multiplicity of voices for the reader to follow and so to gain a more authentic knowledge of what has happened within the Compson family. As a typical work of the stream of consciousness, the novel resorts to some non-rationalist means, such as the congenitally idiotic and hallucinatory voices, in addition to traditional narrative and descriptive methods, and some instinctive and therefore more credible and innermost ideas. Comparatively, *hong-lou-meng* is limited in its narrative form and technique, which adheres, overall, to the normal chronological sequence of narration. Its perspective is still taken from the omnipotent author. Its narration and description are still controlled by an omniscient narrator and appear insufficient in flexibility and mobility. But of course this does not mean *hong-lou-meng* is deprived of all psychological descriptions. As a matter of fact, there are many passages with very vivid and insightful psychological portrayals of the characters concerned, such as the passage about Daiyu collecting and covering up flowers, and the passage where Baoyu is mourning over Daiyu's death. After all, there is a two-century gap between them, making up for the difference in writing techniques.

Given the different cultural background for the two novels, there are some expected diversities in the use of language. *Hong-lou-meng*, for instance, seems more encyclopaedic in its wide coverage of different types of knowledge and full of metaphors, allusions, proverbs, slang expressions and other language characteristics, which could only be matched by those in *Ulysses*, which is unfortunately not a saga. *The Sound and the Fury* has its own merit as a novel, such as its inventiveness in narrative perspective and psychological penetration, but certainly could not match *hong-lou-meng* in its extended structure and insightful thematic exploration as well as poetic language and breadth of cultural implication. This is perhaps the restriction of comparative study: one could never expect to find exactly the target of the same weight.

Questions for comprehension and discussion

1. Describe the development of Chinese and Western fictions.
2. Try to find the basic discrepancies between Chinese and Western ways of writing stories.
3. Choose one story or novel respectively from Chinese and Western fictions for a discussion of either their thematic concerns or writing techniques.

List of proposed books for further reading

1. 鲁迅,2006,《中国小说史略》,上海:上海古籍出版社。
2. 何永康,2006,《二十世纪中西比较小说学》,南京:江苏教育出版社。
3. 饶芃子等,1994,《中西小说比较》,合肥:安徽教育出版社。
4. Gu Mingdong, *Chinese Theories of Fiction: A Non-Western Narrative System*, Albany, NY: State University of New York Press, 2006.
5. Ed. Mongia, Padmini, *Contemporary Postcolonial Theory: A Reader*, London: Arnold, 1996.
6. Chow, Rey, *Women and Chinese Modernity: The Politics of Reading between West and East*, Minneapolis: University of Minnesota Press, 1991.
7. Cornelia N. Moore, Raymond A. Moody, *Comparative Literature East and West: Traditions and Trends*, Hawaii: University of Hawaii Press, 1989.

Chapter 8

A Comparison of Chinese and Western Paintings

Both China and the West have a long tradition of painting, confirmed by the archaeological finds dated to about 4000 years ago. China's earliest artefact painting is a drawing of axe, fish and crane on a piece of coloured pottery excavated in an area famous for her pre-historical artefacts called Yangshao Culture.① The first artefact painting of Western art is perhaps the rock fresco with human and bull images found in the ruined palace of Knossos at Crete. The discovery of the early artistic work has brought together the common aesthetic sense detected from the artistic production and evaluation which therefore marked an important phase in human intellectual and cultural developments by demonstrating and highlighting the creative talent existing in both civilizations. Nonetheless, the production of paintings, as part of the artistic achievement, is not limited to these discoveries. As a matter of fact, both China and the West have a long history of art, which is embodied in the marvellous accomplishment of a variety of artistic works scattered in various stages of cultural development. It might be of some significance to make a brief account of painting development along with the major achievements in this area on both sides for a better understanding of artistic merit as part of human civilization.

 8.1 The development and main features of Chinese painting

8.1.1 Beginning of Chinese painting and its early development

Though the initial painting made its appearance as early as in the pre-historical society, many years had elapsed before some further progress was

---

① See *General History of Chinese Art*, p.33, Wang Qisong, Jiangsu Press for Art and Literature, 1999.

achieved in form and effect in Chinese painting. It is in the Shang and Zhou Dynasties that the paintings found expressions in such material form as on bronze, silk and the walls or in other ornamental designs. They were not exactly images based on reality, but illusive objects or idols like those in myth or legend. Examples are the texture of *haotian* on bronze articles used for ancient ceremonial rites. ① The bronze picture was endowed with a sense of mystery and an utterly fierce image, highlighting a close relationship with ancient social development. In the final analysis, the bronze image reflected the psychological state of the slave owner at the time, who was both worried about and scared by slaves and other poor people.

Several hundred years passed after the popularity of bronze painting that had once dominated cultural life of the Shang Dynasty and early period of the Zhou Dynasty. Towards the end of the Zhou, however, new forms of painting came to the fore, such as murals, silk paintings and actual painted pictures. Murals were recorded in some ancient books, like the description of Confucius watching a mural in *Confucius Talking with His Family*. But unfortunately none of the murals has survived to the present. Painted pictures refer to the coloured drawings painted on different kinds of utensils or articles. Large quantities of painted crafts were excavated in the past two centuries, including pictures about hunting, dancing, inspection tours, playing music, arrow-shooting and banquets, all in relation to social reality in addition to the traditional images about legendary myths, dragon, phoenix, deer and geometric and textual ornaments.

However, more remarkable achievements in painting during this period were still those on silk. The two pieces of silk painting unearthed in 1949 from the tombs of the Spring-Autumn Period demonstrate the rich imagination, strict design and vivid imagery conveyed by a lady with her hands stretching outwards and holding together as if in a gesture of prayer, dressed in a long robe touching the ground. Over her is a phoenix in opposition to a one-legged dragon. In terms of representational skills or attractive designs, the picture is of fine quality and could rival any similar artwork in the same period.

Silk painting seemed fashionable in the following years, for it went on as a principal form of painting subsequent to what was discovered in the Han Dynasty. The five excavated pieces of silk painting from Mawangdui Tomb, Changsha, confirmed this tendency. The most representative among the five is the T-shaped piece which provides the three components of human imagination: heaven, human world and underground. Heaven is represented by a two-part door and two door-keepers seated opposite each other, surrounded by the sun, the moon and curved dragons which appear to prepare for the arrival of the dead matron

---

① *Haotian* is a kind of legendary animal in ancient China. It is said to have one foot and resemble cattle, ram, tiger and deer, but is none of them as a matter of fact. It is absolutely a result of hypothesis.

who is the central figure in the middle section — the human world. The matron is obviously the hostess of the tomb, supported by a stick and accompanied by the three humble maid-servants behind and met by two petty officials stooping to greet her.

Many of the murals of the Han Dynasty are well kept and could be observed in the tombs. Most of these murals describe superstitious beliefs: the dead ascending to the heaven or the ritual ceremonies for the dead.

One of the inventions during this period was stone and brick painting. Some of these stone and brick paintings have constituted a series, forming an independent group of pictures. For instance, some pictures are based on historical stories like *The Prince of the Zhou Offering Assistance to the King of the Zhou*, *Retrieving the Ritual Pot*, *Acrobatic Dance*, *Hunting on the Carriage*, *Confucius Meeting Lao Zi*, *Jing Ke Assassinating the King of the Qin*, *Lin Xiangru Returning the Jade Safely to the Zhao*, etc. Some of the images are vividly portrayed and conveyed, showing the skillful techniques of those painters and carvers as part of the artistic achievements during those days.

Generally the paintings before and during the Han Dynasty established the basic form of the Chinese drawing and provided the material, methods as well as creative experiences for the later development of Chinese painting though these paintings, except for a few, still lacked sophistication and appeared simple and immature in design, representation and use of light and colour, all of which had to be solved or improved in the later period.

8.1.2 Vigour and variety of Chinese painting in the middle period

When history moved on to the period of the Three Kingdoms and the Jin Dynasty, social turmoil and political chaos prevailed to the extent that many intellectuals and scholars were bored by current affairs and indulged themselves in excessive drinking and attempted to seek an escape from social reality, manifesting rebellious spirit against the traditional concept of studying for an official career but instead choosing to focus on cultural amusement and even sensuous and sensual hedonism, such as playing chess, drinking wine, exchanging poems, discussing about Buddhism and Chan meditation and other self-relaxing activities. Drawing was one of these self-amusements and was thus brought to the attention of quite some intellectuals. Among the best-known painters were Gu Kaizhi and Xie He.

Strictly speaking, painting by individuals or scholars started from Gu Kaizhi (about 345 − 406 AC), because none of the drawings before him was ever marked with the painter's name. Gu, in that sense, is perhaps the earliest famous Chinese painter. Gu's representative works are *An Illustration for Melody to Goddess Luo* and *Illustration for Monitor of Woman Officials* as well as quite some other pictures. But unfortunately all of his original works are lost but the duplicates of the two above-mentioned drawings that are still extant. *Illustration for Monitor of Woman Officials* is of a portrait series, consisting of a number of ancient royal ladies famous for their virtues. The portraits are delicately drawn and highlighted with coloured touches.

An Illustration for Melody to Goddess Luo is based on Cao Zhi's famous poem, *Melody to Goddess Luo*, and chooses to depict the chance encounter by Cao Zhi with his hallucinated goddess, Zhen Shi, whom he loved deeply yet could not win. The painter's subtle touches create sophisticated expressions by degrees, truly according to the central ideas of Cao Zhi's original poem.

Apart from the individual paintings, the murals in Mogao Cave of Dunhuang are also reputable for conveying the interpretation of Buddhist Sanskrit scripture. The images are vividly conveyed but capable of striking terror by focusing on the reward for good and the retribution for evil and the cyclical movement of life and death.

If painting began to be more individualistic during the Three Kingdoms and the Jin Dynasty, the Tang Dynasty certainly brought forward more talented painters and more fine pictures with a wider range of subjects and styles. Paintings during this period made divisions in terms of painting objects, like figures, landscape, and flowers and birds.

Among the figure painters were Yan Liben, Wu Daozi, Zhang Xuan and Zhou Fang. The most famous was Wu Daozi who was nicknamed "the Painting Saint". He showed his high talents using ink, colours and proportion. His best-known work, *The Heavenly King Offering His Son*, powerfully defines for the eye the expressions of the figures, characteristic of their manners and their personal identities.

In the area of landscape were also several famous painters like Li Sixun, Li Zhaodao, Wang Wei and Zhang Zao. Among them Li Sixun and Li Zhaodao were father and son, Li the senior was well known for his use of colours while Li the junior approached the emptiness of landscape by focusing on the sense of peculiarity, charm and vagueness, which was based on what he learned from his father. Wang Wei, as a famous poet, put what he observed into the picture by naturalistically combining literary beauty with formal beauty in landscape.

As to the painting group of flowers and birds or animals, the Tang Dynasty also produced quite a number of painters. Many of them were subtle and original in representing the animals in all their shapes and movements. One of the best-known examples was perhaps the horse drawn by Han Gan. Its prototype was said to be from the royal horse owned by Tang Taizong, a famous emperor of the dynasty and the painting offered the dynamic and powerful movements of the horse, according to the painter's observation.

Closely following the Tang Dynasty was a comparatively short period called "the Five Dynasties and Ten Kingdoms" where quite some painters came up with their works on figures, landscape, and flowers and birds. The most commanding achievements, however, were those in landscape, represented by four great figures, namely Jing Hao, Guan Tong, Dong Yuan and Ju Ran. Closely associated with the appearance of the famous painters, the painting house was established in these dynasties and kingdoms, which doubtless promoted the development of Chinese paintings. A more fruitful period was the following Song and Yuan Dynasties.

During the Song and Yuan Dynasties, there were quite a number of famous painters, such as Li Gonglin, Liang Kai, Zhang Zeduan, Ma Yuan, Xia Gui and Zhao Mengfu. On the other hand, Li Gonglin and Liang Kai were both figure painters. Li was famous for his plain sketches while Liang was famous for his ink splash technique. Zhang Zeduan's reputation was founded on the long scroll *The Panorama of Upriver Scene during the Qing-Ming Festival*, which included hundreds of characters, shops, carriages and houses alongside the Yellow River with the boats passing up and down. It presents a variety of images of different manners and daily life typical of social culture at the time. It therefore provides a strong sense of realism.

One of the most famous painters of the period was perhaps Zhao Mengfu. Zhao was a versatile talent, expert in painting, poetry, seal carving and calligraphy. His work shows him to be a successor to the tradition by providing either a sense of neatness and beauty or a style of consistent charm and dynamism.

Ma Yuan and Xia Gui were united in a spirit of innovation. They chose to represent social reality. By selecting a quarter or half of the object for detailing it and leaving empty the rest of space for drawing, they thus achieved an effect symbolic of the political situation at the time when the Southern Song Dynasty was established. The dynasty only had a territory half the original area ruled by the Northern Song because of the intrusions by the Jin troops. Therefore, the symbolic and satirical sense of the painting is not difficult to detect.

Painting was somewhat affected by political changes during the Yuan Dynasty, on account of the reign by a different ethnic group — the Mongol nationality. The Yuan Dynasty painting was hence characterized by landscape drawings, as represented by four famous painters, namely Huang Gongwang, Wang Meng, Ni Zan and Wu Zhen. They lived contemporaneously and shared similar aesthetic pursuits. Since they all came from the south of the Yangtze River, there was much they had in common, such as aesthetic appreciation, love of nature, particular ways of observing and drawing, etc. All these four painters often visited the scenic mountains and famous landscapes, such as Mount Fuchun, Mount Lu and Tai Lake so that they were much impressed by and very familiar with these scenic spots which supplied much raw material for their creative work.

In the meantime they devoted themselves to a careful and serious study of technical aspects in drawing. For instance, they all favoured the use of ink as well as the utilization of brush and consequently produced a kind of idealistic effect.

Their technical achievements worked in hand with their spiritual alienation and disillusionment, as a result of their long-term depression under the alien rule. The simplicity, profundity and symbolism in the design of their drawings, such as a gnarled tree or two growing in the foreground, looking across a vast expansion of lake to distant mountains in the background, reflected their mood and subjects. Typical examples included Ni Zan's *An Autumn Scene of a Fishing Village* which indicates their preference for a hermit's way of life with its simplicity and pursuit of the quietude of nature.

The middle period of Chinese painting illuminated further development and brought forward a large number of established painters and works. The three fundamental genres of painting, namely figures, landscape, and flowers and birds gained popularity and substantial progress. Each of the groups in the long years of practice shaped its own features and specific focus, based on the creative power and specific circumstances pertinent to the talented painters and their numerous representative works which helped to erect the Chinese cultural and artistic tradition.

Theoretical exploration and summary as a necessary compliment to painting development, on the other hand, contributed to the establishment of an artistic framework and discipline for the later painters to follow and to define a Chinese painting imprinted with her own identifiable features. The famous painting theoretical works included Xie He's *Assessment and Records of Ancient Paintings*, Zhang Yuan's *An Annotated Collection of Famous Paintings of Different Generations*, Guo Ruoxu's *A History of the Paintings Witnessed*, Guo Xi's *A Comment on Landscape Painting*, etc. Their theories provided insightful principles of explanation for Chinese painting and contributed much to the systematic way of drawings typical of Chinese national style though they were still somewhat incomplete and insufficient in one way or the other.

The Ming Dynasty was born out of the peasants' armed revolt against the Yuan ruler. Its establishment derived benefit from the temporary relaxation of social disunity and to a degree, promoted social, economic and cultural developments. Well-known painters appeared one after another, such as Shen Zhou, Wen Zhengming, Tang Bohu, Lin Liang and Xu Wei, whose works were famous for their achievements in depicting landscapes, flowers and birds. But compared with the painters in the Qing Dynasty, their works were mostly traditional and lacked a sense of originality except for few, like those of Tang Bohu and Xu Wei, which showed a certain rebellious spirit in their drawings.

There were more established painters in the Qing Dynasty. In the early period appeared so-called four Wangs who were favoured by the royal court and there were, on the other hand, four Buddhist monks who took a rebellious and even hostile attitude towards the royal court. The four monks, especially Ba Da Shan Ren and Shi Tao, displayed a strong sense of depression and suffering in their creative work. For instance, Ba Da Shan Ren was wild in temperament, took to drinking wine and became an eccentric. His painting was forcefully characterized by its oddity and simplicity in structural design, sharp sense of individuality and straight-forwardness and resoluteness. Ba Da Shan Ren was so individualistic in his style that even the image of his signature suggested he could have been either laughing or crying. Shi Tao was very close to Ba Da Shan Ren. Both came from aristocratic families of the previous dynasty. Both liked to visit landscape and both shared much in their aesthetic pursuits. Shi Tao demonstrates his talent for drawing on both landscape and flowers, which communicates a touch of similarity and dissimilarity between his drawing and the chosen subjects. They displayed an air of quiet solitude and apparent breadth and refreshing spirit. However, such a style did not persist till the end of the Qing Dynasty.

Another group of famous painters was "The Odd Eight of Yangzhou". This title referred to a number of talented artists, living around Yangzhou, who produced a large amount of pictures with national influences. Among them were Wang Shishen, Li Shan, Huang Shen, Jin Nong, Gao Xiang, Zheng Xie and some others. The best-known was Zheng Xie whose other name was Zheng Banqiao. Zheng had passed the Imperial Palace Examination and was appointed a county magistrate before he was the victim of a false charge and removed from office. Then he settled in Yangzhou to continue his career as a painter by concentrating on bamboo drawing and calligraphy. He intended to establish his own style as he said: "My writing would form the basis of an independent school once it came out, and I do not want my hand to produce words or pictures to be praised by the ordinary people. Decadent and depressed as they are, they illustrate different manners. The ordinary (people) often ridicule Banqiao as wild tempered." His bamboo painting achieved a very high state of sophistication and attracted much interest, as is represented by *An Illustrated Bamboo in Ink*. Those stems and branches he sketched are vigorously stretching out, while leaves are naturally scattered either densely or sparsely, indicating both the prominence and the extravagance of the living plant.

8.1.3   The signs of change in the modern Chinese painting

The latter period of painting was represented principally by two painting masters, Ren Bainian and Wu Changshuo, whose prime creative years were spent in Shanghai which served to name after the group headed by them as "Shanghai School". They and their group manifested a new tendency and original style in Chinese painting. On the one hand, they adopted different kinds of techniques to add to the variety and freshness of both method and subject, determined to seek a breakthrough in the conventional Chinese painting in their artistic career. On the other hand, their creative work had to face up the challenge from the market place because their success would to a large extent depend on whether they could sell their works. Both of them were famous for their drawings of flowers and birds. Ren's flowers and birds have a natural charm and reflect his elegant manners, confirmed by delicate colourful touches and energetic strokes of brush. He was also good at figure painting when focusing on environmental foil and highlighting human personality and manners. One of his representative works is *Plum Wife and Crane Son*, which depicts an association between a hermit, a plum tree and a crane, in a triangular composition to illustrate and reveal the chief character's haughty and desolate state of mind.

Wu was even more versatile and showed his talent at calligraphy and seal-making as well as painting, which came later than the other forms of art. His painting is an embodiment of momentum and rhythm imprinted with his strength built up in calligraphy and seal-making. One is impressed by his powerful perception and vigorous touches in addition to his rich colours. These combined to signal the beginning of a new situation for the intimate but understated portrayal of flowers. His work contained much of seal and wild cursive calligraphy completed beyond his reaching middle age. It culminated in a stage of maturity which combined vigorous force and romantic eccentricity, putting to effect his aesthetic claim that "I assume everything material varies in appearance because it is born out of nature. I assume all strokes of brushwork vary in shape because they are all soul imparting."[①] His representative paintings, such as *Red Plum*, manifest an air of magnitude based on a design of bizarre imagination. His *Lotus* completed by brushwork of the "splash ink" kind and his *Peony and Daffodil* with its strong sense of contrasting colour, as that between daffodil in watery green and utter verdant below and peony in luxurious red above, are both featured with the lively yet subtle temperament of the south of Yangtze River.

Research in painting techniques went on after the 17th century together with further achievements in the exploration of certain theoretical tenets. The most important work was Shi Tao's *Quotations from Paintings of the Monk Ku Gua*. This book, comprised of 18 chapters, presents a spirit of invention and attempts to handle both the guiding principles of art and specific techniques of painting. One of his key theses emphasizes that no law applies to the ancient times. Once a law was established, it worked on a line of painting. A line of painting is based on public possession and rooted in the universe. He also proposes that a painter needs to collect raw material from nature or from "the images of all odd peaks for drafting so that a painter could immerse himself in the material world and harmonize both emotion and reason."[②] Eventually the painter could depict both natural beauty and situational beauty in his creation and theory revealing a strong sense of originality through bringing more freedom into full play.

In addition, there was Zheng Banqiao's theory about the three kinds of

---

① 详见《中国艺术通史》，445 页，王琪森，江苏文艺出版社，1999。
② 详见《中国艺术通史》，447 页，王琪森，江苏文艺出版社，1999。

bamboo, i. e. "bamboo in the eyes, bamboo in the mind and bamboo in the hand"①. He suggests and reveals three phases in the process of painting (or artistic production) by pointing out a generalized universal law for aesthetic appreciation and expression in the production of all forms of art.

The Chinese painting started to shift its attention to the outside world by getting in touch with Japan where the Tokyo Fine Arts School was set up in 1889, blending native and Western cultural traditions. Among the first group of Chinese artists who travelled to Japan were Gao Jianfu, his brother Gao Qifeng, and Chen Shuren. Gao Jianfu studied art for four years in Japan and met Sun Yatsen there. They inaugurated a "New National Painting" movement, which in turn gave rise to a Cantonese (or Lingnan) regional style that incorporated Euro-Japanese characteristics. Although the new style did not produce distinctive results, it was a significant step and continued to thrive in Hong Kong. The first establishment of Western-style art instruction also dated from this period. A small art department was opened in Nanjing High Normal School in 1906, and the first art academy, which was later to become the Shanghai Art School, was initiated in 1911 by the 16-year-old Liu Haisu. Liu pioneered in the next decade the first public art exhibitions and the use of live models, first clothed and then nude, shocking the country newly freed from her feudal bondage.

By the mid-1920s, some young Chinese artists were attracted not just to Japan but also to Paris and German art centres. Liu Haisu was first attracted by impressionist art. Lin Fengmian was inspired by postimpressionist experiments in colour and pattern by Henri Matisse and the fauvists. Lin advocated a synthesis combining Western techniques and Chinese expressiveness and left a lasting mark on the modern Chinese use of the brush.

Xu Beihong eschewed European modernist movements in favour of Parisian academism. He developed his facility in drawing and oils, later learning to imitate pencil and chalk with the Chinese brush and establishing his own style, such as his drawing of horses. By the 1930s, all these modern trends were clearly developed and institutionalized. Qi Baishi combined Shanghai style with an infusion of folk-derived vitality, producing such works as transparent shrimps and lifelike flowers. Huang Binhong was relatively conservative in his landscape drawings and illustrated the value of the old tradition. Overall, most of the major artists of the time advocated modernism while still cherishing memories and feelings of traditional styles, which related to the development of Chinese art and painting in the early decades of the 20th century.

Consequently, the large numbers of paintings and theoretical expositions underwent tremendous changes under the impact of Western painting and started to present some new features, together with its social and cultural developments

---

① 详见《中国艺术通史》, 448 页, 王琪森, 江苏文艺出版社, 1999。

in the new era.

The origin and development of Western painting

8.2.1 The initial stage of Western painting

The earliest paintings in the West appeared about 1500 BC in Crete, an island some distance from the Greek mainland. They were in the form of a mural, showing a scene when humans were in sporting combat with a bull. It is a magnificent picture, beautifully drawn, in which the young man is trying to hold the bull's horns while a girl, beside him, seems to provoke the bull by hand gestures at the risk of being hurt. The figures are so lively in the fresco that if not for its antiquity, it could have been mistaken for a modern painting, on account of the sharp contrasts of light and darkness as well as the long and slim shapes of the human bodies. Other pictures, mostly murals and decorations on urns, extended throughout the Cretan and Mycenaean Civilizations. Indeed, they illustrate surprising levels of artistic achievement.

The most "modern" figure in the classical period came from a Roman drawing inscribed on a mosaic pavement, entitled *Girl Athlete*. At the first sight, the half-naked lady only wearing what looks like a bra and shorts and with the rest part of her body exposed, appears in terms of apparel exactly like a woman athlete of the present day. Maybe it was one of the last such modern pictures in the days before the birth of Christianity.

Overall, Greek and Roman painting had much in common because the Romans still owed much to Greek art from which they had learned and perhaps imitated a lot. From the many Roman pictures discovered, one might even form a better notion of the lost masterpieces of Greece, such as those in the Roman mural found out in a small town near Naples, Italy.

When the Roman Empire was toppled by the Goth and Vandal, the Roman leadership changed hands to the barbarians who would mark the long period of the Middle Ages with their ignorance and negligence of civilized human values.

The Middle Ages can not be separated from the rise of Christianity, which provided some degree of intellectual control over the continuing development of Western society. As a matter of fact, the Christian influence had been discerned long before the Roman collapse for it started to exert control over the Roman intellectual development from the time it became the Roman state religion in the 4th century. From then on Jesus Christ became almost the only object of worship for nearly all Romans. As Christian influences grew in depth and breadth, more and more social and cultural concerns began to involve Christianity and Jesus

Christ in their major business and daily life. Thus the story of Jesus Christ and the associated religious concerns would dominate the Western painting as a whole, for the coming thousand-odd years.

The early Christians were therefore concerned principally with the Saviour and the spiritual life of the hereafter, without caring so much about the secular world which had provided so much artistic subject matter for the Greeks and Romans, especially in their depiction of the human body. Instead, the Christian painters tried mostly to show the power and glory of Christ, the only figure they respected and cared for. Even with the non-Christian figures they occasionally drew, there was also a sense of artificiality. For instance, the remains of a ceiling decoration found from a catacomb that had been completed about 200 years after Jesus was crucified, indicated a style borrowed from Roman painting. Yet its characters appear rigid and lack vigour and strength. This kind of painting style remained unchanged for a very long time and was even further developed in the Byzantine time as manifested in the depictions of Madonna and child (the Virgin Mary with her son the Infant Christ), which was on a wooden panel with the subject solemnly and emotionlessly drawn.

The rigid style of Byzantine painting continued for many years in the Middle Ages before it began to be displaced by Gothic painting. Gothic painting arose in France as a result of the development of urban society and expansion of the "burghers" — a new class composed of skilled handicraft workers and merchants. Apart from the fact that many Gothic pictures were still concerned with religious subjects, some of them were inclined to manifest ordinary people and their lives, and used different colours and forms to decorate stained glass windows in churches. These artists explored more of the spiritual depth of the subjects of their paintings. Giotto the Italian painter was an example. He greatly developed the art of fresco and his representative work *Lamentation over Christ* shows the true sorrowful feelings of human beings over Jesus' crucifixion. Both the gestures and expressions of the characters in Giotto's paintings are vividly presented in a kind of human spirit, which marks a totally different style from Byzantine art.

8.2.2 Vigorous growth in Western painting since the Renaissance

Beginning from Giotto, Western painting eventually moved into a new era called the Renaissance. The Renaissance generally suggests the rebirth of classical culture that had been buried or hidden or ignored in the long and dark years of the Middle Ages. It was initiated principally in Florence, an Italian city famous for her artistic activities and which produced in the early period many reputed painters like Giotto, Masaccio and then Piero Della Francesca. Their paintings still concentrated on religious subjects, yet the way the artists represented religious figures were quite different from those in the Middle Ages, even substantially different from Gothic painting. For instance, Masaccio's fresco *The Holy Trinity with St John*, *St Mary and Two Donors* is presented both naturally and vividly with figures drawn like real human beings. Saint John and Saint Mary are depicted with human physiques though they are wrapped in heavy cloaks. Even Christ, with his body mostly naked and in pain, exhibits a severity and seems more like a human than a deity. These subtle touches help to offer substantial changes in art, marking the breakthrough into a new era.

The climax of the Renaissance painting did not come until the 16th century when Leonardo da Vinci, Michelangelo and Raphael established their reputations with their remarkable genius and productions of works of art. To a large extent, da Vinci was a genius in almost all the subjects he touched on: mathematics, physics, biology and literature in addition to painting. This is confirmed by his output of paintings and notebooks alike. He believes strongly that to see is to know. He is perhaps the first of the human race to sketch flying machines and to sketch the details of human anatomy. His *Mona Lisa* is well known for her mysterious smile, which is evidence of his desire for truthful resemblance of figures in painting and the social reality of their lives.

Representation of real life in da Vinci's work is also characteristic of both Michelangelo and Raphael. Michelangelo's masterpiece is the huge fresco covering the entire ceiling of the Sistine Chapel in Vatican. It was commissioned by Pope Julius II, who encouraged the development of Italian art. One of the typical scenes in Michelangelo's fresco is *God's Creation of the World and of Man* selected from *Genesis of the Old Testament*. The mighty figures, with their forms physically stronger and handsomer than ordinary men, came doubtless from the painter's own rich imagination which was tremendously inspired by his humanist ideals. God's figure is modelled on an almighty image set against a mythological background in which he is flying over the clouds and is purely imaginative while Adam's human form is still related to the early ideal of men. The attempt to reach each other shows the close relationship between God and men and their mutual need of each other as well as the painter's acute sense and grasp of the critical moment in the Christian story.

Comparatively, Raphael was happier and perhaps less complicated than da Vinci and Michelangelo. He was best-known for his depictions of the Madonna which highlighted the tenderness and calm beauty of the Virgin Mary by following the subtle representation of da Vinci's *Mona Lisa*. His other famous work is *The Expulsion of Heliodorus*, a fresco he painted in the Vatican Palace. It illustrates a story about a Greek pagan soldier trying to go into the Temple in Jerusalem and carry off the treasures. His infidel action gave rise to the prayer by the High Priest to God for help and which led to the three armed messengers' chasing Heliodorus and his men. The stable and well-balanced design of many figures in the picture shows Michelangelo's stylistic influence from the Sistine Chapel Ceiling, but Raphael's figures are generally less sophisticated in facial expression than those depicted in Michelangelo's work.

Apart from these three great painters from Florence and Rome and other groups of remarkable artists, another Italian city Venice was also famous for its artistic activities. The first master of the Venetian painting was Giorgione who brought most of the special qualities which set apart the Venetian school from the rest of Italian art in the 16th century, even though he died at an early age. His representative work *Concert* combined organically the naked beauty and splendour of music in a kind of harmony which was set against the golden rays of the setting sun.

Giorgione's originality in using light and colour was successfully inherited and developed by another Venetian painter Titian, who became the most brilliant and established among all Venetian painters. Titian was particularly famed for his portraits that ranged from the Pope and emperors down to aristocrats and ordinary people. *The Man with Gloves* reflects the quick, feathery strokes administered by the painter who observed acutely and grasped instantly the natural manner, especially the eye movements of the chosen figure. The portrait is so attractive that one could reasonably believe that the subject is more beautiful than he actually was.

One of the important contributions by the Venetian painters was the popularization of the use of canvas, that brought greater convenience to the artists and lowered the prices of paintings. From then on, oil painting was accepted as a constantly-used mode and principal form of art in the Western world, replacing mural and other forms of painting. As well as the convenience it offered, the use of oil on canvas encouraged the expression of light and colour, and helped to evoke sensuous human feelings of the secular world, and thus in a way reduced the religious influences. This tendency is manifest in many works by the Venetian artists, including those of Biblical figures, such as *Christ in the House of Levi* by Paolo Veronese, which demonstrates sparkling costumes and rich architectural settings, more symbolic of a secular festive mood and material comforts, in contrast with its meagre representation of religious figures.

8.2.3 The dawn of the modern painting and modernist achievement

With the passage of time and social change, painting was no longer performed in the service of Christianity but became more associated with social function and entertainment. In the meantime it was recognized by society as an important component of art and played a more and more important role. This is not only confirmed by the appearance of increasing numbers of schools of painting and individual painters, but by the social recognition of their status in terms of their honour and payment. All these changes, however, occurred slowly but steadily until the later years of the 18th century when life began to change more significantly.

During those years many Europeans, especially the French, envied the English who had undergone a time of political revolution in the 17th century and had forced the king to hand most of his power over to parliament, thus to a certain extent representing the voice of the common people in England. At the same time English wealth was growing steadily, with her overseas colonies expanded increasingly and her trade strongly promoted. Under such circumstance, it was not surprising that English fine art, including painting, came to prominence in the Western world. One of the most famous British painters was William Hogarth who demonstrates a satirical sense of humour as well as an observer's sharp eye for detail in his works, such as *The Rake's Progress*. One more example is the delightful portrait of the *Graham Children*. In spite of the fine texture of the children's costume conveyed successfully through bright colours, the painter also manages to avoid any stiffness on such a scene. The group, like the two elder girls' funny appearance in pretending to be ladies and the boy apparently playing pranks with his music box for the bird in the cage, contribute to a picture of merriment. The same kind of light heartedness could be identified perhaps in other painters' works, such as those of Thomas Gainsborough, Benjamin West and John Singleton Copley from the United States.

These realistic tendencies infused works by the French painters Jacques Louis David and his star student Dominique Ingres. The latter exhibited a concern for truthfulness or even exact likeness, such as in *The Death of Marat and Madame Riviere*. At the same time, the Baroque-Rococo style, with its emphasis on imagination rather than on truth, on light and colour rather than on form, continued to develop and achieved new results. These were tendencies extended, often in startling ways, by Spanish painter Francisco Goya and Velazquez.

If Goya shows his strong and sincere feelings in choosing some authentic and significant historical subject matter, such as that in *The Third of May, 1808*, the later Romantic School focuses even more on representation of emotion. This can be seen in Theodore Gericault's *Mounted Officer of Guard*, which manifests a spiritual devotion to a certain ideal. Yet few Romantic artists regard art as having to conform to a fixed ideal. To them, the important thing is not the object itself, but how one feels about it. Like the Romantic poets, they believe in living dangerously or at least thrillingly. In a sense they are born rebels reacting against set rules or values. The more important Romantic painter is Eugene Delacroix, a French painter whose work like *Arab Attacked by a Lion* and *Freedom Leads the People*, *Dante and Virgil in the Hell* exhibits traits of both violence and emotion. In Britain, the highly accomplished landscape painter was Joseph Turner, whose work shows how dramatically Western art has changed.

The unfolding of the Industrial Revolution not only did away with a great many old beliefs, habits and institutions but made people seek new values and ideas. In opposition to the Romantics' pursuit of freedom of feeling and imagination, some painters believe art should only deal with contemporary objects in the times of science of industrial development. These realist painters focus on portraying the life of workers and peasants in a serious spirit, as was exemplified by Gustave Courbet in his *Stone Breaker*. While Courbet and his followers, like those in earlier period relied on modelling and shading to give their work more solidity and roundness, Edouard Manet, another French painter claimed this should be done by the use of different colours. Manet's pictures, like *In the Boat*, through his impressionistic brushwork, were flooded with sunlight and made all the earlier paintings seem murky by comparison through his impressionistic brushwork. For the traditional and conservative critics, his work therefore seems at best no more than quick impressions and unfinished sketches which are not worthy of serious attention. Hence it is called "impressionism".

The birth of impressionism ushered in a new era in painting and was to be joined by a group of younger painters, including Claude Monet, Auguste Renoir, Edgar Degas and Paul Cezanne. Paul Cezanne, however, also introduced some newer styles in his work in addition to his impressionistic brushwork of fresh colour and free strokes. There are dark outlines drawn around most of the shapes which are simpler than their prototypes in nature. This new style was soon followed by other painters and developed into postimpressionism with a number of world-renowned painters like Georges Seurat, Vincent van Gogh and Paul Gauguin, whose works are endowed with more powerful subjective feelings. Vincent van Gogh, a Dutch painter, believes impressionism does not grant artists adequate freedom to express inner feelings and tries to reshape nature by picking out some distinctive natural elements, which could reveal his personal emotions. His works like *Sunflower* and several portraits are all characteristic of this trend. Gauguin was in a sense more radical than van Gogh. In escaping the bounds of impressionism, he asserts very strongly that Western civilization is "out of joint" and the Industrial Revolution forced men into a kind of incomplete life in which their emotions were ignored. His painting *Yellow Christ* and woodcut *Gratitude* use simplification and exaggeration to impart such a style. Both van Gogh and Gauguin are characterized by symbolism, which would point to and merge into the modernist movement.

Modernist painting may be said to be characterized by expressionism, abstraction and fantasy, all of which came from impressionism. Expressionism emphasizes the artist's feelings, while abstraction cares more about order of form within a picture. But fantasy mainly explores the painter's imagination.

Expressionism was seen first in some impressionist or postimpressionist works, like those of van Gogh, Gauguin and then Pablo Picasso. Picasso's feeling of depression and despoliation found expression in *The Old Guitarist* which used gloomy blue colour and conveyed the painter's sense of pathos and homeless feelings in his early days when as a poor youth from another country he was penniless and helpless in Paris. However, the tone of expressionism changed to a kind of gaiety in the paintings of Henri Matisse who represents the fauves ("wild beasts") and discloses some extreme simplicity with no evidence of personal anguish, such as in his *Goldfish and Sculpture*. This work presents a delightful interior by foreshortening details of the bowl, the vase and the figure while flattening the room and the curtain and therefore constitutes a graceful integration, a unity of all the disparate objects.

Abstraction is another important feature of the modernist painting in the early 20th century. It means a state or process of drawing away or separation. In a sense, abstraction exists anywhere and at any time because the human is always able to represent the meaning or image by some generalization. Abstraction had formed part of making of any work of art created down the ages. Both the ancient Egyptians and ancient Greeks demonstrated obvious geometric forms in the early ages. The Renaissance artists presented abstract and simple geometric shapes in a more conscious way. However, the climax of abstraction did not come till the turn of the 20th century when some young artists like Cezanne, Seurat, Picasso and Braque rediscovered the technique of abstraction and imparted it with a new life force.

If Cezanne and Seurat imitated the movement of abstraction, Picasso and Braque brought the movement to the peak of art by creating a new painting style called "cubism". They used lines, angles and planes to demonstrate the gravely separated parts of figures or objects, such as Picasso's *Nude*, *Still Life with Chair Caning*. Further on, they simplified the ways of painting by using collage. Braque's *Le Courrier* shows a design of several parts pasted together out of odd pieces of paper added to only by a few drawn lines. Yet the technique of collage did not last long. Instead they took up a new way to present pictures that looked like collage but were really painted with a brush. One of the successful pieces with the new method is Picasso's *Three Musicians* which looks like a mural with its scale and the monumental appearance. The precisely "cut" shapes are fitted together just as solidly as building blocks, yet with sufficient depth of implication for the viewer to observe and reflect.

The cubist influence was not limited to painting but spread soon to sculpture, decorative art and architecture and was established as one of the most important schools in modernist development.

The third feature of modernism, fantasy, refers to the painter's inner mind of imagination and creation which is based on the belief that "seeing with the inner eye" is more important than looking at the world outside. To some artists, this unconscious part of mind is just as important as proper digesting of food though it does not bring back the experiences the way they actually happened. It often produced some fairy-tale effect in the works with such a tendency. Henry Rousseau's *The Sleeping Gypsy*, for instance, achieves a kind of innocence and strength by building up a dreamlike environment with the bright moon, the grazing cow, the sleeping Gypsy and his guitar. Another famous picture *Melancholy and Mystery of a Street* by the Italian painter Giorgio de Chirico shows more of mystery and perhaps even depression in a city street. The girl's dark silhouette following her circle emerges as a lonely image in the whole of a long and deserted street lined with two rows of the same small-windowed buildings. These are dominated by large tracts of shadow including that of an unknown figure in front of the girl. Obviously the picture is laden with more of a sense of hidden fear and depression alike. The contrastive effect is light and dark, tall and low, normal and abnormal.

Another picture by the Russian-Jewish Marc Chagall is a dreamlike vision and memory of Russian folk stories and country life and also enchants by reaching the experiences of his childhood manifested through an immensely-shaped eye.

Similar representations could be detected in the Swiss painter Paul Klee's *Conquest of Mountains* which shows the behaviours of a machine in human fashion, and in the Spanish painter Joan Miro's *Harlequin's Carnival* which looks like a miniature view under a fairy tale microscope — everything concerned with magic tricks.

One of the most imaginative painting groups is Dadaism or surrealism as it was later called. The well-known painters of this group included Max Ernst and Salvador Dali. They possessed a strong spirit of revolt against Western civilization and regarded their own imagination, reality and chance as law. Typical work is Dali's *Landscape with Figures* which was produced in ink blots made by chance and supplemented by his later lines to fill in the missing strokes. This clarifies the fact that the modern artist retains links to the primitive caveman in terms of imaginative and creative power since it is only the imagined subjects that have changed.

8.3 Comparative comments

8.3.1 The origin and development of paintings

Early paintings in both China and the West were inclined to represent social and natural life with the intention of maintaining a good record of certain images of ordinary life at the time. The first picture in Chinese painting history has taken the images such as fish, crane and axe directly drawn from nature and human life. The first Western picture is a Cretan fresco that manifests how humans played with or worshipped a bull as a holy animal. As a scene based on daily human life of the time, both drawings have provided the evidence that early art was closely related to reality. However, to take reality as a standard does not mean to do it merely for the sake of being true to the real object itself. Rather, one is expected to appreciate something beautiful and hence an aesthetic sense ensued. Therefore, the artist was motivated by two intentions in making a drawing. The first was to truthfully register the object and the second was to choose to present it in a beautiful way. It means these two intentions were performed under the painter's world outlook, including his faith and aesthetic sense which was shaped as early as the ancient time.

For a rather long period of historical development, Western painting was dominated by the above dual-purpose standard all the way through to the modern age until the arrival of modernism. Modernist art no longer regards formal resemblance or verisimilitude as a necessity, but rather sees subjectivity as an essential factor in artistic creation. Such a breakthrough initiated an artistic revolution — an entirely diverse perspective and ways of creation — and makes Western art take a direction different from a traditional concept of art, including that of China. Beginning from impressionist art, Western painting has been through such a development that it often totally ignores objective reality and presents the distortions of formal objects, such as the use of strong colours, dynamic coarse lines and absolutely exaggerated shapes. In a word the modernist artist tried to indicate his subjective perception in his artistic representation or creation.

Comparatively, Chinese painting hardly took such great steps towards a radical and drastic change or rebellion in its modern development, till well into the 20th century, though the Chinese painter showed a different way of representation long before modernism. Except for some few occasions, nonetheless, most Chinese painters did not try to seek that kind of accurate resemblance between the target of painting and its representation. It is especially so in those works of landscape. Vagueness and monotonous or limited use of colour would often suggest some kind of hidden implications symbolic of the painter's intended wishes. For instance, it is very common to have some strokes of black ink set against a point of red in a Chinese traditional drawing of landscape, suggesting the plum fearing no cold in snowy mountains, symbolic of high integrity of an intellectual. In a sense it is also a form of representation but is quite different from those typical of the realist style, which seeks to achieve a detailed resemblance in representation, an accurate conformity between the target and product of the drawing. However, the so-called *xie-yi-fa* (写意法, notional way of representation) which is peculiar to Chinese traditional painting, could scarcely be viewed as tantamount to the modernist way of painting. But maybe they are a bit similar for they both relate to subjective representation though Chinese notional way of painting has never been set apart from realistic representation. Meanwhile China has also got *gong-bi-hua* (工笔画, accurate stroke drawing), emphasizing the accurate resemblance between target and painting. To a certain extent, one could say that the Chinese traditional painting, as part of Chinese culture, is probably bound up by Confucius' "the doctrine of the mean" (中庸之道). Most Chinese painters would refuse to go to such extremes and would choose to keep to the traditional form which would tolerate some minor innovations such as notional painting and accurate drawing. However, obviously Western painting found its way gradually into China and exerted its influence on both the taste of Chinese customers and the techniques of Chinese painters. No one would doubt that Chinese painting with such a wealth of heritage in cultural tradition would be well nourished and evolve into a more vigorous, powerful and popular art after the necessary absorption of fine elements from the West and other countries.

8.3.2 Form and style of paintings

Though the basic form of painting of the two cultures are related to each other, some important distinctions are obvious in the practice of Chinese and Western paintings.

1 Medium and colour for painting

The use of colour was seen in the early Chinese paintings. Though the Chinese painter uses more than one colour, most of his work, nonetheless, is expressed with black ink which serves as the major colour and medium of his work, together with the Chinese brush and a kind of special paper as the only standard painting medium for the Chinese painter. In contrast to the Chinese strict demand for painting instrument and materials, Western painting is dominated by the use first of wood, then canvas, brushes and oil paints, which consequently provides the way or preconditions and foundation for the diverse forms and styles since the Renaissance. However, fresco painters used water-based paints in fresh plaster and water colourists painted on paper too.

2 Form of painting

From the very beginning, the Westerners have been inclined to work on murals or frescoes. It is one of the reasons why quite some paintings survived for the later generations to enjoy. But since the later period of the Byzantine, the painters began to use canvas and painted on it as the major medium for their art. Comparatively, the Chinese painters seemed to care more for bronze, brick and then silk and paper as medium for their paintings though they occasionally also chose walls for drawings like those in Mogao Cave, Dunhuang. (Again it appears to come under the foreign influence of Buddhism.) If the Chinese painter prefers more to work on paper and black ink, the Western painter seems to put more emphasis on colours and space for his production. The long-preserved Chinese ancient paintings are mostly illustrations based on pottery or bronze, or carvings associated with murals and silk pictures, most of which survived the ravage of time in graves.

3 Realistic tradition

For the earlier part of their development, both Chinese and Western paintings kept to realist tradition except for those of religious nature, perhaps for economic, social and intellectual reasons. Retarded development in production and ideology was the basis for the worship for nature and heaven or God. Autocracy and blind faith, as a result of concurrences of certain historical factors, determined the continuation of particular cultural forms within some kinds of social mode subject to economic and intellectual developments. It is little wonder then that Chinese painting remained unchanged in its traditional form for a rather long time due to its slow changes in social, economic and intellectual growth. Western painting, in spite of sluggish evolvement in the early period, underwent rapid changes and advances following the tremendous social and economic and intellectual developments in the years after the Renaissance, especially after the Industrial Revolution and the Renaissance. The prosperous development in painting and other forms of culture from the middle of the 19th century, demonstrates the powerful need for spiritual advances by a society after it made enormous headway in ideological and political arenas. Different styles of painting met with the different needs of social and intellectual developments at the time.

4 Painting schools and styles

Consequently a host of schools and styles, like realism, impressionism, postimpressionism, expressionism, symbolism, cubism and abstraction, fauvism, surrealism and then postmodernism, came into Western art one after another. The age of machines and information has made life pretty much the same throughout the Western world. Today people are so involved with each other that no man, no nation can remain as an isolated island any more, which provides more possibilities for the people to promote and expand artistic creation.

There had been no division for Chinese painting schools until the Ming and Qing Dynasties when such schools as Zhejiang, Suzhou, Yangzhou and Shanghai appeared sooner or later. With a continuous development of many centuries, Chinese painting has set up a glorious and sophisticated tradition based on the picturesque landscape of the vast land and rich heritage of artistic products from its forerunners confronted with an unprecedentedly favourable situation in the era of globalization. The Chinese painters are more confident and successful in their engagement with artistic creation, merging more consciously and enthusiastically into the international current, which offers them more opportunities to pick up new ideas and methods and to heighten their status and ability as an artist. They also try to refer to or convey Chinese traditional ideas by some symbolic designs or special techniques like the use of bamboo to signify high morale of literary figures, splash ink for a sense of strength, *xie-yi-fa* and *gong-bi-hua* of robustness and magnitude. Such temperaments and techniques made their paintings more and more typical and characteristic of their own portrayal and style, though short of some drastic, daring and radical changes as what happened to Western art in the past two or three centuries. If Chinese painters had achieved considerable accomplishments before the modern age, they were somewhat inadequate in the innovation of methods and styles of painting in the recent two centuries when the West moved into the modern age. However, the gap was greatly narrowed with more of the younger artists going abroad for acquiring more knowledge about Western art and culture before they acquire more steady and solid success while more Western works and theories were introduced into China.

5   Painters' changed status and income

For the last two centuries or so, both Chinese and Western painters' status has changed remarkably, from obscure to renowned, from poor to rich, which has been affected and decided by social and economic advances. The Chinese painters used to live two kinds of lives, depending on their social status rather than on their artistic achievement, because painting was separate from public life. Official painters or officially employed painters never worried about their life while the self-employed painters never expected to make money out of their painting career. Both groups could never expect to profit from selling their works, though some, if lucky, might be rewarded or commissioned by emperors or high-ranking officials. Such a situation could also occur in the West when painters had to live on patronage which was a frequent practice for a long period both before and after the Renaissance. The dependant way of life for painters came to an end much earlier in the West than in China because painting was recognized in the West as a decent profession that should keep the artist in an independent position. Nowadays painting is certainly one of the few occupations that could bring painters tremendous wealth and fame.

6   The traditional type of painting

Perhaps not till the Western Renaissance, did painting find much in common between China and the West. In China, prior to the modern age, the subjects of painting basically centred around human figures, landscape, flowers and birds. In the West, most of paintings were also concerned with such topics as human figure and landscape though perhaps the long period of the Middle Ages focused on Christian topics, especially the image of Jesus Christ. As well, in China, Buddhist images appeared in enormous numbers for a short while during the Northern and Southern Dynasties, but were not so dominant as the Christian influence in the Medieval West.

8.3.3 Subject and object

As mentioned above, Chinese painting, throughout its long process of historical development, established three dimensions as the major areas of painting, namely human figures, landscape and flowers and birds. In other words, political, social, ethnic and cultural issues can hardly find any space in paintings, which are either ignored or forbidden to the astonishment of the present audience.

Generally, the Chinese traditional painters fall into two groups, one group being officially-recognized and the other non-official and independent. The former consisted of either government officials or those employed by the imperial court or government. China started to run the official painting house from the Southern Dynasties onward. The official involvement in painting provided the necessary material conditions for artistic development, which reached its climax during the Song Dynasty when the emperor Song Huizong incorporated the painting house into the Civil Service Examination System. On the one hand the new system promoted the development of painting, but on the other it limited the range of artistic creation and the evolvement of style. The famous story of Wang Zhaojun involved an incident where a royal painter Mao Yanshou was killed by the emperor because his portrait did not please the latter. No matter whether the legend is true or not, the story certainly shows that the painter was unable to decide his own style in the early days. It was not only the officially-paid painters who had to be careful in their works, most of the painters in China at the time had to limit their subjects to landscape or flowers or birds or at least humble personage to avoid offending the emperor or the official like the intellectuals in other fields. Such a purely aesthetic pursuit of art was the popular trend among the Chinese painters for a relatively long time.

Moreover, the political and religious influences were visible or perceivable in painting as well as in a variety of literary and cultural media and genres. For instance, in the earlier silk pictures, as were excavated respectively from the Warring States Period and the Han Dynasty tombs, were the images of either the lady with dragon and phoenix, or the gentleman driving a dragon or the lady being guided to heaven, so all of them indicate the ideas of deity at the time.

As to the social and political influences, they could be located in different periods. One typical example is Gu Kaizhi's *An Illustration for Melody to Goddess Luo*, based on the well-known story of Cao Zhi, the younger son of Cao Cao, in his conflict with his elder brother Cao Pi for the heart of a beautiful lady. If this picture is about political influence, Zhang Zeduan's *The Panorama of Upriver Scene during the Qing-Ming Festival* is a good example to demonstrate how social development left its traces on paintings. Of course sometimes political and social influences are rather hard to separate. Ma Yuan and Xia Gui's "Corner and Half of Landscape" style is an illustration of their political nostalgia during the national frustration at the time.

Western painting was closely related to social development in its earliest stage, finding representations in frescoes, decorated pottery utensils or mosaics. Already we have mentioned the Cretan fresco of a young man fighting a bull and Roman illustrations of women displaying their beautiful manners or costumes. Painting subjects and styles show the freedom a painter could enjoy in those days, in strong contrast to what was to happen later in the Medieval Ages. The subsequent narrow focus on the image of Jesus Christ and religious subjects in the thousand-odd year span following the downfall of the Graeco-Roman Classical period, was a result of Christian dominance over Western intellectual development. One could observe that painting, like the rest of the arts, had to be subject to political and ideological sway, in the sense that no artistic achievements can be expected once artistic freedom is lost. The changes in painting subjects and styles in the Renaissance period did, however, ensure renewed progress in painting, which proves from an opposite aspect that the intellectual conditions for the artist is the decisive factor in the development of painting.

Comparatively speaking, Western art is more directly and frequently influenced by religion, especially by Christianity as happened in the Middle Ages and even in the Renaissance. It is not just in the choice of subjects, but in the highly stylized conventions, for painting. The Chinese feudal society or "Middle Period" persisted longer than that of the West, yet it appears that there was more tolerance of different subjects and styles, even though the autocratic ruler occasionally tightened control over the political and ideological arenas. Otherwise no one could explain why China achieved such tremendous artistic accomplishments in the two-thousand-odd-year feudal society. The diversity of artistic results in the two cultures might also be owed to the differences in painting styles. The subtlety and understatement of Chinese painting might have helped retain some secretiveness and reserve as well as a kind of self-protection. Of course the more blunt and courageous representation of human life by Western painters led to a breakthrough in the Western artistic development. The so-called "doctrine of the mean" is the Chinese traditional way of thinking and behaving, which has offered not only a different mode of social development, but also has brought forward different forms of artistic accomplishment.

8.3.4 Practice and theory

Despite some similarities between Chinese and Western paintings in their theoretical exploration and artistic practice, differences are inevitably involved in long-term historical development.

Chinese painting seems to have benefited from its theoretical studies earlier than that of the Western painting. For instance, the first important theoretical work on painting appeared in the Southern Dynasties, produced by the famous art critic and painter Xie He (479 – 502). His work, *Assessment and Records of Ancient Paintings*, was based on an analysis of the pictures by 27 painters of the previous period, and generalized into the six ways of painting by advancing a complete artistic mechanism for systematic composition. Furthermore, it is more than a theory of artistic production but also a theory of appreciation and assessment, pointing out a pluralist and multi-polar direction for presenting and describing the part played by various factors in artistic development. These included: the relationships between the use of brush and work schedule, personal temperament and vividness, objectives and drawn forms, fixed position and distance of drawing, models and transition, etc. However, Chinese art history was not completed till the Tang Dynasty when Zhang Yanyuan finished his ten volumes of artistic commentaries and biographies as well as a collection of art works. Its greatness resides not just in its size, but in a series of remarks, such as his claims for the function of painting in achieving moral education, its ethical assistance to human beings, its limitlessness in mental changes and its fostering of cultured manners and wisdom as well as its ability to guard against stupidity.

Later painting theory, like that in the Song Dynasty, presents more details about both general and specific descriptions of certain kind of drawings such as the landscape principles of Guo Xi. Referring to the principles of observation and aesthetic factors in landscape pictures, he remarks that in observing a genuine landscape, one should take care of its momentum at a long distance and of quality at close quarters. His theoretical focus is the use of a kind of perspective which highlights the three distances, namely "high distance", "deep distance" and "level distance", suggesting the three ways of representing different distances for a painter. Painting theory was pushed to a new high towards the end of the Qing Dynasty. Both Shi Tao and Zheng Banqiao stressed the use of unusually picturesque technique to add to other styles of Chinese traditional pictures. Shi Tao's "make a draft by collecting adequate number of wondrous cliffs" and Zheng Banqiao's theory of "three bamboos" (such as those in the eyes, in the mind and in the hand), all of which contributed to the Chinese artistic development.

Western painting did not seem to have any influential theoretical statement or works in its earlier artistic development though its significant works of art appeared, if not earlier than, just as early as that in China. However, its art practice appeared quite impressive in quality, with some outstanding creations, such as *Venus of Milo*, a marvellously carved statue of Greek antiquity and many others, especially those before the downfall of the Roman Empire. The Medieval period restricted further development of classical art due to the suffocating intellectual and religious control over ideological and cultural growth. The "darkness" of this period left little of artistic importance but some stiff and lifeless figurines of Jesus Christ. However, the Western world woke up from its thousand-odd-year sleep and became aware of the aesthetical and intellectual insufficiency of its civilization. The art of the Renaissance was proof that the Westerner was capable enough to create anything he desired, so long as he had the courage to break the bondage restricting his perspective and action.

The practical spirit and critical attitude of Western culture has contributed to its high levels of artistic achievement of the recent centuries. The rapid social and intellectual developments after the Renaissance assured the people all over the world that the West had ushered in a new epoch where artists would eventually ignore ideological restrictions imposed by Christian and autocratic dominance, choosing more varieties of ways of representation and fully manifesting its potential power and hidden energy and talent. The later development of the West not only satisfied the Europeans but shocked and amazed the whole world.

Compared with painting theory in China, modern theory in Western art shifts its attention from its care for external effects to the expression of internal effects as part of modernist trend. The old preoccupation with plain and formal presentations and restricted colours were regarded as being disadvantageous by the classical painters but came to be seen as advantageous by the modernist artist. Classical Western painters, like Chinese painters, used to value more the content of paintings, but the modernist would value more the expressive value of painting itself or the individualistic form of painting. Therefore it is form rather than the idea or implication of a drawing that the modernist artist would prefer. This is perhaps why so much experimental work was done and achieved in the last century and half. As occurred to the development of modern art of the West, practical art work always preceded theory of art though the latter could apply as guidance to more practice as in the case of fiction. For instance, expressionism made its appearance first in Germany with strong lines and colours to express the painter's feelings of despair and anxiety and produced the first batch of entirely new work of art. Not until the new form of art touched more artists and spread to drama were some theoretical principles advanced to the public and expressionism was thus established as a new mode of art. The German scholar Herman Bahr once said: "Expressionism is in our mind a symbol of the unknown world where we would express our inner ideas and which we expect to save ourselves. It is just the symbol of imprisoned mind that would make an effort to break the prison as the alarm for all those souls who suffer from tortures and hardships. It is the content of Expressionism."[①] Obviously Bahr's statement is based on the experimental work of the expressionist artists and indicated his understanding of the school which had survived the trials of various kinds in the development of modernist art. it was also true of the other groups, such as impressionism, postimpressionism, abstractionism, fantasy, fauvism and cubism,

---

① See *Modern Art and Modernism*, pp. 71−72, F. Frascina & C. Harrison, Harper & Row, 1982.

nearly all had the same experience in terms of theoretical exploration and establishment.

At first sight, one might fear Western art did not care much about theory, but with a more careful examination one could understand that the practical is usually prior to the theoretical and hence appears more significant than the theoretical. The theoretical principle could only be drawn out of practical experience. So far little established theoretical interpretation could perfectly match the remarkable achievements in modernist art. But certainly Western art is practice-based in its daring spirit and actual creation of a large number of artistic styles and products by a variety of schools.

8.3.5 Tradition and experiment

Art, like other branches of the humanities, has to face the challenge of how to handle the relationship between tradition and creation. Experiences of the historical development of human civilization have assured us of the significance of this issue in almost every area of art. The development of painting is a process of continuous interaction of tradition and creation.

Chinese painting seems to care more for tradition on account of its long history and for stability on account of the long-term centralized system and unified ideology. For a fairly long time, Chinese painting proceeded within a traditional framework, environment and identity, defined and restricted by its established rules, aesthetic value and social circumstances. This is confirmed by the three categories of Chinese painting, namely, landscape, figures, flowers and birds, which remained unchanged for thousands of years. Of course it does not mean that Chinese art did not undergo any change at all, rather, such change was quite subtle and limited, hardly comparable with the drastic changes in Western art over the modern period.

Western art appeared also very slow in its development in the long years of the Middle Ages. Doubtless artistic progress is closely related to the progress of social conditions and the advance of intellectual freedom. A society could grant its members these conditions although some accidental factors, like the individual genius, are also important. Hence, it does not seem so strange to witness the abrupt appearance of experimental painting, represented by, for instance, impressionism following the drastic social changes and political turmoil occurring in the Western countries during the bourgeois revolution after the Renaissance.

Generally, experimental art as the major form of creation, has been stronger since the 19th century in the West, despite the diversities of the claims and creative techniques of particular "movements", thanks to a focus on changes of spatial representation, for example, from two dimensions to three dimensions. The abstract method and cubist style were a result of such a trend. As a matter of fact, painting moves more towards sculpture following the awareness of abstraction being shaped. Modernist art also cares much for fantasy, that is, works produced through visionary or illusive perceptions, either in cubist form or by the use of striking colours. Chinese painting also used some fantasy techniques, such as images of supernatural beings, or the use of so-called "splashes of ink". But such imagination and techniques are not exactly the same as the West's modernist fantasy, such as that in surrealism and Dadaism. Experimental art is no longer limited to a partial or methodical modification, without any theoretical evidence or support, but is radical, total and thorough in revolution. It is no longer a matter of readjustments to colour, light or form, but a total breakthrough, a substitution and the establishment of a new tradition. Hence, in a way modernist art seems totally radical, totally rebellious and totally new and original. But experimental art does not necessarily suggest to give up all traditions. Actually it continually tries to keep a sense that all its creations emerge from past eras of Western culture, both material and spiritual. If not the recent past, then inspiration could be drawn from the distant past, like some primitive archetypes (such as geometrical drawings in Egyptian or Greek pictures) as have occurred in some postmodernist operations.

Comparatively speaking, Chinese painting usually tried to avoid radicalism, and chose to keep its traditional position and mode and culture. It underwent the historically long process of slow change and appeared politically cautious and even neutral by evading anything violent and radical. Obviously, it was influenced by its traditional culture and ideology with Confucianism at its core. But with the introduction of modernist works from the West in the recent centuries, many artists of the younger generations have attempted to produce some original work by resorting to a combination of traditional Chinese art and new methods from Western art. Some of them have made some considerable achievements though it is still a long way to go before such experimental work could match their Western counterparts.

Chinese and Western paintings have benefited from interaction with each other since the turn of the 20th century when a few Chinese artists either scholastically visited Europe or introduced Western art at home. Though Chinese painters benefited more from Western art and promoted the development of Chinese modern art by putting into their works Western techniques and styles, the Chinese way of painting was also brought to the Western countries by those expatriate Chinese artists. Perhaps it is a bit too early to make the judgment about the quality and status of these two painting traditions. But certainly it would do both sides good to approach and understand each other, especially when we are located in the process of globalization and feel the breath of multiculturalism.

Questions for comprehension and discussion

1. Describe the general situation of Chinese painting.
2. Tell briefly the historical development of Western painting.
3. Try to find out some similar and dissimilar points between Chinese and Western paintings.
4. Why is it that Western painting met with its modernist development in the latter half of the 19th century? What are the major features of modernist art? Say something about modernist influences on Chinese painting and art.

List of proposed books for further reading

1. 杨新、高居翰、巫鸿、班宗华、聂崇正、郎绍君合著,1996,《中国绘画三千年》,台北:联经出版事业。
2. 王伯敏,1988,《中国美术通史》,济南:山东教育出版社。
3. 俞剑华,1977,《中国绘画史》,台北:台湾商务印书馆。
4. Cahill, James, *The Distant Mountains: Chinese Painting of the Late Ming Dynasty*, New York: Weatherhill, 1982.
5. Gombrich, Ernst, *The Story of Art*, Oxford: Phaidon, 1950.
6. Janson, Hirst, Janson, Anthony F., *History of Art: The Western Tradition*, Upper Saddle River, NJ: Pearson Education, 2004.
7. Arnason, H. H., *History of Modern Art: Painting, Sculpture, Architecture, Photography*, Upper Saddle River, NJ: Prentice Hall, 2004.

Chapter 9

A Comparison of Science between China and the West

Science is an old as well as a popular business which arose from human special needs in dealing with nature in addition to the daily necessity of gaining food, clothing and shelter, such as the practice of metallurgy, foretelling of seasons and the weather and treatment of the sick. This is true of both China and the West.

As part of human creative activities, science is produced and developed with rational and established ways of thinking and acting. It is, in this sense, a kind of culture, which performs to affect human behaviours and lifestyles and contributes to modifying ways of human development.

Science came from the Latin word *scire*, meaning "to know or understand". In those days to acquire knowledge of the outside world, especially the natural world, was an arduous and rewarding undertaking. It involves both exploration and creation. It is especially the case with modern science, which has evolved and opened new possibilities with more knowledge derived from research into and contact with the unknown world.

Science is probably one of the most frequently used words today as a symbol of the advanced or progressive level of modern civilization together with another word "technology", serving as the one-way road towards a better tomorrow for human beings. Therefore it is necessary to know about different aspects of science, not only in terms of creative intellectual ability such as that in material improvement, but also in terms of its influence on social and cultural developments. To make a comparison of science between China and the West involves seeking both similar and dissimilar points in relation of science to the previous social and intellectual experience. The study of science in a comparative way could help shape a better view of the essence of science based on a historical reflection on human intellectual attitudes and development as part of human civilization. Technoscience, a combination of science and technology, is not only a representation of human endeavour to know about and conquer nature, but also indicates human ability to build up a substantial and rational way of thinking and create a more idealistic and fruitful future.

As one of the decisive factors in human development, science works both as a guarantee of the quality of our life and as an indicator of the significance of our existence. Presumably few would doubt the role science has played, but many might argue if science would be totally subject to human will. Maybe this is the charm of studying science comparatively as a culture.

A survey of Chinese scientific development

The history of Chinese scientific development had been obscured or received little attention outside the country from the West for a long time until it came to light in the middle of the 20th century and became known to the international public thanks to the publication of *Science and Civilization in China* by the English historian of science Joseph Needham. Based on the long-term study of Chinese achievements in science and technology, Needham pointed out that Chinese inventions went far beyond what was achieved by contemporary Europeans, more so before the 15th century. Dr Needham backed up his points by providing a systematic and comprehensive list of the accomplishments of Chinese scholars in mathematics, astronomy, geography, agriculture, medicine, biology, metallurgy and meteorology. The following is a summary of major points based on Needham's research.

9.1.1 The early achievement in Chinese maths and astronomy

In mathematics, the Chinese began to use the decimal system as early as in the Zhou Dynasty during the 14th century BC. The concept of mathematical figures came into use in the 2nd century BC. Its earlier appearance occurred in the Western Zhou, about 6 – 10 centuries BC while its eventual establishment was made in *jiu-zhang-suan-shu* (《九章算术》, Nine-Chapter Arithmetic) during the Western Han, about the 3rd century BC to the 1st century AD.

As to the counting of the ratio of the circumference of a circle to its diametre, the Chinese mathematician Liu Hui did it into 3.141599 in the 3rd century BC and Zu Chongzhi improved it and so did his son during the 5th century by getting 3.1415926~3.1415927 which remained the world's best value for about 1000 years. In algebra the Chinese mathematician Wang Xiaotong was the first in the world to be able to solve a cubic equation, 600 years earlier than the Europeans. The forerunner of the binary system, *yi-jing* (《易经》, The Classic of Change) was a work produced in the Zhou Dynasty, providing the basis for modern computer science.

In astronomy, the Chinese began heavenly observations long before the

Arabians. From the 5th century BC to the 10th century AD, Chinese astronomical records were the only surviving documents in the world for registering all the heavenly events, covering solar eclipses, the solar black spots and comets as well as the explosions of supernovae. All of these accomplishments were quite unknown to the Europeans at the time and established a basis for the new development of astronomy. Chinese royal courts kept long ago an official post for heavenly observation, not because they took an interest in the study of nature or the sky, but of their interest in astrology which seemed to be able to predict their own future. This could explain the motivation for the early recorded observations and the invention of some astronomical devices, such as Zhang Heng's *hun-tian-yi* (浑天仪, Heavenly-Observing Instrument).

Other astronomical achievements include the initial concept of an unlimited universe, which regards stars as substantial objects floating in the void of space, the establishment of the equatorial coordinate axis system equipped with heavenly poles (different obviously from the Greek one albeit logically similar), the development of the counting value for astronomy and the application of equatorial coordinate axes in the star catalogue, operating continuously for about 2000 years; the manufacturing of sophisticated astronomical instruments peaked with the birth of an equatorial observation device invented in the 13th century, the continuous and correct registry of astronomical phenomena, such as lunar eclipses, new stars, comets and solar spots.

9.1.2 Contributions of Chinese earth science and medicine

In earth science (geography) Chinese scientists scored such results as the normalization of mapmaking proposed by Pei Xiu during the Wei and Jin Dynasties (about the 3rd — 4th centuries), the production of *shan-hai-jing* (《山海经》, The Classics of Mountains and Seas) consisting of *shan-jing*, *hai-jing* and *da-huang-jing* with *shan-jing* as the earliest work of geography in China though its writing and publishing dates remain undecided. The date and writer of *shui-jing* are also unknown but it was annotated by Li Daoyuan, giving detailed explanatory notes for natural geographical conditions and agricultural values. As well the digging of the Grand Canal improved tremendously the Chinese water transportation system. The publication of the Chinese Buddhist monk Xuanzang's *da-tang-xi-yu-ji* (《大唐西域记》, The Tale of Western Pilgrimage of the Great Tang Dynasty), made available the largest map since the Wei and Jin Dynasties drawn by Jia Dan during the Tang Dynasty, called *hai-nei-hua-yi-tu* (《海内华夷图》, The World Map of Chinese and Foreign Lands). Subsequently *A Record of Sea Tide* by Du Shumeng of the Tang Dynasty presented a theory about the transformation between the sea and land as well as the causes of the formation of tide. In addition, the well-known travel book, *xu-xia-ke-you-ji* (《徐霞客游记》, Xu Xiake's Travels), one of the many of the same type, offered a detailed account of geographical and geological conditions of many places in China, including limestone, watery terrain, hydrology and plants aside from a research on subtropical geomorphology in southwestern China.

As a farming country, China has a rich heritage in agriculture from her ancestors. The earliest document in this area was the papers collected in *lu-shi-chun-qiu*(《鲁氏春秋》, Lu's Annals) about 2300 years ago, dealing with agricultural policy and the farming experiences of tilling land and growing crops.

9.1.3 Scientific records in Chinese agriculture

A large number of books on agriculture followed, such as *si-sheng-zhi-shu* (《汜胜之书》, Si Shengzhi's Book), a summary in the Western Han period of a variety of farming techniques, including the method of distinguishing seeds, the method of soaking seeds and the readjustment of water temperature in rice fields. The ten-volume *qi-min-yao-shu* (《齐民要术》, Key Points in Farming) is perhaps one of the most reputable classic of agriculture. It principally summed up the farming experiences along the lower and middle reaches of the Yellow River as well as the techniques of breeding domestic animals with a range of both farming and husbandry, somewhat like an agricultural encyclopedia.

Lu Yu's monograph *cha-jing* (《茶经》, The Tea Classic) is the earliest writing of the kind, based on the legends of tea from its origin to the various types: growing and manufacturing, tea leaves, tea containers and water type in addition to tea-making methods and effects of tea.

Other writings include *can-shu* (《蚕书》, Book of Silkworms) by Qin Guan from the Song Dynasty, *nong-shu* (《农书》, Farming Book) by Wang Zhen from the Yuan Dynasty, and Xu Guangqi's *nong-zheng-quan-shu* (《农政全书》, A Complete Book of Agricultural Affairs) from the Ming Dynasty. Among these publications, Xu's book, totalling 60 volumes, is notable for both a complete overview of the Chinese traditional agriculture and the introduction of Western agricultural techniques. It covers such a wide-ranging area as farming, water conservancy, farm tools, transplantation of crops and fruit trees, silkworm-raising, husbandry, breeding, processing of food and preparation for famine, etc.

Chinese medical achievements are registered in a number of Chinese medical classics. The earliest is *huang-di-nei-jing* (《黄帝内经》, Huangdi's Internal Classics), supposedly composed 2000 years ago, a collection of 162 essays handling separately such areas as the anatomy of the human body, physiology, pathology, causes of disease and diagnosis. As well, it includes acupuncture, health care and *jing-luo*(经络, nervous network). *Shen-nong-ben-cao-jing* (《神农本草经》, The Shennong Classic of Local Herbs) was said to be from the Eastern Han Dynasty, while *shang-han-lun* (《伤寒论》, On Typhoid Fever and Other Diseases) by Zhang Zhongjing came from the end of the Eastern Han Dynasty. The magical doctor Hua Tuo, a legendary surgeon famous for his use of anesthesia in operation, also came from the same period as Zhang Zhongjing.

The next important medical work is *ben-cao-gang-mu* (《本草纲目》, An Outline Survey of Chinese Herbs) by Li Shizhen, an outstanding doctor from the Ming Dynasty. The book, altogether 52 volumes and 1.9 million words, admits 1,892 kinds of herbs and 110,960 prescriptions of Chinese medicine. Its reputation lies not only in its all-round collection of Chinese herbs and summary of traditional Chinese medical treatment, but in its academic contribution to other subjects like botany, mineralogy, metallurgy, geology and meteorology.

As well, the Chinese applied vaccination to guard against smallpox in the middle of the 16th century.

9.1.4 Chinese early inventions in comparison with those of the West

In addition, Chinese scientists acquired quite a number of inventions and discoveries in the fields of mechanical devices and other techniques. They contributed to the improvement of work efficiencies in a way that their Western counterparts did not. These inventions are partly listed here, for a general view of the scientific and technological achievements in ancient China, in contrast to the equivalent or similar items in the West.

Inventions	Compared with the West
dragon-bone water lifter	15 centuries earlier
water-powered roller for grinding grain	13 centuries earlier
water-powered wheel and winnower	14 centuries earlier
piston bellows	about 14 centuries earlier
cotton-ginned device	about 4 centuries earlier
one-wheel handcart	9 − 10 centuries earlier
sail-added barrow	11 centuries earlier
grinding cart	12 centuries earlier
animal-driven harness	8 centuries earlier
mechanical bow	13 centuries earlier
kite	about 12 centuries earlier
bamboo dragonfly	about 14 centuries earlier
hot-air-powered lamp	10 centuries earlier
mechanical deep-poring technique	11 centuries earlier
cast iron	10 − 12 centuries earlier
shelf for constant suspension	8 − 9 centuries earlier
bow-shaped arched bridge	7 centuries earlier
iron-chain suspension bridge	10 − 13 centuries earlier

(续表)

Inventions	Compared with the West
gunpowder	5－6 centuries earlier
magnetic compass	11 centuries earlier
printing technique	6 centuries earlier
china	11－13 centuries earlier
paper	10 centuries earlier[①]

Generally speaking, all these inventions have contributed a lot to the development of economic production and greatly promoted technological progress. Compared with Western developments in the similar areas, Chinese technological achievements were no less noticeable or sophisticated, but certainly much earlier in terms of their initial manufacturing and application. However, the Chinese scientific and technological developments did not make a breakthrough, in the sense that these results were generally isolated, separate and were unable to change China's social and economic status as a whole. Due to the obscure status of science in society at the time, no one or rather, few could live on science by providing scientific services for economic and intellectual developments. The few scholars who handled science were either officials or part-time inventors whose principal concerns were unfortunately not science. Consequently, science as a profession had to work secretly or underground and greatly suffered from social prejudice and made little progress in the discouraging years of the long-term feudal society.

Another important reason for slow development in science was the shortage of funding and equipment required for scientific research and experiments, such as occurred in the West. The old cultural tradition in China cared more for literary practice or studies than for practical work, as was confirmed by the fact that Chinese officials were selected from those involved in literary study, like composition of poems or prose arguments. The third reason had much to do with the intellectual dominance over the average people who had to tolerate the influence of Confucianism. The latter emphasized loyalty and devotion to the emperor and his court, resulting in a popular submissiveness and obedience to the bureaucratic authorities and a lack of critical spirit, which, in a way, hindered the development of science. Consequently, Chinese science did not have a kind of enduring motivation nor made persistent endeavour in promoting its long-term progress. Rather, it had to slow down its steps in the later development due to the insufficient structure and powerless support in relation to the then social and intellectual circumstances.

Generally, Chinese science was in need of the rational tradition which

---

① 详见《科学技术概念》，9－10 页，胡显章、曾国屏（主编），高等教育出版社，1998。

helped the West get rid of the suffocating effects on its intellectual development from autocracy and divinity since the Renaissance and gradually establish its central ideology in the interests of the bourgeoisie, such as empiricism, positivism, utilitarianism and pragmatism. These factors worked partly to explain why China was left behind on the threshold of the modern age, in spite of the fact that the Chinese civilization had been once more accomplished in her earlier scientific development.

A survey of Western scientific development

9.2.1 The birth of Western science and its early development

No one can tell exactly when and how science started in the West, though Greece is generally regarded as the birth place just as it is acknowledged as the origin of the Western civilization. It is said that Thales, the distinguished philosopher from Miletus, once asserted that water was the origin of all things. His statement certainly touched on the essence of nature and hence marked the beginning of science as a subject dealing with nature.

Indeed there were a number of scholars in ancient Greece, who were famous not only for their philosophical contributions but for their work in science. Thales was an example who was talented in astronomy and mathematics as well as in philosophy as a materialist thinker. Likewise Pythagoras and Aristotle both made notable achievements in the study of science, Aristotle in biology and Pythagoras in mathematics.

It was not a single phenomenon that science was treated favourably by a few individuals. Indeed the early history of Greece was as restless as the curiosity of its people. From the Minoan Cretan civilization to the creation of the acropolis by the Mycenaeans and the glorious city-states scattered over Greece, Italy and Asia Minor, the Greek people navigated the sparkling blue waters of the Mediterranean and Aegean Seas, bringing back in their extended contact with other peoples (like Egyptians) and traditions, a wealth of geometrical and mathematical knowledge. The trading among the coastal seafaring peoples provided the stimulus for a new outlook and a desire to pick up more knowledge as a motive force and instrument for more profits.

When the people shifted the focus of attention from their interest in social affairs and human relationships to nature, their field of vision was much broadened and expected to profit much from the change. This was demonstrated by their discovery of duality, like two sexes, two eyes, two ears, two arms, two legs as well as night and day, the sun and the moon. Such human experiences suggested that number was more than abstract but practical and fundamental. Such knowledge was further extended to the trinity of the family (father, mother and child), the sky, earth and humanity and to practical uses like keeping accounts and grouping the tribes.

In many fields, the Romans inherited Greek culture and tradition. Many of Rome's cultural achievements could be traced to the days of Greek civilization, such as the Roman philosophy (Epicureanism and Stoicism in particular) and their myths and literature. It is also true of Roman science as well as rationalism. It was rational thinking that led to the further development of science in the Roman period.

The Romans were a practical people and valued applied knowledge, such as in feats of engineering, law and political and military organization. However, with its triumph over Macedonia, Sicily and Carthage, Rome built up and sealed its hegemony over the Hellenistic world. At the same time Rome itself was also transformed and became heir to the Greek and oriental cultures.

The Romans found much to admire about the Greeks, not only in their science, but in their art and literature. Greek became the language of the intellectuals in the Empire as much as Latin would be the language of scholarship in the Middle Ages. A group of distinguished scientists appeared in the Roman age, including biologists Herophilus, Galen and Erasistratus. Herophilus contributed much to anatomy and Galen was the most important representative of science, who further researched into the function of the heart and found out that the tricuspid valve allows blood to enter the right ventricle but prevents it from backing up into the right atrium and vena cava. As well he recognized the coronary blood vessels. Erasistratus established the distinction between the sensory and motor nerves.

Another famous figure was Posidonius, a native of Syria and a resident of Rhodes in Greece. He studied mathematics and the ocean tides, and became aware that the tides are fullest at the new moon when the moon and the sun are in conjunction and at the full moon when they are at opposition.

One of the most notable Roman achievements was the calendar reform initiated under Julius Caesar, which utilized the expertise of Helenistic astronomy. In spite of the fact that much intellectual progress was made in pursuit of knowledge in natural science, it was generally believed that all things were a vast system of signs that must be decoded by a mind that thinks in a kind of Divine Mind. For them, mathematics, physics and astronomy were signs (the sun, the moon, the order of the stars, the unit of numbers) that manifested God.

9.2.2　Western scientific development in the Middle Ages

The following stage is the Middle Ages which was intellectually dominated by Christianity and showed few signs of social progress or scientific achievements. However, some of the theologians or church people took an interest in science.

One of them was St Augustine who was interested in science in so far as it provided a formula to reach the ultimate goal of all knowledge, God. He endeavoured to use reason in the defence of faith whenever possible. He mustered a number of arguments for the celestial waters. His primary task was to combat heresies. In so doing he created a theology with its doctrines of hierarchy, original sin, predestination. This was the Christian science of the western half of the Empire. In the eastern half of the Empire was a greater desire to preserve scientific texts.

When Christians were trying to build up a new centre in Constantinople — the capital of the Eastern Roman Empire — they found their faith challenged by Islam — a new religion which emphasized the power of Allah and cared about the study of nature. The first Muslim believers in Allah were Arabs who had formed into a powerful empire by the 8th century, which ranged from Spain to the borders of India and included many non-Arabic peoples. Muslim territories were united linguistically because Arabic was the language of the Koran. Straddling such diverse cultures, however, the science they eventually transmitted to the West was a massive synthesis of Greek, Persian, Hindu and even Chinese thought.

In Spain Omayyad① held sway still and set up a scientific centre of learning at Cordova. From the late 8th century to the early 10th century the translation and assimilation of Greek science proceeded at a rapid pace. The doctrines of Pythagoras, Plato and the Neoplatonists were specially interesting to the Brethren of Purity and Jabir ibn Hayyan (Geber in the West). Jabir lived from about 721 to 815 as one of the earliest Islamic philosopher-scientists.

Once in a while the Middle Ages produced a few remarkable figures who either made some scientific discoveries or dared to challenge the established order of the old traditions against the background of theology. But generally in the West, the barbarian tribes settled across western Europe in this period and retarded social and intellectual developments in spite of the emergence of a few accomplished scholars.

Among these few figures was Ibn Sina (980 – 1037, Avicenna in the West) who was one of the greatest Muslim scientists and philosophers. He tried to reconcile some natural phenomena (like gravity) with God. Ibn Sina's experience was not his own, but based on the European general conditions of history. Under the influences of Arabic science, the natural science of the West gained much headway in the 12th century which witnessed the high development of the medical school at Salerno in southern Italy where some Arabic medical and especially anatomical texts were translated. During this period Spain became quickly the centre of astronomy and Toledo, a Spanish city, became the meridian

---

① Also Umayyad, member of a Muslim caliphate (a political and religious power) which reigned Spain (756 – 1031) and Damascus (661 – 750).

standard for 13th-century Europe. In the course of astronomical development, Arabic numerals, methods of computation and even instruments, such as the astrolabe, had all come to the West.

The 12th century also saw the rise of the universities which replaced monasteries and cathedral schools as the chief centres of learning. Among the earliest were the universities of Paris, Oxford, Bologna, Montpellier (a city in France), Padua (a city in Italy), Salamanca (a city in Spain) and Cambridge. They set up such faculties as theology, law, medicine and the liberal arts. With the growing interest in and popular acceptance of natural science, Ptolemy, Euclid, Archimedes, Galen and the Arab scientists slowly found their way into the curriculum of the Faculty of Arts in the new universities.

One of the pioneering transitional figures from the Middle Ages to the modern era was Roger Bacon (1214 – 1292) whose reputation rests on his stress on the importance of experimental science in addition to his criticism of and opposition to scholasticism. His work upon optics arose from a long tradition that included the nature and propagation of light and the nature of visual perception. He accepted and developed the ideas of earlier scholars from Plato and Aristotle to Euclid and Ptolemy. Those who followed him, like John Pecham and Witelo, furthered the work by synthesizing the various optical traditions.

One of the most significant uses of the experimental method and of mathematical explanation was an account of the rainbow by Theodoric of Freiberg, who demonstrated mathematically that the rainbow and its colours could be explained by assuming both refraction and reflection of light inside individual drops of water.

9.2.3 The awakening of the Western sense of science on the threshold of the modern age

The following period, the Renaissance, brought forward more genius with creative ideas and dynamic interactions with nature occurring on a wider scale. The craftsmen, engineers and even artists dealt with nature directly. The power of science and technology struck more practical areas like warfare as indicated in the Hundred Years' War where cannon replaced the catapult as the major weapon, or in navigation where more accurate mathematical techniques and astronomical observations were employed.

The scientific progress in these areas helped lead to the expansion of trade and colonial settlement initiated by Columbus who discovered the American continent with his fleet and therefore started the long process of colonization, the dawn of capitalist development.

One of the marvellous talents who combined scientific technique and artistic wit was Leonardo da Vinci (1452 – 1519) who adopted the technique of perspective in association with his ideas of painting. He looked into and uncovered nature layer by layer till it revealed its secrets, by applying himself to anatomy, mechanics, biology and botany. He dissected and observed, seeking not only form but the very origin of movement in the animated body and produced ultimately paintings of lasting value based on mechanical science and mathematical laws.

The next important figure of the Renaissance was perhaps Copernicus, a Polish priest who studied medicine and astronomy in Italy, leading to his famous claim that the earth was not the centre of the universe but moved around the sun.

Together with Martin Luther's Reformation, Copernicus' discovery certainly shocked the Western world and Christendom both intellectually and religiously. There followed a series of important scientists and scientific discoveries and theories. The best-known among them were Francis Bacon, Galileo and Isaac Newton.

Francis Bacon was not exactly a scientist, in the sense that he did not achieve any substantial scientific result though he engaged himself in scientific experiments. His reputation in relation to science was largely dependent on his awareness of science. He maintains that the purpose of science is to give human beings power over nature and to extend the power of man. He also tried to extinguish the gloom coming from the backwardness of human beings. He argues that man must seek new pathways if the senses deceive, if education has failed and if the ancients hold us in thrall; that only experiment is able to shed light upon the true causes of things.

Copernicus' theory of a sun-centred universe needed further testimony and substantial theoretical support. However, the Aristotelian theory of physics had become weatherbeaten and could no longer play the role it had done. The time had come to construct a new theory to make up for what was lacking. Galileo's contribution filled up the gap.

Few would deny Galileo's profound influence upon the course of Western science. It is he who finally changed the language of physics from causes and qualities to quantity, measurement and description. He proposed that experiments, designed to answer specific questions, should be the deciding tests of hypothesis. He defended the Copernican system publicly.

Like Aristotle, Galileo assumes that science must give knowledge of the real sensate world, that nature itself is rational, not a chaotic receptacle. Galileo was himself a good Catholic and was certain that any conflicts between his science and his religion must lie in interpretation. But the authorities, smarting from his attacks for many years, were not adverse to using theology and the considerable power of the church in order to find the weak spots in his armour. He appeared to keep a sense of humour in spite of the attacks and persecutions from his enemy.

Galileo died in 1642, the year in which Isaac Newton (1642 − 1727) was born in England. Newton, one of the giants of Western science, was heir to the new astronomy, Baconian experimentation, English Puritanism and alchemy. Few people were aware that Newton's personal opinion of his accomplishment is thoroughly soaked in theological and alchemist beliefs, for he holds that he has restored the pure, uncorrupted doctrine of the ancients.

Newton has indeed done something unique. He made marvelous achievements in the early stage of such science subjects as modern mathematics, physics and astronomy. He developed the theory of differential calculus. He discovered the dispersion of light into coloured spectrum by refraction through a prism. He studied the diffraction and refraction of light and invented the reflecting telescope. He also developed the inverse square law of gravitation and applied it to the planetary motions. He banished mystery from the universe and demonstrated for the first time the true law of nature governing the universe, when all was hidden in the darkest ignorance. The 18th century created the modern word "revolution" and did so in Newton's name. But the subsequent 18th-century revolution in both science and politics was surely not the revolution Newton had foreseen or desired. As a matter of fact, the development of physical science after Newton was much more complex. Perhaps Newton's science was the centre of the garden for Western civilization, yet it was not the only part for there were other contributors to the garden such as Descartes, Leibniz and Huygens[①].

Newton's work marked a demarcation line in the history of human development when science was about to enter social consciousness. His achievements assumed different perspectives, with mathematical, mechanical, speculative, experimental and even religious aspects.

England presented to Western science another genius no more than 100 years after Newton's death. His name is Charles Darwin (1809 – 1882). Darwin founded the theory of evolution in the organic world. His mechanism of evolution fostered one of the greatest revolutions in Western thought, for he dispensed with the ancient and religious doctrine of divinity or teleology, replacing it with continuous variation of forms and purely mechanical selection of those variations, based solely upon natural causes. These life selections and modifications served to reduce the ideas of premeditated design and final cause to the status of vestigial organs in the evolving body of biological knowledge. Darwin's theory was a philosophical and intellectual revolution as much as a biological one.

Another prominent figure in the 19th century was the Frenchman Auguste Comte whose positivism became the new scientific philosophy of the machine age where progress was a determined fact. The word "determinism" no longer means fatalism without free will at the mercy of stoic astrology or original sin. Rather it refers to the inevitable chain of cause and effect and the temporal chain of matter

---

① Huygens (1629 – 1695), Dutch physicist and astronomer.

in motion, leading to positive knowledge of the given social structure. The laws of cause and effect deduced from historical observation would yield knowledge of an inevitable future social configuration.

Comte's theory in a way offered some new perspective into the developments of both society and nature, but he himself is not exactly a scientist in terms of experimental practice. A number of theories were stimulated by imagination, as Comte's positivism was, or originated from the ideas of ancient thinkers. The latter could be confirmed by development of the concept of the atom. The concept of the atom was one of the most influential theories Western scientists took over and used in broad outline from the 1600s until about 1900. The concept was traced to Greek philosophers in the 5th century BC. The original speculation about a hard, indivisible fundamental particle of nature gave way slowly to a new idea confirmed and supported by scientific experiment and mathematical deduction. It took 2000 years for modern physicists to be aware that the atom is neither divisible nor hard or immutable.

The great discovery in the development of atomic theory is obviously that of electrons which was perhaps owed largely to the English scientist Michael Faraday (1791 – 1867). Until Faraday's electrolysis experiments, scientists had had no idea at all about the nature of the forces binding atoms together in a molecule. Faraday's reputation lies in his discovery of electromagnetic induction and the principle of electrolysis. He believed that electricity is not a fluid, but an inherent property of matter as a force. He inferred that electrical forces exist inside the molecule after he produced an electric current and a chemical reaction in a solution with the electrodes of a voltaic cell, and came to the conclusion that each ion of a given chemical compound has exactly the same charge. Furthermore, he found the ionic charges to be integral multiples, never separated.

Research on physics gained a vital result in finding the principle of conservation of energy. The German scientist Rudolf Julius Clausius summed up by following the results from previous scholars, that some heat is converted into work and some passes to a lower state and denies the possibility of perpetual motion. Later he developed a mathematical equivalence value and hence brought forward the term entropy as a measure to embrace the amount of energy of the universe.

9.2.4 Western science in the modern age

The entropy of the universe tends to increase after it marked the founding of the science of thermodynamics. But it gave rise to controversial problems with some 19th-century physics theory, like Newtonian mechanics. In spite of some heated argument, the question remained unsolved till Albert Einstein (1879 – 1955) grew and took up the challenge.

At about 12 Einstein fell in love with the beauty and certainty of "holy geometry (Euclid)". His publication of five articles later called "On the Electrodynamics", provided the basic theoretical ground for his restricted or special Theory of Relativity.

The principle of equivalence was also the first step into a series of problems. He realized space must be warped by gravity. He argues that in a large gravitational field, lines of fall would converge towards the centre. However, the bending of light, the distorting of bodies, the slowing of clocks, all represent relativistic effects, not on the things themselves, but on the space-time coordinate system. Different fields would mean different coordinate systems. All are relative. Even the speed of light is no longer fixed.

After many years of struggling with general relativity, Einstein, guided by mathematical thinking, began to realize that human beings could uncover the sublime structure of the world hidden from immediate experience. He came to believe that pure thought could reach beyond mere economical associations of sensations. Beneath those sensations lay a world constructed by a mathematical plan open to the human mind.

The great beauty of General Relativity lies with the field geometry, the metric tensor equating the energy momentum tensor because all fields carry energy. Therefore the laws of motion are already contained within the law of the gravitational field, as were the laws of energy. Hence $E = MC^2$, which suggests the metric tensor relates to the energy tensor, therefore matter is a continuum, a density of field energy.

Einstein's theory is obviously a further extension of ancient scientific thought, such as that of Greek imagination about the existence of matter and universe, based on the vast, holy vision of the essential unity and holism. Though the ancient Greeks had first seen what seemed to be separate chunks of matter — this or that it is just a vision of a mask over reality.

Einstein demonstrates that if matter is the density of the field, a non-linear continuum of all existence, then it must include the electromagnetic field, and henceforth the atomic theory. This means that somehow atomism must finally give way to continuum physics and the two fields merge into one. Somehow Einstein had to find a Unified Field Theory, which seems to suffer from the cold shoulder of many people.

Einstein died in 1955, but scientific exploration goes on continuously with more results coming out and changing the human ways of living and thinking. They include galaxy's discovery, the bang of the cosmos, DNA theory and biological engineering, information technology, space flight and research technology.

The theory of the earth has manifested rapid progress in recent decades. It was established to elucidate and handle the dynamics of the earth's outer shell, the lithosphere. The theory claims that the lithosphere consists of about a dozen large plates and several small ones. These plates move relative to each other and interact at their boundaries, where they diverge, converge or slip relatively harmlessly past one another. Such interactions are thought to give rise to most of the seismic and volcanic activity of the earth, including earthquakes that have brought great disasters to human beings.

The theory of plate tectonics was shaped during the late 1960s as a broad synthesis of geological and geophysical data. A huge impact on the development of earth science, it represents a true scientific revolution, analogous in its consequences to the Rutherford and Bohr atomic models in physics or the discovery of the genetic code in biology. Its influence on the scientific understanding of the earth's history could never be overestimated, such as the preliminary interpretation of ancient oceans and climates, and of the evolution of life.

The advances in Western medical science are also remarkable, such as those in curing heart disease. As the principal cause and killer of heart attacks, strokes and circulatory insufficiencies, atherosclerosis remained one of the serious concerns of medical workers. Work in the late 1990s led to the view that plaque formation may be a response to chronic inflammation of the innermost arterial layer. It has become clear that treatment aimed at diminishing inflammation could be a new and effective means of treating the disease.

Scientists have resorted to mice for experiments to find ways to decrease inflammation and reduce the formation and development of atherosclerotic plaques. Such work has also increased the structural stability of existing plaques and helped heighten the understanding of the causes of atherosclerosis, which promised to lead to more effective methods of treatment and prevention.

For the last few decades or so, eye-catching achievements have occurred in the field of chemical structures and the processes of biological phenomena at the molecular level. Of growing importance since the 1940s, molecular biology developed out of the related fields of biochemistry, genetics and biophysics. The discipline is particularly concerned with the study of proteins, nucleic acids and enzymes — i.e., the macromolecules that are essential to life processes. Molecular biology seeks to understand the three-dimensional structure of these macromolecules through such techniques as X-ray diffraction and electron microscopy. The discipline particularly seeks to understand the molecular basis of genetic processes; molecular biologists map the location of genes on specific chromosomes, associate these genes with particular characters of an organism, and use recombinant-DNA technology to isolate and modify specific genes.

In its early period during the 1940s, the field was concerned with elucidating the basic three-dimensional structure of proteins. Growing knowledge of the structure of proteins in the early 1950s enabled the structure of deoxyribonucleic acid (DNA) — the genetic blueprint found in all living things — to be described in 1953. Further research enabled scientists to gain an increasingly detailed knowledge not only of DNA and ribonucleic acid (RNA) but also of the chemical sequences within these substances that instruct the cells and viruses to make proteins.

Molecular biology remained a pure science with few practical applications until the 1970s, when certain types of enzymes were discovered that could cut and recombine segments of DNA in the chromosomes of certain bacteria. The resulting recombinant-DNA technology became one of the most potential and promising branches of molecular biology because it promised the ability to modify the genetic sequences that determine the basic characters of plants and animals. Therefore, the new technology has provided a broad prospect for seeking secrets of human life and is bringing more possibilities of various solutions for the developments of human beings as a race of high intelligence.

For the past few decades since the World War II, the influence of Western scientists upon political decision-making values, religion and social issues has increased drastically. The pronouncements of science carry more weight and authority than did papal bulls[①] in the Middle Ages.

Many values that may appear irrational from the perspective of science have arisen from living social experiences and conceal social as well as psychologically useful functions. There are possibly some traditions or other sophisticated ways of understanding the universe that are in conflict within Western rationalism, the loss of which results in spiritual impoverishment of humanity in respect of rational science. Consequently, science has been recognized consciously or unconsciously as the core of rational thinking, determining the social and individual life of the West. These tendencies have apparently given impetus to and helped identify new developments of science which keep pace with economic prosperity and social progress.

9.3 Comparative comments

Science cannot be separated or abstracted from its cultural milieu. It is not value-free nor does it escape from the impact or intervention of the social and cultural environment where it is undertaken or free from the influence of the temperament of the people directly involved. In a word, science is the product of the actual needs of certain social and intellectual conditions of human development. In that sense, science is decided and restricted by real circumstances of human lifestyle and certain levels of intellectual development or rather, rational aspect of thinking and behaviour.

The history of science manifests that people think differently about our actual needs. Only those activities which could help solve actual problems in human life

---

① Refer to papal documents of Roman Catholic church.

are proved to be of value and knowledge of science. Thus we build up the concepts of science and rationalism in general. Like the photon, science is embedded in the greater context of its existence, its value of truth, falsity and reality, cannot be discussed outside the context, nor can it be measured apart from the lustrous framework. Modern science is an objective view of nature, unbiased and fundamentally true to reality, confirmed by the application of experiments and observations.

In view of its notable achievements in the long historical river, Chinese science could be said to have scored a similar or even more fruitful results in ancient times than what the West has. Such a basically balanced development between the two sides continued many centuries, from the early days of the two civilizations till perhaps the Renaissance or approximately the 16th century. In mathematics, astronomy, agriculture, medicine or in other practical areas like geography and ship-building or mining, both sides have made marvellous contributions. One can find quite a few similarities as well as dissimilarities between the two sides in terms of type, degree, effect, awareness and significance.

9.3.1 Initiation of science from mathematics

Both sides started their serious research in science from their interest in mathematics and then shifted to other more practical areas though algebra seemed stronger on the Chinese side while the Westerners were more capable in geometry. This is because human beings are established in their intellectual development by undergoing a process from taking care of simple and specific things to considering more complicated and abstract things. Such a process, occurring to both China and the West, required that they should do some abstract thinking as a summary of practical work they had performed. For instance, the ancients of both sides had to work on the problem of numbers in daily life, such as counting of days, area of land, weight of grain, etc., which initiated the early stage of scientific study. Thus they improved enormously their working efficiency, with a result of mathematics coming into being to meet this demand in spite of the diversities in actual conditions.

9.3.2 Part-time engagement with scientific research

In ancient times, both in China and in the West, few of the scientists could focus only on science but had to take up other jobs either to raise necessary living expenses or to keep a decent position. The most accomplished scientists were often philosophers who tried to choose a particular perspective or method to observe natural phenomena or abstract figures as something substantial to support their philosophical points of view or to expand the ground of their concerns for more knowledge. They included Mo Zi and Lao Zi in China, Thales and Aristotle in the West. This tendency shows that science secured its important status to the mind of the limited elite minority due to the philosopher's solitary endeavour and demonstrated a potentially brilliant and fruitful prospect. At the same time the rational aspect of science has been an inherent part in philosophical development from the ancient times onwards, working practically to convince more and more people of its encouraging results and hence emerging as a solid part of intellectual tradition in the West since the Renaissance. Chinese science, while meeting discouraging and sometimes even prejudicial treatment in its long-term feudal society, overcame countless neglects and setbacks from the landlord class controlled society and made a number of invention or creations based on individual and isolated endeavours.

9.3.3　Close relation between science and practice

Most of the previous scientific discoveries were closely related to production or practical needs in either China or the West. For instance, the use of numerals and the development of arithmetic and algebra came from the need for measurement in the project of water control during Dayu's time and Li Bing's famous Dujiangyan Dam during the Warring States Period. In the West, such need of mathematics, especially geometry, was seen in the measurement of newly piled up land of the Nile Delta by the Egyptians and the public constructions, like water pipes and large-sized bridges in the Roman Empire.

Such practical tradition was further developed in the modern age, as evidenced in economic production and the actual needs of social development as well as the advances of science and technology in all human activities. On the part of Western civilization, scientific development was certainly stepped up during the Industrial Revolution when steam engine was invented and applied to various industrial departments and thus greatly pushed forward the progress of the whole Western civilization. For China, the link between science and practice was not so close after its early spontaneous practical performance in Chinese society. Consequently, science showed signs of slowing down its steps in terms of evoking great enthusiasm for its development from the ordinary people as it did in the West during the Enlightenment due to the political and intellectual bondage set by autocracy and ideological conservatism affected or imposed by Confucianism, which obviously restricted Chinese development, including scientific advance. Once such barriers were lifted, as what has happened since the late 1970s, China would have every opportunity to celebrate the arrival of its scientific spring, which would in turn greatly promote the economic development based on the combination of science and practice.

9.3.4 Dependence of science on economy and other developments

Because of the underdevelopment of social and economic conditions, early scientific research and its results were still quite limited in terms of popularity, scale, range, academic level and practical effects. Scientific research was not yet an area independent of economic production or other occupations. In old China, scientific research did not receive adequate attention from government and public as it deserved in terms of funding and material conditions, even in comparison with cultural affairs. Confucian and other classical works were listed as part of compulsory reading for the candidates of the Civil Service Examination during the feudal society. Some painters in the Song Dynasty were supported financially by being enlisted into a painting house. But scientists were never granted such a favourable working environment. Only those with a particular interest would engage themselves in part-time and isolated research.

In the West the situation was similar, which greatly restricted the social, economic and intellectual effect of science and technology before the Renaissance. It was not till the modern age that science obtained its social status and won its national reputation by its great contribution to the development of the country in both China and the West, as witnessed in the social and intellectual transformations in the transitional period from the 14th century to the 19th century.

9.3.5 Intellectual and rational influences

Beginning from the Renaissance (approximately the 14th − 16th centuries), however, differences appeared between China and the West in terms of social and intellectual developments. In China, it was the turn from the Ming Dynasty to the Qing Dynasty, a period with drastic social and political changes yet with few signs of relaxing intellectual control. In the West, intellectual concern together with social and economic developments, gradually turned into a disfavour and repudiation of medieval darkness, providing the necessary conditions for spiritual emancipation and scientific progress as shown in the Reformation. Obviously the intellectual gap between China and the West was enlarged at the end of the Middle Ages. Chinese emperors tried to hold their autocratic rule over both the ordinary people and intellectuals by enforcing a heavy taxation and building up large numbers of troops at an attempt to deprive the ordinary people, especially the intellectuals, of any right to speak or write about anything against or different from the imperial and Confucian authorities. Consequently, intellectual development was checked and rationalism could hardly be fostered as the necessary environment for the promotion of science and technology. This could explain why Chinese scientific and technological developments proceeded very slowly, making few substantial achievements for no scientist or technician wanted to waste his time or risk his life doing anything which did not hold any hope of success in such spiritual and social circumstances peculiar to the Chinese autocracy from the end of the Ming Dynasty to the Qing Dynasty though some intellectuals became aware of the significance of science and technology and started to deal with a number of individual projects and produced some results.

Comparatively, the West underwent a succession of new challenges and thorough-going and drastic changes and hence relaxed the monolithic frozen totalitarianism which had reigned for over a thousand years. Such events as seafaring adventures, colonization, the Renaissance and the Religious Reformation, industrialization, the Enlightenment and the Encyclopaedia Movement, etc., worked together to bring about a widespread and forceful spiritual emancipation which eventually helped alter the Western world and promote Western intellectual development. These events and developments provided direct motive forces and produced epoch-making effects on Western society where spiritual and intellectual emancipation led to a prosperous development of science and technology.

9.3.6 Practical effects and social status

The early form of modern Western civilization gradually came into shape as the bourgeoisie were getting things ready to take over political power approximately from the end of the Renaissance and foster science into a useful instrument for a better tomorrow. Science from then on was no longer tolerant of its humble status but granted a more glorious mission to search for more efficient and effective ways for human beings to solve problems in dealing with nature and acquiring various kinds of knowledge to build up a fortune unprecedented in human history.

1 Setting for the birth of science

In spite of some social and economic changes, no favourable factors and conditions arose for the prosperous development of a science that still had to tolerate an obscure, dependent and even declining position, contributing little if any to the social and economic developments of the country as a whole, in the long years after the end of China's feudal society. This was partly because of the social turmoil arising out of the civil wars, foreign invasions and natural disasters, and partly because of a retarded awareness of the powerful effect and advantage of science. Such a situation has been basically changed due to the implementation of the open policy and China has caught up at a surprisingly rapid pace in the last few decades since the end of the 1970s.

2 The status of science

An increasingly important status for science has been assumed and recognized universally by Western society. Therefore, a positive attitude and an advanced method different from the traditional one, has promoted scientific development to an unparallelled level in the modern age, as a result of scientific and technological contributions to social and economic developments. A new view of science merged into a new world outlook as part of intellectual changes adapted to the capitalist mode of production and social and economic developments, speeding up all the while in the last few centuries. To guarantee the irreplaceable role of science is more than just a lip service, but requires a consideration of how to provide motivation and specific measures to ensure the effects of science and technology as a practical project in relation to market economy. This is how Western science could gain a remarkable headway in the past two or three centuries since the dawn of the modern age. If China was behind in the previous two or three centuries the advancing steps of the world trend, she is now catching up for Chinese science has a glorious tradition and is ready to meet new challenges in science and technology. China has every reason to believe that, with the continuation of open policy and increasing benefit from scientific and technological developments, she would take great strides in the next few decades to bridge the gap with the West first and then will overtake the Western powers in both scientific and economic developments.

3 The status of science

Tottering in the shadow of Confucianism and feudalist autocracy, Chinese science could hardly find any opportunity to play a positive role or make any substantial contribution or commitment to society in a fairly long historical period before the middle of the 20th century. But occasionally a few scientists might have made some notable achievements, either in their personal research or in the introduction of Western science, as Xu Guangqi did in the Ming Dynasty[1]. Even so, such results were limited in their significance and influence and science was generally excluded from Chinese traditional culture.

Western science, ever since the establishment of its dominant role as *au fait*[2] a successor to classical rationalism, acquired a series of fruitful results after breaking down the barriers set by the Christian church and its Inquisition. Such achievements helped to expand and consolidate its status. Scientific influences

---

[1] Xu Guangqi (1562 – 1633), a scientist and politician during the Ming Dynasty, was famous for his research on agriculture and astronomy as well as his introduction of Western science, associated with Matteo Ricci in their translation into Chinese of Greek mathematician Euclid's *Elements* of plain geometry.

[2] *Au fait*, French word, means "having experience or knowledge of a thing".

grew continuously through the work of great scientists or thinkers such as Copernicus, Kepler, Galileo, Newton, Francis Bacon and Descartes, whose efforts and accomplishments led to the formation and continuation of a scientific and rational tradition as the core of Western intellectual development. The appearance of these distinguished figures of course should be ascribed partly to the change of social environment from autocracy and theology to a freedom to devote themselves to scientific research.

4 Scientific tradition and application

It takes time to build up a scientific tradition. Chinese and Western traditions in science take shape through long years of practical experience.

Chinese history of science was not short of examples of practical application of science and technology, as evident in numerous discoveries or inventions scattered across the centuries. For instance, the dragon-bone water lifter, the water-powered roller for grinding grain, the mechanical bow, the mechanical deep-poring technique, gunpowder, the moveable type for printing, paper-making and the magnetic compass. Each of these inventions was a marvellous accomplishment at the time and was a successful example of productive development. However, these practical results of science did not extend to a chain reaction that could continue automatically as a tradition or as a whole set of conditions or mode or soil for later development. The surface reason related apparently to social turmoil and political instability China suffered in her recent history. Nonetheless, the more substantial and deep-rooted causes might reside in an absolute and radical way of thinking which refused to accept the different points of view, especially the opponents' ideas concerning the attitude towards general values of happiness and fortune as well as the sense of science and economic development. This is perhaps an important reason why China's scientific development was frustrated several times after it moved into the modern period when the country suffered from long-term social turmoil and endless wars or conflicts. China's modern sense of scientific tradition was gradually shaped under the enduring influence of Western science and rationalism in the prolonged period after the last feudal dynasty was overthrown.

Western science and technology started to go through a rapid and vigorous development, stimulated by its spiritual emancipation derived first from the Renaissance and then from the Enlightenment. Though Western science did not seem to accomplish much in the long years before the Renaissance, yet the tradition of rationalism and a practical spirit prompted the pursuit of intellectual emancipation and led to the breakthrough first in ideological development initiated by the Religious Reformation and then in capitalist production. Perhaps it is the capitalist mode of production that provided the motivation and stimulation for continuous scientific development, which needed to proceed in close combination with practical application because of the nature of capitalist production. Examples could be found in the invention and popularization of the steam engine, which had been improved three times before Watt established his final version that greatly promoted the development of the textile industry and introduced it into other industrial departments, as the most important dynamic force.

5 Different focuses in scientific research

Though China and the West are different in their scientific traditions, they started to approach each other in the last two or three centuries. However, their focus in science is not exactly the same.

Generally, ancient Chinese science cared more for research into numerals than into visual form in terms of scientific concerns. This is why algebra received more attention and made more progress than geometry. In physics the Chinese seemed better at magnetism than at mechanics. With respect to research into magnetism, the Chinese invented the compass that helped seafaring over long journeys. Yet they had little research on mechanics which appeared capable of yielding a good view of the universe and nature. This could explain why Chinese philosophy lacked a natural or materialistic theory to deal with the world.

In contrast, the Westerners were probably more interested in mechanics which not only helped them to establish a more scientific and practical world view, but opened a new world based on scientific exploration, the Industrial Revolution and colonial expansion. The tradition was further fortified by Bacon's emphasis on the function of scientific experiments to produce practical results and confirm the truthfulness of these results, such as the invention and wide application of steam engine and other mechanical devices during the Industrial Revolution.

6 Different guiding principles and values

Different focuses of scientific development depend on different guiding principles and values. China's backwardness and poverty were gradually manifested in the last three or four centuries when its monarchs refused to adapt to social and intellectual changes of the world trend as were witnessed in the West. This was not exactly a fault committed by a single emperor or prime minister, but a consequence resulting of certain cultural tradition which could be traced to earlier sources, such as the closed-door tradition and the indifferent attitude towards or prejudice against science and technology, highlighted and hailed by the West.

In a sense, Chinese scientific inventions were largely ascribed to individual efforts, decided by no one or nothing but individual interest or need of certain external circumstances. Such values were limited by the then social conventions dominated by feudal autocracy and Confucianism, which emphasizes biased ideological value and imposed autocratic reign while ignoring the significance of practical experiences, like those of science and technology in promoting economic production. The lack of a strong desire for material accumulation or social progress, ill motivated scientific research in the long years of the ancient and middle periods of China. Hence it was slow, separate and of low-efficiency, stifled by the bureaucracy of feudalistic administration and sluggish social and intellectual developments. Overall, the closed-door policy, narrow-mindedness, lack of contact both domestically and externally, an insufficient theoretical framework and ignorance of material movements in nature were typical of old China.

Western science had also proceeded through a slow and inefficient stage and demonstrated an even slower and poorer performance than Chinese science. However, the Renaissance and the Enlightenment helped remove social and intellectual hindrances and supplied a sound environment in which intellectual and academic freedom was granted for the execution of scientific experiments and the announcement of factual results or theoretical explorations, regarded previously by Christianity as a possible infidelity. Close links between scientific research and economic development have been made on the basis of market demand. It is much easier and more effective to put into operation what is achieved in scientific research. It is the market mechanism that has given impetus to the rapid development of science and technology and pushed forward social and economic growth.

7 Critical spirit

Scientific achievement is always related to critical spirit. The sluggish advance of Chinese science in the later years of feudal society was attributed partly to the lack of critical spirit in handling traditional Chinese ideas of science and culture. Few of the Chinese scientists dared to say or do anything against orthodox thinking epitomized by Confucianism or other forms of autocratic ideology. For instance, none of the Chinese scholars attempted to break from the traditional astrology in their heavenly observations though they made quite a number of astronomical discoveries, including the identification of some stars and their positions as well as the lunar calendar. Consequently the Chinese sense of astronomy had perhaps never been much dissimilar to that of astrology till the introduction of astronomy by Western missionaries in the 16th century or so. This is also true of the development of other subjects of natural science, such as geography and physics.

In geography, the Chinese had made some contributions like the rectangular network mapping method①, the identification of direction by compass and of magnetic poles, etc. However, the Chinese map-makers had never been able to erect an astronomical coordinate system due to the influence of traditional culture, both Confucianism and Taoism, till the 16th century when the Western missionaries brought the new technique to China and helped to make a Western-typed modern map, as in the World Map by Matteo Ricci (利玛窦), an Italian missionary, through a plain projection method of drawing parallel meridians and curved parallels.

Comparatively, Chinese research on mechanics and dynamics was much ignored in the long process of history though Mo Zi had started his preliminary study long before his Western counterparts. Presumably, it was because of the disfavour of Mo Zi in later intellectual and ideological developments that the study of nature and science as a whole, mechanics and dynamics included, did not receive due attention. It really appears incomprehensible or even ridiculous that no Chinese scholars or only a few, challenged such a tendency and consequently that the whole field of mechanics and dynamics saw no substantial progress in the long process of history till the modern age. Such insufficiencies certainly checked the development of Chinese science and technology, especially the practical part which directly restrained economic growth.

The Westerners, in contrast, manifested a good sense of critical spirit. Many scholars dared to challenge the established views held by the authorities. This was particularly so after the Renaissance. One of the examples came from the arguments about the wave theory of light. The wave theory of light was first posed by T. Young (1773 — 1829) who tried to explain the nature of light and determined the wave length of light by interference techniques. The new theory, entirely different from the traditional particle theory by Newton, met with violent attack and sarcasm from other scholars. Young suffered so much from the opposition that he resigned and moved to other areas of investigation. It was not till thirteen years later that a French scholar A. J. Fresnel② proposed the same method and they worked together and firmly established the wave theory that was eventually united with particle theory in Einstein's quantum mechanics at the beginning of the 20th century.

8 National temper and scientific method

Methodology contributes decisively to scientific achievement, once guiding principles are determined in the objective and target of research. Apart from a

---

① The rectangular network mapping method refers to a special way of making maps in ancient time, which used rectangular network to produce the basic structure of the map before the final version of the map was eventually made.

② A. J. Fresnel (1788 — 1827), French engineer, inventor of methods of obtaining interference of light and explained both the apparently rectilinear propagation of light and the phenomenon of diffraction.

diversity in some guiding principles, a difference in methods could also explain the divergence between China and the West.

The Chinese people are well known for their hardworking and capable disposition in the sense of sharing a good living habit and keeping a good discipline. These good points helped unite the Chinese people as a nation and create a fairly large fortune in both material and spirit. Yet at the same time the inclination to be disciplined contributed to the fostering of conservatism and restraint upon courage and creativity when discipline was not balanced by democracy. Too much emphasis on discipline obviously would check one's initiative and talent in times when creative teamwork is demanded, for instance, in times of some important decisionmaking occasions. Such weakness was demonstrated in the long period of autocratic rule and in scientific research. For instance, excessive care for book knowledge and neglect of production and practice, as advocated by Confucianism and feudal monarchs, remained unchanged and unchallenged as a cultural tradition in the closed Chinese society. Also too much emphasis on loyalty and discipline or obedience would lead to the overlook of different opinions or democracy which is universally acknowledged as a basic necessity for scientific research in modern society, but unfortunately was ignored in the long-term tradition of Chinese social and intellectual developments. Obviously it hindered and retarded Chinese intellectual development and the promotion of science despite the emergence of many individual talents, some of whom broke the customary boundaries and restrictions and made large quantities of inventions and creations. In the final analysis, the less dynamic tendency and less practical or creative method were a result of long-term feudal autocratic rule, which focused on political dominance and refused to offer adequate individual freedom. The latter was exactly an absolute must for the training of the ability and the formation of method of scientific research.

Western science had also similar experiences in the early part of its development when it was faced up with spiritual pressure, political intervention and intellectual misguidance, imposed by the Church of Christianity and autocratic monarch. But things have been greatly improved since Francis Bacon deemed it necessary to manipulate nature and benefit from science by means of experiment. Bacon is consequently honoured as the father of experimental science, the modern empiricist methodology that has influenced tremendously later generations of scientists who would make new scientific contributions based on his ideas. Bacon's ideas and methods spread far and wide as a tremendous influence through the ideas and practice of a number of great scientists, which shaped, in the comparatively more tolerable intellectual climate after the Religious Reformation, into a new cultural and democratic tradition for scientific development while assailing old conservative forces impeding scientific advances. Followed by the discovery of the sun-centred universe, Galileo's location of the laws of motion, Newton's successful observation of light and finding of the law of gravity along with Einstein's theory of relativity, Western science relied mainly on practical experiments for a series of major achievements in rapid and efficient development. Such ideas and methods were derived from the ancient classical tradition as a continuation of rationalism, which has provided both fuel and fodder for more historical events leading to thorough-going social and political transformations as well as economic and cultural prosperity. We could say that Bacon's claim for experimental science helped to define a totally new direction in scientific development, as well as a new method of scientific research. In a way, the experimental trend in science marked the foundation for modern science and led to the increasingly different conditions of scientific development between China and the West.

The concept of experimental science found its way into China at the turn of the 20th century when some Chinese scholars returned home with the idea they had picked up from the West. Experimental science was established and further developed in a number of universities newly founded at that time and began to alter first intellectual and cultural circumstances and then impacted social and economic developments in China. From then on, China began to embark on a new route, at an attempt to embrace a new era of modernization with science as a conspicuous and unbreakable factor contributing more considerably in the process of modernization in spite of some twists and turns in terms of social and political transformation and influence.

Questions for comprehension and discussion

1. Tell the scientific achievements in China before the 20th century.
2. Give the major facts of the Western scientific development.
3. Try to provide some comparative comments on the Chinese and Western scientific achievements or developments by focusing on some specific areas.

List of proposed books for further reading

1. 段治文,2001,《中国现代科学文化的兴起》,上海:上海人民出版社。
2. 胡显章、曾国屏(主编),2002,《科学技术概论》,北京:高等教育出版社。

3. Needham, Joseph, *Science and Civilization in China*, Volume 6, Cambridge: Cambridge University Press, 2000.
4. McClellan, James E., Harold Don, *Science and Technology in World History*, The Johns Hopkins University Press, 1999.
5. Sivin, Nathan, *Science in Ancient China: Researches and Reflections*, Variorum, 1995.
6. Hutten, Ernest H., *The Origin of Science*, George Allen and Unwin Ltd, 1962.
7. Alioto, Anthony M., *A History of Western Science*, Prentice-Hall, Inc., 1993.

Epilogue

I had a sense of relief after devoting nearly five years, first to the teaching and then to the drafting of these chapters, which had been submitted to the publisher as an end of a period of hard work. However, I now doubt if I could, for the mission to deal with the issue of Western culture seems just opened to such a large audience. With a continuous introduction of Western science and culture, our country has been admitted into the ranks of rapidly developing countries modelled on the market economy in the past three decades. As part of cultural globalization, the process of acquiring and handling Western culture while maintaining Chinese national identity has received more and more attention from public and academic circles at once. In this sense, the comparison of cultures meets the need as well as the challenge of the current situation, as a project of both interest and significance.

A comparative study of cultures is an extensive area and could embrace many choices, depending on one's intention. For graduate studies in the humanities at large, particularly for those students whose major is concerned with Western language or culture, it seems to me that the choice apparently has to focus on some principal branches within a cultural tradition. Maybe that is why I choose philosophy, literature, art, language and science as the objects of study.

I would not be so stubborn as to insist that this should be the only choice, but it inclines me to say that this could be the necessary and also secure boundary and stance one could start from if one does not really want to trespass on culture. Therefore, ideological development, divided roughly into three stages, appears to be of tremendous significance as it is the source and basis of all human behaviours. Art and literature, as traditional areas of culture, are selected to be discussed under this title though only painting, fiction and poetry are specifically embraced. Another area, the significance of which is generally agreed on, is the great contribution to human intellectual development by language. The role of language can never be replaced by any other science as one of the earliest subjects of the humanities, which lays the foundation for a substantial study of different cultures since it concerns the possibilities of building up initial communication between them. The last section in my selection is science in general, since its appearance and application has changed our traditional styles of thinking and living in its increasingly expanding role to transform the world we are related to. All these choices are of course quite subjective. Time will tell whether they are adequately reasonable and whether they need to be modified in the future. Whether or not we have left out some more important unexplored areas I must leave to the judgment of the scholars and readers who are interested in this field.

One more thing I would like to mention is the principle I followed to consider the division of historical period and the accommodation of the events or figures to temporal arrangement. Generally speaking, chronological order is primarily set in parallel with historical period as adopted popularly in most of academic works. For instance, the terms like "ancient" and "modern", all came from such a routine though their implications might vary slightly between China and the West. An exception is perhaps the term "Middle Ages" or "medieval" which is generally replaced instead by "feudal period" in Chinese history, suggesting the similar period between the ancient and the modern though with some little difference between. For the sake of convenience, I occasionally choose the English term "Middle Ages" or "medieval" to address the similar span of Chinese history.

Also I took the freedom to seek the flexibility of choosing the specific examples or figures beyond the fixed boundary between the periods because my focus resides in ideological or cultural elucidation rather than in the strict agreement with historical divisions. Thus despite the fact that historically the division of the ancient and middle periods is marked by the use of iron instruments and serfs to replace that of bronze instruments and slaves occurring during the Warring States Period, I, for the sake of convenience, propose the Qin Dynasty as the beginning of the Chinese middle period, approximately a hundred years or two later than the division in some history books, and its decline on the 17th-19th centuries though its final fall did not occur till the end of the Qing Dynasty in the beginning of the 20th century. For the same reason, the beginning of the Western medieval period is roughly fixed at the end of the Western Roman Empire, and the end of the Renaissance basically agrees with the beginning of Chinese capitalist mode which budded from the end of the Ming Dynasty, indicating the foreboding of the modern age.

The same principle applies to the selection of samples, depending on whether the ideological tendency of the case in study suits the central concerns of the chapter rather than the strict agreement with fixed time. Hence, I chose to include Neo-Platonism and its founder Plotinus to represent the medieval ideology though his lifetime lay within the Roman period. This is because Neo-Platonist ideas worked more popularly in Byzantium where its influence extended far beyond the end of the Western Roman Empire, as representation of mysterious trend featuring principally medieval ideology instead of the ancient.

As well, I put Wang Fuzhi, Huang Zongxi and Gong Zizhen in the modern period as the pioneering figures for, in my mind, their ideas worked more appropriately in line with the budding phase of Chinese early democracy against autocracy as advocated by many scholars, than being located in the middle or feudal period, which focused on the promotion of Confucianism. For the similar reason, I believe Russian literature before the October Revolution of 1917 was part of the Western tradition because Russia was then ethnically and intellectually linked more closely to European history and culture, as what are represented in the works of Turgenev, Gogal and Tolstoy. Hopefully these ideas and modifications could attain the understanding and acceptance from the general reader as an attempt to probe the depth and width of the ideological and intellectual developments of both China and the West.

From the early days of lecturing to my graduate students in the course that provided the basis of the current book, I started to cherish a hope that it might be improved and adapted to the general needs of those who take an interest in both comparative cultures and the study of English. It is of course not just designed for English majors, many of whom doubtless wish to pick up more information in this area. It is also intended for non-English majors who might have built up an adequate reservoir of professional knowledge but hope to improve their English language competence through certain channels.

In many ways, the present book is a result of friendship and cooperation. I would like to extend my thanks first of all to my students who were actively involved in the class discussions of all the questions concerned with the major ideas and events of each chapter and their enthusiasm for an inquiry into the issues of cultural exchange and interactions between the two sides. Some of them have made actual contribution to the eventual fruit of this book, such as Lily and Zhang Guannan who drafted the *Chronological Table of Major Chinese and Western Cultural Events / Figures* as an appendix.

I am also grateful to my Australian friends, especially Professor Rod Home from Melbourne University and Professor Glen Phillips from Edith Cowan University. Both of them offered their precious time reading the manuscript carefully and critically, and provided constructive advice on both language and content, which helped much polish the book and could hopefully guarantee its quality. Rod focused on the four chapters of philosophy and science in addition to the introduction and epilogue while Glen focused on the other four chapters. Their kindness is acknowledged appreciatively with the permanent record of their contribution herein.

Last of all, I would like to express my debt of thanks to the Office of Graduate Studies of the Shanghai Municipal Government (上海市学位办) and the editors for their assistance to the writing and publication of this work.

Chronological Table of Major Chinese and Western Cultural Events / Figures

Time	Events / Figures in Western Culture	Events / Figures in Chinese Culture
About 1,000,000 – 500,000 years ago	The earliest race of man at sites near Vertesszolos in Hungary and at Isernia in Italy	Beijing man
About 500,000 – 50,000 years ago	The Neanderthals, the use of "Mousterian" stone technology	Mountain-top caveman
About 50,000 to 10,000 years ago	The Palaeolithic Age and The Mesolithic Age	The Palaeolithic Age and The Mesolithic Age
About 10,000 to 5,000 years ago	Neolithic Age	Neolithic Culture, Yangshao Culture, probably the origin of the legendary leader Huangdi, the earliest leader of the Chinese as a nation
About 2500 BC and earlier	Birth of Minoan Civilization and Culture	Longshan Culture
About 2000 BC and earlier	Birth of Mycenaean Civilization and Culture	Appearance of the private ownership
About 2000 – 1500 BC	Appearance of the Jews	Legends about the Chinese pioneering figures Huangdi, Yao, Shun and Yu; the Xia Dynasty, the first dynasty reigned by a family; the invention of Chinese characters by Cangjie
About 1500 – 1100 BC	The Trojan War	The Shang Dynasty; appearance of written characters on tortoise shells and animal bones
11th – 9th centuries BC	Homeric Age: appearance of *The Iliad* and *The Odyssey*	
800 – 700 BC	Early Rome coming into being	
722 BC	Israel fell to Assyria	Chinese history book *chun-qiu* (《春秋》, Spring and Autumn) began to record facts from this year and ended in 481 BC, as the earliest written annal in the world

Chronological Table of Major Chinese and Western Cultural Events / Figures

(续表)

Time	Events / Figures in Western Culture	Events / Figures in Chinese Culture
630 – 560 BC	Solon, Athenian statesman	
624 – 548 or 545 BC	Thales of Miletus, Greek philosopher and father of the Milesian School	
621 BC	Draco, maker of *The Laws of Athens*	
620 – 560 BC	Aesop, writer of *Aesop's Fables*	
About 604 – 531 BC		Lao Zi, Chinese philosopher and founder of Taoism
600 – 527 BC	Peisistratus, Athenian statesman	
586 BC	The Jewish southern kingdom, Judah, fell to Babylon	
570 – 507 BC	Cleisthenes, Greek statesman known as founder of Athenian democracy	
Middle of the 6th century BC	The rise of Greek drama	
551 – 479 BC		Confucius, Chinese philosopher, scholar and educator, founder of Confucianism, with his statements collected and edited by his followers into a book entitled *lun-yu* (《论语》, The Analects).
540 – 480 BC	Heracleitus, Greek philosopher	
538 BC	The fall of Babylon	
525 – 456 BC	Aeschylus, father of Greek tragedy	
520 – 423 BC	Cratinus, author of Greek comedies	
496 – 406 BC	Sophocles, Greek tragedy writer	
476 BC		The first Chinese collection of poems *shi-jing* (《诗经》, The Book of Songs) edited by Confucius
About 475 – 395 BC		Mo Zi, philosopher of the Spring-Autumn Period, the writer of *mo-zi* (《墨子》)
469 – 399 BC	Socrates, Greek philosopher	
459 – 404 BC	The Peloponnesian War	
480 – 406 BC	Euripides, Greek tragedy writer	
480 – 425 BC	Herodotus, Greek historian	
464 BC		*zuo-zhuan* (《左传》), one of the earliest books of Chinese history

(续表)

Time	Events / Figures in Western Culture	Events / Figures in Chinese Culture
460-395 BC	Thucydides, Greek historian and writer of *History of the Peloponnesian War*	
448-380 BC	Aristophanes, Greek writer of comedies	
446?-411? BC	Eupolis, Greek writer of comedies	
430-355 BC	Xenophon, Greek writer of *The Persian Expedition*	
427-347 BC	Plato, Greek philosopher and founder of Academy	
About the 4th century BC	The beginning of the Hellenistic Period	
About 400 BC	Diogenes, chief representative and founder of Cynicism	
384-322 BC	Aristotle, Greek philosopher and founder of Peripatetic School	
372-289 BC		Mencius, philosopher of Confucianism, writer of *meng-zi* (《孟子》, Mencius)
About 369-286 BC		Zhuang Zi, philosopher of Taoism
341-270 BC	Epicurus, Greek philosopher and founder of Epicureanism	
339-278 BC		Qu Yuan, poet and writer of *li-sao* (《离骚》, Worrying Experiences)
336-264 BC	Zeno, Greek philosopher and founder of Stoicism	
333 BC	Conquest of Jerusalem by Alexander the Great	
325-265 BC	Euclid, Greek mathematician and founder of geometry	
End of the 4th century BC	Birth of Skepticism	
310-230 BC	Aristarchus, Greek astronomer and mathematician	
298-238 BC		Xun Zi, Chinese philosopher, writer of *xun-zi* (《荀子》)
287-212 BC	Archimedes, Greek mathematician	
280-233 BC		Han Fei, Chinese philosopher

Chronological Table of Major Chinese and Western Cultural Events / Figures

(续表)

Time	Events / Figures in Western Culture	Events / Figures in Chinese Culture
About 276 – 195 BC	Eratosthene, Greek mathematician and astronomer, inventor of *The Sieve of Eratosthenes*	
254 – 184 BC	Plautus, Roman playwright	
239 BC		*lü-shi-chun-qiu* (《吕氏春秋》, Lü's Spring and Autumn), a historical book completed by the disciples of Lü Buwei, the prime minister of the Qin, a kingdom of the Warring States Period
221 BC		*huang-di-nei-jing* (《黄帝内经》, Huangdi's Internal Classics)
213 BC		Qin Shihuang, emperor of the Qin Dynasty, who ordered burning of books and burying of scholars alive
190 – 159 BC	Terence, Roman playwright	
160 – 125 BC	Hipparachus, Greek astronomer, geographer and mathematician	
145 – ? BC		Sima Qian, historian of the Han Dynasty, writer of *shi-ji* (《史记》, The Historical Annals)
138 BC		Zhang Qian dispatched as the first envoy to the western regions of China during the Han Dynasty
106 – 43 BC	Cicero, Roman politician and orator	
100 BC		*zhou-bi-suan-jing* (《周髀算经》, Zhou Bi Counting Classics)
99 – 55 BC	Lucretius, writer of *On the Nature of Things*	
70 – 19 BC	Virgil, Roman poet and author of *Aeneid*	
65 – 8 BC	Horace, Roman poet	
63 BC	Pompey took over the city of Jerusalem	
59 BC – 17 AD	Livy, Roman historian and author of *History of Rome*	
43 BC – 18 AD	Ovid, Roman poet and author of *Metamorphoses*	
4 BC – 65 AD	Seneca, Roman playwright	
23 or 24 – 79 AD	Pliny the Elder, writer of *Natural History*	

(续表)

Time	Events / Figures in Western Culture	Events / Figures in Chinese Culture
32 – 92 AD		Ban Gu, historian and writer of *han-shu* (《汉书》, The Annals of the Han Dynasty)
46 – 120 AD	Plutarch, Roman biographer and philosopher	
50 – 100 AD		*jiu-zhang-suan-shu* (《九章算术》, Nine-Chapter Arithmetic)
About 58 – 147 AD		Xu Shen, writer of *shuo-wen-jie-zi* (《说文解字》, Interpretation of Chinese Characters and Texts)
88 AD		Wang Chong finished *lun-heng* (《论衡》, On Balance)
8th century AD	Pepin, founder of the Carolingian Dynasty	
Late 1st century AD	Revelation of John	
105 AD		Cai Lun, inventor of paper-making technology
117 AD		Zhang Heng, inventor of *hun-tian-yi* (浑天仪, Heavenly-Observing Instrument)
121 – 180 AD	Marcus Aurelius Antoninus, military leader of the Roman Empire	
123 – 170 AD	Lucius Apuleius, author of *The Golden Ass*	
150 – 219 AD		Zhang Zhongjing, writer of *shang-han-za-bing-lun* (《伤寒杂病论》, Miscellaneous Disease Theory of the Typhoid Fever)
164 – 190 AD		Chinese invented china
205 – 270 AD	Plotinus, founder of Neoplatonism	
285 AD		Chen Shou completed *san-guo-zhi* (《三国志》, The Annals of The Three Kingdoms)
303 – 361 AD		Wang Xizhi, calligrapher of the Jin Dynasty
346 – 395 AD	Theodosius I, Roman emperor who made Christianity the state religion of the Roman Empire	
365 – 427 AD		Tao Yuanming, poet of the Jin Dynasty

Chronological Table of Major Chinese and Western Cultural Events / Figures

(续表)

Time	Events / Figures in Western Culture	Events / Figures in Chinese Culture
Around 409 AD		Death of Gu Kaizhi, painter of the Jin Dynasty
440 – 461 AD	Leo I, Italian Pope offering Elucidation of tenets of Christianity	
445 AD		Death of Fan Ye, writer of *hou-han-shu* (《后汉书》, The Annals of the Latter Han Dynasty)
450 – 400 AD	The Greek Enlightenment	
450 – 515 AD		Fan Zhen, writer of *shen-mie-lun* (《神灭论》, On the Destruction of Divinity)
About 466 – 527 AD		Li Daoyuan, writer of *shui-jing-zhu* (《水经注》, Annotations to Water Classics)
About 473 – 550 AD		Jia Sixie, writer of *qi-min-yao-shu* (《齐民要术》, Key Points in Farming)
476 – 493 AD	Italy under the rule of Odoacer	
483 – 565 AD	Justinian I, Byzantine emperor famous for commissioning the making of *The Code of Justinian* and rebuilding of Sophia Cathedral	
493 AD	Founding of Ostrogoth Kingdom	
494 AD		The start of Longmen Grottoes construction
495 AD		Shaolin Monastery was established
502 AD		Completion of *wen-xin-diao-long* (《文心雕龙》, A Book of Literary Criticism) by Liu Xie
540 AD	Ravenna turned to the capital of Italy under the Byzantine rule	
557 – 641 AD		Ouyang Xun, calligrapher of the Tang Dynasty
570 – 632 AD	Mohammed, founder of Islam	
581 – 682 AD		Sun Simiao, writer of *bei-ji-qian-jin-yao-fang* (《备急千金要方》, Essential Prescriptions Prepared for Urgent Cases)
4th – 6th centuries AD	Production of *Talmud*, a collection of Jewish documents	
590 – 604 AD	Gregory I, Pope famous for establishing Medieval Papacy	

Time	Events / Figures in Western Culture	Events / Figures in Chinese Culture
595 – 605 AD		Built by Li Chun of the Sui Dynasty, the Zhaozhou Bridge was the earliest mono-hole stone arch type
606 AD		Formulation of the Imperial Civil Service Examination System (科举制度)
629 AD		Xuan Zang's pilgrimage journey to India for Buddhist scriptures
634 AD		The Daming Palace built in the Tang Dynasty
638 AD		The Daqin Temple built in the Tang Dynasty
641 AD		Princess Wencheng of the Tang Dynasty was married off to Tibet, where the Potala Palace began to be built in Lhasa
671 AD		Yi Jing of the Tang Dynasty went on pilgrimage to India for Buddhist scriptures and returned to Luoyang in 695
672 AD		Death of Yan Liben, painter of the Tang Dyansty, who painted *gu-di-wang-tu* (《古帝王图》, The Pictures of the Ancient Emperors)
701 – 761 AD		Wang Wei, poet of the Tang Dynasty
701 – 762 AD		Li Bai, poet of the Tang Dynasty
709 – 785 AD		Yan Zhenqing, calligrapher of the Tang Dynasty
712 – 770 AD		Du Fu, poet of the Tang Dynasty
Before the 9th century AD	Baghdad Observatory came into being	
713 AD		The Leshan Statue of Buddha built in the Tang Dynasty
713 – 755 AD		The dancing troupe set up in the Tang Dynasty to offer music and dance performance
742 – 814 AD	Charlemagne, emperor of the Holy Roman Empire, who led a movement of learning and restoring classical art and culture	
754 AD		Monk Jian Zhen of the Tang Dynasty travelling across the sea to Japan

(续表)

Time	Events / Figures in Western Culture	Events / Figures in Chinese Culture
Around 760 AD		Death of Wu Daozi, painter of the Tang Dynasty
768－824 AD		Han Yu, writer of the Tang Dynasty
772－842 AD		Liu Yuxi, writer of the Tang Dynasty
772－846 AD		Bai Juyi, poet of the Tang Dynasty
773－819 AD		Liu Zongyuan, writer of the Tang Dynasty
778－865 AD		Liu Gongquan, calligrapher of the Tang Dynasty
About 813－858 AD		Li Shangyin, poet of the Tang Dynasty
843 AD	The Treaty of Verdun which divided Charlemagne's empire into three parts	
868 AD		Wang Jie, inscribing and printing *Vajiraccedika-sutra*, the earliest survived carved version of print in the world
892 AD		Dazu Caves for fresco, dug in the Tang Dynasty
983 AD		Appearance of *tai-ping-yu-lan* (《太平御览》, Eternal Peace Reader for the Emperor)
984 AD		The Guanyin Tower built in Ji County as the earliest wooden tower extant in China
10th century AD	Transference of Jews to Spain	
1007－1072 AD		Ouyang Xiu, writer of the Song Dynasty, who wrote *zui-weng-ting-ji* (《醉翁亭记》, An Account of the Pavilion by an Old Drunk)
1017－1073 AD		Zhou Dunyi, philosopher of the Song Dynasty
1019－1086 AD		Sima Guang, historian of the Song Dynasty, who wrote *zi-zhi-tong-jian* (《资治通鉴》, The History as a Mirror for Government), the first chronological history in China
1021－1086 AD		Wang Anshi, politician and writer of the Song Dynasty
1033－1097 AD		Shen Kuo, scientist of the Song Dynasty, writer of *meng-xi-bi-tan* (《梦溪笔谈》, Essays of Meng Xi)

(续表)

Time	Events / Figures in Western Culture	Events / Figures in Chinese Culture
1037 – 1101 AD		Su Shi, poet, essayist and calligrapher of the Song Dynasty
1041 – 1048 AD		Bi Sheng of the Song Dynasty, inventor of type printing
1045 AD		Canglang Pavilion built in Suzhou
1045 – 1105 AD		Huang Tingjian, poet and calligrapher of the Song Dynasty
1049 AD		Youguo Tower built in Kaifeng
1054 AD	The split of Christianity into the Roman Catholic Church and the Orthodox Eastern Church	
Mid-11th century AD	Foundation of Dukedom of Moscow	
1056 AD		Shijia Tower in Fogong Temple built as the tallest wooden building extant in the world
1059 AD		Luoyang Bridge, China's first harbour stone bridge, built in Quanzhou
1060 AD		Yuquan Iron Tower built in Danyang, the tallest of the kind in China
1084 – 1155 AD		Li Qingzhao, poetess of the Song Dynasty
1096 AD		Lama Tower built in Miaoying Temple, Tibet
1100 AD		Li Jie of the Song Dynasty, writer of *ying-zao-fa-shi* (《营造法式》, Methods of Architecture) as the earliest book of the kind in the world
1125 – 1210 AD		Lu You, poet of the Song Dynasty
1130 – 1200 AD		Zhu Xi, philosopher and educator of the Song Dynasty
1136 AD		Liu Yu's engraved stones *hua-yi-tu* (《华夷图》, Picture of Chinese and Foreign Visitors) and *yu-ji-tu* (《禹迹图》, Picture of Yu's Traces) were the oldest map printing plates in the world
1140 – 1207 AD		Xin Qiji, poet of the Song Dynasty
1152 AD		Anping Bridge built in Quanzhou, the longest stone bridge extant in China

(续表)

Time	Events / Figures in Western Culture	Events / Figures in Chinese Culture
1169 AD		Guangji Bridge built in present Chaoan, Guangdong.
1190 – 1257 AD		Yuan Haowen, writer and historian of the Jin Dynasty
1192 AD		Lugou Bridge built as the earliest arch stone bridge in China
Early 12th century AD		Zhang Zeduan's long roll of drawing *qing-ming-shang-he-tu* (《清明上河图》, The Panorama of Upriver Scene during the Qing Ming Festival)
1214 – 1294 AD	Roger Bacon, English philosopher and scientist	
1225 – 1274 AD	Thomas Aquinas, representative of Scholasticism and the Italian theologist	
1265 – 1321 AD	Alighieri Dante, Italian poet and politician, writer of *The Divine Comedy*	
1267 – 1337 AD	The start and early development of the Renaissance in Florence, Italy	
1286 AD		Publication of *nong-sang-ji-yao* (《农桑辑要》, Key Records of Crops and Mulberry)
About 1296 – 1370 AD		Shi Naian of the Ming Dynasty, writer of *shui-hu* (《水浒》, The Water Margin)
About 1330 – 1400 AD		Luo Guanzhong, writer of *san-guo-yan-yi* (《三国演义》, The Historical Romances of the Three Kingdoms)
1304 – 1374 AD	Francesco Petrarch, Italian poet, famous for inventing the form of sonnets	
1313 AD		Official recovery of the Imperial Civil Service Examination System
1313 – 1375 AD	Giovanni Boccaccio, Italian writer of *Decameron*	
1331 AD		Completion of *jing-shi-da-dian* (《经世大典》, Permanent Anthology)
1340 – 1400 AD	Geoffrey Chaucer, English poet, writer of *The Canterbury Tales*	
1345 AD		Completion of *liao-shi* (《辽史》, History of the Liao Kingdom), *jin-shi* (《金史》, History of the Jin Kingdom) and *song-shi* (《宋史》, History of the Song Dynasty)

(续表)

Time	Events / Figures in Western Culture	Events / Figures in Chinese Culture
1350s – 14th century AD		Opera writers of the Yuan Dynasty: Guan Hanqing and *dou-e-yuan* (《窦娥冤》, Dou E's Wrongs), Bai Pu and *han-gong-qiu* (《汉宫秋》, Chinese Palace Autumn), Ma Zhiyuan, Wang Shifu and *xi-xiang-ji* (《西厢记》, Romance of Western Chamber)
1370 AD		Appearance of the eight-legged essay at the Imperial Civil Service Examination
1370 AD		Song Lian of the Ming Dynasty, successor to the writing of *yuan-shi* (《元史》, History of the Yuan Dynasty)
1371 AD		Building of the Jiayu Fortress at the western end of the Great Wall
1376 – 1382 AD		Beamless Palace of the Linggu Temple built in Nanjing
1377 AD		Yansheng Mansion built as the largest group building extant in Beijing
1377 – 1446 AD	Filipp Brunelleschi, sculptor and architect from Florence, Italy	
1381 AD		Building of Shanhai Fortress in the Ming Dynasty
1386 – 1466 AD	Donatello, sculptor of Renaissance from Florence	
1401 – 1428 AD	Masaccio, Italian painter, Florentine School	
1405 – 1433 AD		Zheng He of the Ming Dynasty and his fleet sailing seven times overseas, pioneering foreign trade and voyage in China
1407 AD		Completion of *yong-le-da-dian* (《永乐大典》, Yongle Encyclopedia of the Ming Dynasty)
1411 AD		The Ming Tombs were built
1414 AD		The revision of *si-shu* (《四书》, The Four Books) and *wu-jing* (《五经》, The Five Classics)
1417 AD		Cheng-tian-men built in Beijing in the Ming Dynasty, later renamed as Tian-an-men

Chronological Table of Major Chinese and Western Cultural Events / Figures

(续表)

Time	Events / Figures in Western Culture	Events / Figures in Chinese Culture
1420 AD		The largest palace building groups built in Beijing in the Ming Dynasty; Taimiao Temple built in Beijing; The Sky Temples built, among which the Qinian Palace Hall was the largest temple extant in China
1421 AD		Sheji Temple built in Beijing
1429 – 1516 AD	Giovanni Bellini, founder of the Venetian painting school	
1446 – 1506 AD	Christopher Columbus, Italian navigator in Spanish service and the first European to discover American continent	
1452 – 1519 AD	Leonardo da Vinci, Italian scientist and artist during the Renaissance	
1450 – 1500 AD	Bartoleme Dias, Portuguese navigator and the first European who discovered Cape of Good Hope	
1469 – 1527 AD	Niccolo Machiavelli, political writer of Florence during the Renaissance, writer of *Prince and Discourse*	
1471 – 1528 AD	Albrecht Durer, German artist of the Renaissance	
1472 – 1529 AD		Wang Shouren, official and philosopher of the Ming Dynasty
1473 – 1543 AD	Nicolaus Copernicus, Polish astronomer famous for declaring the earth moving around the sun	
1475 – 1564 AD	Michelangelo Buonarroti, Italian painter, sculptor, architect and poet	
1477 – 1535 AD	Thomas More, English writer of *Utopian*	
1483 – 1520 AD	Raphael Sanzio, Italian painter	
1483 – 1546 AD	Martin Luther, leader of the Religious Reformation	
1490 – 1576 AD	Titian, painter of Venice during the Renaissance	
1490 – 1553 AD	Francois Rabelais, French novelist, writer of *Gargantua and Pantagruel*	

（续表）

Time	Events / Figures in Western Culture	Events / Figures in Chinese Culture
1497－1543 AD	Hans Holbein, German artist of the Northern Renaissance	
1509－1564 AD	John Calvin, French theologian and head of Calvinism	
1510?－1582? AD		Wu Chengen, writer of *xi-you-ji*,(《西游记》, The Western Pilgrimage)
Around 1513 AD		Zhuozheng Garden built in Suzhou
1518－1593 AD		Li Shizhen of the Ming Dynasty, writer of *ben-cao-gang-mu* (《本草纲目》, An Outline Survey of Chinese Herbs)
1522 AD		Publication of Luo Guanzhong's *san-guo-yan-yi* (《三国演义》, The Historical Romances of the Three Kingdoms)
1525?－1569 AD	Pieter Bruegel and his sons, the famous Netherlandish artists	
1532 AD		Tianyi Garret built in Ningbo, Zhejiang, which was the oldest library extant today
1533－1592 AD	Michel Montaigne, French essayist	
1534－1536 AD		The Imperial Archives built in Beijing
1547－1616 AD	Miguel de Cervantes, Spanish novelist famous for his *Don Quixote*	
1550－1616 AD		Tang Xianzu, playwright of the Ming Dynasty, writer of *mu-dan-ting* (《牡丹亭》, The Peony Pavilion)
1561－1626 AD	Francis Bacon, English politician, scientist and essayist	
1562－1633 AD		Xu Guangqi, scientist of the Ming Dynasty, writer of *nong-zheng-quan-shu* (《农政全书》, A Complete Book of Agricultural Affairs)
1564－1616 AD	William Shakespeare, English dramatist and poet	
1564－1642 AD	Galileo, Italian scientist after the Renaissance	
1569－1632 AD	Alexandre Hardy, French dramatist	

Chronological Table of Major Chinese and Western Cultural Events / Figures

(续表)

Time	Events / Figures in Western Culture	Events / Figures in Chinese Culture
1571 – 1630 AD	Johannes Kepler, German astronomer and mathematician	
1573 – 1610 AD	Michelangelo Caravaggio, representative of Baroque Art	
1574 – 1646 AD		Feng Menglong, writer of the Qing Dynasty, whose works include *yu-shi-ming-yan* (《喻世明言》, Enlightening Remarks about the World), *jing-shi-tong-yan* (《警世通言》, Warning Remarks about the World), *xing-shi-heng-yan* (《醒世恒言》, Awakening Remarks about the World)
1577 – 1640 AD	Peter Rubens, representative of Baroque Art	
1586 – 1641 AD		Xu Xiake, geographer and traveller of the Ming Dynasty, writer of *xu-xia-ke-you-ji* (《徐霞客游记》, Xu Xiake's Travels)
1587 – 1661 AD		Song Yingxing, scientist of the Ming Dynasty, writer of *tian-gong-kai-wu* (《天工开物》, The Application of Natural Objects)
1588 – 1679 AD	Thomas Hobbes, English philosopher reputed for his *Leviathan*	
1596 – 1650 AD	Rene Descartes, French philosopher	
1598 – 1680 AD	Gionanni Lorenzo Bernini, Italian painter, representative of Baroque Art	
1599 – 1660 AD	Diego Velazquez, Spanish painter, representative of Baroque Art	
17th century AD	Mentalism represented by Rene Descartes, etc.	
17th century AD	Dutch School of Painting	
Late 16th – 17th centuries AD	Baroque Period in architecture, painting, sculpture, music and literature	
1606 – 1669 AD	Rembrandt van Rijn, Dutch painter	
1606 – 1684 AD	Pierre Corneille, French dramatist	
1608 – 1674 AD	John Milton, English poet and political writer	
1610 – 1695 AD		Huang Zongxi, thinker and historian of the Qing Dynasty

(续表)

Time	Events / Figures in Western Culture	Events / Figures in Chinese Culture
1613 – 1682 AD		Gu Yanwu, thinker and scholar of the Qing Dynasty
1619 – 1692 AD		Wang Fuzhi, thinker and writer of the Qing Dynasty
1622 – 1673 AD	Jean-Baptiste P. Moliere, French dramatist	
1628 AD	Appearance of salon culture in France	
1628 – 1688 AD	John Bunyan, English writer, famous for his novel *Pilgrims' Progress*	
1632 – 1677 AD	Baruch Spinoza, Dutch philosopher, well known for religious rationalism	
1632 – 1704 AD	John Locke, English philosopher, famous for his empiricism	
1633 – 1721 AD		Mei Wending, scientist of the Qing Dynasty
1634 – 1635 AD	French Academy, established by Cardinal de Richelieu	
1639 – 1699 AD	Jean Racine, French dramatist	
1640 – 1715 AD		Pu Songling, story writer of the Qing Dynasty, writer of *liao-zhai-zhi-yi* (《聊斋志异》, The Odd Stories of Liao Zhai)
1642 – 1727 AD	Isaac Newton, English mathematician and physicist	
1645 – 1704 AD		Hong Sheng, playwright of the Qing Dynasty, writer of *chang-sheng-dian* (《长生殿》, Long-Life Palace)
1648 – 1718 AD		Kong Shangren, playwright of the Qing Dynasty, writer of *tao-hua-shan* (《桃花扇》, The Peach Flower Fan)
1660 – 1731 AD	Daniel Defoe, English novelist, writer of *Robinson Crusoe*	
1667 – 1745 AD	Jonathan Swift, English novelist, famous for his *Gulliver's Travels*	
1672 AD		Rong Baozhai Publishing House, established in Beijing
1684 – 1721 AD	Antoine Watteau, French painter, famous for Rococo style	

(续表)

Time	Events / Figures in Western Culture	Events / Figures in Chinese Culture
1685－1750 AD	Johann Sebastian Bach, German musician	
1685－1753 AD	George Berkeley, English philosopher and theologist	
1685－1759 AD	George Frideric Handel, German-born English composer	
1688 AD	The Glorious Revolution, England	
1688－1744 AD	Alexander Pope, English poet	
1689－1755 AD	Charles L. Montesquieu, French thinker of the Enlightenment	
1689－1761 AD	Samuel Richardson, English novelist	
1693－1765 AD		Zheng Banqiao, painter of the Qing Dynasty
1694 AD		Yonghe Palace began to be built in Beijing
1694－1778 AD	Francois-Marie A. Voltaire, French thinker of the Enlightenment	
18th century AD	English School of Painting	
18th century AD	Rococo Art, France	
18th century AD	The Movement of Enlightenment in Europe	
1701－1754 AD		Wu Jingzi, novelist of the Qing Dynasty, writer of *ru-lin-wai-shi* (《儒林外史》, The Scholars)
1703 AD		Rehe Abode began to be built in Chengde
1703－1770 AD	Francois Boucher, French painter of Rococo style	
1707 AD		Peng Dingqiu, compiler of *quan-tang-shi* (《全唐诗》, The Complete Poetry of the Tang Dynasty)
1707－1754 AD	Henry Fielding, English novelist	
1709－1784 AD	Samuel Johnson, English scholar and editor of *The Dictionary of the English Language*	

(续表)

Time	Events / Figures in Western Culture	Events / Figures in Chinese Culture
1711 – 1776 AD	David Hume, Scottish philosopher and historian	
1712 – 1778 AD	Jean Rousseau, French thinker	
1713 – 1784 AD	D. Diderot, French thinker and editor of *The Encyclopaedia*	
1715 – 1763 AD		Cao Xueqin, novelist of the Qing Dynasty, writer of *hong-lou-meng* (《红楼梦》, The Dream of Red Mansions)
1716 AD		Completion of *kang-xi-zi-dian* (《康熙字典》, The Kangxi Dictionary)
1723 – 1790 AD	Adam Smith, English scholar of economics and cofounder of political economics	
1724 – 1804 AD	Immanuel Kant, German philosopher	
1724 – 1805 AD		Ji Yun, official and scholar of the Qing Dynasty
1726 AD		*gu-jin-tu-shu-ji-cheng* (《古今图书集成》, A Collection of the Ancient and Contemporary Books), the first book printed by movable copper type
1729 – 1781 AD	Gotthold Ephraim Lessing, German dramatist	
1732 – 1809 AD	Franz Joseph Haydn, Austrian composer	
1737 – 1809 AD	Thomas Paine, British political writer and radical propagandist	
1738 – 1801 AD		Zhang Xuecheng, historian of the Qing Dynasty
1739 AD		Completion of *ming-shi* (《明史》, History of the Ming Dynasty)
1743 – 1826 AD	Thomas Jefferson, US former President, famous for drafting *The Declaration of Independence*	
1744 – 1832 AD		Wang Niansun, scholar of the Qing Dynasty
1746 – 1828 AD	Goya y Lucientes, Spanish painter	
1748 – 1832 AD	Jeremy Bentham, English philosopher and founder of utilitarianism	

(续表)

Time	Events / Figures in Western Culture	Events / Figures in Chinese Culture
1749 – 1832 AD	Johann Wolfgang von Geothe, German poet and dramatist	
1750 AD		Qingyi Palace began to be built in Beijing, later called the Summer Palace
1756 – 1791 AD	Wolfgang Amadeus Mozart, Austrian composer	
1759 – 1805 AD	Johamm Christoph Friedrich von Schiller, German dramatist and poet	
1760 – 1825 AD	Saint Simons, French utopian socialist	
1762 – 1814 AD	Johannn G. Fichte, German philosopher	
1760s – 1830s AD	The Industrial Revolution in England	
1763 – 1830 AD		Li Ruzhen, novelist of the Qing Dynasty, writer of *jing-hua-yuan* (《镜花缘》, The Tales of Visionary Land)
1766 – 1834 AD	Thomas Malthus, British economist	
1768 – 1797 AD		Wang Zhenyi, scientist of the Qing Dynasty
1770 AD	The Movement of Stress and Storm in Germany	
1770 – 1827 AD	Ludwig van Beethoven, German composer	
1770 – 1831 AD	George W. F. Hegel, German philosopher	
1770 – 1850 AD	William Wordsworth, English romantic poet	
1771 – 1858 AD	Robert Owen, English utopian socialist	
1772 – 1823 AD	David Ricardo, British economist	
1772 – 1829 AD	Friedriech von Schlegel, German poet and one of the founders of German romanticism	
1772 – 1837 AD	Charles Fourier, French utopian socialist	
1773 AD		The start of *si-ku-quan-shu* (《四库全书》, The Four Completely Stored Collections of Books)

(续表)

Time	Events / Figures in Western Culture	Events / Figures in Chinese Culture
1783 – 1842 AD	Marie Henri Beyle Stendhal, French novelist and writer of Red and Black	
1784 – 1855 AD	Francois Rude, French sculptor	
1785 – 1850 AD		Lin Zexu, politician and poet of the Qing Dynasty
1788 – 1824 AD	George Byron, English romantic poet	
1788 – 1860 AD	Arthur Schopenhauer, German philosopher	
1792 – 1822 AD	Percy Bysshe Shelley, English romantic poet	
1792 – 1841 AD		Gong Zizhen, poet and thinker of the Qing Dynasty
1794 – 1859 AD		Wei Yuan, thinker of the Qing Dynasty and writer of *hai-guo-tu-zhi* (《海国图志》, Illustrated Tales of Foreign Countries)
1795 – 1821 AD	John Keats, English romantic poet	
1797 – 1856 AD	Heinrich Hein, German romantic poet	
1798 – 1824 AD	Theodore Gericault, French romantic painter	
1798 – 1857 AD	Auguste Comte, French philosopher and founder of positivism	
1799 – 1850 AD	Honore de Balzac, French novelist	
1799 – 1873 AD		He Shaoji, calligrapher of the Qing Dynasty
Late 18th century – early 19th century AD	The Movement of Romanticism in Europe	
Early 19th century AD	Further development of utopian socialism	
19th century AD	Social realism in literature	
19th century AD	Spanish Revolution against feudalism	
1802 – 1885 AD	Victor Hugo, French poet and novelist, writer of *Notre Dame de Paris* and *Les Misérables*	
1803 – 1883 AD	R. W. Emerson, American philosopher and poet	

Chronological Table of Major Chinese and Western Cultural Events / Figures

(续表)

Time	Events / Figures in Western Culture	Events / Figures in Chinese Culture
1804 – 1872 AD	Ludwig Feuerbach, German philosopher	
1806 – 1873 AD	John Mill, English philosopher and economist	
1809 – 1852 AD	Nicolai V. Gogol, Russian novelist, writer of *Dead Souls*	
1809 – 1882 AD	Charles Robert Darwin, English biologist and founder of Darwinism	
1810 – 1856 AD	Robert Alexander Schumann, German composer	
1811 – 1863 AD	William Thackery, English novelist, author of *Vanity Fair*	
1811 – 1882 AD		Li Shanlan, mathematician of the Qing Dynasty
1812 – 1870 AD	Charles Dickens, English novelist, author of *Bleak House*	
1813 – 1855 AD	Seren A. Kierkegaard, Danish philosopher and founder of existentialism	
1813 – 1883 AD	Richard Wagner, German playwright	
1814 – 1841 AD	Mikhail Y. Lermontov, Russian poet and novelist	
1814 – 1875 AD	Jean-Francois Millet, French painter	
1814 – 1896 AD	Jules Simon, French philosopher	
1816 – 1855 AD	Charlot Bronte, English novelist and author of *Jane Eyre*	
1818 – 1883 AD	Karl Marx, German thinker and founder of Marxism	
1819 – 1877 AD	Gustave Courbet, French painter	
1819 – 1880 AD	George Eliot, English novelist and author of *Middlemarch*	
1820 – 1895 AD	Friedrich Engels, Marxist thinker and cofounder of Marxism	
1821 – 1867 AD	Charles Baudelaire, French pioneering poet of symbolism and writer of *les Fleurs du Mal*	
1821 – 1880 AD	Gustave Flaubert, French novelist and author of *Madam Bovary*	

(续表)

Time	Events / Figures in Western Culture	Events / Figures in Chinese Culture
1821 – 1881 AD	Fyodor Mikhaylovich Dostoyevsky, Russian novelist, author of *Crime and Punishment*	
1828 – 1910 AD	Leo Tolstoy, Russian novelist, author of *Anna Karenina* and *War and Peace*	
1832 – 1883 AD	Edouard Manet, French impressionist painter	
1833 – 1902 AD		Hua Hengfang, mathematician of the Qing Dynasty
1833 – 1911 AD	Wilhelm Dilthey, German philosopher	
1835 – 1902 AD		Wu Dacheng, scholar of the Qing Dynasty
1835 – 1910 AD	Mark Twain, American novelist and author of *The Adventures of Huckleberry Finn*	
1837 – 1909 AD		Zhang Zhidong, politician and educator of the Qing Dynasty
1839 – 1906 AD	Paul Cezanne, French impressionist painter	
1839 – 1914 AD	Charles Peirce, American pragmatist philosopher	
1840 – 1928 AD	Thomas Hardy, English novelist and poet, author of *Tess of the d'Urbervilles*	
1841 – 1904 AD	Antonin Dvorak, Czech composer	
1842 – 1910 AD	William James, American philosopher and psychologist	
1844 – 1900 AD	Friedrich Nietzsche, German philosopher, famous for the theory of will of power	
1848 AD	Publication of *The Communist Manifesto*	
1848 – 1903 AD	Paul Gauguin, French impressionist painter	
1848 – 1905 AD		Huang Zunxian, diplomat and poet of the Qing Dynasty
1848 – 1908 AD		Sun Yirang, scholar of the Qing Dynasty
1850 – 1893 AD	Guy de Maupassant, French writer	
1852 – 1924 AD		Lin Shu, translator of the Qing Dynasty

(续表)

Time	Events / Figures in Western Culture	Events / Figures in Chinese Culture
1853 – 1890 AD	Vincent van Gogh, Dutch post-impressionist painter	
1853 – 1926 AD		Zhang Jian, industrialist of the Qing Dynasty
1856 – 1939 AD	Sigmund Freud, Austrian psychologist and founder of psychoanalysis theory	
1857 – 1909 AD		Liu E, novelist of the Qing Dynasty, writer of *lao-can-you-ji* (《老残游记》, The Tale of Lao Can's Travels)
1857 – 1913 AD	Ferdinand de Saussure, Swiss linguist and founder of structuralism	
1858 – 1927 AD		Kang Youwei, politician, scholar and poet of the Qing Dynasty
1859 – 1891 AD	Georges Seurat, French impressionist painter	
1859 – 1938 AD	Edmund Husserl, German philosopher and founder of phenomenology	
1859 – 1941 AD	Henri Bergson, French philosopher and founder of intuitionism	
1859 – 1952 AD	John Dewey, American philosopher	
1860 AD	Convening of the world congress of the Jewish people	
1861 – 1919 AD		Zhan Tianyou, designer of Jing-Zhang Railway, the first Chinese-built railway
1862 AD		Tongwen Institute, established in Beijing to train translators
1862 – 1910 AD	O'Henry, American short story writer	
1862 – 1918 AD	Claude Achille Debussy, French composer	
1863 – 1935 AD	Paul Signac, neo-impressionist painter	
1863 – 1957 AD		Qi Baishi, Chinese painter
1865 – 1898 AD		Tan Sitong, scholar and thinker of the Qing Dynasty, one of the participants of the Wuxu Reform

Time	Events / Figures in Western Culture	Events / Figures in Chinese Culture
1866 – 1910 AD		Wu Jianren, writer of *er-shi-nian-mu-du-zhi-guai-xian-zhuang* (《二十年目睹之怪现状》, Twenty Years' Witness of Strange Phenomena)
1867 – 1906 AD		Li Boyuan, novelist of the Qing Dynasty, writer of *guan-chang-xian-xing-ji* (《官场现形记》, The Tale of Exposing the Official World)
1867 – 1936 AD		Zhang Binglin, writer of the Qing Dynasty
1869 – 1954 AD	Henri Matisse, French painter and founder of fauvism	
1871 – 1922 AD	Marcel Proust, French novelist and author of *A la recherché du temps perdu*	
1871 – 1935 AD		Zeng Pu, novelist and writer of *nie-hai-hua* (《孽海花》, Flowers of the Adverse Sea)
1872 – 1970 AD	Bertrand Russell, English philosopher	
1873 – 1958 AD	G. E. Moore, English philosopher	
1875 – 1905 AD		Chen Tianhua, writer of the Qing Dynasty
1875 – 1961 AD	Carl Gustav Jung, Swiss philosopher and psychologist	
1876 – 1944 AD	Filippo Tommaso Marinetti, Italian poet and founder of futurism	
1876 – 1916 AD	Jack London, American novelist	
1878 – 1907 AD		Qiu Jin, poetess and woman revolutionary
1878 – 1927 AD	Isadora Duncan, American dancer	
1878 – 1935 AD	Kazimir Malevich, Russian painter and founder of supremacist school of abstract painting	
1881 – 1936 AD		Lu Xun (Zhou Shuren), Chinese story writer and critic
1881 – 1973 AD	Pablo Picasso, Spanish-born French painter and founder of cubism	
1882 – 1941 AD	Virginia Woolf, English novelist and critic	
1882 – 1941 AD	James Joyce, Irish novelist and author of *Ulysses* and *Finnegans Wake*	

(续表)

Time	Events / Figures in Western Culture	Events / Figures in Chinese Culture
1883 – 1969 AD	Karl Jaspers, French philosopher	
1884 – 1918 AD		Su Manshu, writer of the Qing Dynasty
1885 – 1971 AD	Georg Lukacs, Hungary Marxist literary critic	
1887 – 1958 AD		Liu Yazi, Chinese poet
1888 – 1965 AD	T. S. Eliot, poet and critic, author of *The Waste Land* and *Four Quartets*	
1889 – 1976 AD	Martin Heidegger, German philosopher	
1890 AD		Zhao Yuanren, Chinese linguist
1891 – 1962 AD		Hu Shi, Chinese poet and scholar
1892 – 1978 AD		Guo Moruo, Chinese poet, historian and politician
1894 AD	Film first released by Thomas Edison, an American inventor	
1894 – 1961 AD		Mei Lanfang, Chinese actor of Beijing opera
1895 – 1975 AD		Zhou Xinfang, Chinese actor of Beijing opera
1895 – 1953 AD		Xu Beihong, Chinese painter
1896 – 1981 AD		Mao Dun (Shen Yanbing), Chinese novelist and critic
1897 AD	The beginning of Zionism as a political movement	The commercial press was established
1897 – 1962 AD	William Faulkner, American novelist and author of *The Sound and the Fury*, *As I Lay Dying* and *Absalom, Absalom*	
1898 AD		Publication of the Chinese version of *Zoological Evidences as to Man's Place in Nature* translated by Yan Fu
1898 – 1979 AD	Herbert Marcuse, German philosopher of Frankfurt School	
1899 AD		Discovery of the hiding-place for Chinese classics at Dunhuang Caves
1899 – 1966 AD		Lao She (Shu Qingchun), Chinese novelist and playwright, famous for *luo-tuo-xiang-zi* (《骆驼祥子》, The Rickshaw Rider) and *cha-guan* (《茶馆》, Tea House)

(续表)

Time	Events / Figures in Western Culture	Events / Figures in Chinese Culture
1899 – 1983 AD		Zhang Daqian, Chinese painter
End of the 19th century AD	Birth of naturalism	
1900 – 2002 AD	Hans-Georg Gadamer, German philosopher and leading figure of hermeneutics in the 20th century	
1900 – 1999 AD	Nathalie Sarraute, French novelist, famous for new fiction	Bing Xin (Xie Wanying), Chinese woman writer of children literature
1901 AD	John Steinbeck, American writer who won the Nobel Prize for *The Grapes of Wrath*	
1904 AD	Birth of Salvador Dali, Spanish painter and sculptor	Publication of *tie-yun-cang-gui* (《铁云藏龟》, Turtles Hidden from Iron Cloud), the first monograph on Chinese characters on turtle and animal bones by Liu E
1904 – 1987 AD		Ding Ling, Chinese woman novelist and writer of *tai-yang-zhao-zai-sang-gan-he-shang* (《太阳照在桑干河上》, The Sun Shining on the Sanggan River)
1904 AD		The Qing court abolished the Imperial Civil Service Examination System
1904 – 2005 AD		Ba Jin (Li Yaotang), Chinese novelist and short story writer
1905 – 1980 AD	Jean-Paul Sartre, French philosopher and writer	
1905 – 1980 AD	Mikhail A. Sholokhov, the Soviet writer, Nobel Prize winner for his *Quiet Flows the Don*	
1905 – 1984 AD	The first cinema of the world, established in Paris	
1906 – 1970 AD		Zhao Shuli, Chinese short story writer
1906 – 1985 AD		Zhang Tianyi, Chinese writer
1906 – 1991 AD	Samuel Beckett, Irish writer, awarded with the 1969 Nobel Prize and leading figure of the theatre of the absurd	
1906 – 1989 AD	Herbert von Karajan, Austrian conductor	

(续表)

Time	Events / Figures in Western Culture	Events / Figures in Chinese Culture
1908 – 1989 AD	Claude Levi-Strauss, French anthropologist and structural theorist	
1911 – 1993 AD	William Golding, English writer of *The Lord of Flies* and Nobel Prize winner in 1980	
1910 – 1998 AD		Qian Zhongshu, Chinese scholar and novelist
1911 – 2009 AD		Ji Xianlin, Chinese scholar
1912 – 1990 AD	Patrick White, Australian novelist and winner of the 1973 Nobel Prize for literature	
1913 – 1960 AD	Albert Camus, French existentialist writer of *The Stranger* and *Plague*, Nobel Prize winner in 1957	
1913 – 2006 AD	Claude Simon, French new fiction writer and Nobel Prize winner in 1985	
1914 – 1986 AD	Bernard Malamud, American writer	
1913 – 1994 AD	Ralph Ellison, American writer, author of *Invisible Man*	
1915 – 2005 AD	Saul Bellow, American Jewish writer and winner of the 1976 Nobel Prize for literature	
1915 AD	Birth of jazz music in the US	
1916 – 2009 AD		Ren Jiyu, Chinese scholar
1920 AD	Publication of *Economy and Society* by Max Weber	Publication of Hu Shi's *chang-shi-ji* (《尝试集》, A Collection of Tentative Writings)
1921 AD	Mario Puzo, American writer of *God Father*	Publication of Guo Moruo's *Goddess* (《女神》)
1922 – 2008 AD	Alain Robbe-Grillet, French new fiction writer	
1922 AD	Jack Kerouac, writer of *Beat Generation*	
1922 – 1969 AD	W. Disney produced cartoon film in Hollywood	
1923 – 1925 AD	Surrealism was popular in France and then in Europe	Publication of Lu Xun's two collections of short stories, *na-han* (《呐喊》, Calling) and *pang-huang* (《彷徨》, Hesitation)
1924 AD		Founding of Beijing Palace Museum
1924 – 1987 AD	Jean-Francois Lyotard, French philosopher	

(续表)

Time	Events / Figures in Western Culture	Events / Figures in Chinese Culture
1925 AD		Publication of Xu Zhimo's *zhi-mo-de-shi* (《志摩的诗》, Zhimo's Poems)
1926 – 1984 AD	Michel Foucault, French philosopher	
1926 – 1984 AD	Allen Ginsberg, poet laureate of the Beat Generation	
1927 AD	Publication of M. Heidegger's *Being and Time*	
1928 AD		Publication of Wen Yiduo's *si-shui* (《死水》, Stagnant Water)
1929 AD	The rise of Imperial Building in New York as the first over hundred floor superstructure in the world	Discovery of the first Peking skull at Zhoukoudian, China
1929 AD	Jurgen Habermas, German philosopher	
1929 AD	Founding of Frankfurt School of Western Marxism	
Late 1920s – early 1930s AD	Birth of magical realism	
1930 AD		Publication of Ba Jin's *jia* (《家》, Family)
1930 – 1998 AD	Ted Hughes, English poet laureate	
1930 – 1998 AD	Jacques Derrida, French philosopher	
1930 – 2004 AD	Morrison, American black writer, winner of the 1993 Nobel Prize for literature and writer of *The Bluest Eye*, *Beloved*, *Paradise*	
1933 AD		Mao Dun's *zi-ye* (《子夜》, Midnight) was published
1934 AD		Cao Yu's play *lei-yu* (《雷雨》, Thunderstorm) was published and staged
1935 AD		*yi-yong-jun-jin-xing-qu* (《义勇军进行曲》, Tune to Marching Volunteers), words by Tian Han and music by Nie Er
1935 – 2005 AD	Edward Said, American Post-Colonial critic	
1935 – 2002 AD	Colleen McCullough, Australian writer of *The Thorn Birds*	
1935 – AD		Li Ao, historian and essayist in Chinese Taiwan

Chronological Table of Major Chinese and Western Cultural Events / Figures

(续表)

Time	Events / Figures in Western Culture	Events / Figures in Chinese Culture
1935 – 1977 AD	Elvis Presley, American rock and roll star singer	
1936 AD		Publication of Xia Yan's *shanghai-wu-yan-xia* (《上海屋檐下》, Under the Eaves of Shanghai)
1937 AD		Building of Qiantang River Bridge
1937 AD		Stage of Zhao Shuli's *xiao-er-hei-jie-hun* (《小二黑结婚》, Xiaoerhei Marriage)
1939 AD	Seamus Heaney, Irish poet and winner of the 1995 Nobel Prize for literature	
1940s – 1950s AD		Publication of Lao She's *si-shi-tong-tang* (《四世同堂》, Four Generations of a Family Living Together)
1945 AD		Publication of Qian Zhongshu's *wei-cheng* (《围城》, The Besieged)
1946 – AD		Yu Qiuyu, Chinese essayist
1946 – 2005 AD		Chen Yifei, Chinese painter
1948 AD	Founding of Israel	
1949 AD	The theatre of the Absurd founded in France	
1940s – 1950s AD	The School of Abstract Art in the US	
1950 AD	Appearance of Angry Young Men, a literary school in England	
1951 AD	Publication of J. D. Salinger's *The Catcher in the Rye*	
1952 AD		Jia Pingwa, Chinese writer
1955 AD	Publication of Australian novelist Patrick White's *Voss*	Mo Yan, novelist and writer of *hong-gao-liang* (《红高粱》, The Red Sorghum)
1957 AD	Fashion of rock and roll music in the US	Publication of Lao She's *cha-guan* (《茶馆》, Tea House)
1957 AD	Building of Sydney Opera House	
1950s – 1960s AD	Fashion of Black Humour, a literary school in the US	
1960s AD	Emergence of Pop Art	
1960s AD	Reemergence of feminism	

(续表)

Time	Events / Figures in Western Culture	Events / Figures in Chinese Culture
1966 – 1976 AD		The Chinese Cultural Revolution
Late 1960s AD	Cultural upheavals in France and other European countries	
1975 AD	The Twin Towers of World Trade Centre were established in New York; Bill Gates invented Microsoft software and established Microsoft company	
1976 AD		Publication of Shu Ting's *zhi-xiang-shu* (《致橡树》, To the Oak)
1979 AD		Convening of the 3rd Session of the 11th Congress of the Chinese Communist Party, marking the start of Chinese open and reform period
1970 – 1974 AD	Building of Sears Tower in Chicago, the highest building of the world at that time	
1977 AD	Fluffy Truman Centre established in France	
1970s – early 1980s AD	Ideological trend of new expression appeared in Germany and the US	
1986 AD		Publication of Gu Cheng's *hei-yan-jing* (《黑眼睛》, Eyes of Darkness)
1987 AD		Publication of Mo Yan's *hong-gao-liang* (《红高粱》, The Red Sorghum)
1996 AD		Publication of Wang Anyi's *chang-hen-ge* (《长恨歌》, The Song of Lasting Hatred)
1996 AD		Publication of Zhang Kangkang's *yin-xing-ban-lü* (《隐形伴侣》, The Invisible Companion)
1997 AD		Tie Ning, writer of *mei-gui-men* (《玫瑰门》, Rose Gate)
2001 AD	The Twin Towers of World Trade Centre in New York was struck and destroyed by terrorist attack	
2003 AD		Ye Zhaoyan, novelist and writer of *yi-jiu-san-qi-nian-de-ai-qing* (《一九三七年的爱情》, Nanjing 1937: A Love Story)

Bibliography

Audi, Robert (general ed.), 1999, *The Cambridge Dictionary of Philosophy*, Cambridge: Cambridge University Press.
Alioto, Anthony M., 1993, *A History of Western Science*, New York: Prentice-Hall, Inc.
Bassnett, Susan, 1993, *Comparative Literature: A Critical Introduction*, Oxford and Cambridge: Blackwell Publishers.
Cooper, David E., 1996, *World Philosophies: An Historical Introduction*, London: Blackwell Publishers.
During, Simon (ed.), 1999, *The Cultural Studies Reader*, London: Routledge.
Davies, Norman, 1997, *Europe: A History*, London: Pimplico.
Duro, Paul and Greenhalgh, Michael, 1994, *Essential Art History*, London: Bloomsbury Publishing Plc.
Deeney, John (ed.), 1980, *Chinese-Western Comparative Literature: Theory and Strategy*, Hong Kong: The Chinese University Press.
Eagleton, Terry, 1985, *Literary Theory: An Introduction*, Basil London: Blackwell Publisher.
Fernandez-Armesto, Felipe, Scribners Sons, Charles, 1995, *Millennium: A History of the Last Thousand Years*, New York: Simon and Schuster Inc.
Frow, John and Morris, Meaghan, 1993, *Australian Cultural Studies: A Reader*, Sydney: Allen and Unwin Pty Ltd.
Goff, Richard D., etc., 1987, *A Survey of Western Civilization*, Chicago: West Publishing Company.
Goetz, Philip W. (editor-in-chief), 1985, *The New Encyclopaedia Britannica* (15th edition), London: Encyclopaedia Britannica, Inc.
Glanville Price (ed.), 1998, *Encyclopaedia of the Languages of Europe*, Oxford: Oxford University Press.
Habermas, Jurgen, 1981, *The Philosophical Discourse of Modernity*, Massachusetts, USA: The MIT Press Cambridge.
H. W. Janson, Dora Jane, 1963, *The Picture History of Painting*, London: Thames and Hudson.
Honour, Hugh, Fleming, John, 1999, *A World History of Art*, London: Lawrence King Publishing.
Hutten, Ernest H., Sydney, George, 1962, *The Origin of Science*, Sydney: Allen and Unwin Ltd.
Jacqueline de Romilly, 1985, *A Short History of Greek Literature*, Chicago: The University of Chicago Press.
Kundera, Milan, 1999, *The Art of the Novel*, New York: Grove Press.
Kiernan Ryan (ed.), 1996, *New Historicism and Cultural Materialism: A Reader*, London: Arnold Press.
Mark Robson, Albert Bauth, Thomas Cable, 2002, *A History of the English Language* (5th edition), Upper Saddle River, NJ: Pearson Education, Inc., as Prentice Hall Inc.
McArthur, Tom, 1998, *The English Language*, Cambridge: Cambridge University Press.
Miner, Earl, 1990, *Comparative Poetics: An Intercultural Essay on Theories of Literature*, Boston: Princeton University Press.

Needham, Joseph, 2000, *Science and Civilization in China*, Volume 6, Cambridge: Cambridge University Press.
Peter, Dash, Joseph Jung, 2005, *Theories in English Language Learning*, London: Routledge.
Robson, Mark, Stockwell, Peter, 2005, *Language in Theory: A Resource Book for Students*, London: Routledge.
Soloman, Robert C., Higgins, Kathleen M., 1996, *A Short History of Philosophy*, Oxford: Oxford University Press.
Said, Edward W., 1991, *Orientalism*, London: Penguin Books.
Sir Harvey, Paul (ed.), 1984, *The Oxford Companion to Classical Literature*, Oxford: Oxford University Press.
Smith, S. C. Kaines, 1985, *An Outline History of Painting in Europe*, Medici Society.
Sivin, Nathan, 1995, *Science in Ancient China: Researches and Reflections*, London: Variorum.
Smith, Jeremy, 1996, *A Historical Study of English*, London: Routledge.
Thorlby, Anthony, 1969, *The Penguin Companion to European Literature*, London: Penguin Books.
Walkowitz, Judith, 1992, *City of Dreadful Delight: Narratives of Sexual Danger in Late-Victorian London*, Chicago: The University of Chicago Press.
Wilson, T. Elizabeth, 1991, *The Sphinx in the City: Urban Life, the Control of Disorder and Women*, London: Virago.
Ye Shengnian, 2005, *Western Culture: An Introduction*, Shanghai Foreign Language Education Press.
Zhang Longxi, 1997, *The Tao and the Logos —— Literary Hermeneutics, East and West* (second edition), Durham & London: Duke University Press.
北京大学哲学系中国哲学教研室,2003,《中国哲学史》(第二版),北京:北京大学出版社。
伯特兰·罗素,1992,《西方的智慧》,北京:世界知识出版社。
鲍诗度,1993,《西方现代派美术》,北京:中国青年出版社。
迟轲,1983,《西方美术史话》,北京:中国青年出版社。
敦尼克等,1972,《哲学史》(欧洲哲学史部分),北京:三联书店。
段治文,2001,《中国现代科学文化的兴起》,上海:上海人民出版社。
冯友兰,2000,《中国哲学史》(上下册),上海:华东师范大学出版社。
高名凯、刘正埮,1958,《现代汉语外来词研究》,北京:文字改革出版社。
亨利·皮朗(乐文译),1986,《中世纪欧洲经济社会史》,上海:上海人民出版社。
胡显章、曾国屏(主编),2002,《科学技术概论》,北京:高等教育出版社。
何九盈,1995,《中国现代语言学史》,广州:广东教育出版社。
金观涛、刘青峰,2000,《中国现代思想的起源》,香港:中文大学。
李霖灿,1987,《中国绘画史稿》,台北:雄狮图书股份有限公司。
李约琴原著(上海交通大学科学史系译),2002,《中华科学文明史》(2),上海:上海人民出版社。
濮之珍,1990,《中国语言学史》,台北:书林出版有限公司。
任继愈(主编),1999,《中国哲学史》,北京:人民出版社。
饶芃子等,1994,《中西小说比较》,合肥:安徽教育出版社。
帅培天等,1996,《圣经文学词典》,成都:四川人民出版社。
王琪森,1999,《中国艺术通史》,南京:江苏文艺出版社。
王力,1958,《汉语史稿》,北京:科学出版社。
许苏民,1992,《比较文化研究史》,昆明:云南人民出版社。
袁华音,1988,《西方社会思想史》,天津:南开大学出版社。
叶胜年,2002,《西方文化史鉴》,上海:上海外语教育出版社。
雅各布·布克哈特(何新译),1992,《意大利文艺复兴时期的文化》,北京:商务印书馆。

杨周翰、吴达元、赵萝蕤,1979,《欧洲文学史》(上下册),北京:人民文学出版社。
兹拉特科夫斯卡雅(陈筠、沈澄译),1984,《欧洲文化的起源》,北京:三联书店。
狄兆俊,1992,《中英比较诗学》,上海:上海外语教育出版社。
中央美术学院外国美术史教研室,1990,《外国美术简史》,北京:高等教育出版社。
张再林,1997,《中西哲学比较论》,兰州:西北大学出版社。
周一良(主编),1987,《中外文化交流史》,郑州:河南人民出版社。